— *Asian Law Center* —
UNIVERSITY OF WASHINGTON
SCHOOL OF LAW
ASIAN LAW SERIES
NUMBER 18

The Asian Law Series was initiated in 1969, with the cooperation of the University of Washington Press and the Institute for Comparative and Foreign Area Studies (now the Henry M. Jackson School of International Studies). A complete listing of the books in the series appears at the end of the book.

The members of the editorial committee are Veronica L. Taylor (chair), Susan Whiting, Saadia Pekkanen, Toshiko Takenaka, and Dongsheng Zang.

Writing and Law in Late Imperial China

Crime, Conflict, and Judgment

Edited by
ROBERT E. HEGEL
AND KATHERINE CARLITZ

UNIVERSITY OF WASHINGTON PRESS
Seattle and London

© 2007 by the University of Washington Press
Printed in the United States of America
Designed by Pamela Canell
12 11 10 09 08 07 5 4 3 2 1

All rights reserved. No part of this publication may be reproduced or transmitted in any form or by any means, electronic or mechanical, including photocopy, recording, or any information storage or retrieval system, without permission in writing from the publisher.

University of Washington Press
P.O. Box 50096, Seattle, WA 98145 U.S.A.
www.washington.edu/uwpress

Library of Congress Cataloging-in-Publication Data
Writing and law in late imperial china : crime, conflict, and judgment / edited by Robert E. Hegel and Katherine Carlitz.
  p. cm. — (Asian law series)
Includes bibliographical references and index.
ISBN-13: 978-0-295-98691-3 (hardback : alk. paper)
ISBN-10: 0-295-98691-3 (hardback : alk. paper)
  1. Law—China—History. 2. Legal stories, Chinese—History and criticism. 3. Legal composition. 4. Law and literature. 5. Law in literature. I. Hegel, Robert E., 1943– II. Carlitz, Katherine.
KNQ48.7.W75 2007   349.5109—dc22   2007002520

The paper used in this publication is acid-free and 90 percent recycled from at least 50 percent post-consumer waste. It meets the minimum requirements of American National Standard for Information Sciences—Permanence of Paper for Printed Library Materials, ANSI Z39.48-1984.♾

TO THE MEMORY OF WILLIAM CATRON JONES (1926–2005),

esteemed colleague, man of insight and good counsel,

and translator of *The Great Qing Code*

Contents

Preface ix

Abbreviations and Terminology xiii

Introduction
Writing and Law 3
ROBERT E. HEGEL

PART I *Rhetoric and Persuasion*

1 Making a Case
   Characterizing the Filial Son 27
   MARAM EPSTEIN

2 Explaining the Shrew
   Narratives of Spousal Violence and the Critique of Masculinity in Eighteenth-Century Criminal Cases 44
   JANET THEISS

3 Between Oral and Written Cultures
   Buddhist Monks in Qing Legal Plaints 64
   YASUHIKO KARASAWA

4 The Art of Persuasion in Literature and Law 81
ROBERT E. HEGEL

PART II *Legal Discourse and the Power of the State*

5 Filial Felons
Leniency and Legal Reasoning in Qing China 109
THOMAS BUOYE

6 The Discourse on Insolvency and Negligence
in Eighteenth-Century China 125
PENGSHENG CHIU

7 Poverty Tales and Statutory Politics
in Mid-Qing Fraud Cases 143
MARK MCNICHOLAS

8 Indictment Rituals and the Judicial Continuum
in Late Imperial China 161
PAUL R. KATZ

PART III *Literature and Legal Procedure*

9 Reading Court Cases from the Song and the Ming
Fact and Fiction, Law and Literature 189
JAMES ST. ANDRÉ

10 Beyond *Bao*
*Moral Ambiguity and the Law in Late Imperial Chinese
Narrative Literature* 215
DANIEL M. YOUD

11 Genre and Justice in Late Qing China
Wu Woyao's *Strange Case of Nine Murders and Its Antecedents* 234
KATHERINE CARLITZ

PART IV *Retrospective*

12 Interpretive Communities
    Legal Meaning in Qing Law 261
    JONATHAN OCKO

Glossary 285

Bibliography 297

Contributors 329

Index 333

Preface

Writing was central to early modern Chinese legal culture, not only because law codes are written documents but especially because legal procedure engendered so much writing. Proceedings of judicial hearings, no matter how trivial the case, had to be kept in several copies in preparation for periodical reviews. The judicial review process produced voluminous case narratives, and at the local level the accused and the aggrieved submitted ever more inventive complaints, all of which had to be investigated and commented upon. Even the imperial penal codes themselves required augmentation by numerous substatutes, as the judiciary struggled to find appropriate punishments for crimes not accounted for by articles of law. Likewise, the rightness of those very laws was endlessly debated in writing among successive generations of judicial administrators.

The establishment of early modern judicial norms in the eleventh century during the Song period gave rise almost immediately to court-case plays and later fiction, which soon became vehicles for venting outrage over official corruption, and for demanding a heavenly justice that would transcend the decisions of earthly courts. Early modern China also saw a radical refashioning of religious understanding that paralleled the new judicial norms. The Song dynasty witnessed not only the rise of the early modern judiciary, but a concomitant systematization of the Ten Courts of the Underworld, complete with written indictments and judicial rituals modeled on their secular counterparts.

The chapters here all began as papers presented at a conference held at Washington University in St. Louis, October 3–5, 2003. Our purpose was to examine written law and writing about law in late Ming and Qing China, with the goal of understanding the place of law in the traditional Chinese social imaginary. Our interests were first explored in two panels on writing and law at the 2002 annual meeting of the Association for Asian Studies, after which a number of panelists felt a need to pursue this research further. We realized that interdisciplinary perspectives and approaches were necessary to illuminate the study of law, legal practice, and the representation of legal practice in imaginative literature. In particular, historians have come to understand that case records in Chinese archives were constructed to meet specific political and social ends, and responded to the norms of other elite written genres. Students of literature have observed how crime fiction frequently departed from accurate reflection of judicial practice to wildly imaginative depictions of crime and punishment. Yet both groups of specialists have generally been ignorant of the role of legal language and documents in religious ritual, to say nothing of the religious beliefs supporting legal language and practice. Only by sharing our research could we illumine the complex intersections between writing as a cultural practice and the administration of justice.

The Washington University conference was a multidisciplinary meeting, a chance for historians, literature specialists, and scholars of Chinese religion to learn from each other. It was a great success in this regard, and the sharing of ideas begun there continued unabated as we revised our papers into a more unified collection for this volume.

Most obviously, these studies will enhance awareness of the intertextual nature of the Ming-Qing universe of writing; this intertextuality suggests that we must also think in terms of the interpenetration of different groups of writing and reading subjects. In the field of *religious studies*, juxtaposing religious indictment rituals with the wider world of legal writing illumines both the bureaucratic character of popular religion and the religious justification sought by the secular bureaucracy. In terms of the *history and sociology of Chinese law*, essays here demonstrate the continuing power of both China's Legalist standards (in the form of a Code that tries to cover all eventualities) and its Confucian values (a generalized mistrust of law in favor of paternalistic guidance on the part of local administrators); the parallels between legal writing and fiction is fresh evidence for how widely disseminated legal knowledge was in Qing China. This cultural contextualization of indigenous laws also contributes significantly to the most hotly contested topic in current Chinese legal studies, namely the potential for achieving the rule of law in the

People's Republic. Work like ours can play a significant role in keeping such discussion from being myopically centered only on the Western experience by situating these debates within historical practice.

Significantly, these chapters call for a reconsideration of the *cultural role of writing* itself, especially in a hyperliterary culture like that of late imperial China. On the one hand, literary texts show us the transgressive tendencies of imaginative literature: the Qing Code was certainly considered majestic, but the fiction considered below treats it as vulnerable to manipulation and corruption. More fundamentally, writing and law are always inherent in each other. Law ostensibly aims at fixity and stasis, whereas writing is inherently innovative: each new text revises what has gone before. Yet literary texts embrace the established conventions of writing, the acknowledged "rules" of the chosen literary form, while substatutes are intended to subvert the Code, making it fit better with messy reality. Case reports—however strictly they seem to apply the law—effectively supplement and undermine its certainties. By examining writing and law together, we bring out the ceaseless dynamism in late imperial Chinese culture.

A number of common questions recur in the chapters below. Although not all focus on rhetoric, each chapter draws attention to the way rhetoric is deployed: whose voice is represented, who creates the speaker on the page, what is the intended effect of the speech? This approach involves considerations of authorship and intended audience for all of our materials.

Our essays are also meant to form a foundation upon which we can all build a better understanding of a broad range of topics that have been raised about other times and other cultures: how are human problems—and transgressions—best represented in writing? How does the need to describe human actions in words shape our perceptions? Where is the "truth" in human motivations? Are all reports of violent emotions and activity necessarily "fictionalized" to some degree? Readers will not find definitive answers to these questions here, but these chapters, individually and collectively, present some of the best observations to date on this range of concerns. We hope that they serve to instigate broad comparative study of cultures as well as to further, and deepen, the understanding of writing and law in late imperial China.

Our St. Louis conference was enlivened and enhanced by the commentary and questions provided by two Washington University School of Law colleagues: John Haley, Wiley Rutledge Professor of Law and Director of the Institute for Global Legal Studies, and the late William C. Jones, Professor Emeritus and the translator of *The Great Qing Code*. It is to Bill's memory that this volume is respectfully dedicated.

ACKNOWLEDGMENTS

The editors gratefully acknowledge the generous financial support received from the China and Inner Asia Council of the Association for Asian Studies and the Graduate School of Arts and Sciences and the Sesquicentennial Year and International Affairs funds of Washington University for help with the conference from which this volume developed.

Abbreviations and Terminology

BXDA   *Baxian dang'an* 巴縣檔案 (Ba County Archives, Sichuan)

DLCY   Xue Yunsheng 薛允升, *Du li cunyi* 讀例存疑 (Remaining doubts after reading the substatutes)

DQLL   *Da Qing lüli* 大清律例 (The Great Qing penal code)

ECCP   *Eminent Chinese of the Ch'ing Period*, ed. Arthur W. Hummel

GZDQL *Gongzhongdang Qianlong chao zouzhe* 宮中檔乾隆朝奏摺 (Secret palace memorials of the Qianlong reign)

HDSL   *Da Qing huidian shili* 大清會典實例 (Institutes of the Qing dynasty)

LFZZ   *Lufu zouzhe* 錄副奏摺 ([Grand Council] file copies of confidential palace memorials)

XKTB   *Xingke tiben* 刑科題本 (Board of Punishments routine memorials)

ZPZZ   *Zhupi zouzhe* 硃批奏摺 (Confidential palace memorials)

REIGNS DURING THE QING 清 PERIOD

SZ   Shunzhi 順治, 1644–1661

KX   Kangxi 康熙, 1662–1722

YZ   Yongzheng 雍正, 1723–1735

QL   Qianlong 乾隆, 1736–1795

JQ   Jiaqing 嘉慶, 1796–1820

DG   Daoguang 道光, 1821–1850

XF   Xianfeng 咸豐, 1851–1861

TZ   Tongzhi 同治, 1862–1874

GX   Guangxu 光緒, 1875–1908

XT   Xuantong 宣統, 1909–1911

A date written in traditional Chinese order gives the year of the reign period followed by the lunar month and then the day (e.g., QL 36.9.15) and is followed by the corresponding date in the Western calendar.

FREQUENTLY USED CHINESE TERMS

li 里: a unit of distance, about half a kilometer or roughly 1/3 mile

sui 歲: a year of age, counted as one at birth and two at the next lunar new year, thus one to two years greater than actual age

tael or liang 兩: "ounces," a unit of measurement for silver used as currency; its value fluctuated in numbers of copper coins

wen 文 or "cash": a coin, usually made of copper, the basic unit of currency

yamen 衙門: administrative office or office compound, including the court and the official's residence

NOTE ON WOMEN'S NAMES IN LEGAL DOCUMENTS

Chinese crime reports and other documents rarely identify women by their given names. Instead, a woman is identified only by her surname followed by the term shi 氏 or by her husband's surname followed by her own surname and the term shi. Here, we refer to, for example, Zhang Yue shi as "Mrs. Zhang née Yue" and to Zhao shi as "Ms. Zhao."

Writing and Law in Late Imperial China

Introduction

Writing and Law

ROBERT E. HEGEL

When the archives of the last imperial dynasty were opened in Beijing in the 1980s, China scholars from around the world came to learn of a vast treasury of materials that even Chinese scholars had only begun to explore. By some accounts, as many as nine million records (ranging in size from single sheets of paper to numerous volumes) document the daily activity of thousands of bureaucrats, both those working in the capital and those in positions scattered throughout the vast Qing empire. The events and personages of major national importance were already well known from other, more public sources. But of particular interest among these documents were those dealing with China's common subjects, its hundreds of millions of farmers, craftsmen, laborers, and, most particularly, the women of the lower social strata. Not surprisingly, many members of these groups came to the attention of administrators only when they were involved in major crimes, when their lives figured in the case reports sent from across the country to Beijing for review.

Around the time that this archive was becoming available to Chinese and foreign scholars, other sources were also gaining academic attention. First were the legal documents found elsewhere: not all of the Qing imperial archives are still in Beijing. In the rush to protect the contents of the Qing Forbidden City (now the Palace Museum) from the Japanese invasion in the 1930s, the imperial art collection was crated and shipped away. Most of it moved from place to place on railroad cars throughout the war, and some of this trove was later transferred to Taiwan, as Chiang Kai-shek's Nationalist Party forces retreated there in the late 1940s. Sizable quantities of documents from the imperial archives were among that collection of art. Likewise, major collections of local legal records were discovered in Sichuan and Taiwan.[1] These documents record petty criminal activity, but far more interesting are the thousands of records of legal suits between area residents. Scholars have only begun to mine these treasures, but the views they have obtained of daily life during late imperial China—which was a very litigious society—are stunning.

During the 1980s, libraries in all parts of China (including Hong Kong and Taiwan) became more accessible to researchers than ever before. Large reprint series also made widely available books that had been virtually lost, among them works of literature, religious texts, and legal advice manuals. Through the 1980s and 1990s, scholars explored these newfound materials within disciplinary borders, but, with the turn of the new millennium, they have to an increasing extent carried on multidisciplinary and humanistic investigations of late imperial China's documentary record. Our chapters represent just this sort of intellectual quest: they use the insights and critical approaches of a variety of disciplines to explore, in an unprecedented fashion, Qing period descriptive, narrative, and expository writing. Our materials are legal, fictional, and religious texts dating mostly from the middle of the seventeenth century to the end of the dynasty, at the turn of the twentieth century. All the chapters deal directly or indirectly with legal practice, but our shared focus is on the *texts* of, and about, that practice.

STUDIES OF LAW, SOCIETY, AND LITERATURE:
CHINA VERSUS THE WEST

The interfaces of creative and legal writing, and their similarities, are relatively new concerns for students of China. Literature (even when conceived broadly) and legal history have been two separate fields, with far more attention given to the former than to the latter, even when legal history is conceived as a branch of Chinese institutional history. Only in recent decades has legal history become an active area of China studies, and then primarily by social scientists. Few scholars have used the insights of literary analysis to examine the texts of the legal tradition, and most of them have contributed to this volume.

But beyond China studies, mentioning law and writing in the same breath is hardly a novel idea. "Law and Literature" has been an active field for academic inquiry in the United States and Great Britain for several decades; by consensus, its seminal work is James Boyd White's book *The Legal Imagination*, of 1973. British students of the law take courses in this area, and many of the law reviews produced at major law schools in this country have published critical surveys of the Law and Literature movement.[2] A growing number of important books and essay collections have been devoted to the subject.[3] Much of the discourse of that field is instructive to the study of writing and law in late imperial China.

Initially, British and American scholars divided their studies between law *in* literature and law *as* literature. Many have examined literary texts for reflections on all aspects of the law, especially such concerns as justice and ethical standards; Western writers have often used law as an emblem of an orderly world. As Richard Posner has observed, "Law's techniques [of argumentation] and imagery have permeated Western culture from its earliest days."[4] (This has also been true of China, although scholars have not recognized the fact until recently.) The efforts of literary studies have been directed, it would seem, toward encouraging legal scholars (including Judge Posner) to look outside the law library for ways of understanding their profession and for better ways of carrying out their practice. But perhaps the more interesting direction has been to examine laws and especially legal opinions as *texts* that may profitably be subjected to the types of analysis previously reserved for literature.

This approach has led critics to deconstruct the stories told by legal writing, to reveal their assumptions, and their often unexplored implications, about human character and motivations for action. These studies have revealed a "professional voice" that budding attorneys had to learn in order to write conventional legal opinions and have explored the confession from a variety of perspectives. Richard Weisberg, for example, has noted that even when summarizing a client's case, the Anglo-American lawyer relies on "the linguistic necessities of the formalized legal act of adversarial representation."[5] Other scholars have demonstrated how "prescripted" conceptions of human behavior—violent actions committed by women or minority men, for example—have on occasion precluded alternative, and more authentic, descriptions of those acts. These "common knowledge" stories stem in large part from popular culture, from the conventional ways in which the causes and frequency of crime are reported in contemporary media. Such representations are directly involved in developing popular notions of deviance and identity formation as well.[6] Reading legal documents as texts has also brought the rhetoric of legal opinions by U.S. Supreme Court justices and other judges under intense analytical scrutiny.

In more recent writing on Anglo-American laws and legal practice, the Law and Literature movement has led to the broad range of approaches referred to as "Critical Legal Studies." Scholars in this camp use insights and methodology adapted from cultural theory. They are divided, although not to the point of mutual exclusion, between those who apply the tools of literary criticism to texts and those whose approaches are more New Historicist.[7] These studies share a concern with the original contexts of the texts, concluding that all legal decisions and texts are dependent upon a variety of contingencies, in the production of which law also participates. Guyora Binder and Robert Weisberg have noted that "familiar myths" are often cited to explain the motivations behind laws and have concluded, "So too can we judge law aesthetically, according to the society it forms, the identities it defines, the preferences it encourages, and the subjective experience it enables. We can 'read' and criticize law as part of the making of a culture."[8] This trend applies the tools of literary criticism in order to discover the use of conventions in legal process as well as constant invention in legal exchanges. Reading itself is recognized as contingent upon a multiplicity of factors: judges' reading of laws and opinions as well as scholars' reading of legal history. In both cases, the conventions of reading are as significant for scholarly understanding as are the conventions of writing.[9] In reading court reports both as social rituals and as social texts, these new legal critics discover that criminal trials frequently fail to address the psychology of the accused, or the social efficacy of the trial for public education, and thus the ability of the trial to deter further crimes. But perhaps most importantly, these legal historians decline to see law or legal practice as unchanging; they are quick to demonstrate that even central concepts are constantly being revised and can be understood only in the particular circumstances of specific times and places. The changing role of the English merchant in both social and legal terms is a relevant example for the study of China.[10]

These trends in the critical study of Western law are reflected to one degree or another in this volume. However, these essays do not attempt to function as "forensic history"; that is, they do not refer to China's past to solve the problems of the present, either in China or elsewhere.[11] Nor are they deliberately comparative in nature. Although each contributor to this book does certainly have a legal tradition under whose strictures she or he lives, none makes an extensive contrastive study between the Qing penal code and Qing period legal practice and, for example, Anglo-American traditions. We have endeavored to explain our uses of English terms and concepts drawn from those traditions by indicating the specific sense of the original term for which a translation is used. Although none of our chapters attempts the sort of inquiries that engage legal scholars of Anglo-American traditions, our sensitivities as students of China based in the humanities and social sciences have helped us avoid both the politics of the legal profession and the sort of "legal orientalism" practiced by non-China specialists who often dismiss other legal systems as unworthy of serious comparison.[12]

Given the extent of the secondary literature of the Anglo-American fields of law and literature and critical historical studies, it would be difficult to survey briefly. Central to all approaches, however, is the awareness of how deeply law is embedded—and implicated—in its social context. In this, the individual chapters are similar. Many Anglo-American legal critics focus on the recent and the contemporary; this is true in the China studies field as well.[13] However, our concern here is limited to late imperial China, especially the Qing period, from around 1650 to the early twentieth century.

STUDIES OF WRITING AND LAW IN QING CHINA

Our chapters explore not only textual representations of, and the recorded treatment received by, men of prominence who ran afoul of the law but also the experiences of women and men of lower or marginal social status in the legal system. Although we have no direct access to testimony from those who were mistreated by that system, we are not precluded from tracing patterns of social discrimination in legal texts. Thomas Buoye and others have shown that men are more likely to be identified as liable to lose control of themselves and women to be represented as rational and calculating.[14] Several have noted that people brought to trial for major crimes such as murder during the Qing period were generally *not* members of China's elite. Those writing in this field have begun to interrogate the effect of popular culture on the legal system—and the reflections of the judicial process in literary texts—as well as the ethics and politics of torture in judicial investigations and punishment of the condemned. Of course, we cannot draw upon the subsequent testimony of survivors or interview readers to gauge their understandings of fictional crime stories, as can our colleagues who study law in contemporary societies.

Studies here can be simultaneously humanistic and social scientific, without fear of compromising one allegiance for the other; our investigations are guided by the larger humanistic mission of understanding the human past in all of its complexity. We can raise questions specific to the Chinese past, such as the efficacy of obligatory judicial review of major crime cases, as well as more general concerns for fairness and impartiality in the judgment of transgression. Our distance in time also facilitates the reconsideration of stereotypes and misunderstandings held by previous generations of scholars concerning the legal systems of old China. The following chapters thus facilitate comparative studies of unprecedented complexity with more recent systems in China and elsewhere.

Studies of writing and law in China generally focus on the Qing simply because of the wealth of available information. Pioneering students of judicial procedure initially mined summaries of difficult cases. The best known of these casebooks is the *Conspectus of Legal Cases* (Xing'an huilan), compiled in 1834, with supplements added in 1840 and again in 1886 to make a total of more than 7,600 cases.[15] The voluminous collections of the First Historical Archives in Beijing and the Taipei Palace Museum include many thousands of original legal documents and case records.[16] These texts present in detail every step of the judicial process, from the reporting of a crime to the final disposition of the sentence, as a major case was referred upward through the judicial review process from the local level to the center of power in Beijing. Moreover, access to hundreds of plaints and decisions in local historical archives, such as the Baxian Archives in Sichuan and the Dan-Xin (Tamsui-Hsinchu) Archives in Taiwan, has allowed complex understandings of lawsuits and other minor legal cases as well.

One might describe this field as still in an early stage. Basic legal texts have been located, organized, studied, and, in some cases, translated into European languages. The collaborative efforts of scholars and bibliographers on both sides of the Taiwan Strait and abroad have resulted in collections of major documents. Chang Wejen is currently editing a massive compendium of perhaps as many as eight hundred volumes of archival materials of the Ming and Qing periods to join those published in Beijing. *The Qing Penal Code* (Da Qing lüli), as edited by Xue Yunsheng (1820–1901), one of the last "presidents" (*shangshu*) of the Board of Punishments (Xingbu), in Beijing, was reprinted in 1970, and now there is a recent translation by William C. Jones, (which joins earlier efforts by Ernest Alabaster and George Thomas Staunton). *The Ming Penal Code* (Da Ming lü) has just appeared in an English translation by Jiang Yonglin. Reprints of memoirs and advice to magistrates by such writers as Huang Liuhong (ca. 1633–after 1705) and Lan Dingyuan (1680–1733) are a boon to those who do not have access to rare Qing editions. And Pierre-Étienne Will's guide to administrative handbooks in circulation during the Ming and Qing provides an excellent view of what men studied in preparation for becoming local administrators and legal assistants.[17] After a few pioneering studies that appeared during the 1950s and 1960s (by Ch'ü T'ung-tsu, Derk Bodde and Clarence Morris, and Sybille van der Sprenkel), Western research on China's premodern legal tradition languished until scholars, including Philip Huang, began to probe newly accessible archives—and to direct their graduate students to do the same. Such efforts have resulted in a flurry of excellent monographs on particular aspects of legal culture. These include recent books by Mark Allee, Jérôme Bourgon, Thomas Buoye, Valerie Hansen, Melissa Macauley, Marinus Johan Meijer, Bradly Reed, Matthew Sommer, and Janet Theiss. In addition, William Alford, Robert Antony, Beatrice Bartlett, Jonathan Ocko, Nancy Park, Joanna Waley-Cohen, and Zhou Guangyuan have all published essential articles in the field—to list only China scholars who write in English. For their part, Pengsheng Chiu and his colleagues at the Institute of History and Philology at the Academia Sinica in Taiwan have produced an impressive series of important studies of all aspects of China's legal history, as have archivists and scholars working in the historical archives in Beijing. Their work has ranged from explorations of criminal laws, civil cases, types of offenses (adultery, murder), to those who litigated (magistrates, their "legal secretaries" [*muyou*], and "litigation masters" [*songshi*]), and to the positions of women under law. And writing in Japanese, Yasuhiko Karasawa has carried on the foundational work of Niida Noboru and others to explore the conventions in legal documents.

Official archives constitute but one source of material, of course. Recent reprints of texts of all sorts from late imperial China have been a boon to students of all historical fields. Hundreds of novels and short stories, to select only one form of writing, previously known only as entries in bibliographies are now available in libraries around the world. The opening of rare-book collections and the creation of new printed and electronic catalogs of the major library collections in China and abroad have brought to light dozens of previously overlooked titles relevant to our study, such as the fiction that Daniel Youd and Katherine Carlitz discuss in chapters 10 and 11, respectively.[18] Novels, stories, and informal writings have been contrasted with courtroom procedures outlined in the plethora of handbooks for magistrates and legal secretaries. These texts complicate all previous understandings of legal practice and how people wrote about it as well as the degree to which knowledge of the law permeated late imperial Chinese society.

The study of law in China must encompass religious beliefs and practices along with legal and fictional texts. This is because the language style, documentary format, and acts of formal supplication seem to have been generally standardized, whether one was begging for the sympathetic attention and authoritative intervention of a local magistrate or of a deity. Paul Katz demonstrates in chapter 8, for example, that people commonly filed plaints in civil and divine courts simultaneously, a practice that continues in Taiwan even today. Likewise, his observations on the "continuum of justice" in late imperial China bring attention to the degree to which writers of the period simply assumed, based on recorded experience, that China's judges could rely on supernatural aid in solving crimes. It was taken for granted that their work paralleled and complemented that of underworld judges, presuming a kind of divine justice that extended beyond the here and now.

However, this new area of China studies is not so well formulated or energetic as to be considered a "movement." The multidisciplinary approaches employed here do not share a common theory, nor do our contributions have a common agenda. There is simply too much to be discovered at this point; our diverse and separate approaches have been so wonderfully productive as to preclude even searching for any artificial limit to our project. This collection is the first attempt to bring together in one volume a representative sample of current research in this field. To that end, all of our contributors have focused on the complex discourse of the judicial system in its many overlapping manifestations.

LAW AND JUDICIAL PRACTICE IN LATE IMPERIAL CHINESE SOCIETY

Writing late in the nineteenth century, Arthur H. Smith expressed an opinion not commonly shared by other Westerners in China at the time: "One of the admirable qualities of the Chinese is their innate respect for the law. Whether this element in their character is the effect of their institutions, or the cause of them, we do not know. But what we do know is that the Chinese are by nature and education a law-abiding people."[19] Modern socioanthropologist Arthur Wolf interpreted this quality as the result of the appropriation of religious authority by the Qing state. He observed that even though the Qing government was not able to exert substantial control locally, it "appears to have been one of the most potent governments ever known, for it created a religion in its own image."[20] More recently, other scholars have posited a general respect for the coercive power of central authorities as the reason why China's people were so "law-abiding." One might well take exception to Wolf's assumption that the state had little control at the local level; numerous more recent studies indicate just the opposite.[21]

Newer studies suggest that China's subjects generally knew about law and, through that knowledge, were well aware of the state's power to control their activities. More to the point, people generally understood which acts were punishable. One might posit several causes for this state of affairs.

First, China's laws changed only gradually through time, to judge from the existing codes. During the Ming, the legal code was based on Song and Yuan predecessors; the Qing penal code was drawn directly from that of the Ming and generally only expanded upon it. The *li* (substatutes) of *The Qing Code* elaborated the fundamental statutes without contradicting them, for the most part.[22] Thus, legal codes were cumulative, apparently reflecting hoary tradition rather than the decisions of individual rulers, even though interpretations and applications varied over time. Popular, general knowledge of the laws as transmitted through oral and performance traditions, whether accurate or not, was undoubtedly cumulative as well. (Chapters 9 and 11 demonstrate that even when the judicial procedure was romanticized or fantasized, most popular literature assumed that wrongdoers would inevitably be punished, although Daniel Youd shows, in chapter 10, that fiction also celebrated those who evaded the law.)

Second, the consequences of legally punishable offenses were unambiguous. Seduction could result in a beating for the perpetrator, but the penalty for rape was strangulation. Those who plotted treason would be put to death with maximum destruction to the body ("death by slicing" [*lingchi*]). Punishment for injuries caused during an affray varied with the degree of relationship between those involved.[23] Handbooks for legal secretaries and others rephrased the laws in rhyming lines using simpler language that could be repeated and memorized. Such jingles may have circulated outside the magistrate's yamen. Common people also knew about the laws because it was the duty of local officials to publicize them: it behooved people to be informed if the magistrates were to care for the citizens of their jurisdiction appropriately. Moreover, the laws of the land simply put coercive force behind common ethical standards.[24]

Nor was judicial procedure unfamiliar. Many plays treat courtroom scenes (often fancifully), but popular novels could be quite explicit in their representations. A case in point occurs in the Ming period *Outlaws of the Marsh*, or, more commonly, *Water Margin* (Shuihu zhuan), when the burly hero Wu Song takes revenge for the murder of his elder brother, an ill-favored dwarf. The killers are his brother's faithless wife, Pan Jinlian, and her paramour Ximen Qing. When Wu Song figures this out, he files a complaint with the local magistrate. But after the official refuses to accept the case because he has been bribed, Wu Song takes matters into his own hands. First, he forces Jinlian and the matchmaker who brought the pair together to make complete confessions in the presence of neighbors, one of whom records the confessions, after being instructed to do so by Wu Song. Then, Wu Song slays Jinlian and tracks down and kills Ximen Qing as well.

After placing the adulterers' bloody heads before his brother's memorial tablet and offering a sacrifice of wine to his spirit, Wu Song surrenders himself to the local court. Appropriately, the magistrate reads the confessions and interrogates the matchmaker and the neighbors so as to corroborate the written record. The magistrate then goes with the coroner to examine both bodies. With the requisite procedures and forms completed, he jails both Wu Song and the matchmaker and confines the witnesses as well. Fully armed with the facts, the magistrate writes out his interpretation of the case, the *zhaozhuang*, but modifies the facts to ensure that Wu Song will be treated leniently during subsequent judicial reviews. To that end, his report portrays Pan Jinlian as having forcibly tried to stop Wu Song from sacrificing to his deceased brother; during the struggle, Wu Song killed her. At that point, this revised document declares, the adulterer Ximen Qing intervened, and after a prolonged battle, he, too, was killed. At the next level of review, the charges are lightened further, and the final decision on the case, reached in the capital, focuses the blame on the matchmaker, who is to be executed slowly and painfully. Wu Song is beaten and exiled for homicides that are now considered justified, not for the carefully planned execution-style murders he actually committed.[25]

This story is fiction, to be sure. Scholars of China's legal administration give adequate evidence to suggest that discrepancies between the evidence and its interpretation were simply not allowed in legal cases (see chapter 5, by Thomas Buoye). But even though its hero escapes with an implausibly light sentence for a double murder, the novel reflects detailed knowledge of both the documents and the procedures involved in a major criminal case. By attributing to the judges (the magistrate, the prefect, and the capital officials) the ability to recast events in ways that can ensure *moral* justice, even if it requires bending the law, the novel shares with other crime tales (*gong'an xiaoshuo*) of late imperial China the confidence that wrongdoing will always be punished and the innocent exonerated. In chapter 11, Katherine Carlitz demonstrates that *Water Margin* was certainly not the only late imperial Chinese novel to provide detailed—and accurate—information on court procedures. (For a discussion of the "interpretive community" for popular fiction, see chapter 12, by Jonathan Ocko.)

Knowledge of what might be called "civil law," those regulations and practices governing local disputes and minor offenses, was probably even more widespread than was familiarity with criminal procedures. There were legal specialists among the public scribes in county and market towns who drafted plaints and other documents for a fee, and printed guidebooks on how to compose legal forms could be purchased at low cost. Although most people might never sue another person themselves, legal language and procedure must have become familiar to them as word spread among relatives and friends from those who were involved in civil suits. Likewise, to judge from the research of Yasuhiko Karasawa (see chapter 3), Paul Katz (see chapter 8), and others, many learned about formal complaints from public legal hearings and religious rituals. In practice, there were no sharp divisions between personal morality, religious practice, and the political values of the state. All shared the same ethical discourse, and all were seen as interwoven, relying on a common set of standards.[26] Although it has been conventional to describe premodern China's working masses as uneducated and thus unsophisticated, from the middle of the sixteenth century onward, travel was increasingly commonplace. Likewise, trade brought people from the countryside into contact with market town activity and merchants from smaller towns into the large urban centers. Popular entertainers wandered from cities into rural areas. Literacy spread ever further through Chinese society, and books of all kinds (including practical handbooks) were peddled to small, local market towns and sold in metropolitan book shops. Government notices generally applied everywhere and were posted in prominent places for all to read.[27] In a society of this complexity, with this degree of integration, it seems logical that many of the individuals discussed in the following chapters possessed at least a working knowledge of the laws being brought to bear upon them and might have used it to their advantage.

True as all this may have been for society at large, knowledge of specific laws may not have played a significant role in shaping individual behavior or social harmony during late imperial times. In his survey of legal education during the Qing period, Chang Wejen discovered diminishing emphasis on formal education in law or legal practices among prospective local administrators (those who took the higher-level civil service examinations) and their assistants in administrative centers. In 1729, students for those degrees in government schools were required by imperial edict to study *The Qing Code*; for the provincial and capital examinations, they had to write five hypothetical judicial decisions. But by 1745, this requirement was altered to require argumentation on the basis of classical moral principles rather than contemporary laws. Apparently in an effort to preclude answers that might be embarrassing to the Qing regime, questions in this area were often very long, as anxious examiners sought to shape the candidates' responses. Despite the central government's efforts to stem this weakening of legal training, law was not a serious subject in the official curriculum, Chang concludes.[28]

Moreover, the position of legal clerk was generally hereditary, which kept knowledge in family lines, and even legal scribes were required to write down exactly what plaintiffs had told them, making detailed knowledge of the laws irrelevant. Even the much-maligned litigation masters who made their living with clever presentations of their clients' cases neither referred to Qing law nor made legal arguments. Furthermore, "most civil matters were regulated not by positive law but by customary rules and moral principles, and traditional China's elaborate ways of teaching these rules and principles are famous." But "they were not taught as 'laws'; they were taught as norms higher than or parallel to law," Chang Wejen affirms.[29]

Even so, a regulation of the Board of Civil Office (Libu Zeli) stipulated that every village and town should have a hall for twice-monthly lectures on law and moral education. These presentations were to be made by elders selected by local officials, but the regulation did not indicate how the elders were to get their legal information. It may be that these lectures were never carried out regularly. And in application, laws did not always embody conventional moral principles; the contradiction between personal ethical standards and the needs of the state was an age-old concern in China.[30] One might argue that a general knowledge of canonical standards for behavior did not make people law-abiding, in a modern sense, but that law confirmed those standards.

Legal secretaries employed by county magistrates were probably the only people truly knowledgeable about the laws at the local and provincial levels. These men were professionals, hired and paid by the magistrates themselves. The memoirs of Wang Huizu (1730–1807), particularly his *Advice to Those Who Assist in Administration* (Zuozhi yaoyan), note how dangerous this position could be: Any mistake in the presentation of a legal case could bring harm to defendants and possible retribution to the magistrate's family. Thus, even though the secretary was entrusted with the drafting of important legal documents, ostensibly the local magistrate had to review every one carefully in order to protect himself from prosecution. To that end, Wang Huizu advised legal secretaries simply to memorize the entire legal code. Even so, according to Wang, the more important preparation was to read a variety of books in order to imbibe elite standards for behavior and their classical justifications— beyond the statutes and substatutes. Thus, despite Chang's observation that specific legal knowledge was monopolized by a very few professionals, a variety of texts and practices contributed to a general understanding of punishable behavior—and the procedures by which legal standards were enforced—in society as a whole.[31]

LEGAL ADMINISTRATIVE STRUCTURES IN LATE IMPERIAL CHINA

The fair administration of the laws seems to have been a primary concern for bureaucrats at all levels. One might argue that this was a product of their common education in the humanistic Confucian canonical texts, but clearly, the punishments for dereliction of official duty were not lost on anyone in a position of authority.[32] Nor, would it appear, was there any appreciable amount of flexibility allowed in the administrative performance of local governors. Substantial portions of *The Qing Code* were devoted to administrative law. It stipulated deadlines and some procedures; others were clearly prescribed by the handbooks created for that purpose, which circulated widely during the Qing.

Although specific practices are explained as relevant in chapters 3, 5, 6, and 7, a general understanding of judicial administrative structures and procedures is implied in all of them. Those structures were hierarchically and vertically arranged, from the emperor at the apex to the 1,200 to 1,300 "county magistrates" (*zhixian*) at the bottom, with few lateral connections. Each magistrate was appointed in the name of the emperor and represented imperial authority on the local level.[33]

Crime required complex official responses. Various members of the magistrate's staff were responsible for assembling all relevant information about a crime, from the first complaint, through the collection of all physical evidence, to the forensic examinations (if needed), to the arrest and detention of the accused and the assembly of relevant witnesses. Magistrates were to oversee the examination of the bodies of homicide victims so as to verify the validity of the examiners' conclusions. Then magistrates had to conduct a thorough review of all evidence, closely question all the principals and all witnesses, and reach conclusions concerning the criminal events, the motivations behind them, and the punishments appropriate to the crimes.

Trials generally were conducted in public, with the yamen open and plaintiffs, defendants, and witnesses all present. The interrogation process, whether or not it included torture, was a spectacle designed to demonstrate the power of the state and to apply the authority of the cosmic moral order vested in the magistrate by his imperial appointment. Although the guidebooks generally cautioned against it, magistrates could legally torture anyone brought to testify before them if the witnesses seemed reluctant to tell the truth. Torture was probably threatened more frequently than it was applied. As Buoye suggests, most major criminal cases involved people who knew one another: family members, neighbors, partners in small businesses. Thus, the details of most crimes were familiar to neighbors, who sometimes knew about dangerous situations long before violence resulted. (The local headman was responsible for reporting such situations to the magistrate before violence erupted.) Consequently, the culprits' identity was seldom at issue.³⁴ Only in the most serious cases—of national prominence or of the most heinous acts of unfiliality such as parricide—was torture used as judicial punishment before sentencing, during interrogation.³⁵ Procedures to be followed during a trial were carefully stipulated by the penal code, and each stage of the investigation had to be completed within a specified period of time. Otherwise, the magistrate and his staff could be punished for delay. Thus, cases moved relatively quickly from the discovery of the crime through the trial process at the local level. In fact, however, only a preliminary review was carried out at the county yamen; the magistrate's findings and judgment were subjected to mandatory reconsideration at several levels of the bureaucracy.

The magistrate's report was submitted to the district (*fu*) administration for the requisite retrial. With the judgment of the prefect (*zhifu*) duly recorded, the magistrate's report was quickly forwarded, along with the defendant, while most witnesses were allowed to return home. The next level of review was the provincial surveillance commissioner (*anchashi*), sometimes referred to in English as the "judicial commissioner." The commissioner heard the criminal, checked his testimony against the written record, verified the accuracy of all elements, and then submitted the case to the provincial governor (*xunfu*) or governor-general (*zongdu*), the military commander of one or two provinces who simultaneously held the nominal position of censor (*du yushi*). The case could be reheard at this level but generally was simply passed forward to Beijing in the form of a memorial containing the magistrate's original report (along with the results of subsequent investigations, if any) and the sentences recommended by all reviewing officials.

Ostensibly, this memorial was directed to the emperor himself. However, given the number of such serious cases among China's large population, all were remanded for review to the Three Judicial Offices (Sanfasi), composed of the Censorate (Duchayuan), the Board of Punishments (Xingbu), and the Court of Judicial Review (Dalisi). Their recommendation was forwarded in a memorial to the emperor, whose decision, in his hand or at his direction, was then written on the outside fold of the document. Execution of the punishment could be ordered to take place immediately or with delay. In the majority of cases, the condemned were jailed pending review at the Autumn Assizes (Qiushen). There, the question was not whether the criminals were guilty but only whether the suggested punishment was appropriate.

For delayed punishments, the case was referred back to the original provincial surveillance commissioner for reconsideration. He had to meet a strictly maintained deadline for reporting to the governor, who completed his review and passed it back to the Board of Punishments, where the highest officials of the land could debate the law before they recommended a sentence to the emperor. Or they could delay debate for another year while the criminal languished in prison. Sometimes, their indecision resulted in a lengthy prison term, but in many cases, if the appropriate punishment could not be decided upon after several successive assizes, the criminal was given some lesser punishment or was released.[36] Thus, theoretically, in the majority of cases, there could be no rush to judgment that ignored the specifics of individual cases, nor would the accused lack adequate opportunities to represent his side of the story before a number of investigators.

Procedures in minor criminal or civil cases did not involve such a lengthy and repetitious review process. On certain days of each month, petitioners could submit written plaints of all sorts at the county level; scribes were available near the official yamen for those who were unable to draft their own documents. Magistrates' decisions normally were final but could be appealed to the district level of administration.[37]

WRITING ABOUT LEGAL PROCEDURES IN LATE IMPERIAL CHINA

The case reports for major crimes, homicides, contained among routine memorials to the throne are the archival documents most frequently utilized in the following chapters. This is because they are relatively numerous, given the enormous size of China's population, even though such acts of violence occurred infrequently in any locality. These texts are also the most striking in their content: many (especially those compiled during the first half of the Qing) contain extensive testimony from all parties involved in a case. Matthew Sommer describes their appeal:

> Most of the ethnographic evidence in both local and central cases can be found in records of testimony by witnesses at court hearings, including the confessions of convicted criminals. These records are probably as close as we will ever get to the "voice" of the illiterate in late imperial China.

> [However,] ... they are not verbatim transcriptions of witnesses' utterances; rather, they are summaries of testimony crafted from witnesses' answers to questions posed during interrogation. The answers were strung together in the form of a monologue in the "voice" of the witness.... These statements were shaped by the priorities of the magistrate, and should not be mistaken for purely spontaneous declarations.[38]

Depositions not only were reformulated but were all rewritten from the deponents' original dialect into standard Chinese (*guanhua* or Mandarin), the language of administration throughout the realm. In this process, language was standardized, and so, to a certain extent, was what one might call the "characterization" of the deponent. That is, in order to make a clear-cut match between the criminal act described and the categories of the penal code, perpetrators frequently were described in similar, conventional terms.[39] Even so, these recorded statements had to accord with the deponent's original "story": defendants were required to sign these written versions of their testimony, thereby indicating their concurrence with the content. And they would be questioned repeatedly throughout the mandatory judicial review. Although most reports were drafted by legal secretaries, any magistrate who falsified or misrepresented testimony could himself be punished.[40]

Standardized writing has broader implications as well. In chapter 1, Maram Epstein traces the trope of the filial son as it is reproduced in routine memorials supporting recommendations of appropriate punishment for aberrant behavior, and in chapter 2, Janet Theiss examines the way in which common notions of shrewish women are drawn upon to rationalize violence between husbands and wives. But standardized language occurs not only in the reports of major cases. As with all bureaucracies, formal documents of every kind required legal language, as Pengsheng Chiu demonstrates in chapter 6. In chapter 3, Yasuhiko Karasawa explores the conventional elements in plaints filed against defendants, and, in chapter 8, Paul Katz reveals the reliance on standardized diction in plaints filed with judicial gods. Mark McNicholas demonstrates, in chapter 7, how "characterization" of offenders shaped both legislation and assigned punishments.

Despite necessary standardization, there are several levels of narrative in crime reports that had their parallels in other forms of writing. The overall outline of the investigation and the trial found fictional counterparts in crime tales originally written in classical Chinese during the middle of the Ming; the genre was subsequently developed into vernacular-language stories, novels, and plays, as in the *Water Margin* episode summarized above. The central figure in most of these stories is the insightful judge, often a literary fabrication based on the historical Bao Zheng, a reportedly discerning but not particularly successful civil administrator during the Song period. In fiction, he became all knowing and extremely crafty in discovering evildoers and according justice to the innocent (see chapter 9, by James St. André).

The recorded testimony of the principals in crime reports has its parallels as well, but in the more developed narratives of late imperial "short stories" (*huaben xiaoshuo*) and "novels" (*zhanghui xiaoshuo*). Like their crime-report counterparts, these vernacular-language texts reveal motivations and the details of action. Unlike the legal documents, however, they leave most of the violence to the reader's imagination.[41] Daniel Youd and Katherine Carlitz discuss later novels of crime and detection in chapters 10 and 11, respectively.

Stories of extreme behavior, in which normal people committed socially and legally unacceptable acts, either unwittingly or by premeditation, were compelling and ultimately defied standardization. Consequently, many of the former magistrates who wrote about their experiences in guides for their successors related stories of memorable cases. These texts may be cast in spare classical style, but the motivations, and the specific actions taken by criminals, are narrated with attention to significant detail. Similar brief stories of crimes occur throughout the *biji xiaoshuo* (informal writings) of Qing period authors; crime stories clearly attracted many types of readers.[42] Here, as in so many other intersections between writing and law, a great range of writers both inside and well beyond the judicial system drew upon the art of writing—and the tricks of the writer's trade. As I demonstrate in chapter 4, many relied on common oratorical flourishes to embellish their arguments. And in chapter 12, Jonathan Ocko suggests that many of these writers had their intended readers firmly in mind as they put brush to paper. Indeed, when we consider how all of these writers wrote to fulfill conventional expectations for their respective forms of writing, the craft of literary writing and the craft of producing legal documents are clearly close and worthy of careful comparisons.

In sum, there is no single analytical or theoretical approach in this volume. However, all chapters are shaped by a humanistic concern for the contexts in which judicial procedures occurred and were described in writing. Many contributors have profited from the critical insights of contemporary literary and cultural theory. And certainly all share a sensitivity to our documents as texts and to their embeddedness in the world of writing—and reading—of late imperial China. Our range of topics and approaches is deliberately broad, to suggest some of the potential this field holds for further research.

NOTES

1. For brief descriptions of these collections, see *Zhongguo diyi lishi dang'an guan*; Zhuang, *Gugong dang'an shuyao*; and Ye and Esherick, *Chinese Archives*, 33–45, 279–81, 327–30, 338–39.

2. A sample of the journal essays includes Massaro, "Empathy, Legal Storytelling, and the Rule of Law"; Getman, "Colloquy"; West, "Communities, Texts and Law"; Koffler, "Forged Alliance"; and Farber and Sherry, "Telling Stories Out of School." In addition, see Aristodemou, "Studies in Law and Literature"; Ward, "Law and Literature"; and Thomas, "Reflections on the Law and Literature Revival."

3. See, for example, Posner, *Law and Literature*; Weisberg, *Poethics*; West, *Narrative, Authority, and Law*; Ward, *Law and Literature*; Brooks, *Troubling Confessions*; Morison and Bell, *Tall Stories?*; Brooks and Gewirtz, *Law's Stories*; and Sarat, Douglas, and Umphrey, *Law on the Screen*.

4. Posner, *Law and Literature*, 3.

5. Weisberg, *Poethics*, 248.

6. See, for example, the essays collected in Morison and Bell, *Tall Stories?* On law and literature in general, see Bell, "Teaching Law as Kafkaesque," 11–38; and Murphy, "Bursting Binary Bubbles," 57–82. On law in literature, see Robson, "Images of Law," 201–22; and Ingram, "Victorian Values," 223–43. On law as literature, see O'Donovan, "Identification with Whom?" esp. 46–48; Fox, "Crime and Punishment," esp. 145–47; and McEvoy, "Newspapers and Crime," 179, 182–84, 190. Dawson's provocatively titled "The Law of Literature: Folklore and the Law," 245–66, takes up such issues as copyright and the use of material for which there is no identified, or identifiable, author. In *Narrative, Authority, and Law*, West, like Weisberg in *Poethics*, insists on the ethical content appropriate to such research, in contrast to the rhetorical focus of Richard Posner and James Boyd White.

7. See, for example, Fisher, "Texts and Contexts"; and Binder and Weisberg, *Literary Criticisms of Law*. An extremely useful survey is Binder and Weisberg, "Cultural Criticism of Law"; this issue contains other essays relevant to these approaches, including "Foreword: The Arrival of Critical Historicism," by Robert W. Gordon, 1023–29. I am grateful to an anonymous reader for the University

of Washington Press who pointed out these materials to me. Binder has also written an extensive critique of the "pragmatic" economic approach to the study of law upheld primarily by the prolific Judge Richard Posner in "Poetics of the Pragmatic"; Binder summarizes his coauthored book *Literary Criticisms of Law* here as well, 1511–15 and 1521–26.

8. Binder and Weisberg, "Cultural Criticism," 1151–52. Theiss, *Disgraceful Matters*, an important recent study, demonstrates just this point in the Chinese context: that legal texts, in this case *The Qing Penal Code*, embody compromises produced to meet contemporary needs, and when the needs changed, so, too, did interpretations of the laws.

9. Binder and Weisberg, "Cultural Criticism," 1166.

10. Ibid., 1168. In this essay, Binder and Weisberg trace the changing role of the merchant in English society by referencing a variety of studies on usury laws and laws governing commercial activity, 1201–6.

11. See Gordon, "Foreword," 1026, which quotes Reid, "Jurisprudence of Liberty," 167.

12. Surely the most thorough study of this phenomenon is Ruskola, "Legal Orientalism"; Ruskola provides a noteworthy list of recent comparative studies, 180–81n. For others, see Ruskola, "Conceptualizing Corporations and Kinship"; and William Alford, "Law, Law, What Law?"

13. See the exemplary studies cited by Ruskola in "Legal Orientalism." A noteworthy literary example is Kinkley, *Chinese Justice*.

14. A story in the seventeenth-century "short story" (*huaben xiaoshuo*) collection *Even the Rocks Nod* (Shi diantou), 276–309, features a woman who coolly marries and then kills her first husband's murderer, a motif that is not rare in fiction of the late Ming and Qing periods; see Carlitz, "Style and Suffering." It was based on a brief classical-language story in Feng Menglong's (1574–1646) *The History of Feeling* (Qingshi), according to literary scholar Hu Shiying; cf. *Shi diantou*, 334.

15. See Bodde and Morris, *Law in Imperial China*, for translations and discussion of 190 out of the more than 7,600 cases from the years 1736–1885. For a description and the history of the text, see 146–51.

16. Surveys of Qing period archives and guides to their use include Bartlett, "Archival Revival"; Park and Antony, "Archival Research"; and Telford and Finegan, "Qing Archival Materials."

17. See *DLCY*; Jiang, *The Great Ming Code / Da Ming lü*; and Jones, *The Great Qing Code*. Handbooks for magistrates and their assistants are listed and described in Will, *Official Handbooks and Anthologies*, esp. sections 2 and 4.1.

18. For an introduction to the reprints of popular fiction, see Hegel, "Traditional Chinese Fiction."

19. Smith, *Chinese Characteristics*, 237; quoted, along with other similar sentiments, in Wong, Huters, and Yu, "Introduction," 1. Other foreigners in China during the late nineteenth century generally held a far less positive view; in order to protect their citizens from "barbaric" Chinese legal action, England, the United States, and other countries had, from the 1840s onward, demanded extraterritoriality from China in the infamous "unequal treaties" enforced by military action. Meijer, *Murder and Adultery*, 121, suggests that if there were local objections to laws, they had no vehicle for being expressed or recorded. See Ruskola, "Legal Orientalism."

20. Wolf, "Gods, Ghosts, and Ancestors," 135.

21. For a discussion of this question, see Wong, Huters, and Yu, "Introduction," 3–4.

22. See Yongping Liu, *Origins of Chinese Law*; and Bodde and Morris, *Law in Imperial China*, 55–68.

23. *DQLL*, Articles 366, 254, and 302–23, respectively; see Jones, *The Great Qing Code*, 347, 237, 285–309.

24. For a discussion of the power relations involved in verbal exchanges in judicial settings, see chapter 4 in this book.

25. "Shuihu zhuan" huipingben (seventy-chapter edition), chapters 25, 26; Shapiro, *Outlaws of the Marsh* (one-hundred-chapter edition), chapters 26, 27.

26. Allee argues for the effect of laws on social organization in the introduction to his *Law and Local Society*, 1–5. See also Macauley, *Social Power and Legal Culture*; and Ch'ü, *Law and Society*. This last point is made forcefully, but somewhat differently, in Wong, Huters, and Yu, "Introduction," 12.

27. Lee and Nathan, "Beginnings of Mass Culture," 361–62.

28. Chang, "Legal Education," 294–96.

29. Ibid., 322 n. 1; see also 296–302. Chiu, "Yi fa wei ming," offers a more complex view of this question.

30. Theiss, *Disgraceful Matters*, provides an extensive discussion of the conflicts between shared moral standards, judicial decisions, and the interests of individuals and families regarding the question of female chastity.

31. Chang, "Legal Education," 319, 314; he also disputes the assertion that late imperial Chinese society was particularly litigious, 314–17. For the specific references to Wang Huizu's ideas, see ibid., 303, 331 n. 71, 332 n. 80, 307, 333 nn. 92, 98; and Chang, "Liangmu xunli Wang Huizu."

32. For the laws concerning proper sentencing, see *DQLL*, Articles 29 and 409; Jones, *The Great Qing Code*, 62–63, 381–92. Chang refers to the *Da Qing huidian* warning to this effect in "Legal Education," 305, with reference on 332 n. 83.

33. On the magistrate's "path to office" and career, see Watt, *District Magis-*

trate, 45–77. On the magistrate's staff, see van der Sprenkel, *Legal Institutions*, 44–46. Chang gives this number of counties in his "Legal Education," 322 n. 2, contradicting van der Sprenkel's number of 1,400.

34. Buoye, "Suddenly Murderous Intent Arose," 65–66.

35. Comparisons might be drawn between the threat of torture in Qing judicial investigations and its punitive use in contemporary European procedures described in Foucault, *Discipline and Punish*, 32–40. Unlike Foucault's presentation of the interrogation and use of torture in European aristocratic courts as a "joust between the accused and the interrogator," this kind of contest is not recorded in Qing court records. The contrast in power between the magistrate and the working man accused of crime was simply too one-sided.

36. For discussions of the judicial review process, see van der Sprenkel, *Legal Institutions*, 66–79; Bodde and Morris, *Law in Imperial China*, esp. 115–22; Ch'ü, *Local Government*, 117–22; and Ocko, "I'll Take It All the Way." Buoye offers a succinct review of the processes and deadlines for handling homicides in *Manslaughter, Markets, and Moral Economy*, 230 ff., as does Meijer, in "Autumn Assizes." On amnesties, see van der Sprenkel, *Legal Institutions*, 68. Alabaster, *Notes and Commentaries*, 21–23, describes the intensity of the final reviews of capital cases.

37. For discussions of civil procedures and minor criminal investigations, see Zelin, Ocko, and Gardella, *Contract and Property in Early Modern China*; and van der Sprenkel, *Legal Institutions*, 66–67.

38. Sommer, *Sex, Law, and Society*, 26–27.

39. See comments to this effect in Karasawa, "Hanasu koto"; Zhou, "Illusion and Reality"; Sommer, *Sex, Law, and Society*, 22; and Buoye, "Suddenly Murderous Intent Arose."

40. Wang Huizu refers to his experience writing reports as a legal secretary and concludes by warning magistrates to protect themselves by carefully scrutinizing their secretaries' drafts. See Chang, "Liangmu xunli Wang Huizu."

41. See Hegel, "Images in Legal and Fictional Texts" and "Imagined Violence."

42. For handbooks and other retellings of crime cases, see the collections by Huang Liuhong, *Fuhui quan shu*; and Lan Dingyuan, *Luzhou gong'an*.

PART I *Rhetoric and Persuasion*

1   Making a Case

Characterizing the Filial Son

MARAM EPSTEIN

Making a compelling legal case in Qing China was similar to telling a good anecdote. This was particularly true of the case summaries prepared by Qing officials, clerks, and legal secretaries that were appended to the *Routine Memorials of the Grand Secretariat's Punishments Office of Scrutiny* (Neige xingke tiben). Routinization of form made the particularities of each case instantly recognizable, and familiarity of character type aided in the comprehension of motivation. In contrast to writers of more complex narratives, in which the layering of details provides much of the meaning and entertainment value, authors of legal documents needed to strip away all extraneous information. The narrower the focus, the better; from an official's perspective, fewer loose ends meant that fewer questions could be raised and the case was less likely to be sent back for reinvestigation. The most important function of a case summary was to "name the crime" (*zuiming*), which it achieved by matching the specifics of each case to an article in *The Qing Code* or by finding the appropriate analogy. Since determining the seriousness of an offense depended on establishing intent—the degree of relationship between the actants and the nature and manner of the injury—summaries were careful to provide enough information to fill in these juridical blanks.

One gets the sense, reading these terse and formulaic summaries, that the vast majority of information provided was necessary for adjudicating the case. Indeed, most of the details are juridically necessary for naming the crime.

Some details that emerge in depositions elsewhere in the file, however, were added to or omitted from the narrative summary in order to make the defendant appear more or less sympathetic. Although the many substatutes added to the *Code* attempted to render it comprehensive enough to establish the proper punishments for all possible situations, officials did have some latitude in reducing sentences when provided with compelling mitigating information.[1] The readings of the case memorials below focus on the narrative manipulation of these details in order to tease out their juridical implications and to get a sense of their effectiveness at gaining reduced sentences for the defendants.

Constructing a male defendant's actions as motivated by filial concerns was a rhetorical maneuver used to portray a defendant in the most sympathetic light possible. The emphasis on filial piety as the dominant affective bond in an adult's life is one of the distinguishing features of Confucian societies. Moreover, the performance of filial piety, through a wide menu of acts, was among the most effective ways of demonstrating virtue in imperial China. Given the broad affective appeal of filial piety and its resonance as a barometer of virtue, it is not surprising that many male defendants in homicide cases were painted as filial sons. The traditional legal system followed ritual norms in privileging the parent-child bond as central among the hierarchical relationships that frame *The Qing Code*. The *Code* was designed to promote and protect a social order based on naturalized hierarchies. It follows that the rights and interests of people with higher hierarchical status were valued more highly than those of their hierarchical juniors. In general, the respect and obligations a son owed his parent outweighed other kinds of ethical and juridical values. Thus, for example, despite the high legal value placed on female chastity, there was no consideration of mitigating circumstances in the sentencing of a son who in 1823 beat his father to death with a rock after his father had raped the son's wife. The son was sentenced to the most severe penalty imaginable, immediate execution by slicing, the standard sentence for parricide.[2]

Most of the cases discussed in this chapter are drawn from the Qianlong reign period (1736–1795), which saw a resurgence of filial themes in the literati novels of the mid-eighteenth and the early nineteenth century. Filial piety is foregrounded as a central moral and emotional value in *The Scholars* (Rulin waishi), by Wu Jingzi (1701–1754); *A Country Codger's Words of Exposure* (Yesou puyan), by Xia Jingqu (1705–1787); *A Lantern for the Crossroads* (Qilu deng), completed around 1777, by Li Lüyuan (1707–1790); *Flowers in the Mirror* (Jinghuayuan), by Li Ruzhen (ca. 1763–1830); and *A Tale of Heroic Lovers* (Ernü yingxiong zhuan), by Wen Kang (fl. 1821–50). The active heroism modeled by the filial protagonists in these novels, however, is very different from the successful characterizations of filial sons in the case memorials discussed below. These sons, who were treated with clemency by the legal system, were largely passive and unwilling participants in events over which they had no control. Many of the details in the case narratives are designed to demonstrate that the defendants acted without intention. More striking, however, is the fact that although filial daughters show up frequently in Qing fiction, the filial daughter is absent from homicide cases.

FILIALLY MOTIVATED HOMICIDE

The largest category of filially motivated homicides is that of wives killed by husbands for showing disrespect to the husbands' parents. There may be at least two explanations. First, there was a high degree of tolerance for a type of discipline (which might well be identified as domestic violence by contemporary American norms) imposed on hierarchically junior members of a household, including servants, younger siblings, wives, and children. Second, filial motivation carried some rhetorical and legal weight in gaining clemency for homicide.

To a greater extent than in other categories of homicide, investigations into the killing of a wife relied on routine structures and formulaic descriptions. In the same way that Vladimir Propp constructed a morphology of the folktale, many of these memorials can be reduced to a number of core events.[3] The husband makes a request of his wife; she fails to respond or refuses. He yells; she yells; he hits her; she yells again; he hits her again and knocks her over; she curses his parents and continues even as he strikes her; he is overcome by rage and strikes the fatal blow. Most case memorials of homicides in which a husband beat his wife to death depict the fatal fight as an anomalous event brought on by the wife's transgressive and shrewish behavior. "Normally harmonious" (hexie, hehao) relations erupt into violent anger. However, from the descriptions of marital relations before the fatal events, it is clear that the description "normally harmonious" is a set legal phrase that functions to rule out the possibility of premeditation, because the term is frequently used to describe domestic situations in which the husband regularly beat his wife.

A typical example is the summary of the events that caused Wang Heixiao, twenty years old, to beat his wife to death after she ignored his request to boil water one summer day in 1736.[4] As narrated in the summary, Ms. Yu had been raised by Heixiao's family since she was twelve; the two had been married six years and normally had amicable relations. On this day, he yelled at her when she did not make him tea, and she yelled back. He then hit her on the right ear with his hand, and she fell to the ground and began to curse his parents. He picked up a wooden stick and hit and wounded her left wrist. Ms. Yu continued to yell and curse without stopping. Heixiao then kicked her in the forehead, and she died. In desperation, he picked her up, carried her inside, and tried to save her, but she did not recover. Left out of the summary is the fact, mentioned in the depositions, that Heixiao, out of fear that Ms. Yu's family would lodge a plaint at the yamen, tried to disguise her death as suicide by hanging.

Ms. Yu's yelling and cursing are markers of shrewish behavior that pushed Wang Heixiao beyond the limits of acceptable violence. The cursing of parents (or a husband's parents) was listed in the "Ten Abominations" (Shi e); it was considered such a great offense that the wife could be punished by strangulation if the aggrieved parent or grandparent filed a complaint (Article 329). It bears mentioning that not all offenses included in the "Ten Abominations" had serious legal consequences. For example, also listed under "lack of filial piety" were the not uncommon practices of dividing the household when the parents were still living or failing to provide for parental support. When these filial shortcomings appeared in case memorials, they invoked a minor judicial response if any at all. It seems, however, that a woman's lack of respect for her husband's parents was perceived as so provocative that it marked a homicide as unintentional—a result of sudden, justified rage—rather than premeditated.

The use in these narratives of cursing as a catalyst for the husband's loss of self-control is a detail worth challenging. As in many domestic homicides, the defendant claimed that his wife raised the level of provocation by cursing his parents once she had been knocked over and was at her most vulnerable; it is as likely that she was screaming for help or for mercy rather than further provoking her husband's anger. Furthermore, unlike other types of evidence collected in case memorials, there is no record of an attempt by the magistrate to corroborate this detail in this or other cases. The image of a shrew with her mouth open, cursing and "throwing a fit" (sapo), brings to mind Keith McMahon's discussions of openings (both architectural and corporeal) as basic causative building blocks in late imperial narratives.[5] The narrative power of the open mouth as trope that leads to disaster may have somehow influenced the frequency with which the detail of a wife cursing without stopping was used in case memorials of wife homicide. The characterization of wife as shrew further emphasized the notion that the wife was a deserving victim who initiated the tragedy, while the husband, who was merely trying to maintain proper domestic order, got caught up in events he could not control. In this particular case, although Wang Heixiao was originally sentenced to strangulation subject to review, the standard punishment for husbands who beat their wives to death, the Three Judicial Offices recommended that Wang be pardoned under the 1736 amnesty.

The next case is a much more violent incident of spousal murder framed in explicitly filial terms. The summary portrays the wife as a shrew worthy of fiction and the ultimate cause of the events. Lü Liu, twenty-seven, of Zhili, hit his wife, Ms. Dong, eight times in the head and face with an ax.[6] Lü and his wife, also twenty-seven, had been married nine years. According to Lü's deposition, there had been no animosity in their marriage. It was "only because his wife was unfilial" (*zhi shi yin nüren bu xiaoshun*) that he lived separately from his parents, who lived in town. In 1736, he brought his mother to the countryside at the time of the melon harvest. When he came back from the fields and gave a basket of melons to his mother and not to his wife, his wife became angry. At that moment, Lü hated her disrespectful behavior but went back to the fields. When he came home later that day, his mother looked angry. He asked her about it, and she explained that Ms. Dong had been complaining. Lü Liu went into the house and heard his wife say: "Some people get to eat melons without doing any of the work." As Ms. Dong continued to insult his mother, Lü picked up an ax, intending to beat her with the handle, but his wife's insults became even more provocative. She goaded him, saying, "If you don't kill me, you were raised by an ass." She then butted him with her head. Lü Liu "hated her shrewishness" (*e qi hanpo*) and struck her in the forehead with the blade of the ax. His wife hit the ground and, "unexpectedly" (*na zhi*), grabbed his leg, throwing a fit, and kept on yelling without stopping. Lü thought to himself, "What's the point of having such an unfilial bitch for a wife?" and hit her seven more times. Lü Liu was sentenced to strangulation after the assizes (Article 315.3) under the statute that applied to a husband who "intentionally kills his wife" (*gusha*), but the case summary is sympathetic to him in its depiction of Ms. Dong as the primary transgressor. The summary begins: "According to the memorial submitted by Li Wei of the Zhifu [yamen], Ms. Dong did not respect the way of women and resided separately from her husband's parents. During the seventh month of 1736, Lü Liu was growing melons...."

Throughout, Lü Liu is portrayed as a passive victim of his wife's shrewishness. It was Ms. Dong who forced him to live separately from his parents, while Lü was doing his best under difficult circumstances to honor his mother. By giving his mother fresh melons, he was furthermore emulating one of the most popular models of virtuous behavior found in the ubiquitous *Twenty-four Exemplars of Filial Piety* (Ershisi xiao); fully one-quarter of the biographies in that collection honor a child for feeding a parent. It was only after Lü realized that his wife's behavior was angering his mother that he moved to confront his wife; until that moment, he had done everything possible to keep the family at peace. The insults Ms. Dong hurled at him, which are quoted verbatim for extra rhetorical power, were so offensive that any reasonable person would have reacted with rage. The summary is expansive in detailing Ms. Dong's transgressions; Lü's violence toward her, however, is treated with far greater narrative economy. The horror of his enraged loss of self-control is lessened by the fact that there is no mention of the blood shed or soft tissue exposed with each cut of the ax. The stark contrast between the expansive characterization of the shrewish wife and the economical treatment of the victimized filial son was so rhetorically persuasive that the magistrate did not question Lü Liu's telling of the events, particularly his blaming his wife for the decision to divide the household when there may have been compelling economic or practical reasons for him to live closer to the fields he tilled. In this instance, the naturalization of Ms. Dong as a shrew out of control was such a powerful narrative component of this memorial that it shut off other narrative threads the magistrate could have explored.[7] The characterization of Lü as a filial son ensured that he would be viewed positively despite the horrific violence of the murder.

The following example shows that ascribing filial motivations to homicide was so rhetorically powerful that it could script the master narrative even though numerous details contradicted the defendant's story. As reported in the case summary, Chen Qianli, forty-five, had been married to Ms. Wang for more than twenty years, and their relationship was harmonious.[8] It was "only because" Chen's mother was over eighty years old and bedridden and needed tea to drink that one night, when Chen was "reading" (*kanshu*) and drinking wine after his wife had gone to bed early, that he discovered that there was no tea on the stove when he went to heat some wine. Chen then locked the door to the bedroom, extinguished the lamp, and went to bed. He found fault with Ms. Wang, and unexpectedly, she responded disrespectfully. Chen tried to hit her, but she blocked him. Under the influence of alcohol, Chen got angry and groped on the table for something he could use to hit her. Unaware, he picked up a knife, and, in the dark and under the influence of alcohol, he struck Ms. Wang with it. Ms. Wang again blocked him and received cuts to her hands; Chen then stabbed her several times in the torso, with some cuts going to the bone. Chen Qianli ran away that night but denied nothing when arrested.

The summary omits several pertinent details that came out in the depositions. First, Ms. Wang's father had registered a plaint at the yamen six years earlier accusing Chen Qianli of beating Ms. Wang and leaving her with serious injuries. The district magistrate repeatedly tried to link the homicide to the earlier incident, claiming there must have been a residual grudge. However, all family members, including Ms. Wang's father, testified that the couple had gotten along well since then and had even had a son during that period. All agreed that the incident had been caused by the fact that there was no tea for Chen's mother. As Yasuhiko Karasawa shows in chapter 3, even when all witnesses agree to a statement, that agreement does not necessarily validate the truth of the statement; rather, it is a sign of the tight composition of the memorials.[9] Also omitted from this summary is the information, given by Chen Qianli's children and neighbors, that Chen was a habitual drinker with a bad temper. The most important detail excluded from the summary is the presence of several women younger than Ms. Wang in the household. It seems reasonable to assume that Chen's younger sister, who had joined his household after her own husband disappeared, and Qianli's fourteen-year-old daughter, who shared a *kang*, or heated brick bed, with her grandmother, were also responsible for supplying tea for the family matriarch.

The master narrative presents only one of Chen Qianli's actions as intentional: his attempt to discipline a lazy wife. This portrayal of Chen, as a man who turned on his wife out of natural filial concern for his aged mother, formed a sufficiently powerful narrative that the magistrate did not feel the need to follow several loose threads that might have been pursued in a different kind of case. Why had Chen attacked his wife on a night when his son was out of the house and only the women were home? Why had he taken the precaution of bolting the bedroom door? Why did he stab his wife three more times after she started screaming? If he was so drunk that he did not realize he was stabbing his wife, how did he have the wits to run away when his daughter and his sister tried to force open the door upon hearing his wife's screams? The summary is crafted in such a way as to make Chen Qianli's actions look reasonable. He had stayed up to read, an activity that seems to have made the judicial system more sympathetic to the defendant.[10] (The literary historian in me wants to know what he was reading; the feminist wants to know why no one questioned his ability to read if he was intoxicated enough not to be aware he was stabbing his wife.) Although the records clearly leave open the possibility that this was a case of premeditated murder, Chen was sentenced for the lesser crime of killing his wife in an affray.

Given the foundational importance of a child's obligations to a parent, it would seem likely that children who killed in order to defend a parent or to obey parental orders would receive special treatment in their sentencing. Acting to save a parent was not a foolproof way to obtain clemency, however. In trying a homicide that occurred during a scuffle between neighbors when one neighbor's cow wandered into the other's fields, the magistrate took no mitigating factors into consideration.[11] The eighteen-year-old defendant, Zhou Demao, was sentenced to strangulation subject to review at the autumn assizes after he struck and killed his neighbor with a pole because the neighbor was having a fistfight with Demao's father. Demao had escalated the level of violence even though his father was not in imminent danger.

The following example similarly demonstrates that magistrates did not automatically reduce sentences for filially motivated crimes, although sentences might be reduced at a higher level of review. Chen Liangfu had raised his younger brother, Lianglu, after the death of their parents. Unfortunately, the younger brother turned out to be a delinquent.[12] He drank heavily, twice tried to rape the wives of Liangfu and Liangfu's son Gongyuan, and beat up Liangfu and his wife after he and Liangfu had divided the household. Finally, Liangfu reached the end of his patience. One night, as Lianglu was lying drunk on Liangfu's wife's bed, Liangfu ordered Gongyuan to help him carry Lianglu outside. Liangfu tied up Lianglu under the pear tree and then ordered Gongyuan to help him strangle Lianglu. Gongyuan hesitated because Lianglu's status as his uncle made him afraid. Liangfu yelled at Gongyuan and called him unfilial. Gongyuan then obeyed, and, together with his father, strangled Lianglu. They then took the corpse and dropped it in the garden.

The first central review of the case followed the initial recommendation that Chen Gongyuan be sentenced to immediate slicing for intentionally murdering an older relative, although it did conclude with the mitigating comment that Gongyuan had acted only under his father's coercion. Liangfu, for his complicity in the crime, was sentenced to exile at a distance of 2,000 *li* and one hundred strokes of the heavy bamboo. (Even though Liangfu was clearly responsible for the homicide, juridical responsibility was shifted, as was typical, onto Gongyuan, the most junior of the relatives involved.) After review, the sentence was found to be so unjust that the case was sent back for reconsideration. On second hearing, the Three Judicial Offices argued that Chen Gongyuan's sentence should be reduced to strangulation after the assizes since he had acted not of his own volition but under his father's orders; his father, Chen Liangfu, was forgiven under the 1736 amnesty.

Significant in this case, as in those above in which filial motivation gained the defendant a reduced sentence, the son's behavior was in no way motivated by his own self-interest or emotions but was totally subordinate to the will or interests of his parent. For example, this memorial contains no mention of Gongyuan's responses to his uncle's harassment of his own wife and his mother, and no suggestion that he might have resented his uncle for economic reasons. The only emotion voiced in the case record is Liangfu's anger toward his "unfilial" son when Gongyuan disobeyed him. A similar nesting of emotions occurs in a case from 1768 in which a forty-six-year-old son unintentionally killed his cousin with two blows of his left arm while supporting his frail father with his right.[13] According to the records, the only reason Yao Tianqing intervened was to de-escalate the conflict between his seventy-six-year-old father and his loutish, drunken cousin, while his father alone expressed anger. The Nine Chief Ministries (Jiu qing) recommended reducing Yao Tianqing's sentence one degree, from beheading after review at the autumn assizes (for striking and killing an older relative) to strangulation subject to review at the autumn assizes, since he had been acting to defend his father and had no intention of striking an older relative. Since only a small percentage of those sentenced to be strangled after review at the assizes were actually executed, the reduced sentences given to Chen Gongyuan and Yao Tianqing literally meant the difference between life and death.

Following Natalie Davis's pioneering research on narrative paradigms in sixteenth-century French pardon tales, and what she described as the importance of framing emotions appropriately, the extremely limited palette of emotions in these Qing memorials deserves comment.[14] The filial sons who appear in the cases are emotionally subordinate to their parents. No matter the relative age of parent and son, the narrative constructs agency as lying with the parent. For the defendant to express anger would mean constructing him as an agent rather than as a victim swept up in events he could not control.

The following memorial is masterful in its depiction of the defendant as victim of fate. One morning in 1768, Liu Jizhao, the son of a local "licentiate" (*shengyuan*), went out to cut grass with a scythe.[15] He saw that Liu Shou, age fourteen, a poor and distant relative outside the bonds of mourning, had already cut a big bundle of grass. Jizhao tried to take some, but Liu Shou ran off with the grass. Jizhao followed, still carrying his scythe. Liu Shou ran home and told his mother what had happened. Ms. Ma began to reason with Liu Jizhao when he ran into her courtyard, but Jizhao ignored her and continued to make a fuss. Ms. Ma picked up a reed switch and swung it in his direction; Jizhao then threw a brick and hit her in the forehead, causing her to bleed. Ms. Ma grabbed him, intending to drag him off to his father; at this point, Liu Shou also joined the fray and grabbed Jizhao. Jizhao, however, was strong enough to grab Ms. Ma by the collar and pull her to the ground. His younger brother Liu Sihan rushed over from where he had been herding cows and started hitting Ms. Ma with his switch. Liu Shou, having witnessed his mother being hit by a brick and now beaten with a switch, suddenly "became frantic" (*yishi qingji*) to save her. He took a wooden pole from a female neighbor and hit Sihan on the back, planning to frighten and drive him off. Unexpectedly, Sihan turned around, and Liu Shou hit him from the front. Liu Sihan died two weeks later.

Although this homicide was less serious than the killings of older relatives discussed above, the case had to be decided with care since the victim was the son of a local licentiate. However, the memorial was compiled in such a way as to make Liu Shou appear to be the passive and unwilling victim of the brothers' bullying. Liu Jizhao was the only litigant to whom anger was attributed; his anger was unjustified and drove him to act improperly. As his deposition states, Jizhao initially chased Liu Shou in order to hit him and vent his anger. In contrast, Liu Shou's testimony contains no emotion other than his desire to save his mother in a moment of desperation. Indeed, his deposition constructs him as a passive participant in the events: "I wanted to scare them off; unexpectedly [*buliao*], he turned around. The pole was curved, and I had no control of it. How could I have known that it would wound him on the head?"

Even though Liu Shou was found guilty of killing someone in an affray, a crime punishable by strangulation subject to review at the assizes, the fact that he was acting in desperation to save his mother was found to be so compelling that his sentence was reduced one degree, to exile. Because of his youth, this sentence was further commuted to forty strokes of the light bamboo and a fine of twenty taels to the victim's family, to pay for funeral expenses. The rescript shows that the commuted sentence was approved.

One last example contradicts this tendency to create sympathetic characterizations of filial sons by portraying them as unwilling actants. A case from Yangzhou prefecture comes closer to fictional norms by depicting an active protagonist, Xu Wu, nineteen, who avenged his father's honor by killing his mother's lover.[16] Despite the extremely sympathetic depiction of the victim, the defendant was pardoned in the 1736 amnesty. Xu Wu's father had died in 1722 when the boy was six. Afterward, his father's close friend, Li Qiansheng, began an illicit sexual relationship with Wu's mother, Ms. Chen; the two were together for three years. Ms. Chen and Wu moved in with Qiansheng after their house burned down. In Xu Wu's words: "Outsiders all said that my mother was acting like Li Qiansheng's wife. At that time, I was furious, but because I was young I had to tolerate it." After his mother's death in 1725, Xu Wu left to apprentice with his maternal uncle. In 1736, when he was twenty, Wu returned to his natal village and made offerings at his parents' graves; he suddenly became aggrieved when he remembered Li Qiansheng and came up with the plan to kill him to help his father "vent his anger" (*ti fuqin chuqi*). Four days later, after he had purchased a vegetable knife, he went to Li's restaurant to confront him. Direct speech marks the climax of Xu Wu's deposition: "I called him outside and asked him: 'Do you recognize me?' He said, 'I know you; you're Xu Wu.' I then asked him, 'Do you remember what happened before?' He said, 'How could I not remember? Your mother and I were together.' I then grabbed his beard with my left hand and stabbed his throat with my right."

Many details in the depositions render Li Qiansheng in a positive light. He had supported the widowed Chen until her death, and his wife at the time of his death, another widow who also brought a son into the marriage, reported that he had burned paper money to Ms. Chen during the New Year's festival.

The case summary omits the fact that eleven years had passed between Xu Wu's mother's death and his act of vengeance. The summary also refines Xu Wu's motivations as a desire to "clear his father's shame" (*wei fu xie chi*) rather than to vent his anger. The legal code was highly sympathetic to a husband who acted out of an uncontrollable rage upon discovering his wife's infidelity and granted him (or a close relative) impunity if he killed his wife and her lover when certain provisions were met. The intent of the law was to cede the authority to impose capital punishment only under narrow conditions—ideally when the husband discovered, apprehended, and killed the fornicators on the spot.[17] However, as time and distance from the act increased, the state's willingness to cede its penal authority diminished rapidly. A series of substatutes debated the exact meaning of the limits placed on the phrases "at the time" (*dengshi*) and "on the spot" (*jiansuo*). As written into the *Code* in 1767, if a husband killed an adulterer who had left the scene and offered no resistance and after the time of the adultery, the crime was analogous to homicide, and the husband was subject to strangulation after review (Article 285.2). In this case, the eleven years Xu Wu had waited before killing his mother's lover clearly exceeded juridical sympathy for homicides committed by closely related family members. Xu Wu was provisionally sentenced to beheading subject to review at the autumn assizes for the crime of "premeditated homicide" (*mousha*). However, the portrait of Xu Wu was sympathetic enough that the rescript approved the request for a pardon under the 1736 amnesty. Critical to the framing of Xu Wu's motivations was the inference that he was acting selflessly on behalf of his father's emotions and not of his own.

ABSENT FILIAL DAUGHTERS

As suggested by the above cases, it was not uncommon for magistrates to help male defendants by depicting them as filial sons whose concern for a parent's welfare was the only named motivation for the commission of an offense. Filial motivations, however, seem to have been the prerogative of sons, whether they truly deserved the characterization or not. Case records clearly demonstrate that many women maintained close relations with their natal families after marrying out: parents stayed with married daughters or supported them and their indigent husbands' parents, who borrowed money from married daughters, and married daughters frequently visited their natal families. But while there might have been sympathy for a daughter's filial bonds with her parents, a daughter's relationship with her parents carried no legal value. Although one magistrate commented favorably on the close affective bonds between mothers and daughters,[18] too many visits from a married woman to her natal family implied that the woman was resisting the authority of her husband's family—even in cases of delayed transfer marriage.[19]

For example, when the eighteen-year-old wife of Bai Can, Ms. Liu, told her husband that she wanted to take some of the apricots they had just harvested to her mother's house and then stay for a couple of days, Bai would not allow her to go because it was the middle of the harvest.[20] Ms. Liu insisted on staying in her natal home for several days, and in his depositions, Bai repeatedly accused his wife of escalating the conflict. He ended up beating her to death with a pole. Of interest is the contrast to the positive depiction of Lü Liu, discussed above, who brought his mother to his home to enjoy the melon harvest. In this case, the narrative summary does not explain Ms. Liu's motivations for wanting to stay at her natal home for several days. Her husband's deposition suggests that her motivation was to get out of helping him during the busiest part of the harvest, although it is just as likely she went home to help her own family with their harvest.

In other cases, when married women made explicit claims that they were motivated by filial intent, their actions were shockingly misguided, undermining their claims to filial motivation. In explaining why she had sexual relations with a hired laborer, Ms. Geng, a thirty-two-year-old concubine living in Zhili, said that she missed her parents and brothers, whom she had not seen in many years, and was afraid that her strict husband would not let her go home.[21] Ms. Geng asked Hu Si, a hired laborer, to keep her company one night when the master and his wife were out visiting the wife's family and she was afraid to be alone. She then asked Hu Si to accompany her to her parents' home in Henan. Their affair came to light when Hu Si poisoned Ms. Geng's seven-year-old son so that the two could travel unencumbered. Ms. Geng is portrayed as unwitting, naive, and without true agency. The summary glosses over her seduction of Hu and states simply: "They then spent the night together." The investigating magistrate did not push either of them for further details about their illicit sexual relationship. By minimizing her agency, the summary heightens the portrayal of Hu Si as the primary criminal transgressor while characterizing Ms. Geng as a naive victim who ultimately remained loyal to her husband when she turned Hu in to the authorities.

In a second example of a woman explicitly naming filial motivations as justification for her actions, Mrs. Sun née Han, from Shuntian prefecture in Zhili, reveals the moral bankruptcy of her claims.[22] In 1857, Mrs. Sun, twenty years of age, poisoned Sun De, her husband of three years. Mrs. Sun's retelling of the events leading to her decision to kill her husband shows her attempt to frame it as sympathetically as possible. In her deposition, Mrs. Sun stated that she often stayed with her father at her natal home because her husband's family was so poor that his parents had been reduced to begging. One day, she realized that her husband's family had no means of support; her own father was both old and sick, and if he should die, she would have no one on whom to rely.

> The more I thought about it, the more [I realized] there was no way out. I thought that I would be better off killing my husband and marrying into a family with food [*inserted on side*: to avoid freezing and starving]. My father could also get enough from the dowry to live on in his old age.

Mrs. Sun convinced her father to buy some arsenic for her as medicine for a pain in her foot and then used it to poison her husband. The magistrate who questioned Mrs. Sun did not fall for her misplaced appeal to filial piety; in fact, that detail was omitted from the case summary. Instead, the magistrate

Characterizing the Filial Son 39

focused much of his questioning on the sexual and economic details of affairs with two lovers with whom she had been involved before she married—although neither of the men had participated in any way in the poisoning of her husband. Pointedly, the case summary links her motivations for the homicide directly to these much earlier events:

> Because her husband was poor and his house small, Mrs. Sun often stayed at her natal home. She did not avoid the gaze of Ma Guifang [her father's landlord]. In the spring of 1852 [two years before she married], the defendant does not remember the exact month or day, she was washing vegetables at her father's house while he was out working in the fields when Yue Lu passed by on a stroll. Seeing that no one was around, his lascivious thoughts were aroused, and so he propositioned Mrs. Sun. From that time, it was more than once that they took advantage of an opportunity to indulge their lust. He gave her money and gifts, but [she] does not remember the exact amount. Later that year, sometime after the fall, Ma Guifang went to the home of Liang Fu [her father] to collect rent. Because Liang Fu had gone out, Ma Guifang then flirted with Mrs. Sun and they engaged in illicit sex.

Although neither Ma nor Yue were in any way involved in the poisoning of Sun De, the narrative of Mrs. Sun's sexual transgressions was used to frame her motivations for this more serious crime. Her desire to be of some support to her father, or at least not to depend on him economically, was omitted from the case summary.

A similar impulse to identify illicit sexual relations as the motivating factor for the killing of a husband informed the magistrate's interrogations in the case of Ms. Peng, age thirty-seven, who had received a parcel of land from her father.[23] Her husband, Gong Ruisi, was a habitual drinker who took no responsibility for his family. Usually, when her husband returned home drunk and yelling, Ms. Peng tolerated his behavior and did not make a fuss. However, one night in the spring of 1736, her husband came home drunk and tried to force her to sign a contract to sell the land that had belonged to her father. When she refused, Ruisi picked up a club and began to hit her. Panicking, she grabbed it from him and hit him back. He fell to the ground and died soon after. Ms. Peng and her daughter (age not given) then buried him on a corner of their land without telling anyone, but a cousin discovered his skeleton and reported it to the village head.

During his interrogation, the magistrate accused Ms. Peng of having had an illicit sexual relationship and then plotting her husband's homicide. The magistrate subjected her to finger presses in order to determine whether her denials of that charge were truthful. He next accused her of harboring some resentment against her husband (which would have provided evidence of intentional homicide). In the magistrate's reasoning, the land was her husband's to sell, so why had she intervened? Ms. Peng explained that the land had been given by her father, a detail indicating that by custom she maintained some control over it. Curiously, the case summary omits the fact that the property had come from her father; including this detail would have suggested that Ms. Peng's obligations to protect own lineage's landholdings somehow legitimated her resistance to her husband's authority.

Case memorials that involve a daughter going to her parents' home—whether it be just to visit, to care for a sick parent, or because her husband was sojourning away from home—do not invoke the language or sentiments of filial affection that would be ascribed to a son. The wife's actions are typically described as "sneaking off to her mother's house" (*sihui niangjia*).[24] Even when the families had some agreement about a wife returning to her natal home, there were still conflicts about which family had rights to the wife's time and labor.[25] There was, it seems, no accepted juridical arena in which crimes committed by married women could be treated more leniently because they had acted out of a sense of filial loyalty to their own families. Within juridical norms, a married woman's allegiance was exclusively to her husband and his parents.

CONCLUSION

In contrast to Qing fictional accounts of heroic sons and daughters who actively seek to promote their parents' honor and interests, the portraits in criminal-case memorials depict sons as secondary characters in the family dramas into which they are swept up. No matter their relative age, the agency of these men is subordinated to that of their parents or of their wives—they react rather than act. Furthermore, in many instances, these sympathetic male defendants are described as having no emotional motivations of their own; implicitly or explicitly, they follow the emotional lead of their parents. The active Xu Wu, who avenged his father's honor by plotting to kill his mother's lover eleven years after her death, stands out from the more common model of sons who were unwillingly forced to act in order to restore proper order. However, the summary explicitly states that he was acting on behalf of his father. We will never know whether events unfolded as narrated in the case memorials, but we can be sure that the motivations that drove these men to act were more complex than the narrow causality outlined in the memorials.

The summaries reveal that magistrates had a great deal of flexibility in shaping these highly formulaic documents. It should not be a surprise that their sympathies fell along predictable gender lines when they dealt with family dramas that pitted husbands against wives. We see magistrates choosing not to follow certain threads that could be damaging to male defendants and ferreting out other details, especially of sexual histories that would be damaging to female defendants, and weaving them into the narrative even though they lay outside the time frame of the crimes. Additionally, magistrates employed certain narrative constructions intended to minimize the agency of male defendants. The summaries frequently employ the male defendant's actions within a chain of events initiated by the victim. The narratives themselves are filled with passive verbal constructions or words such as "unexpectedly," "unaware," "only because" that further limit or shift responsibility for the criminal offense from the defendant onto the victim and the situation. In short, applications of *The Qing Code* clearly favored the patrilineal obligations imagined to be most in accordance with Confucian norms for a harmonious society.

NOTES

1. See chapter 5, by Thomas Buoye, in this volume.
2. Ng, "Sexual Abuse of Daughters-in-law," 385, citing *Xing'an huilan*, 3326.
3. Propp, *Morphology of the Folktale*.
4. "Hunyin jianqing" (Marriage and illicit sex), XKTB, 2/10/10; QL 1.5.29 (film 2: 1776–1802).
5. McMahon, *Causality and Containment*, 25–28.
6. "Hunyin jianqing," XKTB, 2/38/10; QL 2.5.5 (film 6: 2938–60).
7. For a discussion of the shrew as a type in case memorials, see Theiss, *Disgraceful Matters*, 206.
8. "Hunyin jianqing," XKTB, 2/84/10; QL 3.9.12 (film 13: 2611–40).
9. Karasawa, "Orality, Textuality, and Reality."
10. The legal capital of reading is suggested in the following memorial. The death of an ugly wife was reported to the yamen four days after she had drowned. The woman was found face down in a cistern, with blood streaming from her nose and mouth. Her husband presented himself as an aspiring scholar and

nephew of a "licentiate" (shengyuan). The husband explained events this way: he told his wife to make him tea when he was "studying" (dushu), but she replied, "What is so important about studying? I don't have time to get it." Although his family had bribed the coroner with seven taels of silver and the woman's body bore the telltale signs of poisoning (both serious offenses), the husband's claims to social respectability were successful enough that he was pardoned in the 1736 amnesty. "Hunyin jianqing," XKYB, 2/2/2; QL 1.2.20 (film 1: 581–690).

11. "Dousha" (Affrays), XKTB, QL 33, bundle 33; QL 33.9.15.

12. "Hunyin jianqing," XKTB, 2/9/18; QL 1.5.21 (film 2: 1095). Reviewed 2/23/11; QL 1.11.12 (tape 4: 1694–1712).

13. "Dousha," XKTB, QL 33, bundle 36; QL 33.12.16.

14. Davis, Fiction in the Archives.

15. "Dousha," XKTB, QL 33, bundle 33; QL 33.8.26.

16. "Hunyin jianqing," XKTB, 2/28/4; QL 1.12.5 (film 5: 986–1011).

17. DLCY, vol. 4, Article 285, pp. 783–811; discussed in Meijer, Murder and Adultery, 49–50, 68–71.

18. Cited from Paderni, "Appeal Case of Honor," 89. "Hunyin jianqing," XKTB, QL 1.7.1.

19. For example, a Miao husband from Guizhou was involved in a deadly altercation with his wife's brother because his wife spent so little time with his family. In his deposition, the husband, Agui, complained that even though they had been married for two years "[my wife] was never willing to come back and act like an adult [making a family (zuo renjia)]. I would go get her several times, and she would only stay one or two days and then return to her mom's house." "Hunyin jianqing," XKTB, 2/616/3; QL 21.4.20 (film 110: 285–302).

20. Ibid., 28, 2/615/7; QL 21.4 (film 109: 2696–2711); reviewed 2/627/13; QL 21.7.16.

21. Ibid., 2/606/1; QL 21.2.2 (film 108: 371–98).

22. "Shuntian Prefecture Archives," film 4/68, juan 166–68; XF 7.2.27 (1858).

23. "Hunyin jianqing," XKTB, 2/21/18; QL 1.10.23 (film 4: 797–826).

24. See, for example, XKTB, 2/612/10; QL 21.4.17 (film 109: 1207–29); and 2/616/7; QL 21.4.20 (film 110: 516–35).

25. XKTB, "Hunyin jianqing," 2/644/5; QL 21.12.10 (film 115: 2174–92). For a similar case in which a man kills his father-in-law in an affray after his wife stayed away too long, see ibid., 2/607/7; QL 21.3.11 (film 108: 1292–1313); reviewed 2/624/5; QL 21.6.17.

2   Explaining the Shrew

Narratives of Spousal Violence and the Critique of Masculinity in Eighteenth-Century Criminal Cases

JANET THEISS

If criminal cases are any indication, the "shrew" (*pofu, hanfu, yinfu*) was a familiar social category in the Qing period; she was as commonplace in everyday interactions as in late imperial fiction. In "Board of Punishments routine memorials" (*xingke tiben*), judicial officials and case participants routinely used certain phrases to describe shrewish women whose "bad temperament" (*xingqing buhao*) accounts for various kinds of unvirtuous behavior, including the classic elements of the fictional shrew's repertoire: disobedience to family superiors, unfiliality, lasciviousness, argumentativeness, bad temper, verbal and physical aggression, intransigence, laziness, and ineptitude at household chores. Such women were typically said to have a "stubborn and intransigent disposition" (*xingqing jueqiang*) or a "fierce, shrewish temperament" (*suxing hanpo*). They refused to submit to the "discipline and instruction" (*guanjiao*) of their husbands and mothers-in-law and were thus "uncontrollable" (*guanbuzhu*). In the context of arguments, they "throw tantrums" (*sapo*). In the midst of conflicts, they "scream shrewish curses" (*fa poma*).

How are we to understand these judicial characterizations, which are so similar to fictional constructions of the shrew?[1] Tropes of shrewish behavior are especially common in cases of spousal homicide perpetrated by husband or wife. Accusations of shrewishness were thus clearly, on one level, part of rhetorical strategies of enhancing or diminishing culpability: a wife's shrewishness gave her husband a motive for homicidal fury or explained an adulteress's homicidal betrayal of the wifely way. Such emphasis on the moral responsibility of women makes sense in this period when the cult of female chastity was at its height. Yet judicial narratives of spousal homicide also paint quite unflattering portraits of husbands. Magistrates' interrogation questions and case summaries often evince both disdain for men who were violent, hot-tempered, and impatient and a degree of sympathy for women subjected to their husbands' cruelty.

This disapproval is reminiscent of the criticism of family and community authorities that pervades mid-Qing discussions of social policy. Espousing an activist civilizing role for the imperial state, the Yongzheng and Qianlong emperors and their officials saw the moral failings, weakness, and compromised priorities of husbands, fathers, and lineage leaders as the root of social breakdown and moral depravity of all sorts, from crimes to unnecessary female suicides, to excessive litigation, to the degeneration of marriage and funeral customs. Rectification of proper social hierarchy founded on chastity and filiality was the heart of the imperial civilizing mission.[2] Statecraft writings and memorials often mention that officials should expect to encounter shrewishness as a female form of socially disruptive behavior along with the gambling, drunkenness, and thuggery that characterized male immorality. Descriptions of female troublemakers, such as conniving women who trump up lawsuits in criminal cases, evil stepmothers who persecute stepsons, and lascivious adulteresses, are couched in metaphors of shrewishness.[3]

Yet statecraft constructions of male and female forms of moral turpitude did not consider them as parallel problems but rather assumed that women's lack of virtue was due to the failure of men to uphold orthodox social and moral order. Thus, ironically, in this heyday of the chastity cult, dynastic officials found male virtue and authority far more problematic than female virtue. Indeed, much of the impetus for the state's obsession with female virtue was a reaction to disillusionment with family patriarchs.[4] From this perspective, spousal homicides, perpetrated by men or women, appear as one more manifestation of the inability or unwillingness of male authorities to educate their inferiors and enforce moral norms in ways that were conducive not only to the cultivation of morality but also to the maintenance of social order.

Such critique of improper expressions of masculine authority was explicit in the judicial framing of cases of men who killed their wives. Both *The Qing Code* and the adjudication process treated such men as examples of the degradation of proper masculinity, demonstrated by an abusively aberrant exercise of authority and the collapse of proper patriarchal order. In such cases, male virtue was figuratively and literally on trial. Judicial officials often approached such cases with contempt for the ways in which the mostly commoner men they encountered in the courtroom exercised their authority. Their criticisms of male violence and moral failure suggest the broad circulation of the ideal of male self-containment or self-mastery that pervades late imperial fiction. Keith McMahon identifies self-containment as temperance, its opposite being abandonment to the four vices of drink, lust, greed, and wrath: "The tempered self maintains stasis and equilibrium by trying not to take more than the proper allotment of such things as wealth or pleasure and by avoiding altered, unnatural states such as drunkenness or anger." He argues that the ideology of self-containment incorporates both a moral emphasis on virtues such as temperance, chastity, and filiality and an economic focus on frugality rather than wastefulness in all realms.[5] Yet self-containment, embodied in the fictional characters of temperate polygamists, misers, and ascetics, is an "innately male" approach to the regulation of self, women, family, and society, the failure of which allows, among other things, the disastrous ascendance of the shrew.[6] Maram Epstein describes this ideal of masculine self-regulation as "self-mastery" (*zhu*), noting its roots in Neo-Confucian philosophy dating back to the Song dynasty. She interprets the fictional shrew, represented in her most egregious form in the character of Sujie, the vile anti-heroine of the early Qing novel *Marriage Bonds to Awaken the World* (Xingshi yinyuan zhuan), as the product of male failure at self-cultivation: "The narrative lesson taught so clearly by *Xingshi* is that without [her husband] Chao Yuan's initial loss of self-mastery, Sujie would never have come into being."[7]

This same causal logic, by which female immorality is the result of male failures at self-containment and control, also structures the narration of wife-killing cases. Like many authors of late imperial fiction, when mid-Qing judicial officials explained the causes of extreme marital violence, they often blamed the worst consequences of female lack of virtue, if not the existence of unvirtuous women themselves, on the husbands' loss of self-mastery through drunkenness, loss of temper, or dissolute or wastrel behavior. At the same time, however, these cases demonstrate the limited acceptance of this masculine ideal, and of the notion of male responsibility for female behavior, not only among uneducated commoners, but even among the local elites whose family conflicts became severe enough to land them in court. Reading wife-killing cases with the fictional paradigm of containment in mind shows us elite and popular models of masculinity and marital relations that help explain the significance of the shrew as a social and cultural phenomenon in late imperial China.

THE SCHOLAR-OFFICIAL IDEAL OF MASCULINITY

The influential mid-Qing jurist, scholar, and moralist Wang Huizu (1731–1807) offers a useful starting point for piecing together the notions of masculinity that informed the moral standards and judicial judgments of officialdom. Wang's widely read handbook for the regulation of family life, *Simple Precepts from the Hall Enshrining a Pair of Chaste Widows* (Shuangjietang yongxun), not only elaborates his personal ideal of the cultivated mode of masculinity appropriate for elite men but links his own values explicitly to the assumptions that guide his courtroom judgments of male violence. The handbook is dedicated to the two women (his father's second wife and his concubine, Wang Huizu's mother) whose wisdom and virtue supposedly inspired it and is full of commentary on female virtue. Yet anxiety about the fragility of masculine virtue permeates the book, addressed to Wang's sons as future patriarchs. Wang emphasizes throughout that the morality and harmony of the family, especially the virtue of its women, depends chiefly on the "family elder's discipline" (zunzhang yueshu).[8] He also stresses women's crucial role in educating children and managing household affairs and the threat to family stability posed by women's lack of virtue. But in a section titled "Regulation of the family must begin with women," he pointedly notes that it is men who are responsible for cultivating women's virtue: "The moral transformation of men is easy, but the moral transformation of women is difficult. If women are to be completely transformed, then men must guide and educate them [shuaijiao]."[9] For Wang Huizu, female immorality was symbolic of family disorder, just as, in fiction, "the figure of the shrew . . . became emblematic of the breakdown of the sociopolitical order."[10] Yet for Wang, as for fiction writers, the ultimate cause of this breakdown was male failure to exercise patriarchal authority properly. In another section titled "When wives are not virtuous, their husbands are to blame," he reiterates even more explicitly who is at fault when women misbehave: "If the husband controls [his wife] with rectitude, then if the wife is sensible, she will know her place. Even if she is not too sensible, she will gradually come to know fear/awe and become aware [of her place]. Therefore, if a man is filial, his wife surely will not dare to be unfilial and unharmonious. Wives' lack of virtue is caused, for the most part, by men."[11]

Although he does not comment specifically on methods for correcting disobedient wives, Wang Huizu expounds his general views on violent behavior, which he assumes would be a temptation for cultivated gentlemen like his sons only if they were humiliated or provoked by "violent bullies." Quoting Mencius, he explains that there are "evil and unreasonable" people, who "do not know shame, do not cherish life, are not the least bit patient and perversely instigate fights." Yet such people "do not necessarily lack conscience," he argues, "If one is conciliatory toward them, then they will gradually come to know shame."[12] So when confronting them, he counsels, "it is especially appropriate to be patient." "In situations that are most difficult to tolerate, one must force oneself to suffer the humiliation. Then there will be no crisis under Heaven that cannot be resolved."[13] In a section on the prohibition of "physical fighting," he explains the dangers of violence, citing Confucius's comment on dealing with the depraved: "To attack evil as evil and not as evil of a particular man, is that not the way to reform the depraved? To let a sudden fit of anger make you forget the safety of your own person or even that of your parents, is that not misguided judgment?"[14] Wang then opines, "These sagely instructions are to the point and sensible. Do not quarrel with a raised voice. Moreover, it is unnecessary to engage in wanton physical fighting." He concludes the section by explaining how he applied his view of violence as a county magistrate handling criminal cases: "In the homicide cases I adjudicated for many decades as an official, multiple wounds and fatalities were not inevitable. Accidental injuries all too easily result in serious offenses. Therefore, when quarreling, one should under no circumstances raise a hand to punish someone." Wang thus articulates a practical, if elitist ethic of male self-containment, interpreting violent behavior in general as a result of ignorance and lack of self-control, and female misbehavior and marital strife in particular as signs of the failure of masculine authority. The case record suggests that he was unusual in his application of this critique of male violence in the courtroom. In fact, *The Qing Code* itself set the judicial parameters for this critique.

DOMESTIC VIOLENCE IN *THE QING CODE*

The architects of *The Qing Code* imagined three scenarios, aside from adultery, for a husband killing his wife: the unintentional killing of a wife who had committed a minor offense or done nothing wrong, the intentional killing of such a wife, and the deliberate killing of a wife guilty of unfiliality to her husband's parents. In practice, then, magistrates juggled three possible explanations for the husband's violence: a lapse of self-control, an evil personality, or righteous anger. Section 3 of the statute on "wives and concubines who beat their husbands," stipulated that "if a husband beats his wife without causing broken [bones] or wounds, then there is to be no judgment; as for [beatings] that result in broken [bones] or wounds or worse, [the punishment will be] two degrees less than that for [beating] an ordinary person. . . . As for those who kill [their wives], [the punishment is] strangulation after the assizes. Intentional homicide is also [punished with] strangulation."[15] The *Code* also contains a statute on "husbands beating to death guilty wives or concubines," which states that "Husbands who, because their wife or concubine beats or curses their grandparents or parents, does not report to the yamen, but kills [the wife or concubine] without authorization, [are sentenced to] one hundred strokes of the heavy bamboo."[16] Most extant domestic violence cases involve the capital crimes of unintentional or intentional wife killing, making it difficult to assess magisterial attitudes toward nonlethal domestic violence.

However, the capital cases presented in *xingke tiben* are quite revealing of judicial views on marital strife. Despite the uniform sentencing of wife-killing cases, for the purposes of the assizes process, judicial officials had to choose whether to narrate the cases so as to maximize or minimize the husband's guilt. They did this not only by labeling the homicides intentional or unintentional but also by highlighting circumstances that either mitigated the defendant's guilt, like a wife's misbehavior, mental illness, or evidence of the accidental nature of the fatality, or compounded it, like the defendant's immorality or "bad personality" or the wife's virtue. A wife's unfiliality toward her husband's parents, a classic component of the shrew's repertoire, was one prominent mitigating factor, which, in 1762 (Qianlong 27) was incorporated explicitly into the *Code*'s section on the assizes process. The new substatute singled out men convicted of killing in extreme anger "a wife who is unfilial and curses and beats her father-in-law or mother-in-law" as cases "worthy of compassion" and thus eligible for a reduction of sentence to exile or penal servitude. The substatute further explains that such circumstances involving sacred family relationships and "a moment of righteous anger" (*yiji*) "are not the same as ordinary fierce conflicts." Such cases are therefore to be deliberated by the Board of Punishments and the Nine Ministers and considered for an additional reduction in sentence of one degree.[17]

The creation of this exception to the normal standards for judging wife-killers highlights the illegitimacy of all other scenarios of lethal husbandly violence that were not justifiable as righteous anger. Although the *Code*, in effect, condoned what the state considered "minor" levels of wife-beating, it punished injurious domestic violence and killing as serious crimes. As shown below, violence judged to be extreme signaled the possibility that the killing was intentional. So if the verdict was unintentional homicide, this kind of violence had to be explained with reference to the defendant's state of mind, the victim's provocation, or the accidental circumstances of the killing.

In wife-killing cases, magistrates interrogated defendants and witnesses with a standard set of questions about whether the couple was "ordinarily harmonious" (*pingri hehao*); whether they harbored any "resentments" (*xianxi*); what instigated the fatal conflict; how it escalated into lethal violence; and what that violence entailed. Intended to determine whether or not the defendants killed their wives intentionally, the key factor in assessing their eligibility for the assizes, these questions reveal the normative assumptions of elite men about the appropriate tenor of marital relationships, the moral and judicial significance of violence, and its implications for masculinity. As in all homicide cases, magistrates had to justify their sentences with a detailed coroner's report of the sequence, nature, and number of wounds, including size, shape, color and lethality, type of blow, and weapons used. This codification of violence had to match precisely the descriptions of the conflict in the confession, case testimonies, and the magistrate's summation. Yet evaluation of the severity of violence was also entangled with assessment of the defendant's character and the quality of the marital relationship. Since wife-beating was not categorically defined as a crime, the establishment of intent in these cases was tricky.

Magistrates often stressed the ordinariness of marital arguments, suggesting that extreme violence would not and should not occur in harmonious marriages. They frequently commented on the triviality of the issues that triggered fatal quarrels and chastised defendants for their loss of temper and intolerance of normally accepted behavior on the part of their wives. For example, one magistrate challenged a husband's justification for hitting his wife with a knife and unintentionally stabbing her to death in a drunken fury, stating, "Your wife spun some flawed thread, which is a small matter, but you blamed her. She then merely retorted verbally, but did not even strike you. So why did you grab a knife and stab her twice? Clearly there was some other issue."[18] Sometimes, magistrates concluded that the husband had provoked his wife's improper behavior. Interrogating a husband who killed his young wife by hitting her in the head with a piece of firewood when she cursed him for waking her up in the middle of the night to add oil to the lamp for him, one magistrate said, "You told Ms. Li to add oil, but she was unwilling and contrarily put out the light. If you had not cursed her, then why would she have a reason to curse you for nothing?"[19]

As they pieced together a trajectory of escalating violence, magistrates often indicated that a couple of blows struck in anger or intended to punish wrongdoing were no serious matter, but repeated blows, the use of weapons, and injuries to "fatal spots" (*zhi ming*) on the body raised questions about the defendant's motives and character. In a case from Shandong, one Wang San beat his wife to death amidst an argument about her staying too long at her natal family home.[20] The magistrate saw no justification for his anger: "Your wife's desire to stay for a while at her mother's house is a normal thing. . . . As you were walking along the road, you started quarrelling. This was also a normal instance of an argument between husband and wife. So why did you hit her in the fatal spots on her ear and the top of her head with a rock so that she died? Obviously, you intended to kill her." In another typical case, a husband beat his wife to death after he came home to find that lunch was not prepared and his wife was out chatting with neighbor women. He testified that he chastised her and she was unwilling to "submit" to him. The magistrate queried, "Since you and Ms. Li got along well, on that day when [she] did not make lunch, you could easily have stopped after first knocking her to the ground with a wooden stick. Why did you hit her again in the fatal spot on her side, causing her death? Clearly there was another issue. Undoubtedly, you intended to beat her to death."[21]

Even when wives are depicted as vituperously disrespectful of their husbands' authority, magistrates often noted that verbal chastisement and education were the proper ways to punish them, interpreting extreme violence as evidence of intention to kill. Chastised by her husband for dropping a piece of burning charcoal on the floor, one Mrs. Chen née Su caustically retorted, "Burning this thatched house would not be a big loss. Are you afraid I'll burn you?" Her husband, Chen Wenzhang, "furious that she obstinately challenged me with venom," hit her in the back with a rake. She shouted, "I should burn you to death!" Chen then hit her fatally in the temples. Despite her mocking of her husband's authority, the magistrate interpreted Chen's violence as an unjustified reaction to an ordinary marital conflict, suggesting that he must have had some other motive for killing her. The magistrate queried, "Arguments between husband and wife are normal. Why did you beat her in the temples so severely that she died that same day? Is it not true that you wanted to kill her?" Chen insisted that the killing was unintentional, replying, "I rightly chastised her [*zhengyan zebei ta*], but she in turn obstinately challenged me, defying me with venom [*qiangzui duma*]. So I suddenly lost my temper and hit her in the head a couple of times." The magistrate sentenced him for unintentional homicide, accepting this protestation of righteous intent, which, like many similar defenses, stressed that the single fatal blow was a sudden reaction to a serious provocation.[22]

In another case from Guangxi, Wei Junlong (age fifty-four) killed his wife of thirty-six years, Wang Shi, in the midst of an argument that started when she requested that he buy a new pot for the New Year to replace their old broken one. Having put off the purchase because of extra expenses over the New Year, he then became furious when he demanded lunch one day and she said to him, "You didn't buy the pot when you had the money. How am I supposed to boil rice in this broken pot? We'll go hungry together." He retorted, "I spent the silver for expenses to pass the New Year. I didn't waste any of it. And what's more, that pot didn't break today. Why can't you boil rice in it? If you're not willing to make rice, then you shouldn't have let our daughter-in-law go home to greet [her family] for the New Year." Mrs. Wang replied, "What silver do poor families need to pass the New Year? Do you mean to say that buying a pot is not a proper expense? I told our daughter-in-law to go home to greet [her family] for the New Year. Do you mean to tell me that this too is improper? If you want rice, then you boil it." Wei pressed his wife again to make him lunch. She again refused and called him "an old turtle who might as well be dead" (*laowangba buru zao si*). Infuriated, he then began hitting her on the back with a bamboo pole. She collapsed on the floor, smashed her lower abdomen on a brick, and died later that night. The magistrate ignored Mrs. Wang's angry challenge of her husband's judgment, homing in on the nature of the violence as proof of intentionality: "If your wife was unwilling to boil rice, you ought to have reasoned with her. Why did you beat her? Having hit her with a bamboo pole, wounding her in the ribs, you should not have then hit her repeatedly on the back, causing serious injury that knocked her to the ground and led her to die that night. Clearly you intentionally beat her to death." Wei offered another common defense, stressing the length of the marriage and their production of a son and grandsons as proof that he had not intended to kill her: "Wang Shi and I have gotten along well as husband and wife day after day for many years, and we have a son who has brought in a daughter-in-law and even produced a grandson. Why would I want to intentionally beat her to death?" The magistrate accepted his explanation and sentenced him for unintentional wife-killing.[23]

These interrogation strategies reveal the contours of a judicial paradigm of male containment in which lethal violence is an aberrant expression of husbandly authority indicating the defendant's lack of self-control, failure to exercise moral suasion, or simply cruelty. Magistrates saw blows to a fatal spot as evidence of violence that exceeded the limits of normal marital conflict and proper husbandly chastisement, including minor forms of corporal punishment. Yet in each case, the magistrate concluded that the killing was unintentional because the fatal wound was caused by a single blow struck in a moment of fury. The perceived sudden and arbitrary nature of the violence signaled that although violence was an improper exercise of husbandly prerogative, it was not intended to kill. These murders were thus tragic instances of ordinary arguments within harmonious marriages that became lethal, as Wang Huizu warned, because husbands lost control of their tempers and overreacted to their wives' provocation with violence rather than reasoned discipline.

In contrast, when the verdict was intentional homicide, the defendant was usually portrayed as an unvirtuous man with a vicious personality, a portrait of cruelty bolstered by the extreme violence of the killing. Thus, for example, a man from Henan, Li Caoer, who shot his pregnant wife and seven-year-old[24] daughter to death with a gun in a fit of anger because his wife was too sleepy to get out of bed in the middle of the night to make him tea, was convicted of intentional homicide, despite several potential mitigating factors.[25] The couple had been "harmonious" during their ten years of marriage, despite extreme poverty. He stated that he had been sick and unable to work for several days before the murder, so they had nothing to eat or drink, and he was "becoming more anxious and impatient every day." Relatives and neighbors testified that Li had an "extremely bad personality" (*qixing yuan zui buhao*), though this is not further explained. It appears from the husband's confession that he picked up the gun in a moment of mental breakdown and depression: "Seeing her sleeping and not getting up, my mind was full of bad thoughts, and I was consumed with anger and wanted to kill her." After killing his wife, he heard his daughter crying. "I saw that my wife was already dead, so who would take care of this little child? I said, 'You two can go together.'" He then shot his daughter as well. From a judicial standpoint, the use of a gun and the killing of two people made the violence extreme by definition, and his guilt was exacerbated by his attempt to hide his crime by burning the bodies. The magistrate thus described him as "suddenly developing a murderous intent in a moment of fury." Failing to discover any motive for the murder, he suggested that it was the result of the defendant's "violent and vicious" personality. Li then reiterated this interpretation in his confession: "I shot my wife and daughter to death for no reason, only because my disposition is originally bad." The characterization of Li as a vicious man complements the judgment that the violence of the murder was extreme in order to make a case for the intentionality of the crime, despite its sudden and arbitrary nature.

SHREWISHNESS AND MALE VIOLENCE

The judicial significance of accusations of shrewishness becomes clear in the context of the notions of male containment that informed the adjudication of spousal homicides. Critically, despite the disobedience and often caustic argumentativeness of many of the wives in the cases above, none is described as having a shrewish temperament, indicating that there was no automatic labeling of women's improper or aggressive behavior. Even when women were described as shrews, the label was used to different effect in different cases. The rest of this chapter compares the narrative patterns of three cases in which the victim-wife is constructed as the worst type of unfilial shrew, though each case had a different outcome. Intriguingly, none of the cases was sentenced under the substatute on killing an unfilial wife. Indeed, quite a number of cases sentenced under the standard substatute involved wives accused of unfilial shrewishness, suggesting that judicial officials had significant leeway in sentencing such cases as they saw fit. The case memorials below depict shrews as indictments of their husbands' failures in the role of family authorities. Judgments of men who killed their shrewish wives turned on assessments of the degree of self-containment and moral suasion the men exercised in dealing with their wives. As in other wife-killing cases, the unfolding of homicidal violence was narrated to support the portrayal of the defendant as virtuously self-controlled or unvirtuous and wantonly violent.

A Husband Loses His Patience and Kills His Shrewish Wife

The most typical of the three cases, in terms of sentencing, involves a Guangdong farmer named Qiu Weicheng (age thirty-eight), who had been married to Ms. Zhan (age thirty-four) for eighteen years.[26] Although the childless couple, by all accounts, "got on well together" and "did not have any mutual resentments or grudges" (*pingri bing wu xianyuan*), everyone agreed that Ms. Zhan had a "cunning and savage temperament" and "indulged [her] temper a bit" (*xingzi diaoman yao shi qizhi xie*). When chastised by her husband or father-in-law for her impropriety, she often argued back. Still, Qiu emphasized in his confession, "we were not particularly unharmonious." One evening, Qiu returned home from the fields hungry and invited his elderly father, whose care was rotated among his five sons after the division of the family, to eat dinner with them. To his surprise, Ms. Zhan had not prepared the meal. "I was afraid Father, being elderly, would be hungry, so I chastised my wife. Who would have thought that she would throw a shrewish tantrum and curse me bitterly [*sapo fan ba xiaode chou ma*]? Also, she complained that 'an old man like Father is really a burden.'" Qiu confessed, "When I heard this, I was furious and slapped her. She then picked up the wooden handle of the muck rake to hit me. In a moment's consternation, I grabbed the handle from her and hit her. I didn't realize I wounded her in the temples. She immediately fell to the ground." A neighbor came running in to mediate, and the two of them carried her to the bed. She died later that night.

The magistrate, as required, noted that Qiu went straight for a fatal point on her body, indicating intention to kill. He pressed Qiu to confess that his wife's shrewishness drove him to kill her deliberately, saying, "When Ms. Zhan grabbed the wooden muck rake handle to fight with you, you grabbed it and then immediately hit her in a fatal spot on the top of her head. Clearly you considered how cunning and savage she was day in and day out and intentionally beat her to death." Qiu insisted, "Although my wife Ms. Zhan was wily and savage day in and day out, this was the temperament she was born with. Moreover, she was my first and only wife from my youth. I truly did not hate her. How could I intentionally want to beat her to death?" With this response, Qiu blamed his wife's shrewishness on elements of fate beyond his control. But by invoking again the length of the marriage, which he insists was mostly harmonious, he implied his own virtue—the patience and self-control necessary to make a successful marriage with such a woman.

Consonant with Qiu's downplaying of his wife's shrewishness, the magistrate's summary of the case made no mention of her personality, emphasizing instead how Qiu struck his wife in the heat of the moment while she was complaining about the burden of his father, not realizing where he had hit her. He sentenced Qiu to strangulation after the assizes for unintentionally beating his wife to death, although given the limited and sudden nature of the violence, the unfilial implications of the comment that provoked it, and his wife's attempt to strike him, the case seemed well positioned for a reduction in sentence in the assizes process. The characterization of Qiu's violence—a single blow struck as a sudden reflex reaction—is a crucial part of the portrait of Qiu as a man of middling virtue who, though he failed to reform his wayward wife, nevertheless exercised admirable self-control in dealing with her for eighteen years.

An Exemplary Husband Accidentally Kills His Shrewish Wife

In contrast, Yu Chengzhang (age forty-eight) from Fenyang county, Shanxi, who had been married to his wife, Ms. Liu (age forty-two), for more than twenty years, is portrayed as deserving of extraordinary mercy.[27] Like Ms. Zhan, Ms. Liu was described by her husband, other family members, and neighbors as having a bad temperament in that she "did not submit to [her mother-in-law's] instruction and guidance." Her unfiliality had the morally disastrous consequence of driving her mother-in-law from her home. Her mother-in-law explained, "Ms. Liu did not care what I wore or ate. Because of this, I went to live with my eldest son in another courtyard." The incident that sparked the murder was Yu's request that Ms. Liu take some cold noodles she had made over to her mother-in-law. Testifying before her death, she said, "My husband wouldn't let me eat [the noodles] and told me to 'give them to Mother.' I wasn't willing to send them over because there weren't a lot . . . and Mother-in-law lives in another courtyard." Her husband quoted her as saying, "Does this old mother [herself] have to compete with her to eat?" According to Yu, "I cursed her for being an unfilial, disobedient, worthless woman. She then screamed at me at the top of her voice. I was angry and picked up a brick and threw it. Without realizing it, I hit her on top of the head. She started bleeding." The couple's daughter ran out into the street for help as Yu made a poultice for his wife's wound. The constable came to investigate and reported the case to the magistrate, who ordered the family to seek medical treatment for Ms. Liu and declared he would wait to see the effects of the injury before meting out punishment. The next day, Ms. Liu appeared fine and told her husband not to bother calling a doctor. Within a few days, she was back to her normal activities, but two weeks later, she complained that her head was excruciatingly hot and removed her bandage, ripping open the wound. That night, she fell into chills and fever, her speech blurred, and her facial features became contorted. She passed out and soon died, apparently of a stroke.

The magistrate interrogated Yu, asking, "Although your wife was wrong in her unwillingness to take cold noodles over to your mother, this was not an offense deserving of death. Why did you then hit her in a fatal spot on her head with a brick? And why were you then unwilling to call a doctor to treat her? . . . There must be some other grudge you were holding to provoke this." Yu replied, "Because my wife was unwilling to give . . . noodles to Mother, and then also fought with me, I suddenly lost my temper, picked up the brick, and threw it. I absolutely did not intend to beat her to death." He explained that he did not call a doctor right away because he was poor and because his village did not have one. By the next day, his wife claimed she was better, so it seemed unnecessary. "I have been married to Ms. Liu for more than twenty years, and we have always been harmonious. There really is nothing else." Yu, like Qiu Weicheng, suggested that the fact of having been married for so many years indicates a degree of marital harmony that precludes an intent to kill his wife and indicates instead his own virtue. The magistrate's summation of the case, as with Qiu's, did not even mention the victim's shrewish personality.

In an unusual move, the magistrate suggested that Yu be sentenced, not according to the substatute on husbands who unintentionally kill their wives, but instead according to the substatute on people who beat someone and cause minor injuries that result in a stroke. He would thus "not pay with his life" but be sentenced only to one hundred strokes of the heavy bamboo and life exile. In order to justify this sentence, the magistrate emphasized the spontaneous and undeliberate nature of the violence as well as its minimal effects, arguing that "although [the injury] was to a fatal spot, the original examination of the wound after it had swollen showed that it was only one inch deep and did not hit the bone, thus constituting a light wound. Moreover, after being hit, Ms. Liu ate, drank, and moved about as normal." The case was rescripted with the unusual instruction that the Board of Punishments, rather than the usual Three Judicial Offices, review the case specially, indicating the irregularity of and possibility of disagreement with the verdict. Again, as in the case above, the understatement of the wife's shrewish unfiliality worked with the downplaying of conflict within the marriage and minimization of the violence of the killing to build sympathy for the defendant.

A Violent Husband Vengefully Murders His Shrewish Wife

Sympathy for husbands of shrews was not automatic. Yi Yongchang (age twenty-eight) similarly killed his wife, Ms. Qiu (age twenty), in an argument about her unfiliality toward his parents, but the magistrate found this murder to be intentional, issuing the most severe verdict possible.[28] In this case, the depiction of Ms. Qiu's shrewishness is much more dramatic and extensive than the characterizations of the other shrews considered in this chapter, but in contrast to the other cases, which placed emphasis on the harmonious nature of the marriage overall, the testimonies here indicate a context of constant marital and familial conflict. Ms. Qiu's husband, his parents, their neighbors, and her own father described her as having a bad temperament in that she was unfilial and disobedient. She had entered the family as a "child bride" (*tongyangxi*) at the age of ten, and the couple had consummated their marriage four years before the murder. Bitterly hostile to her daughter-in-law, Ms. Qiu's mother-in-law Ms. Zhou said, "I raised Ms. Qiu from the time she entered the gate. I treated her as though she were my own flesh-and-blood daughter. Who would have thought that my daughter-in-law from the time she was a child would never obey my instructions and guidance? She became worse and worse as time went on. Her temperament was that of a vicious shrew [*shengqing pohan*]. I am old and unwell and could not be harmonious with her. I tolerated her in everything, but she just screamed at me." Having painted a picture of the worst kind of shrew, Ms. Zhou then added an unexpected comment on her son's personality, saying, "I also did not dare to speak to my son about this. My son also has a bad temperament. If I had said anything, then he would have beaten her. I was afraid of arousing his anger over trifles, so I went to live with my second son."

Yi Yongchang himself was very blunt about his hatred for his wife and the bad nature of their relationship, indicating that were it not for the intervention of his father, who seems to have had some sympathy for the young wife despite her misbehavior, he would have treated his wife even more harshly. He confessed, "My wife was diligent at eating and lazy at working. She was not willing to be filial and reverential to her mother-in-law and father-in-law, so Mother went to live with my brother. I have never liked her. I often instruct and guide her with a few words, but she perversely wrangles with me. When Father sees her flying into a shrewish tantrum [*sapo qilai*] and shouting, he holds me back, saying, 'She is young, so you should be a bit patient with her.' So I have no choice."

Yi's younger brother also hinted at larger family dysfunction. Noting that the two brothers had divided their households, he claimed to know nothing about the killing. "Although I don't live far from my elder brother, I am a farmer and a woodcutter so I go to work early and come home late. Each of us minds our own family business. . . . My sister-in-law was always fighting and shouting at my mother, so it was hard for Mother to eat her rice. So I take care of Mother." Such perfunctory admissions of early household division were usually followed by statements indicating regular contact between the separate branches of the family so as to downplay the implications of family disharmony. In this context, the brother's matter-of-fact description of the lack of contact suggests that the two brothers actually did not care what happened in each other's households despite their shared responsibility for their parents.

The conflict that led to Ms. Qiu's murder began when Ms. Zhou asked her to do some laundry, and she responded by yelling that her mother-in-law's clothes were "for displaying a corpse." Yi Yongchang overheard this exchange and hit his wife twice on her shoulder blades and arms with the door bar. His mother and father intervened to stop him from beating her further. A few days later, his father was leaving for a trip to Hangzhou to sell some cloth, so Yi bought some pork to be prepared for his father's food along the road. Ms. Qiu took some of it and ate it herself. Her mother-in-law said, "I heard that my eldest son had bought some meat and invited me and my husband to his house to eat it. Unexpectedly, my son was not there. I asked about it, and Ms. Qiu just chattered away loquaciously. I endured this in my stomach."

When he found out about the meat, Yi said, "I yelled at her, and my wife then flew into a shrewish tantrum until my father intervened to stop her before leaving for the provincial capital." The next day, Yi told his wife to accompany him to the mountains to help clear a field for planting. She did not arrive till noon, and when her husband asked her why she was late, she said, "I was arguing again over the meat from yesterday with that old mother of yours who never dies." At this, Yi confessed, "I was furious and cursed her. She wrangled back. I then swung the scythe and cut her right elbow. She tried to grab the scythe, and I cut her again on her shoulders. She fell to the ground, cursing my mother. I was even more furious and hated her. I thought to myself, why should I keep this kind of shrewish wife? It would be better to cut her to death. So I cut her successively in the back of the head and neck. She didn't make a sound. I turned her over and also cut her throat and neck several times . . . cutting off her head." Yi buried her at the spot and returned home, telling his mother, when she asked where Ms. Qiu was, "That unfilial person is already dead. Why still speak of her?" They kept the matter to themselves until two days later, when Ms. Qiu's father came by for a visit, and Yi was forced to tell him she was dead.

Despite Ms. Qiu's deeply immoral behavior, the magistrate did not express any sympathy for Yi Yongchang. Indeed, his interrogation highlighted Yi's failure to deal with his wife's unfiliality properly and the brutal excess of decapitating her. He asked, "You testified that marital quarrelling was an ordinary occurrence. If she cursed your mother, then you should have reported her to the yamen for punishment. Why were you so brutally malicious as to cut her head off? There must have been some other issue." Unlike the husbands of shrews described above, Yi replied that he detested his wife, and his restraint toward her was due only to his father's intervention. He continued:

> I usually tolerated my wife's unfiliality. . . . That day, when she cursed my mother, I took advantage of the fact that Father was not in front of me and suddenly became extremely furious and wanted to cut her a couple

of times to make her afraid of me. How could I know she would fall to the ground still cursing my mother venomously? Because of this, I hated her infinitely and cut her neck several times. I was afraid she wouldn't die, so I also turned her body over and cut her throat twice. It didn't occur to me that the scythe was so sharp I would cut her head off.

The case memorial includes unusually extensive interrogations of neighbors and relatives about the nature of the couple's marital relationship. Such extreme violence required an explanation that included not only the victim's lack of virtue but also her husband's response to her. Pressing a neighbor, the magistrate asked, "How could this quarrel between husband and wife over this trivial issue of eating the meat result in such a brutal and malicious murder and decapitation? Clearly there was some other issue. Do you mean to say you know nothing?" The neighbor commented, "As husband and wife, their harmonious days were few and their days of quarrelling numerous. Although this [murder] was brought on by the argument about stealing the meat, Ms. Qiu always had a recalcitrant temperament and was never willing to be filial and obedient to her mother-in-law. Husband and wife had lost compassion and love for each other." In other words, Yi responded to his wife not with a patient desire to reform her behavior but with hatred. The excessive violence of the murder, though provoked by her, was the culmination of his own lack of both self-control and moral authority, demonstrated by the complete absence of harmony in the marriage and, for that matter, in the family as a whole.

Accordingly, while the magistrate noted the possibility of using the statute on killing unfilial wives, he argued against it. In the words of the summary,

> According to the statutes, "a wife or concubine who curses her husband's grandparents or parents is sentenced to strangulation." Also, "If a wife or concubine beats or curses her husband's grandparents or parents, but the husband does not report this to the yamen and kills her without authorization, [then he] is sentenced to one hundred strokes of the heavy bamboo." The small character commentary states that "if the grandparents or parents report, the husband is still tried." Now although Yi Yongchang testified that Ms. Qiu cursed his mother, he should have reported this to the yamen for punishment, but he immediately killed her and beheaded her. This was brutal and heartless in the extreme. [So] Yi Yongchang should be sentenced to strangulation after the assizes according to the statute on intentional killing of a wife.

The summary recognizes Ms. Qiu's "viciously shrewish" temperament and notes Yi's frequent attempts to educate and admonish her. Yet the Zhejiang judicial commissioner added his own twist to the sentence, concluding that "despite Yi Yongchang's testimony about Ms. Qiu cursing her mother-in-law, Ms. Zhou [the mother-in-law] did not ever report the matter herself, and Ms. Qiu was thus stabbed to death with many wounds." This final take on the murder implicated the mother-in-law herself, as a family authority figure, for failing to deal properly with an unvirtuous daughter-in-law.

CONCLUSION

The judicial system's priority was the maintenance of social and political order based on patriarchal family hierarchy and recognition of the state's prerogatives as the central arbiter of the morality that order assumed. Unfiliality posed the greatest of threats to that order and had to be punished severely. It is thus a prominent focus not only in the statutes on spousal conflict and murder but in many other sections of *The Qing Code*. Given this, the variance in treatment of wifely unfiliality in the adjudication of wife-killing cases, in terms of both sentencing and the narrative construction of the causes and consequences of shrewish unfiliality, is striking and, I would argue, suggestive of the workings of another, competing paradigm of marital failure. In this paradigm, which resonates in interesting ways with fictional theories of marriage, the unfilial shrew is clearly the impetus for social chaos in the form of family conflict, division, violence, and criminality. But she is able to wreak such havoc only because family authorities, chiefly her husband but also his parents, have failed to educate and admonish her effectively. As Wang Huizu and the magistrates who adjudicated in wife-killing cases insisted, violence does not constitute effective admonishment but instead represents a lack of control and moral authority that merely escalates social breakdown rather than prevents it. The critical question in the cases examined here is not whether the husband's homicidal violence was provoked by his wife's unfilial shrewishness, for it was assumed that it was. Instead, the outcome of these cases turned on the attitude and behavior of the husband.

Although the final characterization of wife-killers was clearly shaped by statutory requirements, it is important to consider the effects of judicial narratives of spousal violence not just for the assizes process but also for the broader reproduction of notions of masculine and feminine virtue. For as Wang Huizu noted in his handbook for magistrates, courtroom proceedings were performed for a public audience and thus had enormous educational potential.²⁹ Court cases in a sense functioned as public morality tales. And while the leniency offered by the assizes process was abstract and remote—delayed by several years in most cases—the judgment announced in the courtroom had an immediate audience. Of course, the testimonies and judgments contained in *xingke tiben* are not identical to those heard in the courtroom. But in the diverse portraits of husbands and wives presented in these cases, they seem to preserve something of the public morality tale that the courtroom audience might have seen. The moral of these stories is not that unfiliality deserves punishment but that the path of masculine virtue is one of patience, persuasion, and self-control.

NOTES

1. On fictional depictions of shrews, see McMahon, *Misers, Shrews, and Polygamists*.
2. On the centrality of chastity to the Qing civilizing mission and the relationship between chastity and patriarchy, see Theiss, *Disgraceful Matters*.
3. On women causing trouble in criminal investigations, see, for example, Wang Huizu, *Lun mingan* (On homicide cases), in He Changling, *Huangchao jingshi wenbian*, 94, 8b–9a. On cruel stepmothers, see ZPZZ, QL 2.5, *luli lei*, *bao* 28, *juan* 45 (memorial of Zhao Tingyuan). On lascivious and cruel stepmothers, see ZPZZ, QL 25.11.16, *luli lei*, *bao* 21, *juan* 50 (memorial of Tuo Enduo). On lascivious adulteresses, see ZPZZ, QL 12.5.15, *qita lei*, *bao* 34, *juan* 57 (memorial of Chen Hongmou).
4. See Theiss, *Disgraceful Matters*.
5. McMahon, *Causality and Containment*, 9–10.
6. McMahon, *Misers, Shrews, and Polygamists*, 83.
7. Epstein, *Competing Discourses*, 149.
8. Wang Huizu, *Shuangjietang yongxun*, 18b.
9. Ibid., 22a.
10. Epstein, *Competing Discourses*, 121.
11. Wang Huizu, *Shuangjietang yongxun*, 22b–23a.
12. Ibid., 48a.
13. Ibid., 47b–48a.
14. Ibid., 48b–49a.
15. DLCY, vol. 4, *juan* 36: 929. The statute on beating an ordinary person details many forms of breakage of and injury to various parts of the body, each with

specifically designated punishments entailing various combinations of flogging with light or heavy bamboo and penal servitude. Thus, the punishment for injurious wife-beating, set two degrees lower than these, would amount to some form of flogging. It was administered at the county level with no review by higher levels of the judicial system, and there would be no records of such cases in the central archives in Beijing. There are a few of these cases extant in the Baxian Archives.

16. Ibid., *juan* 34: 864.
17. Ibid., vol. 5, *juan* 49: 1244.
18. *XKTB*, QL 18.
19. Ibid., QL 18.
20. Ibid., QL 18.7.24.
21. Ibid., QL 32.10.10, 226.6.
22. Ibid., QL 5.8.1, 137.5.
23. Ibid., QL 18.6.6.
24. The Chinese text reads *"ba sui."* By Chinese reckoning, which still sometimes holds true today, a child is considered to be one *sui* old at birth; the child then gains one *sui* on each New Year's day.
25. *XKTB*, QL 18.
26. Ibid., QL 5.7.29.
27. Ibid., QL 18.10.9.
28. Ibid., QL 18.6.27.
29. Wang Huizu, "Lun qinmin," 6b–7a.

3   Between Oral and Written Cultures

Buddhist Monks in Qing Legal Plaints

YASUHIKO KARASAWA

On the eleventh day of the tenth month of Daoguang 14 (1834), the Ba county yamen of Sichuan received a Buddhist monk called Tianran and a woman, Mrs. Yue née Zhang, both of whom had been taken into custody by "community leaders" (*tuanyue*). According to the formal report submitted along with the two prisoners, on the evening of the eighth day of that month, Tianran and Ms. Zhang were caught "in the act of illicit sex" (*xingjian*) at Shuikou Temple by two villagers who happened to pass by. Hearing a woman's voice coming from inside the temple, they investigated and interrupted a scene of "illicit sexual intercourse" (*jianyin*) on the bed in Tianran's private room. The report also emphasizes the personality of Tianran as "never abiding by the Buddhist precepts, habitually luring women to commit illicit sexual deeds at the temple" (*bushou qinggui, siyou funü zaimiao jianyin*).

However, after interrogating the various parties, Magistrate Yang concluded that these illicit deeds had never occurred. The facts established at the yamen court were as follows. As twilight approached, Ms. Zhang and her son decided to take a rest under a tree standing just inside the temple gate. Tianran, coming out to close the gate, found them and told them to leave. Two villagers who were passing by misinterpreted the situation. Although Ms. Zhang and the two villagers, in their written records of oral testimony, agreed that Tianran "had made a pass at her and requested illicit sex" (*tiaoxi qiujian*), the magistrate ignored their claims. Both villagers did concede that they, in fact, had not found Tianran and Ms. Zhang inside the private room of the temple, but rather just inside the gate.[1]

This case from the Ba County Archive raises some interesting questions. Why did the two villagers assume that illicit sex was occurring, based solely on hearing a woman's voice inside a temple? When they explained the situation to the community leaders, they embellished theirs account to include a sexual scene in a bedroom. Perhaps they genuinely believed adultery was about to begin, or perhaps they were simply lying. Either way, what made them believe in or invent this particular kind of story? In addition, why did community leaders choose to write a report including such sensational expressions and images, depicting Tianran as a lustful, evil rogue?

Their report narrated a version of what happened on the night of the arrest, but it did more. It also provided background information that supposedly would reinforce the plausibility of this Buddhist monk's illicit sexual behavior. Although we have no idea whether this Buddhist monk was actually a lustful rogue (after all, he might have been), we can be sure that these community leaders of rural Ba county believed that such a sensational depiction would help support their accusation.

This chapter aims to answer the questions raised by the case introduced above. Close examination of narrative elements in legal plaints from local-level case records not only sheds light on litigation strategy but also reveals one type of interface between the cultural spheres of writing and speech in Qing China.

LANGUAGE USE IN LEGAL PLAINTS

In Qing China, local magistrates were familiar with the popular proverb "A plaint without exaggeration will not work" (*wuhuang bucheng zhuang*).[2] The ostensible role of plaints in the legal process was to demonstrate events that had happened in order to initiate and forward a legal case. Legal plaints might include sensational exaggeration and fabrication. The Qing government endeavored to exclude such elements from plaints through institutional safeguards such as (1) "officially authorized scribes" (*guan daishu*) who were expected to write down a straightforward account of the story told by the plaintiffs, (2) the use of official standard "plaint forms" (*zhuangshi*) printed with squares that imposed a maximum limit on the number of Chinese logographs in the text of the plaint, and (3) in some counties, an indication on the plaint form of whether a draft of the plaint had been composed in advance by someone other than an official scribe.

Despite these government efforts, legal plaints did not simply tell the "truth" of the event in question. Focusing on the process of their production reveals complicated tactics of textual manipulation that were designed to advance a case smoothly (though it is questionable whether such manipulation always worked as intended).

A normal plaint includes a concrete description of the incident plus background evidence and some moralistic rhetoric aimed at persuading the magistrate that the plaintiff is honest and good while the accused is evil. This packaging invariably includes specific patterns of plot development, legal terminology, and the inevitable legalistic clichés that appear constantly in written complaints. Texts called "treatises for litigation masters" (*songshi miben*) include many examples of such recurring features. These treatises basically explain how to package an event in an exaggerated or dramatic manner in order to attract the attention and sympathy of a magistrate.

In late imperial China, terms such as "litigation masters" (*songshi*) and "litigation mongers" (*songgun*) were generally used to designate litigation professionals who wrote exaggerated and fabricated plaints that frequently made false accusations. As recent comprehensive studies of these legal specialists show, they are depicted in official documents, handbooks for magistrate and private secretaries, and vernacular fiction as sneaky pettifoggers undertaking litigation procedures so as to benefit their customers.[3] Treatises for litigation masters, which were published underground and were widespread, have been seen as evidence of such manipulation.

Fuma Susumu points out that many litigation professionals were lower-degree holders of the licentiate class.[4] Sources such as government documents and vernacular fiction emphasize the devious and illegal activities of litigation professionals, because in reality they had the opportunity to harm ordinary people by exploiting them. Many licentiates who gave up examination life might have earned a living by advising litigants on their cases and helping them with paperwork. Fuma asserts that there was a similarity in terms of patterns of composition between examination essays (conventionally written in a style called the "eight-legged essay" [*baguwen*]) and legal plaints. Both examination essays and legal plaints combine clichés and specialized terminology within a limited space in order to impress their expected readers (examiners, in the case of examination essays, and magistrates, in the case of plaints).[5] Treatises for litigation masters offered vocabulary lists of such legal terminology and clichés.

The similarities between examination essays and legal plaints, however, may be limited to technical aspects like those just listed. Unlike examination essays, actual plaints in legal case records were written with plain, hybrid language: half classical, half vernacular.[6] Even literates who were not necessarily well grounded in sophisticated literary language could work in this hybrid-language style. Lower-degree holders were, without doubt, outnumbered by literates and semiliterates who had only gone through early stages of composition training. Such training in the elementary level of education was designed to help children acquire the ability to eventually compose an eight-legged essay. Composing legal plaints thus drew on writing skills broadly shared by all literates in late imperial society.

Therefore, even a literate whose ability did not reach the level required to write eight-legged essays still could, in his other sorts of writings, rely on a composition pattern combining technical terms and clichés, a pattern with which he had been familiar since his elementary-level education. In other words, most literates were able to compose a legal plaint by consulting treatises for litigation masters.[7] The common designation of these books does not mean that people had to be litigation masters to make use of them. Most plaints were not necessarily written by people who were legal specialists but by those who performed the service of writing plaints for others, a means of livelihood open to all with some command of the literary language, even if not particularly refined.[8]

Most written complaints, no matter who wrote them, employ narrative skills to package events. In a cognitive sense, it is no simple task, even for a literate and educated person, to present something that has happened in a way that is convincing to other parties. Recognizing what one has experienced and presenting it in narrative form are two different things. Even if several people experience the same event, their perceptions of the truth may differ. Nevertheless, this does not contradict the fact that something actually happened.

During the process of formulation, narrative elements such as consistency, details, and explanatory language—what Natalie Davis calls the "fictional" elements in the archives—are selectively configured. Davis's use of the term "fictional" does not indicate something false or fanciful. Instead, her intent is to indicate narrative skills that formulate, embody, and construct elements in the story.[9] If we regard the stories in Qing plaints as simply fabrications or lies, we would distort a significant aspect of Qing culture. Even if they intended to lie, people could not just say whatever they chose; they needed to present their stories in a manner that would be convincing, and this required the careful use of "fictional" elements. But this was also true if people intended to tell only the truth. Reading plaints from this perspective sheds light on the cultural practice of storytelling in the Qing.

PLAINTS AS AN INTERFACE BETWEEN ORAL AND WRITTEN CULTURES

Written complaints were usually composed by literate individuals, either based on stories told orally by nonliterate litigants or based on these literates' various skills at fabricating stories. Of course, we have no access to the original stories told by nonliterate litigants to plaint writers. In addition, it is difficult to assess to what extent the versions presented in plaints reflect the litigants' original stories.

It is clear, at least, that the plaints we read were constructed through multiple layers of storytelling: first, the oral tales (in many cases); second, the narrative fashioning done by plaint writers; and third, certain changes added by official scribes before filing the plaints.[10] This multilayered feature of plaints shows the interaction between oral and written modes of communication. The methods of packaging events in plaints reveal how the various agents involved in this process shaped reality; this packaging, therefore, sheds light on their sense of reality as well.

In other words, plaints provide us with many examples of multilayered stories in which reality was molded by narrative skills particular to legal prose. The fabrication of a story in a written complaint, whether that complaint is true or false, means shaping reality, inevitably attended by "fictional" elements of narratives. This phenomenon of shaping is *universal* in that all stories are packaged with certain literary devices when experiences are translated into written narratives; at the same time, it is *particular* in that such packaging always occurs within some specific cultural framework.[11] Examining a number of written complaints illuminates how experiences were packaged, a process that occurred at the interface between the oral and the written.

Making effective use of rhetoric in constructing a plausible plaint was part of the process of shaping reality within a textual framework of literary devices and narrative strategies. Most fundamentally, a plaint was composed in order to persuade the magistrate that the litigant was telling the "truth." One theme of this chapter is the meaning and function of "plausibility" and "rhetoric" in this shaping of reality: what kind of storytelling appeared plausible to the people involved?

In the case of China, it is difficult to determine whether conventional phrases derived from the oral tradition or from the written one. Outside the Mandarin-Chinese-speaking region, for example, people used "literary" pronunciation when reading Chinese logographs in classical texts, distinct from the "colloquial" pronunciations of daily speech. With the spread of literacy and publishing after the Tang dynasty (618–907), words with "literary" pronunciations, generally lofty terms for higher culture, began to enter everyday speech. Therefore, by the early twentieth century, Yuen Ren Chao could report that "even from the mouth of an illiterate storyteller, one hears phrases and sentences in *wen-yen* [*wenyan*, the literary language]. Blind fortune-tellers are literally conversant with the literary idioms, which differ widely in vocabulary and to some extent in grammar from everyday speech."[12]

At the same time, fiction in the vernacular language developed in close contact with the tradition of oral storytelling, and literary scholarship has analyzed how particular tales were transformed in the process of transfer from oral to written forms and vice versa; an example frequently discussed is Judge Bao's crime tales.[13] In sum, there was considerable circulation of vocabulary and diction between the oral and written traditions. The clichés and idioms used in plaints came from the sphere of linguistic interaction between the two.

REPRESENTATIONS OF BUDDHIST CLERGY IN LEGAL CASES

In legal plaints from the Qing, it was common to describe the accused in terms we would consider slanderous. The descriptions of people and their deeds are filled with clichés. Cases involving Buddhist monks are no exception. An actual plaint from Xianfeng 5 (1855) reads as follows:

> *Plaint Filer:* Chen Guanglian, Liu Wanfa, Lu Wanyi, and Chen Hongshun, all of whom are neighbors in the same militia company
> *Age:* Diverse
> *Residence:* The sixth tithing group in the Zhi community
> *Originally Registered in:* This county of this province [Ba county, Sichuan]
> *Distance of Residence from the County Seat:* 80 li
> *Lodging at:* The Shuangcheng Inn in Tangna District
> *Subject of Plaint:* To report sinful monks [*nieseng*] violating the precepts and to beg that they be summoned and interrogated
>
> We humbly submit that we are community neighbors belonging to the Fuxing militia company. The Ciyun Temple in our area houses the Buddhist monks Fuwen, Fubu, Fuben, and Dengpin, none of whom ever abides by the Buddhist precepts. They use tobacco in excess and commit all manner of misbehavior. In the twelfth month of last year, Fuwen and Fuben had illicit liaisons with Mrs. Xie née Qin, the wife of their neighbor, Xie

Guozhao. Guozhao accused them at the subcounty yamen, and, after an interrogation to confirm the accusation, the sub-magistrate concluded the case by beating them and expelling them from the temple. Now Fuwen and Fuben, however, are staying on at the temple, in violation of the magistrate's judgment. They have not repented and even dare to take turns practicing adultery with Mrs. Xie. We can no longer bear this scandal they are creating. Unless Your Honor condescends to summon and interrogate them, their outrageous behavior might even result in homicide. That would be a matter of truly serious proportions. Therefore, we entreat Your Honor to hear this case and summon and interrogate them. If Your Honor will rid us of these sinful [monks] and prevent disaster, the whole community will receive the benefit. We beg Your Honor to hear our plea.

It turned out that Chen Guanglian, one of the filers of the above petition, had tried to extort money from monks at Ciyun Temple but had been rebuffed. This failure provoked him to make a false accusation against them.[14] Mrs. Xie herself had previously filed a false accusation against the same monks, because of a grudge she bore them. Chen had heard about Mrs. Xie's false accusation, and this inspired him to file a false accusation of his own against the monks.

Because this file is incomplete, we do not know the conclusion of the case. Nevertheless, it is obvious that Chen Guanglian tried to catch the magistrate's attention by telling a story of illicit sex involving Buddhist monks. Accordingly, the plaint is filled with clichés, such as "never abiding by the Buddhist precepts" (*bushou qinggui*), which frequently appears in plaints during the Qing. In fact, plaints against Buddhist monks usually refer to their nefarious schemes to have illicit sex with women. Some other cases help clarify this point.

In a Ba county case from the year Daoguang 5 (1825), a monk was accused of having illicit sex with the wife of his tenant. The accusing parties (who did not include the tenant) relied on a lofty Confucian discourse emphasizing the need to maintain social morals in their district. After various plaints and counterplaints were filed at the yamen, it turned out that the whole affair began when some ruffians had tried to extort money from the monk. After the extortion attempt failed, the ruffians attacked the monk when he was chatting with his tenant and the tenant's wife at their house. The ruffians beat them up and took away some clothing to use as "proof" of adultery, which they presented to the magistrate together with the above petition.[15]

A written complaint from another case in Daoguang 23 (1843), begins with a phrase that summarizes the accusation: "A sinful monk bullied me and sexually propositioned me" (*nieseng qitiao*). A woman, backed by her husband, accused a monk of pulling her to him and trying to rape her in the hills. Later, a court hearing established that the woman and the monk had just quarreled over firewood they were gathering there.[16]

A case from Daoguang 30 (1850) shows that an accusation of illicit sex was used as a means to get a Buddhist monk fired from his job managing a local charitable school. It is not clear whether adultery actually took place, but that seems to have been beside the point. The true purpose of the accusers was to convince the magistrate that the monk was morally unfit for such a position, and they succeeded in doing so, even though the magistrate never ruled on the question of adultery.[17]

Even Buddhist nuns relied on the common phrases and the stereotype of licentious Buddhist clergy. In one case, a pair of nuns accused each other of engaging in illicit sex with monks. Later, their testimony revealed that their real dispute centered on their competition for the position of chief priestess at a Buddhist temple. The magistrate ordered both nuns expelled from the temple.[18]

Like other plaintiffs, monks used conventional phrases to describe themselves in positive terms: "I am an honest, sincere, and good person," "I always abide by the Buddhist precepts" (*sushou qinggui*) (for commoners, the term would be "the laws" [*tazhi*] instead of "the Buddhist precepts"), and "I have never committed any transgressions" (*haowu guojiu*). Such emphasis on the good character of plaintiffs is often reinforced by the phrase "This [fact] is known by everybody throughout the district" (*tongxiang gongzhi*). In contrast, those who accused Buddhist monks always call them "sinful monks," "ruffian monks" (*sengpi*), or "licentious monks" (*yinseng*). Treatises for litigation masters provide lists of such clichés for use in writing plaints.[19]

Most of the treatises of this kind that survive are filled with examples of simple plaint texts, listed according to the criminal category. A model plaint for suing Buddhist monks over land demonstrates how to describe the accused as habitually "fornicating and violating the precepts" (*jianyin fanjie*).[20] In fact, the subject of land could be easily replaced by any other object of dispute, such as the management of the school in the case cited above. Another model plaint, which demonstrates how to accuse a monk of illicit sex, narrates a scene of a Buddhist monk lurking around the periphery of a village in order to rape a woman.[21]

REPRESENTATIONS OF BUDDHIST CLERGY IN THE WORLD OF FICTION

The last model plaint mentioned above portrays Buddhist monks as would-be seducers or rapists. The genre of crime tales (*gong'an xiaoshuo*) in late imperial vernacular fiction, including the famous Judge Bao stories, shares this unsavory image of monks, according to which, despite the religious prohibition against sex, they are provoked to lust when they see beautiful women. Most crime tales were written beginning in the Ming period (1368–1644) and were widespread during the Qing. This image of Buddhist clergy can be also found in erotic vernacular fiction.

"Cai Yunu Takes Shelter from the Rain and Encounters Licentious Monks" (Cai Yunu biyu zhuang yinseng), a story in the collection of late Ming vernacular fiction *The Lovers Who Cause Both Joy and Pain* (Huanxi yuanjia), follows the same pattern as a number of other works of vernacular fiction. In this story, Cai Yunu, the beautiful nineteen-year-old wife of a petit proprietor, Cai Lin, age twenty-nine, is victimized by Buddhist monks.

The story begins when Cai Yunu and her husband visit her natal parents' house to celebrate her mother's birthday. Cai Lin leaves for home earlier than his wife, who plans to spend a few more days with her parents. As she is traveling home alone two days later, she encounters a severe thunderstorm and is unable either to continue on or to return to her parents' home. Coincidentally, she finds a Buddhist temple and takes shelter under the roof over its gate. After a while, two young monks come out and ask who she is. Cai Yunu's youth and beauty arouse their sexual desire. Therefore, they suggest that she might wait more comfortably inside the temple. Although she declines their offer, the two lascivious monks grab hold of her and carry her into the temple, where she finds an elder monk attended by two other women. Both of these women have been kidnapped like Cai Yunu, raped by the monks, and confined inside the temple ever since; Cai Yunu soon finds herself doomed to the same fate.

As one might expect, her husband Cai Lin starts to worry when his beloved does not come home after several days. He rushes to his wife's natal family to request her return: "Why hasn't Yunu come back home yet?" In this way, a dispute begins between Cai Lin and his father-in-law, Wang Chun.

Wang Chun and his wife say, "Your wife left eight days ago. How dare you come here to ask for her?" Cai Lin goes on, "She never came back. I am sure that you do not like me, because I am nothing more than the penniless manager of a small business. Your daughter is gifted with beauty. You must have remarried her to somebody else, wishing to receive more bride-price." Wang

Chun curses him, "Bullshit! It must have been you, you destitute brute, who sold your wife off to another man. Yet still you dare to come to me and demand her!" The mother-in-law says, "Do not beat my daughter to death and lay the blame upon us to extort money!" She starts to cry in her furious indignation.

Both sides end up filing legal plaints at the local yamen, accusing each other of illegally disposing of Cai Yunu. The magistrate, torn between two different stories, temporarily sides with Wang Chun, who has accused Cai Lin of possibly murdering Yunu.

While her husband is imprisoned in the yamen jail, Cai Yunu shares a similar life confined in the temple. The story then tells about a widow in her mid-thirties, Mrs. Tian, who visits the temple to pray for a better life. One of the lascivious monks takes this opportunity to serve her tea laced with a sedative so that he can rape her as well. Mrs. Tian, however, unlike the other women, turns out to enjoy her sexual pleasure with the monk.

After some time passes, Cai Yunu, imploring the older monk for mercy, finally succeeds in winning her freedom. She immediately returns to her home to find that her husband has been imprisoned. Her appearance and testimony persuade the magistrate to release her husband and to rescue all the women confined at the temple. The two younger monks each receive forty blows and a provisional sentence of execution. The older one, who had showed compassion to Cai Yunu, benefits from her testimony and is simply returned to secular life.

This story shares the retribution plot typical of late Ming fiction, but it also exemplifies the stereotypical representation of "lascivious" Buddhist clergy in late imperial China. A typical crime-tale story pattern of monks is as follows: a Buddhist monk (sometimes more than one) tries to seduce or rape a woman who comes to the temple for such reasons as pilgrimage, prayer, or getting out of the rain; she refuses to satisfy the monk's lewd desire; he, then, is provoked to anger (or is afraid of being accused), so he kills her. Incorrupt, wise magistrates, who are the heroes of these crime tales, usually exercise their extraordinary ability to bring the monks' crimes to light and to vindicate the dead women. In this fashion, vernacular fiction displays the fictional stereotypes of Buddhist monks and the common hope for justice in the end.[22]

BUDDHIST CLERGY IN QING SOCIETY

Although Buddhism attracted the faith of many ordinary people (especially women) in late imperial China, the Confucian tradition relegated Buddhist clergy to the periphery of society. Confucian tradition centers its discourse on the notion of filial piety. A son's filial obligation to his father ought to be expressed even after the father's death. According to the popular belief, if a son does not conduct a proper ritual for his father's soul, it turns into a ghost. Such ghosts wander about and suffer. In order to avoid turning his father into a ghost, a son has to keep performing the proper rituals throughout his entire life. The chain of responsibility for such ritual obligations between father and son is ancestor worship: male descendants are responsible for performing rituals on behalf of all patrilineal ancestors.

Confucian tradition, with its emphasis on filial piety and ancestor ritual, saw Buddhist clergy as unfilial because they cut off family ties and lived collectively in monasteries in order to maintain celibate, religious lives. Becoming a Buddhist novice was called "leaving the family" (*chujia*). In Confucian eyes, these novices had severed their ties with their families, the most important social unit in China, and refused to continue their family lines. The Buddhist clergy's refusal to create families and maintain the patriarchal line is the primary reason why Confucian discourse socially marginalized them.

The Qing state also expressed a fear of Buddhist monasteries partly for security reasons. In the state's eyes, temples might serve as places of refuge for criminals who shaved their heads and disguised themselves as clergy to conceal their true identity. In order to assure state control, the Qing government tried to force every monk to carry a placard providing information such as his name, the name of the temple to which he belonged, the exact date when he became a monk, and so on.²³ In fact, magistrates of Ba county from at least the Jiaqing through Xianfeng reigns successively issued orders denouncing rogues who squatted inside Juelin Temple, one of the oldest monasteries of the Chongqing region. The following order is typical of this genre:

> Since Juelin Temple is the oldest Buddhist temple in the region of Yu [another name for Chongqing], there are always people visiting from far and wide at the New Year season. I [the magistrate of Ba county] am afraid that unlawful rogues form gangs and spy on women [*kuishi funü*], making a pretense of participating in the ceremonies. Their loitering in the precincts may lead to "breaking off twigs and pulling up flowers" [i.e., seducing women]. Beggars and wandering clergy also practice extortion and keep squatting inside the temple grounds, refusing to leave. . . . ²⁴

This order expresses anxiety that the temple could be exploited as a setting for illicit liaisons between men and women. As noted above, one of the classic story patterns in vernacular fiction describes sexual, and eventually lethal, calamities that befall women who visit Buddhist temples. This magistrate (like dozens of other Ba county magistrates) appears to have shared the same assumptions about the sexual dangers of Buddhist temples.

Readers may be struck by the similarity in plot between the story of Cai Yunu and the written report discussed at the beginning of this chapter. For people in Qing dynasty China, a scene of a Buddhist monk with a woman at a temple gate must have recalled this plot, which had been included in much vernacular fiction, especially in the genre of crime tales.[25] People who had read or heard of such stories might see such a scene through the "interpretive grid" (to use Carlo Ginzburg's term) of culture, which made things familiar and thus plausible in their eyes.[26]

Despite the social marginalization of Buddhist clergy, Buddhism enjoyed significant popularity among women during the late imperial era. Women from elite families found the visit to the temple to be one of their rare chances to travel outside their residences for pleasure.[27] Such women sometimes invited monks or nuns to their homes, asking them to provide consoling sermons and prayers, to exercise ritualistic magic, and to prescribe medicine. A number of women, including those from peasant families, went to temples to pray for the safe birth of a son. The bodhisattva Guanyin was represented in many different forms related to pregnancy and childbirth. Women's intimacy with monks and their visits to temples to pray aroused men's anxiety about the possibility of sexual relations between their women and monks. One story pattern shared by pornographic fiction in late imperial China tells of a young Buddhist monk who falls in love with a beautiful wife and dresses up like a nun in order to take advantage of her loneliness and stay with her for a night.[28]

Monks and Nuns in a Sea of Sin (Sengni niehai), a work of pornography from the late sixteenth century, includes a number of stories of this type. Timothy Brook, in his work on gentry patronage of Buddhist monasteries, argues that such patronage derived from the late Ming local elite's search for alternative sites in which to exercise its power in local society. He sees this pornography as a reflection of the more frequent and closer relationship between local elites and Buddhist clergy observed in the late Ming.[29] Although he does not explicitly point it out, such a closer relationship was also accompanied by a growing anxiety about excessive intimacy between elite family members and Buddhist clergy. Monks' detachment from the family system and the communal fear of wandering clergy exercising ritualistic magic might have reinforced this suspicion.[30]

The growth of print culture during the late imperial period helped to shape the image of Buddhist clergy as dangerous. Plaint writers in the Qing, by consulting treatises for litigation masters and relying on the widespread image of monks, fashioned appropriately plausible stories when the accused party was a monk. Some plaint writers might have read vernacular fiction containing lascivious clergy stories.[31] One treatise for litigation masters includes a model plaint that follows a typical story pattern reflecting husbands' anxiety. This model plaint accuses a Buddhist monk of seducing women into the temple to pray for the birth of a son. As in all other stories of this type, the monk seizes this chance to start illicit relations with these women and maintains the liaisons until their husbands discover them.[32]

BUDDHIST MONKS BETWEEN REALITY AND FICTION

The representation of events in written complaints does not, as noted above, necessarily tell us what actually happened. As the above-cited case from 1825 indicates, a monk seen simply chatting with a woman could arouse suspicion of adultery. A story from the late Ming collection *Judge Bao's Hundred Cases* (Bao Longtu pan baijia gong'an) shows a similar situation in which a husband suspects his wife of adultery when he comes home and finds that she has kindly let a Buddhist monk warm himself at their fire.[33] One facet of an actual event could provide the hint a plaint writer could use to construct a plot both familiar to himself and acceptable to contemporaries as "reality."

The interpretation of reality inevitably involves fictional elements used to create plausibility. Case records show that a stereotype derived from fiction provided plaint writers with a framework within which to depict the accused. In actual cases in which Buddhist monks were involved, a fictional stereotype was not only used as a narrative strategy but also served to shape the representation of reality in plaints, which the magistrate would interpret.

This, of course, does not mean that readers and writers in Qing China could not distinguish between facts and imagination. The presentation and interpretation of reality in legal prose, however, were shaped by a frame of reference that had been developed in fiction genres. In cases involving monks, a fictional stereotype with specific clichés and a typical story pattern played a central role in constructing what would be presented as reality. The textual framework composed of these literary devices grew out of the tension between the interpretation of reality and the reality being interpreted in the process of packaging a story.

CONCLUSION

The terms and plots used in legal case records reveal that plaintiffs accusing Buddhist monks usually relied on a narrative strategy that portrays monks as lustful and always thirsting for women, contriving at rape or adultery. Monks are described as those who essentially violated Confucian social order and morality.

The choice of clichés found in case records involving Buddhist monks was similar to those in cases involving ordinary laymen. Sets of phrases and patterns of terminology attacking one after another were shared by most written complaints, regardless of whether or not monks were involved. However, a strong association with sexual misdeeds was a specific feature typical in descriptions of monks. Although monks may sometimes have committed adultery, the frequency of a fixed plot pattern with sexual deeds seems to indicate a borrowing of the popular fictional image of monks for the purpose of packaging narratives about them in written legal complaints.

No matter who hit on the story of rape or seduction written in plaints, illiterate peasants also participated in the process of composing such narratives. Even if a literate litigation adviser fabricated the story of rape, the illiterate litigant still had to know the story that was written in his or her plaint. Otherwise, the magistrate would find out in the court hearing that the story was fabricated.

Therefore, the stories in plaints had to be culturally acceptable so that every participant in the litigation process, including the magistrate, would be convinced that the plaints were plausible. Presumably, even an illiterate litigant would bridle if his adviser presented a culturally inexplicable plot in his plaint. The magistrate would refuse to endorse the plaint if the story narrated was completely beyond his imagination and comprehension. Resorting to the fictional stereotype of Buddhist monks was part of a litigation strategy for ensuring that all participants acknowledged the plaint's plausibility, regardless of whether it convinced the magistrate of its truth.

At the same time, such use of fictional stereotypes indicates a circulation and exchange between oral and written cultures. The genre of vernacular crime tales grew out of the storytelling and theatrical traditions. Stories transmitted orally and told as entertainment in marketplaces ultimately circulated in the form of published fiction, especially during the Ming period. But in turn, many of these original stories were undoubtedly based on actual cases. Despite its diverse roots, the fictional stereotype of monks became fixed when fictional crime tales became popular reading material.

However, this does not mean that such stereotypes were shared only among literate people. The case from 1825 indicates that illiterate ruffians intended from the beginning to use material evidence of adultery in order to fashion a narrative of illicit sex between a monk and his tenant's wife. The similarity of plot between a crime tale involving Judge Bao and this actual case denotes that those ruffians were also familiar with the stereotype of Buddhist monks. In addition to the spread of the crime fiction genre, neighbors would surely have heard about these stories from actual legal plaints. Thus, even illiterate litigants who knew how to present a plot could use a stereotype as a way of packaging the narrative. This points to the continuous circulation of stereotypes between oral and written traditions, mutually reproducing and reinforcing them.

NOTES

1. BXDA, 6-3-9048.
2. This is cited by an eighteenth-century private secretary (later an official), Wang Huizu, in his warning to his readers not to be fooled by the fabrications included in plaints. See his *Xu Zuozhi yaoyan*, 232–33.
3. Macauley, "Civil and Uncivil Disputes" and *Social Power and Legal Culture*; Fuma Susumu, "Min-Shin jidai," "Shōshi hihon 'Shō-Sō ihitsu' no shutsugen," and "Shōshi hihon no sekai."
4. Fuma, "Min-Shin jidai."
5. Ibid.
6. One of the treatises for litigation masters emphasizes that "the language of legal plaints must be neither too literary nor too vulgar." See *Xinke fajia xinshu, juan* 1: 3b.
7. Fuma, "Shōshi hihon 'Shō-Sō ihitsu' no shutsugen," cites Yu Jianwu's *Zhipu* (Notes on governing published in Chongzhen 12, 1639) observation that most plaints in the regions of Jiangsu, Zhejian, Jiangxi, Hubei, and Hunan were written by "wandering ruffians and fortune-tellers" who consulted "treatises." A detailed account of urban life in Chengdu, Sichuan, in the early twentieth century says that fortune-tellers read personal letters and wrote texts for illiterate customers. See Fu Chongju, *Chengdu tonglan*, 460.
8. These obscure and mediocre literates and semiliterates had received a certain amount of classical education in preparation for taking the civil service examinations but had abandoned the examination route for various reasons (successive failure to pass the exams, poverty, etc.). Given the incomplete level they achieved in composition training, they could not be full-time legal specialists and, instead, simultaneously had to offer their services as, for example, geomancer, fortune-

teller, village schoolteacher, and writer of letters, wills, and contracts. Most actual plaints in local-level case records were not written by eminent litigation professionals, called "litigation masters" or "litigation mongers," given the widespread availability of treatises for plaint writing, the ease with which any nonprofessional might write a plaint by consulting these treatises, and the simplicity of the language. Undeniably, there were real professional legal writers in late imperial society; however, such eminent professionals no doubt collected exorbitant fees. Most commoners probably hired amateur, part-time ghostwriters. Some of them, but not all of them, might have been pejoratively labeled "litigation mongers" by the state, when their litigation advice exceeded some tolerable levels. For the litigation strategies, see Philip C. C. Huang, *Civil Justice in China*, 172–97.

9. Davis, *Fiction in the Archives*.

10. In Ba county during the magistracy of Zhu Fengyun in Daoguang 28–29 (1848–49), a plaint draft either written or edited by an officially authorized notary was attached with the standard plaint form when it was filed at the yamen. Magistrate Zhu also ordered scribes to indicate clearly whether they actually had composed or edited plaints. Plaints from his term of office at Ba county employ either the term "scribe's text" (*daishu zuo*) or the term "scribe's edited draft" (*daishu gao*) at the left side of the notary's official stamp. Zhu maintained this method of clarifying the plaint-writing process during his magistracy in Nanbu county, Sichuan, between 1851 and 1853. See Nambu County Archive (*Nanbu xian dang-'an*), held in Nanchong Municipal Archives.

11. Past scholarship points out that such linguistic elements as formulaic language and clichés are products of the transmission of tales. Works on the oral tradition tell us how oral cultures developed formulas, clichés, rhymes, and other linguistic devices because of the need for memorization of material that cannot be recorded in any other way. These techniques of text transmission received further development under conditions of literacy, when oral storytelling started to be transcribed on paper. See Parry, *Making of Homeric Verse*; Ong, *Orality and Literacy*; and Goody, *Domestication of the Savage Mind* and *Interface*.

12. Yuen Ren Chao, "Chinese Language."

13. See Bauer, "The Tradition of the 'Criminal Cases of Master Pao' *Pao-kung-an (Lung-t'u kung-an)*"; Y. W. Ma, "Themes and Characterization"; Hanan, "*Judge Bao's Hundred Cases* Reconstructed"; and Waltner, "From Casebook to Fiction."

14. BXDA, 6-4-9841.

15. Ibid., 6-3-8708.

16. Ibid., 6-3-9457.

17. Ibid., 6-3-9675.

18. Ibid., 6-3-9701. Another case, in Daoguang 21–22 (1841–42), initiated by Buddhist nuns, also shows that those in the priesthood relied on their own nasty image in their plaints. See BXDA, 6-3-9380.

19. Treatises for litigation masters consulted in this chapter include *Xinjuan fajia toudanhan*; *Zheyu qibian*, *Xinke fajia xinshu*, *Pili shoubi*, *Fabi jingtianlei*, *Fabi tianyou*, *Xue'an mingyuanlu*, *Xiao-Cao yibi*, and *Zheyu mingzhu*.

20. Wu Tianmin and Da Keqi's *Xinke fajia xinshu*, 2.14a–14b. The model plaint is followed by a model counterplaint, which would be filed by the accused Buddhist monk and tells a story completely different from that of the model plaint. *Xinke zhaixuan zengbu zhushi fajia yaolan zheyu mingzhu*, 2.6a–6b, and *Xinke fabi tianyou*, 2.13b–14a, also have similar sets of plaints and counterplaints.

21. *Xinke fabi tianyou*, 1.21b–22a; and *Xinke fabi jingtianlei*, 1.18a–18b.

22. See, for example, Ling Mengchu's *Pai'an jingqi*, story 26, in which a woman flees to a monastery, where a monk and a disciple take turns having sex with her. When she is accidentally killed, they bury her in the courtyard. After the crime is detected, the monk is beaten to death, and the disciple is exiled.

23. Kuhn, *Soulstealers*.

24. BXDA, 6-2-170; 6-4-381.

25. The short pornographic novel *Buddhist Monks Addicted to Love* (Fengliu heshang) is based on the story "Cai Yunu Takes Shelter from the Rain." A number of crime tales include a similar story in which, however, some details were changed slightly. For example, see "Lin Hou qiu Guanyin qiyu" (Lin Hou Prays to Guanyin to Request Rain), in *Mingjing gong'an*, juan 2, from the late Ming.

26. Ginzburg, *Cheese and the Worms*.

27. Ko, *Teachers of the Inner Chambers*.

28. This is the beginning of *Buddhist Monks Addicted to Love* (Fengliu heshang).

29. See Brook, *Praying for Power*, 94–95.

30. See Kuhn, *Soulstealers*, 1–29.

31. For example, one collection, *Gujin Lütiao gong'an*, includes a special section devoted entirely to stories about "licentious monks" (*yinseng*).

32. See Buxiangzi's *Xinjuan fajia toudanhan*, 1.2b–3a.

33. In *Bao Longtu pan baijia gong'an*, story 56 is titled "Zhang jianseng juepei yuanfang" (Beating the rapist monk and exiling him to a remote area). James St. André discusses the collection in chapter 9 of this volume.

4 The Art of Persuasion in Literature and Law

ROBERT E. HEGEL

Acts of violence that offend moral standards and thus merit punishment figure in writings of all kinds from late imperial China. Crime reports frequently represent face-to-face confrontations, generally between interrogators and the accused. Many of these confrontations involve what appear to be oratorical positions taken by speakers who assert their innocence, or their conviction that the other is most certainly not innocent. Skillfully used rhetorical questions, often followed by aphorisms or other bits of folk wisdom, are key elements in creating such authoritative positions. But unanswerable questions and proverbs appear in other narrative situations as well, in texts not involving crimes, whenever persuasive effort is needed. What one can conclude from this apparent ubiquity in prose texts is that the rhetorical question was a standard stylistic tool known to virtually all writers, which one could safely attribute to impassioned speakers of all social levels. To indicate the prevalence of this rhetorical tool will require a brief survey of texts of several forms produced during the seventeenth, eighteenth, and nineteenth centuries. Our concern here is primarily with the writing of crime reports and writing about legal proceedings. As we can see in texts of these types, legal writers of late imperial China drew from the same rhetorical pool as did writers of fiction and prose in other forms, as self-conscious participants in the larger world of writing.

The reason for stylistic commonality within a form is that all writers followed the same models. For some forms of writing, it was obligatory to follow the models; in others, writers did so simply in order that their presentations could be easily understood. A few did so in the spirit of parody. Prefatory and other paratextual materials reveal a common concern among writers over generic clarity in informal writings (for personal expression and entertainment); their aim was to elicit specific responses from intended audiences.

For writers of fiction, the models might be more or less explicitly identified, but these writers also placed implicit emphasis on controlling how readers responded to their texts. By contrast, those who worked in the Qing imperial administration had little access to the creative "space" allotted to the creative writer. Instead, numerous authoritative guidebooks provided advice, guidelines, and even samples to imitate in the drafting of judicial reports.[1] Qing criminal case reports for the most part were written to fit preexisting formulas to a greater extent than were works of fiction; they describe crimes and criminals in generally conventional ways.[2] The models focus on structure and how to represent the principals of a case; rhetorical style is seemingly taken for granted there, as it was by the authors of fiction and other less formal prose.

Thus, in the crafting of narrative, regardless of audience or ostensible purpose for writing, Qing period writers relied perhaps unself-consciously on common rhetorical tools—questions that preclude an answer and appeals to common knowledge—as ways to make their texts seem familiar, serious, and persuasive. Persuasion was as essential in casual or informal writing as it was in serious administrative communications; it functioned to produce complex but generally predictable responses among their respective reading communities. In many kinds of texts, writers utilized rhetorical questions to clarify standards of judgment and, frequently, to develop convincing characterization as well.

Furthermore, oratorically persuasive characters were conventionally coded as morally upright, an essential element in guiding the readings of a variety of types of texts. A similar function for rhetorical questions in diverse contexts suggests a broadly shared conception of how to build a convincing argument in writing. It also suggests a common set of models, drawn most likely from the classic texts memorized in preparation for the civil service examinations, the experience that encouraged all readers to be proficient as writers. Those models, like the canonical principles themselves, upheld the notion of a moral hierarchy in society, a point to which we will return.

Samples for this study have been drawn from a variety of texts. Crime case reports are from *Routine Memorials of the Grand Secretariat's Punishments Office of Scrutiny* (Neige xingke tiben), most of which involve homicide; others are from published collections of memorials and edicts concerning the major corruption cases during the Qing. Other sources include examples of narrative literature circulating at that time; vernacular stories and novels intended for general reading audiences, or "popular fiction" (*tongsu xiaoshuo*); and the classical-language anecdotes, generally termed *biji xiaoshuo*, or informal writings, that circulated in print or in manuscript among the literati. The focus here is on the use of rhetorical questions to exemplify moral and ethical positions in narrative situations for quite different audiences.

(RE)WRITING JUDICIAL REPORTS

The ostensible purpose of the careful investigations and painstaking reasoning reflected in crime reports was to ensure that the appropriate punishment was meted out for improper behavior. On the one hand, given the emperor's status as human representative of the moral order of the cosmos, it was in the interests of the ruling dynasty for its people to feel that justice would be done locally in his name.[3] On the other hand, emperors had to balance the many forces competing for their approval—and seeking to sway their opinions on cases of regional or national significance. Thus, emperors sought a variety of opinions obtained during the mandatory judicial review for all serious cases; there could be no lack of clarity in a report about causation or culpability in an offense. This explicit demand placed even more pressure on those who crafted reports or memorials to write effectively.[4] But a secondary purpose of case reports—and their successive rewritings as they passed through the several obligatory levels of judicial review—was to verify that all the officials involved had done their job scrupulously. The magistrate and his superiors who crafted these reports had more than simply justice on their minds; they were also trying to preclude any disciplinary action against them for dereliction of duty.[5] To do so, their characterization of every individual involved had to be clear and convincing, for the entire case depended on whether readers of the report were persuaded by the total presentation. In short, creating clearly convincing arguments was in the interests of individuals at all levels of the imperial administration.

These legal writers displayed creative genius in drafting the reports for their superiors. This is not to say that the magistrates of Qing China and their legal assistants were self-consciously fictionalizing their material. However, it is now widely recognized that they were expected to edit the relevant information very carefully for their reports. This involved the *creative rewriting* of the oral testimony that served as the cornerstone of every case, and they apparently drew on the pool of common assumptions about how to create convincing stories.

Perhaps the most obvious evidence of editorial work in major criminal case reports is their standardized language format. That is, the introductory and concluding portions of reports written in the first person by various members of the judiciary all appear in standard classical style. Testimony recorded as interrogation, in contrast, appears in the official standard vernacular Chinese regardless of the language or dialect spoken by the deponent. (Written depositions appear in reports of cases involving officials or other obviously literate persons.) Likewise, Qing period guidebooks for magistrates regularly counseled these legal writers to remove all vulgarity and local dialectical expressions from recorded testimony in order to enhance its comprehensibility.[6] Finally, it was considered mandatory that all testimony should reinforce the facts of the case as finally determined by the judicial officials themselves—and as summarized in its introduction.

One can only speculate on precisely what sort of utterances came from witnesses either after the intense, disorienting pain of torture or under immense mental pressure from the magistrate's threats that torture might be applied. Court scribes probably edited and summarized as they took down this testimony in the first place. We do know, from cases that have been preserved in their several drafts, that oral testimony was often heavily rewritten to eliminate all irrelevant comments and to emphasize the consistency of information they conveyed.[7]

RHETORICAL DEFENSES

Many murder reports and other cases of similar gravity include extensive testimony—from the plaintiff, from the defendants, and from many witnesses. The standard format is a dialogue, with the judicial officer asking questions and the deponent responding with complete, consistent answers. Some of these responses seem, initially, to be oratorical gestures of defiance against authority.[8] This is despite the obvious fact that the magistrate had absolute power over them in his courtroom; bailiffs stood at the ready to administer torture to any involved party who seemed to be withholding information or to be lying. After all, the responses of witnesses—the rhetorical questions they apparently fired at their interrogators—do not constitute *their* rhetorical strategy to save themselves; instead, these responses reveal the narrative strategies of those who compiled the case reports.

For example, when four members of a Beijing-area household were murdered in 1674, the *dianshi* (local sheriff) reportedly first questioned the survivors and even the neighbors about what they had seen and heard. One man responded: "Even though we are neighbors, we didn't hear any noise at all. Their dogs are ferocious—if somebody had gotten in, wouldn't the dogs have barked? Furthermore, [the murdered householder] Liu Er was a Bordered Red Bannermen, just like us. If we had heard something, how could we have not gone to lend a hand?!"[9] As represented here, this neighbor was not intimidated by the interrogation; by responding with assertive questions, he appears as one who speaks with confidence and absolute conviction in his own innocence of any involvement in the crime. It seems unlikely that any real village elder would be so brash in the face of possible punishment, if his account of the events were not accepted; instead, his position is meant to be persuasive of his aloofness from the offense. His testimony should be read as part of the magistrate's general textual strategy, designed to highlight the culpability of the individual perpetrator without involving any of his community. Whether the neighbor actually spoke those words in court is quite beside the point; he comes across to the reader as confident in the validity of his comments and in his own moral authority in expressing them. His testimony thus reinforces the magistrate's conclusions about the case.

During his interrogation in a 1696 Shandong murder case, Magistrate Jin Yingdou of Liaocheng county received a combative response from a desperate suspect. This came after an apparently lengthy session in which both this prisoner, Ms. Li, and her erstwhile lover and former landlord, Du Huailiang, were being questioned a second time about the death of the woman's husband, Chen Wenxian. Chen had moved himself and his wife away from Du's house after a quarrel between the households; this physical separation of the lovers necessitated the termination of the affair. Once away from her landlord's importuning, Ms. Li experienced intense remorse for her infidelity, she said, and realized how close she felt to her husband. However, Magistrate Jin was skeptical, and he questioned her again about the depth of her involvement with the killer: in truth, had she not plotted with him to commit the murder? She replied,

> . . . after we moved away to live by ourselves, I felt so ashamed that I could not bear it. How could I be willing to have any contact with him again?! Furthermore, my husband and I had been married for ten years already. Seeing that we'd recently had a child, our feelings for each other were very deep. There's no way I would get somebody to kill him. Now I charge Du Huailiang with killing my husband—I hate that Du Huailiang so much!

The case report does not state explicitly how the magistrate felt about this outburst, but his subsequent line of questioning suggests that he was not persuaded. This was because Widow Li did not file charges against her former lover until three days after the murder. When the magistrate questioned her yet again about this delay, she responded, with even more apparent urgency:

> I am a woman left all alone. And at that time, I also had a fever from malaria. When finally I could get in to file the complaint, Your Honor had gone out to examine the corpses. And because I took the wrong route, I did not meet you along the way. This is why it was only on the third day that I filed the complaint.

Reviewing officials, however, revealed their feelings about the case in two ways. Hou Juguang, the prefect of Dongchang, left all of this testimony in the record as he forwarded it to the next level of review—when clearly he could have deleted or modified it, had he chosen to do so or if his own rehearing of the case had uncovered alternative accounts of the killing. Su Changchen, the Shandong provincial surveillance commissioner (*anchashi*), interrogated the woman again during his automatic review of the case. Her response at that time was only slightly more detailed and equally insistent. Likewise, even though both of these officials agreed with Magistrate Jin that, according to *The Qing Code*, Ms. Li should be strangled for her crimes, upon further consideration, her case was shown to fit nicely within the parameters of an imperial amnesty. Although her suitor should be beheaded, she should be pardoned, the Beijing officials confirmed, and the emperor agreed. And so Ms. Li had successfully been represented to her judges as deserving no punishment for the charges of murder and adultery.[10]

Rhetorical questions in defensive testimony serve to confirm the harmony of the entire neighborhood in a 1728 case from Suining county in Sichuan. Here, the magistrate Xu Ren questioned a neighbor who lived down the street from where a murder had been committed. The magistrate began by demanding,

> How far are you from the place where Ms. Zhang lived? On the twenty-third of the fourth month, whom did you see enter the Zhang house? For what reason did somebody kill Ms. Zhang? Why didn't you even try to save her? Tell the court your reasons in detail.

With what is represented as considerable composure, the elderly Yang Gongyi replied:

> The place where I live on this street is two houses away from Ms. Zhang. Because I'm getting old, I sit quietly in my house and don't go out into the street much. On the twenty-third of the fourth month, I didn't see anybody go toward Ms. Zhang's house. I don't know why it was that somebody murdered her. My nephew Yang Shangda saw Ms. Zhang's child out in the street crying, so he picked him up and took him back home. When he couldn't push the front door open, he went to the back door to drop him off. It was only then that he saw Ms. Zhang murdered on her bed. He screamed to the next-door neighbor Hu Gongshan to come and see. Only after he came home and told me about it did I know that somebody had killed Ms. Zhang. Since Luo Er had gone away, I told the nephew Yang Shangda to go and tell her father-in-law Luo Qisheng to come. At that time, I had no idea who had killed her—so you tell me, how I could have gone to save her?![11]

The old man presumably was not under any suspicion, although neighbors were regularly questioned on the supposition that they might have been involved in, or at least familiar with, the daily activities of the accused.[12] What his deposition reveals, however, is a generally harmonious neighborhood. The old people sit at leisure in their homes; when a child is found wandering in the street, a passerby will take him home and thoughtfully check on his family. Such facts reveal a society at peace, its members living responsibly with one another; it is only the inexplicable, aberrant individual who destroys this peaceful pattern by committing murder. The self-confident representation of an old man gives eloquent testimony to this ideal—and probably idealized—situation.

Why should magistrates and their secretaries include testimony from such witnesses? And why should these bystanders resort to such oratorical gestures in order to drive home their points? As suggested above, the elements of case reports necessarily reflect the assumptions of the Confucian state system for which they were written. With all its authority delegated downward from the autocratic emperor, the Qing government made regular appeals for moral rectitude on the part of all members of society, administrators as well as the citizenry.[13] Such activities dictated the involvement of local administration in the preservation of social order through the maintenance of personal, family, and community morality.

Local administrators also performed this function through public demonstrations of legal procedures as well as public punishments of malefactors—public floggings, exposure of petty criminals in cangues, public executions, and display of the heads of decapitated bandits and rebels—so as to remind everyone of the penalties that awaited others who made the same mistakes. Furthermore, as presumed moral exemplars in their own right, local magistrates were required to maintain social order in their districts. When order broke down, these administrators would seem to be implicated: if they were truly Good in themselves, canonical Confucian teachings would suggest that the area under their control might necessarily be orderly.[14]

This idealistic vision of local administration seems to explain the appearance of righteous self-assertion and self-defense in the testimony of witnesses in capital cases that were sent to the emperor for final review. These witnesses all protest their own innocence; none of them had any knowledge of antisocial or criminal behavior occurring, in effect, right next door. All blame for social disorder is thus heaped on the individual perpetrators; beyond these few sinners, the neighborhood where the crime occurred is peaceful and harmonious. By implication, then, the magistrate, like the neighbors, are all being Good, and only the perpetrator acted antisocially. Thus, it makes far greater sense to attribute these representations of resistance *not* to the individual deponents wishing to escape torture but to magistrates wishing to deflect all blame from themselves and onto the perpetrators alone for interruptions of social harmony. This implication would suggest a clear textual strategy on the part of the report's compiler, the magistrate or a secretary working in his name. To that end, self-confident testimony has a role to play in the case report, and rhetorical questions help strengthen the position of those who use them.

THE RHETORIC OF INTERROGATION

Rhetorical questions regularly appear in interrogation by officiating judges as well. In examining a 1662 case of adultery between an unmarried man and a married woman, both of them Manchus, Korkun of the Gioro clan, the "grand secretary of the Board of Punishments" (*Xingbu daxueshi*), reportedly took a stern tone, relying on rhetorical questions to reveal the strength of his position and the utter untenability of theirs. Of the adulteress, he demanded:

> Your older brother's wife said that you slept in her house on the second and the third and that you went someplace else to sleep on the first and the fourth. On the fifth, you came over with Bisangga and asked him for two hundred cash to give to her to buy something for your child to eat. On the first and the fourth, you didn't go to your brother's house to sleep.

> If you really haven't had illicit sex with Bisangga, why would he be willing to give two hundred cash to buy things for your child to eat? You had illicit sex with Bisangga, and that's the truth. Now confess.

Yet the hapless couple confessed only to a perfunctory affair when subjected to torture (by squeezing the fingers of the woman and the ankles of the man). The judge followed *The Qing Code* and sentenced them both to strangulation, but their execution was postponed until the aggrieved husband returned: he had the right to plead for their lives. When confronted with their guilt as adequately proved, he chose not to appeal, and they were sentenced to immediate execution.[15]

A STRONG ATTACK—AND A STRONG DEFENSE

Given the higher stakes involved for all concerned, it is not surprising that oratorical responses appear even more frequently in court cases of official corruption than in matters involving only common citizens at the local level. Examples abound in the texts generated by the notorious tax and relief grain scandal in Gansu during the 1780s. Wang Danwang (d. 1781) had been financial commissioner there (1774–77) and provincial governor of Zhejiang (1777–80); he was accused of misappropriating nearly a million *liang* of silver from famine relief and from the sale of Imperial Academy student (*jiansheng*) degrees.[16] Wang used persuasive language in his defense to confess to certain offenses but not others. He declared, "My crimes deserve ten thousand deaths. So if in Zhejiang there are yet more cases of corruption, why should I try to prevaricate about them for his benefit?" He concluded, contritely, but with another rhetorical flourish: "These all are my crimes; what could I say in my own defense?"[17] Similarly, apparently to forestall further questioning about accomplices, Liang Guang viceroy Fulehun asked plaintively, "Who would be willing to give up his own life and the lives of his family to cover up for me? [Shei ken shele shenjia xingming ti wo yinji ne?]"[18] In a written deposition, Tao Shilin explained: " . . . after I entered the capital and was summoned for an audience, I begged for sick leave and returned to my native place. If I had offered any bribes, then I would most certainly have expected a transfer. Why should I present a request merely for sick leave?"[19]

Some questions seemingly challenge the deponents on moral grounds, as if to preempt any defense on their part. A confession by Chen Huizu, the viceroy of Fujian and Zhejiang, concerning the Wang Danwang corruption case, includes the following exchange:

The Art of Persuasion in Literature and Law 89

> *Interrogator*: Failing to establish any business in your home area, and wishing to reside in Suzhou, you were "blinded by greed" and abandoned the graves of your forefathers. Was this not a case of "abandoning virtue and forgetting your roots"?
>
> *Deponent*: . . . I am the son of Chen Dashou; our family has "enjoyed the Favor of the State for generations." But because of my "passion for the bustle of the city," I wished to reside in Suzhou, and thus "turned my back on my roots and forgot my kin." I was "disloyal and unfilial." But in fact, "sin arises from within," so much so that "Heaven's goodness could not bear it," and "everything came to light." I can no longer face the world, nor do I have anything to say in my own defense.[20]

Perhaps more than anything, this exchange demonstrates to the reader that the accused could offer no defense against the persuasive rhetoric of his interrogator; he could only resort to timeworn clichés in response. Or, at least, this seemed the most appropriate way, stylistically, in which to record the interview.

But the rhetorical questions of others who testified seemed to protest that their accusers were wrong, or at least misguided in their interrogation. In the 1786 corruption case of the Manchu official Fulehun, his staff member Li Shirong was to plead, "That whole time [three months of incarceration], I could not get home. How could I have transferred the goods over to him to deliver?" He continued: "I only beg that you give my wife Zhou a strenuous interrogation, and then you'll understand. I'm already in deep trouble myself; how could I dare conceal anything else?"[21] Certain retorts seem intended to be amusing. Zhou Jing (a *kuli*, an official at a granary) declared: "Viceroy Wu is hard of hearing; he can't hear clearly even if you shout at him. How could I dare to tell him about such weighty matters as these losses in a loud voice? It would reach the ears and eyes of everybody around—I'd just be bringing everything out into the light myself." However, interrogator Changlin of the Gioro clan was not convinced by his protest and ordered the man tortured.[22]

It appears that prisoners might have relied on rhetorical questions as their last resort, as a final admission of guilt and appeal for mercy. Fulehun himself was to exclaim, "How would I still dare to prevaricate?" Another of the accused resorted to a common aphorism to explain his situation: "'When the water is low, the rocks are exposed.' [Shui luo shi chu.] How could I dare not tell the truth and get myself into deeper trouble?" Likewise, a third testified, "This is all due to my timidity and lack of talent; what could I say in my own defense?" And another confessed, "There's nothing I can do to reduce my crime—why should I deceive you on this matter?" But the most poignant of these questions came from Li Shirong: "Having received such harsh interrogation, dare I still prevaricate? I beg you to release me from torture."[23] Here, in their rhetorical questions, the deponents authoritatively establish their own guilt, contributing to the coherence of the narrative.

PERSUASIONS FOR NEW READERS?

In case records in which the voices represented are speaking generally to their peers rather than for their superiors, a sensitivity to oratorical positions seems even more pronounced. Such records frequently attribute rhetorical questions to judicial officers during interrogation as well as to the officials being interrogated. Legal secretaries, we can assume, transcribed and then edited testimony in these high-level trials.

But we see the same sort of rhetoric in private accounts. Writing in retrospect (from a record of the trial, perhaps) in his published collection of the cases he heard during a brief tenure as district magistrate in Guangzhou, Lan Dingyuan (1680–1733) developed his narratives using the same oratorical flourishes. In structure, his account of events follows clear temporal sequences, precisely as in a formal crime report. One example is an account in his *Luzhou Cases* (Luzhou gong'an), which Lan titled "Private Punishment in the Yunluo Inn" (*Yunluo dian sixing*).[24] In it, Lan first summarizes the events of the case and then mentions that it had been reported to the "village headman" (*xiangzhang*), who duly rounded up the principals and presented his appeal to Lan as magistrate. Lan Dingyuan then tells how he set off in the middle of the night to examine the corpse, a man beaten to death by a "magistrate's clerk" (*xian li*) and his entourage: the hapless man had stolen some four ounces of silver from the clerk, one Li Zhenchuan from Haiyang county.

In the account, Lan is surprised to discover that the body bears many wounds: the bruise from a severe blow on the right temple and clear rope impressions on his thumbs, his head appears to have been squeezed in a bamboo hoop, and his body is covered with burns and with lacerations from having been beaten with vines. Lan writes: "I said, 'Oh my! Who could have been this perverse? No matter whether it is the clerk from a neighboring jurisdiction or some high circuit official, I will order the death of whoever could have done this!'" Thus, he combines his rhetorical question with a further exclamation so as to clarify his assessment of the gravity of this situation.

Lan is not persuaded by the clerk's testimony that a band of soldiers and their sergeant Cai Gao had helped with the beating; initially, Lan is also skeptical about whether this clerk could have hit the victim on the temple with enough force to cause a fatal injury, as Li claims to have done. Thus, he narrates the investigative steps that lead to his conclusion and the penalties he recommends for the culprits. However, the innkeeper's testimony utterly contradicts the version of events given by the others; instead, he recounts a sadistic beating by the clerk and his cousin, to whom he had previously promised to loan the money that had turned up missing. Lan demands of the innkeeper, "[Li] Zhenchuan, Axiong, and Awei have all given the same version. Why do you alone try to prevaricate?" The innkeeper, Xu Abing, adamantly insists on his version of the events, retorting, "As the sun is in the sky, you may squeeze me to death before I would dare lie to you. I beg you to take your time and make a careful investigation; 'when the water is low, the rocks are exposed.' If Zhenchuan's nephew did not do it, then I will pay for his life with mine."[25] Indeed, his testimony is ultimately corroborated by Lan Dingyuan's subsequent interrogations, particularly those of the clerk whose silver had been stolen and the latter's now contrite nephew.

But Lan Dingyuan's superiors are not convinced by his account; they believe that soldiers are far more likely than any clerk and his luggage bearers to have treated the victim so barbarously. The "provincial surveillance commissioner" (Lan uses the common appellation, *niesi*) orders Lan to reinvestigate the case; he does, but his conclusions remain unaltered. When the commissioner threatens impeachment, Lan replies: "To take the life of an innocent man simply to protect my own reputation—how could I do such a thing!" Later, Lan defends changing his mind from his initial report to his final suggested sentence by noting, "Testimony is given by the criminal. In matters of his life or death, how could the interrogator alter the testimony? Since the testimony cannot be changed, of course the investigation report cannot be altered either." Finally, during the commissioner's interrogation, clerk Li responds: "I have worked in administrative offices for many decades; how could I not know that he who kills a person must die? Even if I received a bribe of a thousand in gold, if I could not live to enjoy it, what value would it have for me?"[26]

In the face of this rhetorical defense, the commissioner can only concede that Lan Dingyuan's verdicts are incontrovertible, and he forwards the case to the capital for final review.

Lan presents a retelling of a 1728 case that uses precisely the same rhetorical tricks found in the case reports themselves, as well as proverbial phrases to emphasize their points. Regardless of whether Lan Dingyuan crafted this version on the basis of his original case report, his stylistic markers are unmistakably shared with official documents of that form. Given his lack of sustained success in administrative positions, one might ask, cynically, whether he thought mastery of style was sufficient in itself for further official appointments. Clearly, one of Lan's concerns is to persuade his readers of the rightness of his statements—and his reliability as a judge and writer of case records.

RHETORICAL QUESTIONS IN FICTIONAL NARRATIVES

Contemporary fiction and other informal narratives illustrate that writers of the late Ming and Qing regularly put rhetorical questions into the mouths of their characters in order to assert agency on the part of the speaker; this oratorical stance also serves to enhance the authority and individuality with which those characters speak. These characters are convinced they are right, as are similarly determined speakers in legal documents. Similar rhetorical challenges often appear in the stories about legal cases in informal *biji xiaoshuo* collections such as the compilation of anecdotes and amusing fantasies *Liaozhai's Record of the Strange* (Liaozhai zhi yi), by Pu Songling (1640–1715).[27]

Pu uses this rhetorical tool flexibly. In several cases, its appearance signals resignation on the part of a character. In his famous story about the scholar who enters a wall painting in order to make love to a beautiful maiden depicted there, a monk explains: "Illusion is born in the mind. How can a poor mendicant like me explain it?" [Huan you ren sheng, pindao heneng jie?] In another, Lu, a judge from the underworld, confronts a scholar whose mortal life is drawing to an end. When the scholar asks whether the judge can save him, the judge replies: "What good are personal wishes in the face of Heaven's decree? And anyway, life and death are one in the eyes of a man of broad perspective. Why should you rejoice at life and grieve at death?" [Hebi sheng zhi wei le, si zhi wei bei?]

Sometimes his questions come across as sarcastic: in a second story, a character remarks, "The power to promote or demote is in the hands of my superiors, not with the people. If the higher-ups are pleased with someone, he's a good official. What good is love of the people for winning favor with the higher-ups?"[28]

Other Pu Songling characters refer to commonly shared assumptions through rhetorical questions. Speaking about a betrothal, a mother says, "Now that we have made the offer, why should we go back on it?" [Ji yi you yan, naihe zhong gai?] When she describes a promising young man, a woman remarks, "What is more, young Cheng studies himself ragged night and day. Does he look like the sort to remain on the bottom for long?" [Fu qi jiu wei renxia zhe?][29]

One of the more outstanding writer-scholars of the Qing period is Ji Yun (1724–1805), a *jinshi* (presented scholar) of 1754 who in 1773 was appointed a chief compiler of the imperial manuscript library known as Siku Quanshu; he was in charge of the project until it was completed in 1783. In and out of imperial favor thereafter, in his later years, Ji Yun compiled anecdotes interpreted by some as a way both to seek solace from the vagaries of his times and to satirize pedants and his opponents in philosophical debates through allegories.[30] They were printed in 1800 as *Notes from the Studio for Careful Scrutiny* (Yuewei caotang biji). In a recent study, Leo Chan asserts that Ji Yun used the collection to assert the validity of believing in spirits and ghosts. His method, Chan observes, was to argue on the basis of his own experience. In this regard, Ji Yun's "evidence" (Leo Chan's apt term) is testimony very similar in form to that collected in legal case reports.[31]

Consider a situation in which acceptance of oral testimony is most clearly questioned. This is an anecdote written in the first person about a 1739 conversation Ji Yun had with two friends and fellow students. Li Yunju said that he believed ghosts and spirits exist; Huo Yangzhong scoffed at such beliefs. But after a servant told of his horrifying encounter with the dead, Huo remarked,

> "I can never take what others have seen as something that I have seen myself." To this, Li replied, "Were you to adjudicate a legal case, would you have to witness everything to believe? [Jiang shishi mudu erhou xin hu?] Or would you consider others' testimonies? [Yi yi quzheng zhongkou hu?] Unreasonable as it is to expect to see everything that occurs, would we not accept their testimonies and take what they have seen as what we have seen? [Bu yi ren suojian wei wo suojian hu?]"[32]

The people named in Ji Yun's narratives, his characters, in effect, regularly forestall disbelief and assert the authority of their positions through the use of rhetorical questions.

A similar example can be seen in a story recounted by Fan Jiaxiang, a *jinshi* of 1754, about the judgment of the dead in Hell. Fan concludes: "For the enlightened resolution of difficult cases, the netherworld court is unsurpassed. For comprehensive accuracy of records, the netherworld court is also unsurpassed. In this case, the netherworld king was neither overconfident nor impatient. Is this not what makes a netherworld king a netherworld king?" [Si Mingwang suo yi wei Mingwang yu?][33]

By implying a comparison between the widely accepted objectivity and justice of courts in the underworld and those in reality, Fan's sarcasm is scathing; Ji Yun probably meant it to amuse, and to provoke, his literati readers while revealing something of Fan Jiaxiang's character. But his ironic use of a rhetorical question merely confirms the stylistic similarities between persuasive statements in records of conversations among the literati at their leisure and in their more formal writings.

Story 16 in Feng Menglong's first collection of forty vernacular tales, *Stories Old and New* (Gujin xiaoshuo), printed in 1621, contains the famous tale of extreme loyalty among friends "The Chicken and Millet Dinner for Fan Juqing, Friend in Life and Death" (Fan Juqing jishu sisheng jiao). After Zhang Yuanbo reads the eulogy for his friend Fan, who killed himself in order that his spirit might transverse the impossible distance to meet Zhang at the appointed time, Zhang declares to Fan's widow: "My elder brother died for my sake. How can I live without him?" [Qi neng du sheng ye?] And then Zhang, too, commits suicide so that the friends might be buried together.[34]

Likewise, the last story in Feng's initial collection is one of several that present fictionalized judicial interrogations. In "Shen Xiaoxia Encounters the Expedition Memorials" (Shen Xiaoxia xianghui Chushi biao), when a prefect questions Shen's wife about the disappearance of her husband, she replies, "Today, Zhang Qian was away all morning and returned with Li Wan but not my husband. If those two didn't kill my husband, who did?" [Bushi ta mouhai le shi shui?] If my husband was not in the Feng residence, Li Wan should have looked for him yesterday, and Zhang Qian should have been worried, too. Why did he try to pacify me with nice words?" [Ruhe jiang hao yanyu yinzhu xiaofuren?] Not surprisingly, the prefect is convinced, and he tortures the two runners to learn the truth.[35] Throughout the story, there are numerous other rhetorical questions given in response to questioning. In many, these oratorical flourishes constitute a "parting shot," a comment that ends both the speech and, usually, the writer's efforts at fleshing out the character as confident in her or his own ethical position. Proverbial phrases often are employed to that same effect.

IMPERIAL RHETORIC(AL QUESTIONS)

One might assume that emperors never needed to resort to rhetorical tricks in order to validate their moral positions. Yet edicts on political problems encountered by the Qianlong emperor (1711–1799, r. 1736–96) reveal that even the ultimately authoritative emperor was represented as engaging in persuasive argumentation. Curiously, perhaps, rhetorical questions appear as frequently in his writings as in texts produced by his subjects. In the Gansu corruption scandal, for example, the emperor, expressing dismay at how local officials had misrepresented natural disasters, demanded of Wang Tingzan: "How could it be, when all you had been reporting was that rainfall was so short as to constitute drought, that in this year only Gansu should have enough?" [Qiyou jinnian Gansheng du duozhi zhi li?] In the somewhat later corruption case from South China, the emperor asked, with apparent exasperation, about Fulehun, "How could [his actions] escape Our penetrating scrutiny?" [An neng tao Zhenzhi dong jian hu?][36] Clearly, they could not. The monarch vented his frustration in a further series of rhetorical questions:

> We greatly wanted [Fulehun] to succeed, and this is why We favored him with an appointment where he could prove himself in a frontier area. This is Our frustration over not achieving Our goal in that appointment. Now, since [his crime] has already been revealed, even if We do not investigate and deal with it severely, "when the water is low, the rocks are exposed." If all he were to do is tender his resignation for transgressions, how could We grant him another appointment in the future? What would the world say about Us as a ruler? According to Yade's memorial, this was not the only such case. Since We have treated him as a faithful servant to the point of posting him in Guangdong, how could We change Our tune and treat him differently now?

As we see from these examples—and there are innumerable others—the Qianlong emperor's questions often took the form "How could this [rightly] be?" [Qiyou . . . zhi li?!][37] Here, we might find the clue that reveals the strategy behind the frequent use of rhetorical questions both in fiction and in judicial presentations, the reason why persuasion is such a common element in writing in late imperial China.

As an ethical concept, *li* has been widely explored in past and present by administrators and philosophers, scholars of literature, and cultural historians. Especially when it comes from the imperial pen, *li* clearly conveys the sense of moral or ethical Principle, and thus serves as rationale for the emperor's rule. As the Kangxi emperor sought to demonstrate with his "Sacred Edict" (Shengyu) of 1670, emperors served as the embodiment of ethical standards on Earth, the representative of Tian, the moral order of the cosmos.[38] Imperially authored rhetorical questions asserted what was Right in a cosmic sense: When an emperor asked, "How could this rightly be?" he was clearly indicating that it *could not be right*, because *he was right* in posing the question that way. In insisting on *li*, emperors were demanding orthodox standards. When other writers used this phrase or posed other questions with similar connotations, then, their efforts were meant to provoke the same response in their readers: The speaker is right; what he is questioning is wrong. Only a fool, or worse, would pursue the alternative. The proof is the immediate and unanimous perception of the rightness of his position, as all can see the rocks exposed when a river's water subsides.

When lesser writers used rhetorical questions, their aim paralleled that of the emperor. These stylistic flourishes refer to higher standards, the collective voice of the community, the values shared by writer and reader.[39] This pervasive practice ostensibly suggests unequivocal support of a singular set of values, yet the reality is not so simple.[40] When characters in our sample texts use rhetorical questions, their positions differ from one another in moral or ethical weight, and the arguments they seek to win have quite different aims. What draws them all together would seem to be the various authors' desire to assert authoritative standards, positions that, like the imperial voice, cannot be questioned further. In their use here, rhetorical questions seem to preclude considerations of contingency in the statements presented. These arguments seek to forestall opposition, to elicit agreement on the basis of shared standards and shared assumptions about how to clarify what is right. This is a discourse of morality, one might say, a strategy by which to assemble authority of the sort needed to judge other people, whether they are real people accused of crime or fictional characters fabricated for a story.

And in this final regard, using questions to express the Qianlong emperor's frustrations becomes comprehensible as well. He is in the right; an erstwhile trusted subject is in the wrong. The monarch asserts his position, and yet he seemingly begs for understanding at the same time: he, too, made mistakes here, but they were not selfish or, at the time, ill considered. Curiously, he places himself in the same rhetorical position as the one created for the abject adulteress whose husband was slain. He, like she, has now seen the proper way to act, and he speaks persuasively about how to proceed, difficult though it may be. And we readers are to be persuaded that he is justified in saying so.

CONSIDERING AUDIENCES

The exchanges involving rhetorical questions not only work within texts; in most cases, they must work beyond the text, to persuade the reader of the strength of the questioner's position. This relationship can problematize any simple ostensible meaning. Such double dialogues, within the text and between text and reader, are better understood by considering their analogue in theatrical performance. In traditional storytelling, the narrator regular asks many questions during the presentation, but he or she never expects any verbal response from the audience.[41] Similarly, the purpose of rhetorical questions in texts is to signal the reader that he or she is *supposed* to accept—without resistance—the assertion behind the question. The reader might not be immediately persuaded; indeed, the oratorical stance can signal the reader to question either the speaker taking that stance or the person addressed, or both. As does the storyteller, the writer uses tricks to assure the reader that he is in control of his material, and this control is to be appreciated.

Like the listener attending oral presentations who is talked *at*, but not directly *to*, the intended reader is clearly implicit in each of the texts examined above. Were we to look at the crime-case material from an angle suggested by theoretician and critic Michel de Certeau, we might see the yamen as a theater where fundamental social questions could be addressed. Power was clearly involved there, asserted, demonstrated, and imposed entirely by one side onto the other, wielded by the magistrates and their superiors against the accused, regardless of the prisoners' original social status.[42] It is useful to see in these documents a kind of *textual theater* in which very compelling questions are raised and played out, questions of an ethical or philosophical nature for the most part. And given their seriousness, they demand a thoughtful response on the part of the reader.

Rhetorical outbursts in crime reports seemingly challenge simple categorizations of human affairs, revealing an ironic distance between legal models and lived experience. The unruly material of everyday life is not so easily systematized (hence the constant revision of the *li*, or substatutes, to the more general *lü* laws of *The Qing Code*). *Not all* adulterous wives want their husbands killed. *Not all* bandits seek careers of crime. *Not all* persons accused of dereliction of duty to the state had selfishness as their motive. Writer Milan Kundera's comments seem relevant at this point: "Irony irritates. Not because it mocks or attacks but because it denies us our certainties by unmasking the world as an ambiguity."[43] Rhetorical challenges appearing ironically in the mouths of witnesses and even the accused may have served to contest the penal models and had concrete ramifications in the world beyond the text. In at least a few cases (such as that of Du Huailiang and Ms. Li above), people may have been spared from execution because the texts present their cases sympathetically in order to win the emotional support of the intended readers, the reviewing officials. And Ji Yun's belief in ghosts could not be so easily dismissed, because of *how it was represented*. Nor could one leave unquestioned the assertion that the fictional Fan Juqing had no choice but to die of longing for his friend. It would appear that an oratorical position on the part of a person in a text might signal the author's subversion of that very position.

Who were the players in this textualized theater, the combatants in this struggle over the presentation of human action and its motivations? In the archival documents, they surely did not include the accused: all authors of case records were legal professionals. We probably can also dismiss from the role of responsible author the court scribes and even the unnamed legal secretaries who worked for magistrates, prefects, and supervisory officials. These functionaries had no stake in the system or its rhetoric; they did not have to put their names on these documents, risking their careers and reputations thereby (although they were culpable for errors, they had far less to lose than did court-appointed members of the bureaucracy). The real agents in these dramas must have been the officials whose names figure prominently on them, the county magistrates and the officials above them in the judicial hierarchy, all of whom risked wealth, position, and social status if they were found to have been derelict in their duties.[44]

The formulation presented here rests on this evidence: in most cases, the basic text of the case report was first written for, or perhaps by, the county magistrate. In order to have *his* "voice" heard, that is, to preclude testimony and his legal judgment being rewritten at higher levels, a magistrate had to validate his version of the events. He had to write carefully, as a ventriloquist, using the voices of others as well as speaking from his own defaced position. That is, the magistrate had to use language as dictated by custom and legal necessity, judiciously bending it as needed to shape the messy reality under his jurisdiction.

Carefully constructed argumentation in fiction and informal writings also allowed writers to present—and to challenge—dominant values. Ji Yun commented on the morality of China's judicial system by comparing it to that of the netherworld. His political skepticism is clear. But what of Feng Menglong's story of friendship that results in the deaths of both friends? One might well conclude that he examines the concept in its extreme; posing the moral position so forcefully in effect renders it suspect. In each of these cases, the reader is left to decide whether the explicitly endorsed position is the right one, or whether the opposition implicit in the rhetorical challenge is more reasonable. The story becomes more than just a diversion; rhetorical questions can engage the reader in serious contemplation of the positions represented, thus adding another dimension of appeal.

CONCLUSIONS

In the examples discussed above, there is no more uniformity in language style than there is in genre of texts. The materials are in both vernacular and classical Chinese, with considerable variation in stylistic register in both. But the essential element for a powerful self-assertion or a strong self-defense in any dialogue written during the Qing period seems to be the rhetorical question, regardless of language style. In the mouths of the Qianlong emperor and other interrogators, rhetorical questions can take on a powerful authority, which presents crushing challenges to the assertions of other figures in the text. Such questions may also be used to plead one's case, by asking for understanding of one's (new) position. Through their use, a character may assert a moral position, which, it is hoped, thereby becomes unassailable. Assertions of authority through rhetorical questions appear alike in straightforward fictional narrative, in simulated courtroom interrogation, in official records of legal cases, and even in parodies of all of the above. In an initial sample of Qing capital murder cases, roughly 10 percent include such questions in their oral testimony, and many more examples appear in both vernacular and classical-language fiction and informal writings of the late Ming and Qing. All educated readers would have come in contact with numerous examples; as writers, they relied on rhetorical questions each time they wished to represent a strong conviction on the part of a character. And writers of a variety of social positions relied on this oratorical stance to present their views.[45] Thus, whether in deadly seriousness or in the spirit of fun, the use of rhetorical questions reveals that the fiction of late imperial China self-consciously shares the values of the elite and even the discursive strategies of the state.

And finally, what are the origins of this widely shared rhetorical flourish? Canonical texts provide many models. There, challenging questions function, both explicitly and implicitly, just as in the many texts cited above. Confucius stated it concisely in *The Analects* 12:7: "To govern is to correct. If you sent an example by being correct, who would dare to remain incorrect?" [Zheng zhe, zheng ye. Zi shuai yi zheng, shu gan buzheng?]" Appearing in the basic texts of the education system, such examples were memorized and repeated in the civil service examinations. From there, if not directly from their classical sources, rhetorical questions made their way into every type of narrative or exposition attempted by anyone who ever studied for the examinations—which meant virtually every literate male in late imperial China.[46]

NOTES

1. See Will, *Official Handbooks and Anthologies*, section 4.1, for handbooks on law and the administration of justice.

2. See Sommer, *Sex, Law, and Society*, 27, for example. For studies of repeated uses of stock phrases in case reports, see Buoye, "Suddenly Murderous Intent Arose"; and especially Karasawa, "Hanasu koto." See also Karasawa, "Rethinking Legal Case Records."

3. On popular perceptions of whether justice was done, and efforts to protest perceived injustice, see Alford, "Of Arsenic and Old Laws"; Waley-Cohen, "Politics and the Supernatural"; and Zhou, "Illusion and Reality."

4. Waley-Cohen, in "Politics and the Supernatural," has demonstrated how reframing essentially the same narrative of events allowed several authors to focus the blame on one person or another in a troubling case from 1808–9. For the purpose of clarifying culpability, they referred to a variety of written or traditional sources to support their arguments. Long, "Textual Interpretation as Collective Action," 190–92, argues that reading—of any type of text—is a social activity and must be learned. In "Rhetoric," 204, Stanley Fish expresses the popular, negative conception of rhetoric, particularly in the United States, by stating, "rhetoric's deficiencies are not only epistemological (sundered from truth and fact) and moral (sundered from true knowledge and sincerity) but social: it panders to the worst in people and moves them to base actions. . . . " A similar prejudice against the argumentative tricks attributed to litigation masters, or *songshi*, was common enough in late imperial China; see Macauley, *Social Power and Legal Culture*. However, it is the positive sense of rhetoric as a tool in effective argumentation (Fish, "Rhetoric," 206–9) that concerns us here.

5. A convenient example of a guidebook for magistrates and their clerks is Huang Liuhong (1633–after 1705), *Fuhui quan shu*; see also the translation, Huang Liu-hung, *Complete Book*, 342–43, and for procedure in homicide investigations, see 319–27. Yasuhiko Karasawa has introduced an important handbook for legal secretaries (and probably magistrates as well), *Ban'an yaolue* (Essentials of managing crime cases), written by Wang Youhuai in 1793. Karasawa presents translations of the part of this handbook that concerns testimony in "Between Speech and Narrative," an unpublished essay that formed the basis for his "Hanasu koto." Pierre-Étienne Will also identifies the *Ban'an yaolue* as having been written for clerks; Wang Youhuai was himself a highly respected legal secretary who published several other administrative handbooks. See Will, *Official Handbooks and Anthologies*, 163, entry for Item No. 259. This text has also been reprinted in *Guan-*

zhenshu jicheng. Ch'ü, *Local Government*, 125, 128–29, notes that the final responsibility for accuracy and completeness in case reports lay with the magistrate, who would be harshly punished for any shortcomings. See also Alabaster, *Notes and Commentaries*, lxxi–lxxii.

6. Karasawa goes so far as to posit vernacular fiction as a greater influence than the dialect of the Qing capital on this style of language; see his "Hanasu koto," 212–50. However, the language of testimony is really quite impoverished compared to the language of fiction; there is no close connection between the two forms. Rather, the connection was more in general purpose than in specific detail. For a more nuanced discussion of language styles available to Ming–Qing period writers, including the broadly defined standard vernacular Chinese, see Hanan, *Chinese Vernacular Story*, 1–16.

7. Detailed descriptions of proceedings are found in guidebooks for lower-level legal officials such as that compiled by Huang Liuhong; see *Fuhui quan shu* 14.1a–9b, 365–69, and Huang Liu-hung, *Complete Book*, 319–27, for procedure in homicide investigations. Elaine Scarry has explored in some detail the methodology and effect of torture on the individual. Torture, such as the squeezing of ankles and legs in Qing period courtrooms, produces so much pain that its victim loses all access to language and even to the ability to think. See Scarry, *Body in Pain*, esp. 5–6, 12–18, 35–37. References to torture are frequent in these documents, but never, in my reading, are words attributed to a deponent during its application. Instead, although there is no effort to hide its use, references to torture serve, as here, to demonstrate the questioner's conviction that the version of events he presents is believable. Surely all recorded testimony would appear as conventionally constructed to all readers familiar with court procedure and the effects of torture in reality. Brooks, *Troubling Confessions*, 63, observes that even without the application of physical pain, "confessions rarely are products of a free and rational will." On the uses and limitations of torture during the Qing, see Ch'ü, *Local Government*, 125.

8. Compare the explanation of this concept offered in Metzger, "Foreword," esp. xx; although Metzger refers primarily to twentieth-century cultural responses, he seems, appropriately, to include premodern society in his references. I am grateful to Dr. Nancy Park for her many helpful suggestions on how to read the tenor, and the implicit meaning, of recorded testimony.

9. *Neige Kangxi chao tiben Xingfa lei*: KX 13.3.10 (April 15, 1674), Shuntianfu.

10. *Neige tiben Xingfa lei*, 518–46. Du had also killed his wife so that he and Ms. Li would be free to remarry. Magistrate Jin threatened torture the first time he asked Ms. Li these questions: "*Bu shishuo jiu yao xingshen ni le*"; on this later occasion, there was no reference to torture, and yet her response was more passion-

ate. During the subsequent review by the Shandong surveillance commissioner, Ms. Li added, "Even now I regret it so much—how could I even think of doing that thing with him again?! Talking about feelings—my husband and I were married for over ten years, and we had a child. How could it be that I could have so little feelings for him that I could be willing to have somebody kill him? If I had any feelings for Du Huailiang, then I would cover up for him. How could I be willing to file charges against him? [But] I charge Du Huailiang with killing my husband—I hate that Du Huailiang so much!" In clarifying her reasons for not filing the complaint sooner, she elaborated for the surveillance commissioner: "I am a woman left all alone. And at that time I also had a fever from malaria. And my son is small. Who could I get to stand up for me?"

11. *Neige tiben Xingfa lei*, 2-34-2335-5: YZ 6.10.20 (November 21, 1728).

12. See Alabaster, *Notes and Commentaries*, lxx–lxxi, on the responsibility felt to be shared by family members of the accused; Ch'ü, *Local Government*, 150–51, describes responsibility for knowing one's neighbors' business as rationale for the *baojia* (community self-defense) system of local surveillance.

13. One need only think of the public lectures on moral topics such as those of the "Sacred Edict" (Shengyu), promulgated in 1670 by the youthful Kangxi Emperor Xuanye (1654–1722, r. 1661–1722), and of the numerous memorial arches constructed throughout the country at state expense to honor chaste widows. See Mair, "Language and Ideology"; and Mann, *Precious Records*, esp. 2–3, 23–24, 66.

14. As Confucius reportedly said, in *Lunyu* 2:19: Zi yu shan er min shan yi (Just desire the good yourself, and the common people will be good); Confucius, *The Analects*, 115. Hsu Daulin argues against inferring any connection between individual actions and any higher order in his "Crime and Cosmic Order," esp. 118–23.

15. *Neige tiben Xingfa lei* 522-105: KX 1.10.17 (November 27, 1662); the aggrieved husband was allowed to beg for pardon on KX 2.3.9 (April 16, 1663). Presumably, the errant couple died soon thereafter; the final sentence was immediate execution, rather than a retrial during the autumn assizes. For this chance at a reduction of sentence, see Meijer, "The Autumn Assizes." I am grateful to Nicola Di Cosmo for the romanization of these Manchu names.

16. See *ECCP*, 100. Mark McNicholas pursues this and similar cases in his PhD dissertation (University of California, Berkeley, forthcoming).

17. *Qianlongchao chengban tanwu dang'an xuanbian*, vol. 2, 1343, from Wang Danwang's confession of QL 46.7.29. I gratefully acknowledge the assistance of my former students Luo Manling and Zhang Jing in locating cases for this project.

18. Ibid., 1533, memorial from Fulehun, dated QL 46.9.8.

19. Ibid., 1752, deposition by Tao Shilin attached to a memorial from Li Shiyao, QL 46.12.9.

20. Ibid., vol. 3, 2811, interrogation attached to a memorial from the Grand Council dated QL 47.12.1 (January 3, 1783). Of Chen's testimony, the words chosen as synopsis by the Grand Council were similar to the quotation here: "The aforementioned criminal prostrated himself on the floor and cried bitterly, and he claimed, 'I have "enjoyed the favor of The State for generations." I have even served as a viceroy [of Fujian and Zhejiang]. But unconscionably I have turned my back on [the Emperor's] Favor by doing this "stealing like a rat" business. But "Heaven's goodness could not bear it," and "everything came to light." I can no longer face the world, nor is regret of any avail. My crimes deserve a thousand deaths. I only implore that His Majesty would grant me a quick execution, for in truth I have nothing to say in my own defense.'" The text leaves an obligatory space before references to the dynasty and the ruler as a sign of respect.

21. "Qiken bieyou yinni de?" ibid., vol. 4, 3022–23.

22. Ibid., 3536, interrogation of Zhou Jing, QL 60/10/9.

23. Ibid., 3060, Fulehun in interrogation by Agui attached to memorial of QL 51.7.1; 3063, memorial by Agui of QL 51.7.1; 3431 and 3515–16; 3085, at the end of an extended collection of depositions attached to a memorial from Agui dated QL 51.*run* 7.3.

24. Lan, *Luzhou gong'an*, ed. Kuang, 123–41. For a brief biographical sketch of Lan, see *ECCP*, 440–41; while accompanying his cousin, successful military commander Lan Tingzhen (1664–1730), Lan was able to record copious information about Taiwan during a campaign to suppress the rebel Zhu Yigui in 1721. Because of this and his other accomplishments, Lan was presented to the Yongzheng emperor in 1728.

25. Lan, *Luzhou gong'an*, 125, 131; compare Lan, "Lan Lu-chow's Criminal Cases," 196, 201. The marks on the victim's thumbs were caused by the *shuang feiyan diaofa*, a method of hanging a person up by his two thumbs behind his back to immobilize him for beating.

26. Lan, *Luzhou gong'an*, 136, 139; compare Lan, "Lan Lu-chow's Criminal Cases," 205 and esp. 208. For other, more literal translations from Lan's *Luzhou gong'an*, see the two segments in "Lan Ting-yüan's Casebook."

27. A useful collection of these materials is Chen and Ding, *Anyu juan*, cf. 271, 304–5, 307, 385–86, for instance; these examples are by a variety of hands. For a study of Pu Songling and his famous collection, see Zeitlin, *Historian of the Strange*. For a biographical sketch, see *ECCP*, 628–30.

28. Pu, *Liaozhai*, 16/9; 144/69; 1054/295–96.

29. Ibid., 513/166; 963/261.

30. *ECCP*, 120–23; see biographer Fang Chao-ying's interpretation on 123.

31. Chan, *Discourse on Foxes*, 95.

32. Ji Yun, *Yuewei caotang biji*, 105–6; Chan, *Discourse on Foxes*, 97.

33. Ji Yun, *Yuewei caotang biji*, 377–78; Chi, *Shadows in a Chinese Landscape*, 79–81.

34. Feng, *Gujin xiaoshuo*, 262; Feng, *Stories Old and New*, 289.

35. Feng, *Gujin xiaoshuo*, 675; Feng, *Stories Old and New*, 744.

36. *Qianlongchao chengban tanwu dang'an xuanbian*, 2.1210 (memorial of Qianlong 46.6.17) and 4.2933 (edict of QL 51.5.14). For a biographical sketch, see *ECCP*, 369–73.

37. Examples come from an edict to his favorite minister, Heshen (1750–1799); Heshen's memorial was dated QL 51.4.28 (June 25, 1786). *Qianlongchao chengban*, 4.2905. See, for example, 2.1193, 1210, 1213, 1341, 1725, 1728 and 4.2913, 2933, 3430, 3536.

38. On the "Sacred Edict," see note 13 above. Sybille van der Sprenkel, in *Legal Institutions*, discusses the moral order and the imperial duty to realize it in society, 28–34; Hsu discounts such views in his "Crime and Cosmic Order."

39. These fiction texts seemingly participate, as did popular writings on ritual, in perpetuating social hierarchy. On this, see Ebrey, *Confucianism and Family Rituals*, 5–6. On the assertions of relative power and authority in self-defense through rhetoric, see Foucault, *Discipline and Punish*, 177–84, and Bourdieu, *Language and Symbolic Power*, esp. 66.

40. Although, to a large extent, popular values and the values of the elite did correspond quite closely to the values of the state. For a succinct statement of this commonality, see Ebrey, *Confucianism and Family Rituals*, 10–11.

41. Børdahl, "Narrative Voices," 9. In his *Articulated Ladies*, 214, Paul Rouzer adroitly discusses earlier (Tang period) writers who self-consciously controlled all voices within their texts in order to achieve the desired effect: to provide sexual pleasure and to control the pace at which it might be experienced. Clearly, Qing writers of crime case reports strove for a similar degree of narrative control, despite the difference in readers' responses.

42. See Certeau, *Writing of History*, 244–48, a discussion of the substitution of "prepared" language for the alien words of possessed women by doctors in seventeenth-century France. Nichols, in "Foreword," vii–viii, draws attention to the function of just this sort of rhetoric: "Fiction establishes its *truth* status by the way language turns back on itself, tautologically, to accomplish the expectations it sets up. The narrative need not be judged true because it corresponds to an external image of the world, but because it is consistent with the linguistic usages current in a given social context, at a given moment in time." Clearly, all writers discussed here inherently followed this principle.

43. Kundera, *Art of the Novel*, 134.

44. Chiu, "Yi fa wei ming," argues for the importance of winning cases for a legal secretary to be considered successful.

45. That rhetorical questions are a regular feature of fiction suggests that fiction—as prefaces to novels and story collections often insist—seeks to validate its existence by participating in a discourse shared with the more formal writings of the time. Given the self-consciousness with which most fiction writers of the Qing period produced their texts, this may very well have been the case. Shang "Jin Ping Mei," 197–98, notes that the great Ming novel *Jin Ping Mei cihua* uses a rhetorical question made famous in the very first line of Confucius's classic text *Lunyu*: *Bu yi le hu* . . . (Is it not a joy . . . ?). Confucius may have used the device to assert that everyone should enjoy learning and friendship. By contrast, the author of *Jin Ping Mei* does so repeatedly only to challenge conventional assumptions about pleasure. For the original, see Confucius, *Analects*, 3; Shang, 226 n. 36, cites *Jin Ping Mei cihua*, 24.2b, 61.71, 83.9a–b, and 99.8a. Shang also refers to Peter Rushton, *The "Jin Ping Mei" and the Nonlinear Dimensions of the Traditional Chinese Novel* (Lewiston, N.Y.: Edwin Mellen, 1993), 69–70, for ironic uses of this phrase.

46. Confucius, *The Analects*, 115. The model essay by Wang Ao (1450–1524) provides a ready example of a rhetorical question, on a quotation from *Lunyu* 12:9: "Baixing zu, jun shuyu buzu?" (When the people have enough, how can the ruler alone have too little?) For Wang Ao's text and a translation, see Elman, *Cultural History*, 389–90. See also Elman's discussion of the role of memorization in education, 268–70; on canonical rhetoric, see 396–97.

PART II *Legal Discourse and the Power of the State*

5 Filial Felons

Leniency and Legal Reasoning in Qing China

THOMAS BUOYE

Elaborate, redundant procedures for trying and sentencing capital cases, and a propensity to seek leniency, were hallmarks of eighteenth-century Chinese criminal justice that bespoke a sincere regard for human life. Concern for the cautious application of capital punishment had deep historical roots that predate the imperial era.[1] By the early Qing period, the predilection to seek leniency was well established and openly discussed in administrative manuals for magistrates. For example, Huang Liuhong's *Complete Book Concerning Happiness and Benevolence* (Fuhui quan shu) admonished magistrates to "always lean on the side of leniency."[2] Here, we study four cases in which leniency was formally requested.

While the tendency to seek leniency was often pursued subtly in the representation of the crime, pardons were also obtained under conditions clearly defined in *The Qing Code*. Unlike the rhetorical devices that magistrates employed in the informal pursuit of leniency, a formal request for a statutory pardon was strictly adjudicated in accordance with specific legal criteria. The conditions under which the pardon could be granted were detailed in the *Code* and required exact evidence and precise legal reasoning. Contrary to the Weberian concept of *qadi* justice, the adjudication of capital crimes in eighteenth-century China was anything but arbitrary. Not surprisingly, the criteria for formal pardons also reflected cherished social values; for example, killing in defense of one's parents qualified for consideration. An examination of cases involving pardonable offenses allows us to see the complex interaction between legal reasoning, ideology, and rhetoric.

THE REVIEW OF CAPITAL CASES

Reports of capital crimes cannot be fully understood without consideration of the two-tiered structure of judicial and sentencing reviews as well as the magistrates' general predilection to seek leniency. Nearly all capital cases were subject to two separate and distinct reviews, each of which culminated in the endorsement of the emperor. In the initial round of review, each capital case was tried at the county level and then automatically reexamined at successive administrative levels, starting with the prefecture and continuing upward to the province, central government, and eventually the emperor, who reserved the right to review all capital cases. This stage of review established guilt and assigned specific sentences in accordance with *The Qing Code*. The legal requirements of the first round of judicial review called for straightforward accounts of the essential elements of the crime, forensic evidence, and testimony from the accused and key witnesses, necessary for determining which laws had been violated and what punishments were appropriate. The bureaucratic burden of uniform empirewide review of capital crimes necessitated concision and clarity. As one administrative handbook advises, reports should be composed "so that his superior can understand the contents at a glance, without studying the depositions and confessions."[3] (During the eighteenth century, as unprecedented demographic growth imposed increasing administrative burdens on the judicial bureaucracy, capital-case reports were further streamlined in order to facilitate their transmission.) Serious crimes, such as parricide, were sentenced to "immediate execution" (*lijue*), and such a criminal was "executed without delay after the judgment was given,"[4] but the overwhelming majority of capital sentences were provisional and subject to the next stage of review, the annual autumn assizes.[5] Provisional sentencing for the overwhelming majority of capital cases in effect made the death penalty revisable and debatable, and it created an enormous burden for the judicial bureaucracy. It also provided an opportunity and an incentive for magistrates to compose their case records with an eye toward influencing the ultimate fate of the accused.

THE AUTUMN ASSIZES

The Qing autumn assizes represent the zenith of uniform administration and direct imperial control over capital punishment. The autumn assizes were not an appeal process, nor did the tribunals entail a reinvestigation of the crimes or the introduction of new evidence. Guilt had been irrevocably established in the initial judicial review. At the autumn assizes, the emperor and the highest judicial officials deliberated on provisional death sentences and considered formal requests for pardons and reductions in sentencing. There were four possible dispositions: "execution warranted" (*qingshi*), "indefinite stay" (*huanjue*), "to be left at home to care for aged parents" (*liuyang*), and "worthy of compassion" (*kejin*). Presented with a list of criminals who warranted execution, the emperor personally endorsed death sentences by placing a red checkmark after each name. Criminals granted an indefinite stay would be reviewed again at the following year's autumn assizes.[6] Criminals eligible for a pardon to care for parents were released in their home counties. Those deemed worthy of compassion based on statutory provisions usually received a reduced sentence of banishment and beating with the heavy staff. Ironically, although the Qing autumn assizes centralized review of capital cases to an unprecedented degree, higher-level officials based their decisions largely on the original case records that the county magistrates (*xianzhang*) had prepared. The higher the level of judicial administration and the more removed from the original jurisdiction, the more dependent officials were on the information provided by the district magistrates in their case records.

The two-tiered review of capital cases provided magistrates with opportunities, formal and informal, to seek leniency. By the mid-eighteenth century, thousands of cases were reviewed at the autumn assizes. Most numerous were those crimes that carried provisional death sentences. These cases were open to more wide-ranging debate and deliberation at the autumn assizes. These more subjective judgments were based on the depictions of offenders and victims contained in the county magistrates' initial reports. Influenced by ideological values of benevolence and paternalism, which encouraged leniency, magistrates often interspersed case records with understated observations suggesting psychological states, motivations, and moral standards that could be used to mitigate the final sentencing at the autumn assizes. An accused killer was often depicted as an otherwise decent person who inadvertently caused a death under duress in extraordinary circumstances. These depictions could only have been meant to obtain leniency for the vast majority of capital criminals who received provisional death sentences.[7] Less numerous were direct requests for statutorily defined pardons. As the cases examined below illustrate, the conditions under which requests for formal pardons could be made were specifically defined in law and had to be addressed directly in the case record.

STATUTORY PARDONS

Under Qing law, the determination of fault and causation required a thorough reporting of the relevant circumstances of the crime, an explanation of the apparent motivations of the individuals involved, a complete examination and assessment of all physical injuries and any weapons used, and a clear delineation of the relative status of victims, perpetrators, and other principals. The last criterion was critically important in determining the severity and punishment of the crime under Chinese law. Fault in Chinese law could be understood in terms of intention to kill, the cruelty of the act, or whether the act was due to careless or reckless actions, but it could also be understood as a "failure to observe the behavior demanded by a particular status, that is, by the kin relationship in which the offender stood to the victim."[8] The consideration of kinship might strike modern eyes as inequitable, but the legal code clearly defined the hierarchy of kinship and its relevance in determining fault. As the following cases demonstrate, magistrates rationally and carefully applied this principle in adjudicating capital crimes. Thousands of homicide reports confirm that whether formally presenting evidence for leniency in accordance with the legal code or subtly seeking to influence the final decision of a provisional sentence, Chinese magistrates operated entirely within the framework of *The Qing Code*.

Article 323 of *The Qing Code*, "When the Father or Paternal Grandfather Is Struck [by Another]" (Fumu beiou lüwen), set the conditions under which a formal request for leniency could be considered.[9] "If someone struck a parent or paternal grandparent and a child or grandchild retaliated immediately [*jishi*], the punishment would be reduced depending on the severity of the injuries that the child or grandchild inflicted on the attacker." If death occurred, the killer would be tried under Article 302 of the *Code*, "Affrays and Blows" (Dou'ou). During the Yongzheng reign, a substatute was added to the article allowing for leniency if a son or a grandchild killed the attacker of a parent or a paternal grandparent, provided the "effort to rescue was immediate" (*qingjie qiuhu*).[10] A request for leniency had to be declared in the case report, but leniency could not be granted without imperial approval. The substatute also stated that if the parent or paternal grandparent had "ordered" (*zhuling*) the child or grandchild to beat the attacker to death, or the parents were "seeking trouble" (*xunxin*) and the child or grandchild "followed and assisted under their influence" (*zhong zhi zhu shi*) and together they killed the attacker, they should be punished according to the law without consideration of leniency. The language of the substatute was revised in Qianlong 5

(1740) to state that the parent had to be "under attack and in immediate danger" (*ouda shi xi shi zai weiji*) in order to request leniency. In Qianlong 43 (1778), the language of the substatute was further revised to emphasize that leniency could not be granted if the parent instigated the violence or conspired with the child to engage in violence.[11]

While the tendency to seek leniency permeated the process of judicial review, formal requests for leniency were made only after careful consideration of the facts of a case and the applicable laws. The following four cases, in which killers seem to qualify for formal requests for leniency, demonstrate this point. In each case, an individual committed a homicide while attempting to rescue a parent who was being physically assaulted. In these cases, county magistrates respected the law and rationally applied its provisions. Equally important, this analysis also reveals the limits of leniency. Interestingly, the same ideology that advocated an expansive policy of leniency also imposed strict and unforgiving punishment when a crime impinged on the core values of patriarchal hierarchy. As these cases illustrate, leniency, although common, was not a foregone conclusion even for those who killed in defense of a parent.

CASE RECORDS

In 1770, a dispute over rent collection arose within the Guo lineage of Chaoyang county, Guangdong.[12] One party to the dispute entrusted the rental grain to Chen Ji, the village head (*xiangzhang*), for safekeeping while they sought to convene a meeting of lineage members to address the dispute. When Guo Zhongyi and his son, Guo Changyi, the other parties to the dispute, discovered what had happened, they demanded their share of the grain from Chen Ji. Chen Ji refused, and a struggle ensued. The Guos forced Chen Ji onto a boat that had been used to transport the grain and set off down the river, while Chen Ji and Guo Changyi engaged in a "loud argument" (*zheng dou*). Chen Ji's son, Chen Aang, was working in his field when he saw the struggle between his father and the Guos. "Fearing that his father would be beaten" (*pa fuqin bei ou*), Aang went home to get a "night protection spear" (*fang ye tiaodao*). Running along the bank of the river and shouting curses, Aang followed the boat downriver until it reached a dock. When the boat stopped at the dock, a brief but deadly confrontation ensued. Changyi struck Aang with an oar as he boarded the boat, and Aang stabbed Changyi in the thigh. Changyi later died from the wound.

In a somewhat similar case in 1740 (QL 5.1.25), in Boluo county, Guangdong, Huang Bin and Zhong Youxiang each leased half of a plot of land from the landlord Xie Yijun.[13] Zhong Youxiang discovered that Huang Bin had begun plowing Zhong's half of the land and protested to Xie, claiming that the fields had not yet been demarcated. Zhong Youxiang and Xie Yijun decided to go to Huang Bin's home to discuss the matter. Because Xie Yijun was elderly, he could not keep pace, and Zhong Youxiang arrived at Huang's home first. A loud row ensued, and Zhong struck Huang on the hand with a bamboo rod, drawing blood. Huang then punched Zhong on the shoulder blade. Zhong dropped the bamboo rod, grabbed Huang by his shirt collar, and punched him. At this moment, Huang Yaer, Huang Bin's son, who was returning from working in his field, saw that his father was bleeding and locked in Youxiang's grasp. Fearing that his father would be injured, Yaer tried to separate them, but Youxiang would not let go and continued to punch Yaer's father in the arm. Seeing this, Yaer became "anxious" (*qingji*) and punched Youxiang once in the chest and once in the ribs. At that, Youxiang released Huang Bin, and the fighting ended. Thirteen days later, Zhong Youxiang died.

These two cases occurred almost three decades apart and had no relation to each other, yet the written records illustrate a remarkable consistency in the language and style of crime reporting during the Qing. In part, this reflected the requirements of criminal procedures as well as the "editorial" work of the county magistrate and his staff, but the representation of the crime also indicates a consistency in official attitudes and ideological considerations that informed criminal prosecution. These cases are quite similar in several important respects. Each of the young men (coincidentally, Chen Aang and Huang Yaer were the same age, seventeen *sui*) killed an individual who was assaulting his father. Neither father was at fault in the underlying dispute that set the stage for the violence. Chen Ji appeared to have been fulfilling his duty as village headman. He had no discernible personal interest in the quarrel over rent collection within the Guo clan and was literally dragged into the violent event when Guo Zhongyi and Guo Changyi forced him aboard the boat. In the second case, despite Zhong Youxiang's accusations, Huang Bin was found to be blameless in the disagreement over the land. The landlord Xie Yijun testified that Huang had not encroached on Zhong's half of the field. Similarly, in both cases, the victim of the homicide had initiated the violence. Finally, both Huang Yaer and Chen Aang were found guilty of the same crime, "killing in an affray" (*dou'ou sharen*). In their own depositions (*kougong*), both Aang and Yaer emphatically claim that they had not intended to kill their victims and that they had acted out of concern for the safety of their fathers. Despite these important similarities, Huang Yaer had his sentence reduced to internal exile under the substatute granting leniency to offenders who acted out of concern for a parent "in imminent danger" (*zai weiji*). In Chen Aang's case, leniency was never discussed, and he was sentenced to imprisonment awaiting strangulation "pending final sentencing at the autumn assizes" (*jiao jianhou qiu hou chujue*). Further comparison of the vastly different fates of Chen Aang and Huang Yaer reveals that the circumstances of the crime was the paramount consideration in determining the sentences.

Under Qing law, when an individual committed a homicide while coming to the rescue of a parent, leniency could be granted only if that person had acted spontaneously when the parent was in imminent danger. In this regard, these cases differ significantly. Although Chen Ji had been assaulted and abducted, the Guos did not attack him physically once they were aboard the boat. Conversely, Chen Aang's behavior raised suspicion because he returned home to get a weapon, euphemistically referred to as a "night protection spear," which had obvious lethal potential. Although the magistrate made these observations without additional comment, the experienced reader of case records could draw several critical inferences from this information: the father was not in imminent danger; Aang paused, however briefly, before acting to save his father; and Aang was armed with what was undeniably a dangerous weapon. Without further elaboration, judicial officials reviewing the case record would know immediately that the two criteria for leniency, imminent danger to the parent and a spontaneous response from the son, had not been met. Thus, despite his claim, undoubtedly true, that he acted out of concern for his father, Aang's actions could be deemed excessive, given that his father was not in imminent danger, the Guos were unarmed, and Aang was in possession of a potentially lethal weapon.

Because Huang Yaer's case occurred early in the Qianlong reign and includes a formal request for leniency, this case record provides richer insight into the magistrate's legal reasoning and his handling of the case. In the early years of the Qianlong reign, county-level case reports often included extensive records of the interrogations of all the principals involved. Depending on the complexity of the case, these might include several rounds of questioning. Following a format similar to that recommended in *Styles of Interrogation* (Fengzhen shi), an annotated legal text from the third century B.C.E., the magistrate allowed the accused to develop a version of the crime in the first round of questioning even if the testimony seemed dubious.[14] Subsequent rounds of interrogation would then probe the questionable points. Magistrates often forcefully confronted the accused person, pointing out inconsistencies, suggesting alternative explanations for their actions, and presenting them with material evidence that contradicted their version of events. In this way, the earlier Qianlong documents frequently showcased the magistrates' detective skills. While this technique provided a livelier narrative, it also resulted in a much longer document. By 1745 (QL 10), reports usually included detailed interrogatories or multiple rounds of interrogation of the offenders and sometimes of only the most important witnesses. After 1765 (QL 30), detailed transcriptions of interrogations had largely disappeared, the streamlining of depositions was more pronounced, and case reports became more formulaic. Fortunately, Huang Yaer's case contains two rounds of interrogation that focused attention on elements of the crime with which the magistrate was most concerned.

In the first round of testimony, Yaer was asked standard questions such as his age, marital status, and residency as well as questions regarding the circumstances of the crime. Yaer initially stated that he was "spontaneously motivated owing to his fear that his father was old and was being beaten" (*pa fuqin nian lao bei ta dashang yishi qingqie*). Yaer further stated: "Motivated by concern to save my father, I spontaneously injured [Youxiang] accidentally. [Xiaode yin qiuhu fuqin qingqie yishi shishou ba ta dashang.]" In the subsequent round of questioning, the magistrate noted that Yaer had struck Zhong Youxiang twice in places on the body that, according to forensic manuals, were potentially lethal. From this the magistrate concluded, "It was clear that your father hated Youxiang for beating him and ordered you to beat him to death. [Zhe ming shi ni fuqin hen ta niuou zhuling ni ba ta dashang shen side le.]" By accusing Yaer of following his father's orders, the magistrate directly addressed a specific condition of the law. The magistrate then challenged Yaer, asking: "Do you still dare to contend foolishly that you were saving your father and that it was accidental? [Hai gan hun gong qiu fu shishou de hua ma?]" Yaer repeated that he was on his way home from planting taro, signifying that this had not been a planned ambush. Yaer also reiterated that his father's hand was bleeding, evidence of a serious threat to his father's safety. He emphasized that he feared for his aged father and initially tried to separate the two men. It was only after Zhong refused to release his father that Yaer struck him. In a concluding statement that must have been edited by a legal secretary, Yaer, a seventeen-year-old peasant from Guangdong who presumably had no formal education, used language strikingly similar to that contained in *The Qing Code* when he reiterated that he acted "spontaneously" (*yishi qingie*), and that his father "had not ordered him to attack" (*bushi ting fuqin zhuling*). Whether or not Yaer actually spoke these exact words, the written deposition bolstered the county magistrate's argument for a pardon by using legal language that echoed specific points outlined in the law. The argument for leniency was made in the county-level summary of the case and at each ascending level of review, and the Three Judicial Offices ultimately recommended leniency.

The facts that Zhong Youxiang did not die until thirteen days after the attack (which meant his injuries were not as serious as those in the other cases cited here) and that Huang Yaer was unarmed undoubtedly would have supported an appeal for leniency had the argument for a pardon failed. But in order to justify a formal request for pardon, it was more important to show that Yaer responded to the threat immediately and that his father was bleeding and locked in Youxiang's grip and therefore in imminent danger. These conditions were critical to invoking the specific substatute on leniency for killing while coming to the aid of a parent. Since the circumstances in Chen Aang's case did not meet the legally defined conditions for pardon, the magistrate made no formal request to this end. Given the propensity to seek leniency, however, Chen Aang may have been granted leniency at the autumn assizes.

Interestingly, Aang's testimony did address a key point in the relevant substatute on leniency. Aang clearly stated that his "father had not instigated him to attack" (*fuqin bing meiyou zhushi ouda de shi*). Once again, an uneducated peasant addresses a specific point in *The Qing Code* in his oral testimony, further evidence of official editing. Aang also emphatically insisted that he had reacted to Guo's violent act, that he accidentally wounded Guo, and that he "had no intent whatsoever to kill Guo" (*bing bushi youxin yao zhi si tade*). The magistrate's inclusion of this testimony in his final report indicates that he must have wanted to help Aang obtain leniency in the autumn assizes. While Aang did not qualify for a formal request for leniency, he did have a reasonable chance to avoid the death sentence at the autumn assizes, given the circumstances of his crime.

THE LIMITS ON LENIENCY

Despite the contention that Chinese magistrates evinced a predilection to seek leniency, paradoxically the same values that were used to mitigate punishments could also justify severe sentences. A comparison of two additional cases illustrates this point. In 1749 (QL 14.5.27), in Qujiang county, Guangdong, Liu Sixian was returning home when he saw his uncle, Liu Hanzu, assaulting his mother, Ms. Huang.[15] The two had gotten into an argument after Ms. Huang caught Liu Hanzu, the younger brother of her deceased husband, picking pears from a tree that her husband had planted on the embankment of a fish pond, which the two brothers had jointly inherited. Liu Hanzu had pushed Ms. Huang to the ground and was about to strike her with his hand. When Liu Sixian came to her rescue, Hanzu cursed him for "helping and protecting" (*ma qi banghu*) his mother and threatened him with a wooden spear (*mu qiang*). Sixian fended him off with a wooden carrying pole (*mu bian*), striking him in the ribs and the armpit. At that, Sixian fled, and Hanzu, armed with the spear, pursued him. As Hanzu gained on him, Sixian became "anxious." He turned to ward off Hanzu and, by chance, struck Hanzu on the forehead, causing him to fall and injure his back and spine. Ms. Huang shouted at them to stop, but she was too late. Sixian and Ms. Huang helped Hanzu home. Despite their efforts to treat his injuries, Hanzu died.

The second case occurred in Lufeng county, Guangdong, in 1778 (QL 43.7.10), when the Xie and Ceng families became embroiled in a violent dispute over the control of water for irrigation.[16] When Xie Zhenhui saw Ceng Nengduan drain water from his field, he started a "noisy quarrel" (*zhengnao*). Nengduan struck Zhenhui over the head with his hoe. Xie's younger brother, Xie Yade, then stabbed Nengduan in the thigh with a "pointed bamboo pole" (*zhu jian*). Nengduan returned home and told his eldest brother, Ceng Nengchun. In the afternoon, Ceng Nengchun, carrying a "metal-tipped pole" (*tie zui jian*), went to Xie Zhenhui's home. According to a witness, Nengchun "shouted curses" (*nang ma*) outside the gate of Xie's home until Xie's mother, Ms. Wang, came out to "reason" (*lunli*) with him. Nengchun struck her on the head with his pole, and Ms. Wang turned and fled. Nengchun caught up with her and struck her at the base of the ear, knocking her down. Ms. Wang shouted for help. As Nengchun raised the pole to strike her again, Xie Zhenhui arrived and seized the pole. Wresting the weapon from his mother's attacker, Zhenhui jabbed Nengchun in the navel, knocking him to the ground. "Unexpectedly" (*ju*), Nengchun was seriously injured and died a short while later.

The events in these two homicides share many similarities with the cases described above. Most important, a son intervened to halt an unprovoked physical attack on his mother. The presiding magistrates in both cases clearly stated that the attackers were at fault in the disputes that precipitated the violence. In the case of Ms. Huang, the magistrate noted that, although the pear tree was planted on jointly inherited land, her husband had planted the tree and the fruit therefore belonged to her alone. Regarding the control of water in the skirmish between the Xies and the Cengs, the magistrate ordered that "water should be drawn as before, and, in order to prevent disputes from arising, the destruction of embankments should not be permitted," strongly implying that the Cengs were at fault. Thus, neither of these two women or their family members had done anything to justify an attack. Also important was the behavior of the women before they were battered. Ms. Wang's effort to reason with Ceng Nengchun, despite his rowdy behavior, demonstrated that she was calm and levelheaded, not to mention brave. Both women did not resort to physical violence, nor did they appear capable of self-defense. In both cases, their sons reacted to unprovoked violence against their mothers.

There were also negative depictions of the victims in both cases. In the case of Xie Zhenhui, the magistrate consistently depicted the Cengs less favorably than the Xies. In the initial fracas over the water, it was Ceng Nengduan who first resorted to physical violence. When Ceng Nengchun went to confront the Xies, he created a loud ruckus at their front gate, and when Ms. Wang emerged and attempted to reason with him, he reacted with physical violence. Other facts of the case, which are noted without amplification, were equally important to the negative representation of Nengchun. For example, after Nengchun initially landed a potentially lethal blow to Ms. Wang's head, she fled, but he pursued her and struck her again at the base of her ear. According to traditional Chinese forensic medicine, the locations of both blows were potentially fatal. At the time that Xie Zhenhui intervened, Nengchun was about to strike yet another blow. Furthermore, the metal-tipped pole, which ultimately was the murder weapon, was brought to the crime scene by Nengchun himself. In the terse recounting of violent events, the inferences to be drawn were clear. Nengchun was a crude and violent person, but despite all this, his own death likely would have been averted had he himself not brought the metal-tipped pole to the scene of the crime.

Conversely, the report presents Xie Zhenhui somewhat favorably. In the initial confrontation over control of the water, Xie Zhenhui was himself a victim of violence. He did resort to violence to protect his mother after rushing to the scene upon hearing her cry for help. When he saw his mother lying on the ground about to receive a third blow from Ceng Nengchun, he became "anxious." Unarmed, Zhenhui struggled to seize the pole from Nengchun's grasp. In the course of this struggle, "unexpectedly," the metal tip wounded Nengchun in his navel. After Nengchun fell to the ground, Zhenhui ended the assault and immediately tended to his mother. The contrast between the depictions of Nengchun and Zhenhui did not need further elaboration for the seasoned judicial officials who would review this case. While the brutal Nengchun viciously attacked an older woman, the filial Zhenhui intervened to rescue his mother from a life-threatening situation. Rather than intentionally harm Nengchun, Zhenhui tried to disarm the assailant and, only then, "unexpectedly" injured Nengchun. After Nengchun collapsed and the threat to his mother had ended, Zhenhui desisted from violence and attended to his mother. Here, the inferences to be drawn were also clear. Zhenhui acted out of concern for his mother, and his use of violence was defensive and relatively restrained. In his own deposition, Zhenhui stated this emphatically: "On that day, it was truly because Ceng Nengchun had injured my mother that I anxiously seized the pole and accidentally wounded Ceng. I definitely did not have intent to kill him. [Dang ri xiaode shi yin Ceng Nengchun oushang muqin qingji duotiao shishou zhi shang bing bushi youxin yao zhi si tade.]" As in the case of Huang Yaer, the accused fulfills all the conditions for a formal request of leniency in his deposition.

Xie Zhenhui was found guilty of killing in an affray, which normally carried the penalty of imprisonment awaiting strangulation, pending final sentencing at the autumn assizes; however, his sentence was reduced because his "motivation was to save a close relative" (*qiu qin qingqie*). The fact that Xie Zhenhui acted to save the life of his mother meant that the magistrate could formally request this reduction of sentence in the initial judicial review process. After duly noting that Xie Zhenhui was guilty of killing in an affray, the magistrate made a formal appeal for leniency, citing the substatute that permitted consideration for a son who committed a homicide in an effort to rescue a parent "in imminent danger" from a beating. In support of this request, the magistrate noted that Xie Zhenhui acted after Ms. Wang had received two potentially fatal blows and was on the ground crying out for help. The magistrate also noted that Zhenhui acted "just at the moment" (*zhengzai*) when Ceng Nengchun was about strike again. Clearly, Ms. Wang was in imminent danger. The county magistrate concluded that the facts of the case warranted leniency for Zhenhui, and his argument was repeated verbatim at each succeeding review of the case.

Xie Zhenhui's case sheds light on the benign influence of Confucian values on the adjudication of capital crimes. But when the crime struck at the core of Confucian principles, punishment could be overwhelmingly harsh and unforgiving. Returning to the case of Liu Sixian, although his crime was serious, the county magistrate nevertheless did not attempt to portray him unsympathetically. Regarding motivation, the report noted that Sixian "feared that his mother would be injured" (*kong muqin shang*) when he intervened to stop his uncle, Liu Hanzu. Conversely, the case record unmistakably depicts Liu Hanzu as an aggressor who unjustly bullied the widow of his elder brother, a familiar pattern of behavior in rural society. When Sixian intervened to rescue his mother, Hanzu responded by "cursing" (*ma*) Sixian and threatening him with a wooden spear. When threatened, Sixian acted in self-defense to ward off Hanzu's spear with his own wooden pole. It was noteworthy that Hanzu wielded a spear, a weapon, while Sixian defended himself with a shoulder pole, an item of everyday use. Although Sixian did hit his uncle in the ribs and armpit in the course of this struggle, he took the opportunity to flee, choosing not to continue his attack. The incident could have ended then and there if Hanzu had not picked up the spear and pursued Sixian. As his uncle gained on him, Sixian became "anxious" and turned to defend himself and wrestle the spear from Hanzu. The fatal blow came when the spear "unexpectedly" (*buqi*) struck Hanzu on the forehead and knocked him off his feet, resulting in two additional injuries to his back and spine. Had the victim not been his uncle, the inclusion of the term "unexpectedly" would have helped to build a case for leniency for Sixian. This indication of absence of intent was consistent with general depiction of the crime.

As noted above, individual judicial officials edited depositions for clarity and consistency. Depositions were not verbatim transcripts of testimony, and they could be used to influence opinions of a victim or an offender. As the depositions of Huang Yaer and Chen Aang illustrate, peasant teenagers might even improbably appear to quote *The Great Qing Code*. In the case of Liu Sixian, Ms. Huang testified that her son acted out of fear for her safety, and she emphasized that on that day she "definitely had not ordered her son to aid or attack" (*dang ri xiaofuren bing mei heling zhu ou de*). This declaration was significant because, according to *The Qing Code*, if the parent ordered or incited the son to attack, the son was not eligible for leniency. It was important to establish that the violence was spontaneous. Similarly, Sixian personally testified that "I accidentally wounded him and by no means had intent to kill him. (*Xiaode shizhou dashang bing bushi youxin yao zhi si tade.*) While one would expect such statements from an individual accused of a capital crime, and from the mother he defended, it is important to bear in mind that the magistrate and his staff prepared the report and ultimately decided which statements to include. Any experienced judicial official would have realized that these statements were unambiguously meant to address the specific legal requirements for pardon.

Unfortunately, although the report was relatively sympathetic toward the offender in tenor and presentation, given the Chinese conception of criminal fault, Liu Sixian was doomed because he had caused the death of a senior male relative. For Liu Sixian, it was not a matter of *how or why* he killed but rather of *whom* he killed. Liu Sixian was found guilty as "a nephew killing an uncle in an affray" (*zhi ou qiqin boshu shasi zhe*) and was sentenced to "imminent decapitation" (*zhan lijue*), second only to lingering death in its severity. Because his sentence was not eligible for reconsideration at the autumn assizes, Sixian would have been put to death at the conclusion of the judicial review of his case. Had the victim not been his uncle, Liu Sixian would likely have been convicted of killing in affray and sentenced to imprisonment awaiting strangulation, pending final sentencing at the autumn assizes. Given the fairly favorable account of events, there was a good chance that his life would have been spared.

In Liu Sixian's case record, the magistrate did not make a formal appeal for leniency. This might have been due to the relative status of the victim and the offender, which increased the severity of the crime. And while we can only speculate, the cases discussed above suggest some clues as to why the magistrate chose not to do so. For example, the magistrate may have felt that the standard of "imminent danger" had not been met. While Xie's mother, Ms. Huang, had been struck twice with a metal-tipped pole and the killer was poised to administer a third blow, Liu's mother had been merely pushed to the ground and Liu Hanzu was about to strike with his bare hand. Another important dissimilarity was the number of wounds inflicted on the victims. Both killers were depicted as unintentionally inflicting wounds, but Liu Sixian had caused five wounds, three of which, the blow to the forehead and the injuries to the back and spine sustained in the subsequent fall, were potentially fatal according to traditional forensic manuals; Xie Zhenhui, in contrast, had inadvertently inflicted only one wound. Given these differences, even if the victim had not been a senior male relative, the magistrate might not have explicitly argued for leniency in Liu Sixian's case. Nevertheless, the generally sympathetic portrayal of Sixian's motivations and limited use of force might have obtained leniency for him at the autumn assizes.

These vastly different sentences, based entirely on the relative status of victim and offender, appear to illustrate the supposed inequity of traditional Chinese law and to demonstrate precisely the ascendancy of Confucian ideology over law that Western observers have often criticized. A closer examination of these cases, however, reveals the abiding tendency to seek leniency within the limits of the law and demonstrates the rational adjudication of capital crimes in eighteenth-century China, albeit within the framework of a legal code strongly influenced by Confucian ideology. Although, by modern legal standards, the decision may have been flawed by inequities, the law itself was conscientiously and rationally applied.

Whatever shortcomings modern critics have attributed to traditional Chinese law, the elaborate and redundant procedures for adjudicating and sentencing capital crimes bespeaks a serious concern for justice, a diligent search for the truth, and a sincere regard for the lives of both victims and offenders. All legal codes, traditional or modern, embody the dominant ideology of the society's ruling elite. *The Qing Code* was not exceptional in this regard. To the extent that the *Code* was exceptional, it was the degree to which ideological values were formally and transparently codified. Elite ideology underpinned the law, and despite what is often presumed to be the softer side of Confucian legal philosophy, when the crime violated the core values of the "Confucian creed," punishment could be unremittingly severe. Kinship and status were essential elements in assessing fault and determining punishments in criminal matters, as the comparisons above reveal. The same crime could be punished differently depending on the relationship between victim and offender. Cases in which ideology blatantly overrode equal treatment before the law have frequently been cited as evidence of the cruelty and inequity of the traditional Chinese legal system. Nevertheless, we should not allow extreme examples to color our understanding. Leniency could be obtained based on specific and well-defined criteria contained in *The Qing Code*. The law mattered, and Chinese magistrates adhered to the law.

NOTES

1. For example, the *Lü xing*, which can be dated to the Warring States period (475–221 B.C.E.), urges caution and mercy in the use of all physical punishments. See MacCormack, "The *Lü Hsing*."
2. Huang Liu-hung, *Complete Book*, 288.
3. Ibid., 292.
4. Ch'ü, *Law and Society*, p. 45.
5. The best explanation of the autumn assizes in English is Meijer, "Autumn Assizes"; see also, Na, *Qingdai zhongyang sifa shenban zhidu*.
6. By law, any criminal whose sentence was deferred for ten consecutive years would have his sentence reduced to life exile. Thousands of criminals had their sentences deferred every year, and some even exceeded the ten-year limit. The

successive granting of indefinite stays requires further research, but the practice might indicate an overburdened legal system as well as a reluctance to pass final judgment in doubtful cases.

7. See Buoye, "Suddenly Murderous Intent Arose."

8. MacCormack, "Cause, Status and Fault," 174.

9. See Jones, *The Great Qing Code*, 309, for an English translation of the article.

10. Ma and Yang, *Da Qing lüli tongkao jiaozhu*, 863.

11. Ibid.

12. *XKTB*, 2381; QL 36.4.23. All case records are from the collection of routine memorials to the Board of Punishments that contain reports of homicide cases related to disputes over land and debt.

13. *XKTB*, 0194; QL 5.11.8.

14. Cited in McLeod and Yates, "Forms of Ch'in Law," 130–32.

15. *XKTB*, 0714; QL 15.9.4.

16. Ibid., 3174; QL 44.2.23.

6 The Discourse on Insolvency and Negligence in Eighteenth-Century China

PENGSHENG CHIU

Between the sixteenth and the nineteenth centuries, long-distance trade in China underwent great expansion accompanied by a regional division of labor among the different economic areas of China.[1] As this nationwide division of labor became both deeper and broader, many cities and towns in the Lower Yangzi region emerged as centers of commerce and industry. The production of cotton, silk, agricultural crops, and other goods there and in the surrounding countryside was gradually promoted by the investment of merchant capital. With this input of capital, various kinds of merchants began to have an impact on the material life and work habits of craftsmen, peasants, and other people. If the investment of capital in such goods did not lead to a factory system and mass production, as it did in western Europe, its momentum nevertheless helped reshape late imperial China's economic organizations and its legal discourse in ways we will explore here through the investigation of key tropes introduced in economic and legal discourse during the Qing.

The improvement or transformation of various economic organizations especially during the eighteenth century is evident in the reformation of the "brokerage" (*jingji* or *yahang*) and "pawnshop" (*dangpu* or *diandang*) systems, the establishment of "cotton business firms" (*zihao*) and "silk business firms" (*zhangfang*) engaged in the production system, the evolution of "money exchangers" (*qianzhuang*) and premodern "banks" (*piaohao*), and the creation of "merchant or craftsmen associations" (*huiguan* or *gongsuo*), sometimes called "guilds." Along with these organizational changes, there were probing debates over "protecting wealthy people" (*baofu*) to ensure security in local society, the abstract concept of an "independent principle" (*yiding zhi li*) in the operation of markets,[2] the authentic function of "extravagance and waste" (*shemi*) in a sound economy,[3] and how to "combine common profit with self-interest" (*gongli zhi li*).[4] New discursive treatments of all these questions were articulated in the wake of economic growth in late imperial China.

In this chapter, our main concern is the question of how these changes in economic organizations and discourses became a part of China's legal framework. We will focus on issues of insolvency and negligence that merchants encountered in disputes and litigation as seen in *The Great Qing Code* and other legal texts of the eighteenth century. This textual analysis will clarify the complex relations between law, discourse, and economics in China at that time.

In 1740, the Qianlong emperor (r. 1736–95) approved a regulation banning clerks from acting as brokers.[5] Three years later, the emperor issued a further decree to the Board of Personnel (Libu) banning gentry from being brokers and enabling merchants to reclaim their goods and property from brokers. The emperor not only expressed his sympathy for "merchants far away from home" (*jilü yuan shang*) but also blamed their troubles on the gentry's insolence and the magistrates' indolence.[6] The president of the Board of Personnel reacted promptly and drafted a regulation that increased the officials' obligation to handle lawsuits over merchant losses. The president emphasized that this new regulation resonated well with the previous substatute, which forbade any incumbent clerk from being a broker, and so the law also prohibited gentry from acting as brokers.[7] The regulation also imposed harsh sanctions on officials who failed to help merchants recover their losses. It punished officials in charge of merchant lawsuits according to three degrees of culpability: for not paying enough attention, for not impeding wrongdoing, and for taking bribes.

Clearly, the enforcement of these rulings was the crux of the issue; it is difficult to determine the scale of official sympathy actually shown to merchant victims and the likelihood that their losses would be recovered by means of harsh inspection pressures applied on officials. However, the appearance of a new trope in eighteenth-century insolvency legislation—that is, the frequent deployment of a phrase such as "merchants far away from home," who suffered much—may indicate that sympathy with merchants engaged in long-distance trade became the predominant official norm that fueled the drafting of regulations to resolve insolvency cases in this increasingly commercialized society. In that sense, the change of rhetoric may illuminate changes in legal and social values.

INSOLVENCY DISCOURSES

Questions of merchant insolvency came to be formulated in terms of the trope of the discomforts of long-distance trade. From the sixteenth century onward, long-distance trade drew an increasing number of merchants into travel along the empire's main land and water routes, thereby providing opportunities for brokers dealing with these merchants and their commodities in hundreds of cities and towns along the way.[8] The four most important kinds of commodities transported long distance were rice, salt, cotton, and silk.[9] Cotton and silk could yield profit at each exchange. Consequently, a great amount of "silver ingots" (*wenyin*) circulated in the Lower Yangzi region, the major zone of cotton and silk production, especially during the summer months when peasant family and craftsman workshops produced much of their cotton and silk goods. Merchants brought along silver to buy their cotton or silk products, and brokers functioned to facilitate trade between them and the producers.

SYMPATHY FOR MERCHANTS FAR AWAY FROM HOME

Many historical sources reveal the prosperity of this cotton and silk trade. For example, a scholar who had once been a broker himself, Tang Zhen (1630–1704), described the volume of the silk trade in the Lower Yangzi region, which took place once every fifth lunar month in seventeenth-century Huzhou prefecture; it attracted so many merchants that an enormous amount of silver ingots poured into the market.[10] Ye Mengzhu, a scholar of the late Ming, also recalled scenes of the many cotton brokers doing business in Songjiang prefecture, a famous cotton-textile production area at that time, and having to court those merchants with their hundreds of thousands of silver ingots in order to compete successfully with other brokers.[11] Both of these sources emphasize the huge amount of merchant silver circulating in the Lower Yangzi silk and cotton markets. Groups of brokers, acting as agents between these merchants and their producers, found niches in these and less profitable trades as well. Meanwhile, for merchants in search of lucrative transactions, the choice of a competent and credible broker became crucial to the success of their business.

Manuals for merchants detailed practical criteria by which to identify the ideal broker, providing a typology of characteristics that might distinguish the precarious from the more credible. These tricks became crucial knowledge for merchants.[12] Since the questionable brokers seemed to prevail over the more credible types, merchants had to face the harsh reality of the marketplace. They might encounter conflicts with or even enter into lawsuits against brokers regarding disputes over such matters as the adoption of local or official measurements or the negotiation of miscellaneous fees for accessible storage, transportation, and commission. Even if merchants escaped the misfortune of sinking into a malicious broker's complex web of deceit, they often had no resort but to take legal action.

Some literati and officials, when recording the misfortunes merchants suffered at the hands of brokers, overtly expressed their sympathy for merchants. For example, in the sixteenth century, Li Le blamed merchant problems on deceitful brokers in Wuzhen and Qingzhen market towns, two famous silk production and distribution centers in Huzhou prefecture.[13] Insolvency brought on by a broker's wrongdoing and the merchant's loss of capital became serious concerns for Li Le, as he rhetorically designated the offense of insolvency as something "not allowed by Heaven and Earth, and an extremely bad crime in society." Li Le was not a judge with the power to decide that insolvency is the worst crime, but high-ranking officials with such power did not hesitate to take this offense seriously. The influential official Zhang Boxing (1651–1725) made a similar, albeit more crime-oriented, comment in 1707 when he was governor of Fujian. In accusing a criminal alliance of brokers and clerks of extorting, embezzling, defrauding, and swindling merchants out of their money, Zhang not only expressed his deep sympathy for those "hardworking and frugal merchants far away from home" but also condemned officials and clerks who did not pay enough attention to the merchants' insolvency lawsuits.[14] His concern about merchants' losses and brokers' insolvencies was not atypical in the eighteenth century.

An official's sympathy for "merchant losses in both capital and goods" (benkui huozhe) might increase his willingness to support a merchant's appeal to reclaim those losses in the courts. In addition, the institutional reform of the "broker entitlement system" (guanya zhidu) and a series of "broker insolvency" (keqian) laws were critical policy changes enacted during the eighteenth century to resolve these problems fairly and efficiently.[15]

RHETORICAL RESPONSES TO TRANSACTION COSTS

A deep sympathy for merchants far away from home is a basic, recurring motif in writings about insolvency by the literatus Li Le and in reports from Governor Zhang Boxing to the Qianlong emperor. But this sympathy did not preclude an objective understanding of the broker's positive role in market operations—and the appearance of another important trope, the honest broker. In the 1743 decree quoted above, the Qianlong emperor used the concept of reciprocal profit between a merchant and other people in order to validate the role of the broker.[16] The broker was deemed a useful and necessary agent for determining a suitable price that would complete a transaction between two parties and thus "provide equal benefit to merchants and their customers" (tongshang bianmin). Along with this imperial understanding, we have the brokers' own view of their role in a polished argument presented by a group of Suzhou silk brokers twenty years before the Qianlong emperor's decree. In 1723, these brokers declared that they made an indispensable contribution toward shortening the time needed to find qualified silk producers, thereby benefiting both merchants and producers. If there were not enough brokers, then the profits of merchants, producers, and even brokers would be impaired.[17] One might summarize the rationale of these Suzhou silk brokers as follows: that they met the need of all parties to reduce transaction costs, consisting of, at minimum, search and information costs, bargaining and decision costs, and policing and enforcement costs.[18] In the view of the famous historian Zhao Yi (1721–1814), in addition to linking producers and merchants in profitable deals by cutting the costs of information, brokers were indispensable for effectively handling the diverse measurement standards used in even one local market district.[19] This brokerage function lessened the bargaining and decision costs for merchants and their customers and suppliers.

The issue of policing and enforcement costs in the operation of a brokerage system is too complex to analyze in detail here. Even so, an official order for the use of sale receipts in eighteenth-century Jiangxi indicates the dimension of these policing and enforcement costs. Before 1743, the Jiangxi provincial judicial commissioner Ling Tao devised a system of "certified receipts" (lianpiao), and he forced all brokers, merchants, and retail customers in the province to adopt his newly designed system. Ling believed that the lack of certified receipts in deals between merchants and their customers was the main reason why brokers so often swindled money from and inflicted damage on merchants.[20] Consequently, Ling Tao responded to this insolvency problem by ordering all brokers, merchants, and retail-shop owners to certify and keep their own part of official receipts.[21] Determining to what extent this plan actually worked requires further study. However, this official's detailed blueprint illustrates the broker's intended role of at least facilitating all the tedious but necessary procedures of adjusting, policing, and enforcing the original contracts between merchants and retail customers. Officials such as Ling Tao knew this fact well and hence sought to reduce problems of insolvency with the broker's crucial support.

In sum, the Suzhou silk brokers, the historian Zhao Yi, and the Jiangxi provincial judicial commissioner Ling Tao would certainly all have agreed with the Qianlong emperor's comment that the role of the broker was to foster reciprocal profit between merchants and other people. Whether one deploys the imperial rhetoric of fostering reciprocal profit or applies the modern jargon of cutting transaction costs, the crucial function of economic brokerage had become embedded in the legal and social consciousness of political figures who could affect the drafting and enforcement of insolvency law. Nonetheless, this approval of the broker's economic function was accompanied by the rhetoric of deep sympathy for merchants far away from home.

NEGLIGENCE DISCOURSES: FROM UNINTENDED LIABILITY TO NEGLIGENCE IN PROVINCIAL SUBSTATUTES

The broker system in eighteenth-century China was like a double-edged sword; it could reduce transaction costs, but it could also multiply insolvency problems. Consequently, officials did not overlook the necessity of regulating brokerage in order to assure economic stability. New tropes growing out of the changing world of trade played a central role in the development of legal discourse on this issue.

Among the many regulations and substatutes issued to prevent and remedy those insolvency problems, the substatute issued in 1758 is notable for discriminating between intentional insolvency and unintended liability. In the case of intentional insolvency, the broker was to be punished in accordance with the statute "Obtaining Property from the Government or an Individual by Deceit and Cheating"; however, if insolvency was actually caused by a retail-shop owner and compensation was not recovered within one year, the broker was to be indicted under the statute "Taking Interest in Violation of the Prohibitions."[22] Again, the official in charge of a merchant's insolvency lawsuit faced the pressure of his superior's oversight. If found to have been inattentive or to have hindered a merchant's recovery of his losses, that official faced trouble in gaining promotion in his next appointment.[23]

It is worth noting that a broker might be indicted under the charge of unintended liability if he did not help a merchant regain his losses within one year even if the broker himself had not actually embezzled any money or goods in the transactions he negotiated between the merchant and the debtor. The broker was charged with the responsibility of helping the merchant resolve his insolvency problem; otherwise, the hapless broker, like the debtor, might be indicted and punished according to the debt statute. Therefore, this article may fairly be said to impose liability on a broker who could not help the merchant recover his losses, even though this same article is ambiguous about whether the broker himself should pay for the loss when the shop owner could not fulfill the contract.

This article is even more unclear about the rationale for unintended liability, since it mentions nothing at all about why the broker should eventually compensate the merchant for a loss caused by a specific retail-shop owner; moreover, the article did not explain why the broker should be punished for what he had *not* done. It might be inferred, however, that this indictment would be made for two possible reasons: the broker was responsible for having recommended an unqualified shop owner or was reasonably suspected of conspiring with a deceitful shop owner. Does this article then reflect official concern with the principle of negligence? The question merits further investigation.

A passage in a popular "encyclopedia for daily use" (*riyong leishu*) published at the end of the sixteenth century provides couplets in legal rhetoric for merchants who needed to sue an insolvent broker.[24] In this text, the first and the third of these phrases relate to an article in the "Consumption of Property Received in Deposit" statute, which states that

> one who has received in deposit the property or domestic animals of [another], and who, without authority, consumes them, will be punished for illegally obtained property, reduced one degree. If he falsely claims that [the deposited property or domestic animals] are dead or lost, sentence as if it were non-manifest theft, reduced one degree. Levy on the property, and return it to the owner. If there is clear evidence that the property was consumed or lost by flood, fire, or theft, or that the animals became sick and died, there is no punishment.[25]

The renowned and authoritative *Qing Code* annotator Shen Zhiqi commented on the latter half of this article, saying that one should not be responsible for such "unexpected events."[26]

As a matter of fact, the latter half of this statute contains critical elements of the legal principle of negligence and also exempted the recipient from responsibility for loss or destruction of property due to natural disasters, illness, or theft.[27] Obviously, this exemption provided merchants with legal loopholes, and brokers probably faked evidence that property had been destroyed or stolen in order to avoid their obligation to compensate a merchant for his loss. From this perspective, the 1758 substatute showed reasonable official suspicions toward brokers who claimed not to have embezzled a merchant's property. Strictly speaking, in punishing those brokers who did not deceive a merchant or embezzle his property, the 1758 substatute contradicted the "Consumption of Property Received in Deposit" statute, which exempted the broker from obligatory compensation for unintended damage on deposited property.

During the 1750s, another law appeared that embodied the negligence principle, although this substatute seems to have been enacted only in a few provinces. Not intended to address broker and merchant lawsuits, this ruling decided only on compensation between pawnbrokers and their customers.

During the fifth and sixth lunar months of 1746, high-ranking officials in Zhejiang engaged in a debate over how to regulate the method of compensation in various cases involving a pawnshop that had caught fire. The provincial judicial commissioner Wang and his colleague Pan had noted that the average pawn ticket did include the agreement that "risk by fire loss should not be posited on either party's side" (*fengyan buce ge ting tianming*) in its contract. Nevertheless, depositors whose goods were damaged by fire did not always abide by the contract and might press for compensation with the local government. Mainly because there was no universal rule for levying an acceptable liability on pawnbrokers, clerks might receive bribes that would undermine depositors' struggles.[28] To end this chaos, the provincial judge Wang suggested a uniform regulation that would henceforth apply to all such cases in Zhejiang.[29]

This ruling was the same as in other provincial substatutes; however, controversy arose over its details. Wang suggested that the pawnbroker could be exempted from making any compensation, both when a fire had spread from the neighborhood and when it had been started by the pawnshop itself. Wang's suggestion about the latter eventuality was noteworthy in his emphasis that the exemption should be confined to occasions when the pawnbroker's warehouse for depositing goods and his residence had both burned down. For his part, the governor felt comfortable about exempting pawnbrokers if their shops were lost as the result of a fire that had spread from the neighborhood, but he could not help having reservations about exempting pawnshops if the fires had started on the premises. He commented that this ruling would be "unfair" to poor depositors and too generous to careless pawnbrokers.[30]

In defense of his original suggestion, Provincial Judge Wang detailed his reasoning and tried to persuade the governor and the governor-general of

Zhejiang. Wang's argumentation emphasized two reasons for exempting the pawnbroker even when he was responsible for starting a fire. First, the pawnbroker also had lost all of his property and thus could not afford to compensate others for any large losses of goods. Second, Wang worried that pawnbrokers might prove unwilling to continue in their business if they risked having to pay compensation even when they had suffered huge accidental damages. Wang's hesitation stemmed not only from his concern for the interests of pawnbrokers but also from the fact that pawnshops often played an important role in assisting common people through hard times.[31] The governor and governor-general were persuaded and finally accepted all the legal suggestions proposed by Wang and his colleague.

The 1746 debate among the high-ranking officials in Zhejiang reveal a pervasive tension behind this series of pawnshop compensatory substatutes in eighteenth-century China. The source of this tension was the question of how to balance the interests of pawnbrokers and their customers fairly when losses were incurred because of circumstances beyond the control of both contending parties.

Zhejiang officials created precedents that could be transplanted to other provinces. In 1759, when the Hunan judicial commissioner Yan Youxi requested approval for a ruling from his superior, the Hunan governor, he referred to "provincial substatutes enacted in Jiangsu and Zhejiang" (*Jiang Zhe liang sheng xianxing shengli*).[32] In these substatutes, pawnbrokers or dyeing-shop owners could be exempted from making compensation if the deposited goods were burned by a fire that spread throughout the neighborhood or were stolen by bandits. This kind of provincial substatute accorded well with the latter half of the "Consumption of Property Received in Deposit" statute.

Yan's report invoked these Jiangsu and Zhejiang substatutes in order to strengthen the argument of the Hunan magistrate's ruling and thereby help it gain approval from the province's governor. In 1759, the magistrate Lu Tingcong submitted a case in which a dyeing-shop owner asserted that deposited cloth as well as his own property had been stolen. Although Magistrate Lu was aware of the claims of commoners protesting the lack of compensation for the loss of their deposited goods, he did not downplay the loss to pawnbrokers or dyeing-shop owners. Lu acknowledged that they, too, were victims, and he felt it would be unfair to order them to compensate all of the loss in cases of a genuine accidental fire or an actual robbery. Yet, in spite of his sympathy for shop owners, Lu also had deep concerns about being fooled by deceitful shop owners or being threatened with protests from wrathful commoners. Lu's comments seem sincere and sympathetic; however, as "there was no substatute to abide by," local officials were puzzled by having to consider the interests of both shop owners and commoners. Eventually, Lu resorted to the Jiangsu and Zhejiang substatutes in reaching his decision.[33]

Provincial Judicial Commissioner Yan completely agreed with Magistrate Lu's suggestion to adopt the Jiangsu and Zhejiang legislation. In addition, Yan requested that the Hunan governor endorse the adoption of legislation from other provinces. His recommendation was not intended only to produce a proper ruling in the case of the dyeing shop; he also intended to establish new legislation for Hunan.[34] Subsequently, both of Yan's aims were accomplished. His recommendation for this case was approved by the Hunan governor and was incorporated into the "Collected Hunan Provincial Substatutes."[35]

Aside from adopting the regulatory text of the Jiangsu and Zhejiang substatutes, Yan also added a more nuanced discourse to his 1759 legislative suggestion. Deploying some traditional rhetoric in his analysis of the negligence principle, he emphasized a series of legal reasons for discerning different liabilities in related cases. First, as pawnbrokers and dyeing-shop owners all profited from providing services for customers, they had an essential obligation to take care of deposited goods. Second, if a fire has started or an item has been stolen inside the pawnshop or dyeing shop, the shop owner is obliged to pay for the loss because he has violated his responsibility to protect the deposited goods. Third, when these goods are burned because of a fire from the neighborhood or are stolen with the use of overwhelming force, the shop owner should be exempted from paying compensation because he could not avoid these kinds of losses.[36] In all, these sentences contain the coherent criteria of a "due care" principle, which resonated well with the related regulation in the "Consumption of Property Received in Deposit" statute.

LEGISLATIVE ADJUSTMENTS CONCERNING PAWNBROKERS' NEGLIGENCE IN *THE GREAT QING CODE*

Substatutes enacted in Jiangsu, Zhejiang, Hunan, and Jiangxi were never incorporated into *The Great Qing Code*. Those provincial substatutes had clearly applied the negligence principle in property damage cases from the 1740s to the 1760s for those cases related to pawnshops or dyeing shops at least. Nonetheless, the central government began a similar legislative process in the 1770s, which it initiated with the legislation of 1772, as a consequence of several years of discussion of an accidental pawnshop fire in Beijing in 1769.[37]

Although issued by the central government, the text of the 1772 legislation delimited its area of enactment to the capital, Beijing, and, most importantly, its content was not the same as in the previous provincial substatutes; at present, it is not clear how judges in local and central governments dealt with the contradiction in legislation. The version of legislation issued by the central government was less nuanced than the provincial substatutes enacted decades earlier. The text of the 1772 substatute omitted the original distinctions between fires starting inside the shop and fires that spread from the neighborhood, paying no attention to the question of whether or not the fire damage had been a preventable accident. Rather, it simply ordered that all losses incurred by fire should be compensated at 70 percent of value.[38] Hence, the 1772 substatute showed no concern for negligence cases, unlike the previous provincial substatutes.

Four years later, a revision of the 1772 substatute was issued on lines suggested by the Jiang Zhe governor-general Gao Jin. Gao declared that the 1772 substatute ought to be revised because it did not correspond to the substatutes enacted in Jiangsu and other provinces under his governance. He pointed out that the provincial substatute differentiated among the cases related to damage caused by pawnshop fire and, in particular, determined the amount of fire compensation according to the kind of goods deposited, thereby overtly criticizing the 70 percent compensation regulation in the 1772 substatute.[39] Gao's critique won out and subsequently culminated in a new version of the substatute in 1777.[40]

In comparing the 1777 substatute with its 1772 predecessor, one can see two changes: (1) it revived the policy of differentiating between fires originating inside the pawnshop and those from outside, and (2) it added distinctions between compensation for normal goods and for wholesale goods (raw materials such as rice, wheat, and cotton). In addition to these two major changes, there was one minor but significant modification, which alleviated the obligation to the pawnbroker who suffered from damage caused by a fire that had spread from the neighborhood. As a result, when the loss of deposited goods was caused by fire spread from outside, the pawnshop owner now had to pay compensation at 40 percent of the value for normal goods and at 24 percent for wholesale items.

The significance of the 1777 legislative modification lay not only in the change in compensation rate, from zero to 40 percent and 24 percent, but also in the adjustment of the original negligence principle embodied in the provincial substatutes. This represented a significant shift in the burden of losses allocated to pawnbrokers and their customers. The pawnshops located in Jiangsu, Zhejiang, Hunan, and Jiangxi, at least, might evade all compensatory obligations if they could prove that the fire or robbery had not been caused by their own carelessness; therefore, pawnbrokers in these provinces were freed from the risk of damages due to unpreventable fire and robbery. However, the 1777 substatute did not fully recognize the favors granted pawnbrokers by the provincial substatutes; instead, it imposed on them a compensatory obligation to pay for 40 percent or 24 percent of the current value of the damaged goods on an empirewide basis. In contrast, the 1772 substatute had been limited to pawnbrokers in Beijing.

Nonetheless, the Qianlong emperor chose to side with the opponents of Zhejiang Judicial Commissioner Wang, shifting the balance back toward the pawnbrokers' customers. As a result, the 1777 substatute in the central government code increased the obligatory compensation rate of pawnbrokers from zero to 40 percent or to 24 percent when a pawnshop fell victim to a fire that had originated outside it.

CONCLUSION: THE DISCOURSE ON CONTRIBUTIONS
OF WEALTHY PEOPLE

We can see the role played by pervasive, and persuasive, rhetorical tropes in two important categories of commercial legislation that emerged in eighteenth-century China. In the category of insolvency legislation, rulers expressed the prevailing sympathy for merchants far away from home, a sympathy that had prevailed from at least the sixteenth century and thus enhanced the security of merchant transactions. The other new category of law was designed to differentiate the obligation of pawnshops and dyeing shops to compensate customers' losses according to the degree to which their owners could have avoided risks from fire, robbery, or embezzlement. These two categories of laws—insolvency and negligence—also allowed merchants to preserve more of their resources and to claim legal protection and even privileges in various kinds of commerce. They responded to, and may have incorporated, considerable sympathy and respect for merchants. These laws also reveal a new respect for investors.

Analysis of these discourses reveals the tensions underlying the process of drafting these laws, thereby reflecting the challenges facing officials who sought to balance the contending interests of pawnbrokers and their customers. Among the talk, rulings, and writings of eighteenth-century emperors and high-ranking provincial officials, the chief legislators in late imperial China, one finds a spectrum of ways in which to maintain this balance when dealing with the question of the pawnbroker's risk. This spectrum reflected these legislators' perception of the roles played by wealthy people, including merchants, in their own communities.

In eighteenth-century China, many officials and literati emphasized the contributions wealthy people made to society. A Jiangxi judicial official, for instance, urged peasants who mortgaged their crops to a landlord to follow the common practices accepted by pawnshops and their customers. Aiming to empower landlords with similar security, this provincial judge suggested issuing a regulation that would assure landlords of lawful profit.[41] In 1804, this Jiangxi judicial official expressed a typical High Qing viewpoint about the contribution of wealthy people, using the metaphor of motherhood for those landlords "wealthy enough to nurture the poor" (*fu nai pinzhi mu*). In addition, this Jiangxi official called the wealthy "the vitality of the country" (*guojia yuanqi*).[42] At about the same time, sentiments similar to those of this Jiangxi provincial judge were expressed by the renowned "private secretary" (*muyou*) Wang Huizu (1730–1807): "The wealthy were not only deemed to be the backers of the poor; moreover, they are also the indispensable sponsors of public affairs in local society."[43]

The contributions of the wealthy to the poor and their indispensable role in local affairs—a new trope in these discussions—were clear to some eighteenth-century contemporaries. But how and why had the wealthy acquired their riches? We may direct our attention to a discussion of this question in the record of an eighteenth-century cause célèbre.[44] While interrogating the scholar Zeng Jing (1679–1736), the Yongzheng Emperor (r. 1722–35) made several comments relevant to this issue. The emperor said that the wealthy deserved their riches because they were "frugal and industrious," while the poor had "brought poverty on themselves" (*zizhi jiongpo*).[45] Here, the emperor seems to be lionizing the successes of the rich, yet we should perhaps refrain from reading too much into his comment. His utterance sprang from the specific circumstances; he apparently did not think over the implications of what he was saying. He was concerned primarily with convincing his audience that all the critiques Zeng Jing had voiced were ridiculous and vulnerable to his rebuttal. He even seemed to forget that his ruthless comments about the poor might damage his image among scholar-officials. Nevertheless, his view perhaps unveiled one dimension of his deeply rooted assumption that one's financial fate could be imputed to one's character, namely, that industriousness leads to success and riches, and laziness to failure and poverty.[46]

Could the Yongzheng emperor's comments have just been a slip of the tongue? Or did he really believe that industriousness or laziness determined one's fate of being either rich or poor? Either way, the emperor's words reveal a conceptual change that lessened the probability that the wealthy would be accused of infringing on the commoners' welfare. Conceiving the wealthy as the beneficiaries of their own "frugality and industriousness," the Yongzheng Emperor was expressing a mode of thought that would make it easier to incorporate a sophisticated negligence principle into commercial legislation during the Qianlong period.

As the successor to the throne of Yongzheng, the Qianlong emperor showed more caution than his father in commenting on social and economic inequality. He would not bluntly assert a causal link between a man's character and his fate as rich or poor. In addition, some of the Yongzheng emperor's policies on pawnshops were modified during the Qianlong period.[47] However, the negligence substatutes he issued evidence a shift in attitude toward the responsibilities of the wealthy. The substatutes insist that the poor's misfortunes should not be attributed arbitrarily to the wealthy even as they consider how to share the burdens of compensation for various kinds of unpreventable mishaps.

Claims about the important social contributions of the wealthy were expressed not only by the Yongzheng and Qianlong emperors; they were made by many officials and literati in eighteenth-century China, thus facilitating reforms in the area of insolvency and negligence laws. Merchants could reclaim damages more effectively and pawnbrokers reduce their cost of risk, thanks to this legislation. Discourses stressing the resources wealthy people could use to benefit the poor coexisted with older, contending discourses that urged balancing the welfare of the poor with security for the property of the wealthy. The issue of how to evaluate and adjust the contending interests between merchants and common people had gradually become part of calculated and nuanced discussions in both the legal and economic fields. The stage was set for some of the highly contentious debates and decisions about merchants that would erupt in China over the next two centuries.

NOTES

I would like to thank Professors Joseph P. McDermott and Steven B. Miles for their many helpful suggestions when I first presented this chapter as a conference paper in 2003.

1. On expansion of long-distance trade, see R. Bin Wong, *China Transformed*, 17–22; Wu Chengming, *Zhongguozhibenzhuyi*; and Li Bozhong, "Zhongguo quanguo shichang." On regional division of labor, see Wang Yeh-chien, "Qingdai jingji chulun."

2. Rowe, "State and Market" and *Saving the World*, 204–5. Will, "Discussions about the Market-Place," 331–57.

3. Yang Lien-sheng, "Chimi lun"; Lin Liyue, "Lu Ji chongshe sixiang zaitan" and "Jianjiatang gao"; Chen Kuo-tung, "You guan Lu Ji"; Chao Xiaohong, "Ming Qing ren de 'shemi' guannian."

4. Liu Kuang-ching, "Houxu"; Dunstan, *Conflicting Counsels*, 164–68; Chiu, "Shiba shiji Dian tong shichang," 97–104.

5. *DLCY*, vol. 3, *juan* 17: 406. In 1743, this regulation was upgraded into a substatute recognized by *The Great Qing Code*; see Wu Tan, "Da Qing lüli" tongkao, 530.

6. In *Qinding Da Qing huidian shili*, vol. 133, 718–19.

7. In ibid., 719.

8. Han Dacheng, "Mingdai de fu shang"; Timothy Brook, "The Merchants' Network."

9. Xu and Wu, *Zhongguo zibenzhuyi de mengya*; Fan Jinmin, *Ming Qing Jiangnan shangye*.

10. Tang, *Qian shu*, 428. About the career of Tang Zhen as a broker and his thoughts about political and economic affairs, see Hsiung Ping-chen, "Cong Tang Zhen kan."

11. Ye, *Yueshi bian*, 157–58.

12. "Keshang guijian lun" (Useful advice for merchants), in *Xingke tianxia simin bienlan*, vol. 21, 295.

13. Li Le, *Xu "Jianwen zaji,"* vol. 11.

14. Zhang Boxing, *Zhengyitang ji*, vol. 5, 32.

15. On the broker entitlement system, see Wu Qiyen, "Qingdai qianqi yahang"; Mann, *Local Merchants*; and Kuang-ching Liu, "Chinese Merchant Guilds." As for brokerage insolvency laws, brokerage legislation was issued from the fifteenth to the eighteenth century, most of which can be found in the statute "Monopolizing Market" and its substatutes; see Chiu, "You shi lüli yanbian," 310–18.

16. *Qinding Da Qing huidian shili*, vol. 133, 718–19.

17. *Ming Qing Suzhou gongshangye beike ji*, 14.

18. Coase, *Firm, the Market and the Law*, 38–39, 6. For almost two decades, pioneering scholars have insightfully applied the "transaction cost" as an analyt-

ical tool in order to illuminate how these institutional innovations evolved with the development of merchant associations and "customary law" in late imperial China. See Myers, "Customary Law"; and Chen and Myers, "Coping with Transaction Costs." However, a new agenda for broadening the scope of transaction-cost analysis has recently appeared. Ocko urges focusing on "how group norms rather than contract principles shape the way people imagine, create, sustain, and end exchange relationships"; consequently, he urges examination of how contract and property relationships were formed by "the basic mechanics and language of early modern Chinese economic relationships." Ocko, "Missing Metaphor," 197, 201.

19. Zhao Yi, *Gaiyu congkao*, juan 30: 3. Also see the discussion in Fanzhong Liang, *Zhongguo lidai hukou*, 535; and Chiu, "You Suzhou jingshang," 30–34.

20. Ling Zhu, *Xijiang shinie jishi*, vol. 4, 149.

21. Ibid.

22. For full English translations of these two statutes, "Obtaining Property from the Government or an Individual by Deceit and Cheating" and "Taking Interest in Violation of the Prohibitions," see the text of Articles 274 and 149 in Jones, *The Great Qing Code*, 257, 161–62.

23. DLCY, vol. 3, juan 17: 411–12.

24. *Xingke Tianxia siming beilang Santai wanyong zhengzong*, vol. 8, 348. For an introduction to this genre of Chinese traditional encyclopedias, see Wu Huifang, *Wanbao quanshu*.

25. "Da Qing lüli" tongkao, 526; for an English translation, see Jones, *The Great Qing Code*, 162–63.

26. Shen Zhiqi, "Da Qing lü" jizhu, juan 9: 584.

27. In general, negligence is defined as "failure to exercise that degree of care which a person of ordinary prudence would exercise under the same circumstances." See Gifis, *Law Dictionary*, 315.

28. *Zhi Zhe chenggui*, juan 5: 528.

29. Ibid., 528–29.

30. Ibid., 529.

31. Ibid., 529–30.

32. *Hunan shengli cheng'an*, vol. 33, 25–26. However, Yan's restatement was probably not so accurate; the original regulations about differential compensation in Jiangsu and Zhejiang substatutes could be more complex. I have not yet found the original substatute text from Jiangsu; nonetheless, the Zhejiang substatute issued in 1746 may be found in *Zhi Zhe chenggui*, vol. 5, 528–60.

33. *Hunan shengli cheng'an*, vol. 33, 25.

34. Ibid., 27.

35. After the legislation was issued in Hunan, the Jiangxi provincial governor also approved the enactment of a similar substatute in 1760. The negligence principle, especially as embodied in the original text of the Jiangxi legislation, may be found in *Xijiang zhengyao*, vol. 2, 36.

36. *Hunan shengli cheng'an*, vol. 33, 27.

37. "*Da Qing lüli*" *tongkao*, 982.

38. Ibid.

39. Ibid. Gao's original memorial is now stored in the Neige Daku Archive, and has been published by the Institute of History and Philology, Academia Sinica, with the additional title "A Memorial on Rules for Compensation by Pawnbrokers When Pawned Articles Have Been Destroyed by Fire." See *Zhongyang yanjiuyuan*, vol. 227, 48–55.

40. Ibid., 982. This substatute was appended to the "Accidental Setting of Fires" article in *The Great Qing Code* (356–57), but in 1844, it was removed and included in the article "The Consumption of Property Received in Deposit." The rearrangement of the 1844 substatutes was also accompanied by textual revision, thus erecting additional regulations on the compensation of deposited goods in dyeing shops. Meanwhile, in 1844, another new substatute appeared that regulated compensation for goods burgled, robbed, or embezzled in the specific pawnshop or dyeing shop. See *Qinding Da Qing huidan shili*, vol. 764, 11–12.

41. *Xijiang zhengyao*, vol. 43, 7.

42. Ibid., 6.

43. Wang Huizu, *Xuezhi xushuo*, 125.

44. About this "treason by the book" cause célèbre, see the outstanding discussion in Spence, *Treason by the Book*.

45. *Dayi juemi lu*, vol. 1.

46. Several writers in the Southern Song (1127–1279) expressed the causality between one's character and one's fate as rich or poor. They focus on "a principle in a cyclical moral logic" in which the virtue of thrift could lead to wealth. See McDermott, "Family Financial Plans," 41–42. This discourse seems not to have painted with as broad a brush on the issue of social and economic inequality as the Yongzheng emperor did.

47. It is noteworthy that the Qianlong emperor differed from his father in his attitude toward government investment in pawnshop activities. The Yongzhong and Qianlong emperors both supported making loans to salt merchants and pawnbrokers through an official institution called "loan to merchants to earn interest" (*fashang shengxi*), and allowing the establishment of "official pawnshops

belonging to the inner court" (*Neiwufu guandang*). Even so, the Qianlong emperor showed more reservations about these institutions and closed down some official pawnshops. See Pan Ming-te, *Zhongguo jindai diandang*, 43–51. For the central reason behind the Qianlong emperor's actions, a recent study has demonstrated that he found it more profitable to lend money to salt and copper merchants than to manage official pawnshops. See Lai Huimin, "Qianlong chao Neiwufu de dangpu," 140.

7   Poverty Tales and Statutory Politics
    in Mid-Qing Fraud Cases

MARK MCNICHOLAS

On a September evening in 1805, in the city of Guangzhou, eight men posing as an official street patrol extorted 160 silver dollars from a moneychanger.¹ According to their confessions, the scheme had been hatched earlier that day when seven of them went to visit their friend Kuang Laoqi, an unsuccessful Hunanese merchant who lived outside the city walls. They "began to talk about their poverty" (*jiangqi pinku*), and Kuang spoke up with an idea. He had noticed that a nearby moneychanger often had a female visitor from across the river that ran behind his shop and suspected that the man was keeping a prostitute.² Why not dress up as an official street patrol and squeeze some money out of him?

The others agreed, and Kuang bought some supplies from street vendors: an official's cap, five iron chains and five locks, and a patrol lantern. Thus equipped, the little band set out that evening, with Kuang playing the role of Deputy for Inspecting the Streets and the others posing as guards and runners. Bursting into the moneychanger's shop, they accused him of harboring gamblers and prostitutes and made as if to drag him off to the district magistrate. Then, one of the "guards" offered to plead for leniency on his behalf, in exchange for a fee. The frightened merchant paid 160 silver dollars and was released on the spot. Discarding the hat, chains, and other objects, the phony patrol scattered. The authorities caught all but two of the men within a year, and Kuang Laoqi was sentenced to death by strangulation.

Kuang and his friends were by no means the first to commit such a crime.

The Qing archives in Beijing and Taipei contain scores of similar case records for the Yongzheng, Qianlong, and Jiaqing periods (1723–1820). In 1734, for instance, a Guangdong engraver and three accomplices were caught running a phony tax-remittance scam. Working the countryside in Chaoyang district, they contracted to deliver landowners' taxes but gave forged receipts to the unsuspecting victims and kept all of the money for themselves instead of taking it to local officials. The engraver's confession read in part, "Because my family was poor and I had no way to make a living [*jia pin wuji yingsheng*] . . . I came up with the idea of carving a phony seal for tax collection receipts, to swindle some money to live on."[3]

In another case in 1760, district authorities in Xiangtan, Hunan, arrested one Yu Heng, a suspicious character claiming to be on a mission for the Board of War. In his baggage, they found forged travel permits and the white hat-button and blue plume of an imperial guardsman. Under questioning, Yu admitted that he was a minor yamen underling from the capital. His family was "poverty-stricken" (*jiazhong qiongku*), and recently his father had fallen gravely ill. In desperation, Yu had slipped out of the capital, setting out for Hunan in the hope of borrowing money from in-laws and his father's old friends. The guardsman costume was merely a device to impress his prospective lenders and stimulate their generosity.[4]

These three records share an element common to the vast majority of fraud cases in the archives: a simple economic motivation behind the crime. In 138 of the cases for which motivation is evident, the perpetrators acted either to obtain money or to avoid spending it; forged documents and phony personae were tools for extorting money, freeloading off men of means, and gaining access to lodging, transport, and provisions at official courier stations. Fifty-three of these cases, moreover, have something else in common: a clear statement that the offender acted out of poverty. This number rises to sixty-two—nearly half—with the inclusion of case reports that ascribe the offense to indebtedness.

Unfortunately for the perpetrators of these crimes, the late imperial state took a dim view of frauds who appropriated official authority to carry out their schemes. This chapter explores an apparent contradiction between criminal motivation and its legal interpretation and punishment. Comparison of case summaries and penal statutes in mid-Qing fraud cases reveals that sentencing reflected an awkward convergence of economic narrative and political context. In many cases, a rhetorical depiction of criminals driven to their deeds by poverty helped mediate this tension.[5] Before considering these poverty tales more closely, it will be useful to consider the larger legal and political context that produced them.

FRAUD AS POLITICS: THE *ZHAWEI* STATUTES

When a con man—even a quite petty one—made use of the state, he entered the realm of political crime and punishment. Both *The Ming Code* and *The Qing Code* devoted a special section to such offenders. Titled the *zhawei* (*zha* as in "deception," and *wei* as in "false" or "counterfeit") section, it was one of eleven sections in the "Punishments" division of each *Code*.[6] *Zhawei* has been variously translated into English as "forgeries and frauds," "deception and fraud," "fraud and counterfeit," and, most recently, "forgeries and counterfeiting."[7] It carries similar meanings in modern Chinese, and on first sight one might suppose that the *zhawei* section of the *Code* encompassed confidence games and marketplace deceptions, or simply fraud in general. In fact, it was much narrower in scope.

The *zhawei* article headings in *The Great Qing Code* have been translated as follows: 355, "Counterfeiting an Imperial Written Order" (Zhawei zhishu); 356, "Falsely Transmitting an [Oral] Expression of the Imperial Will" (Zhachuan zhaozhi); 357, "Replying or Addressing a Petition to the Emperor in a Way That Is Not in Accordance with the Facts" (Duizhi shangshu zha buyishi); 358, "Counterfeiting Seals, Almanacs, and the Like" (Weizao yinxin shixianshu deng); 359, "Privately Casting Copper Cash" (Sizhu tongqian); 360, "Falsely Impersonating an Official" (Zha jiaguan); 361, "Falsely Claiming to Be One in Close Attendance on the Emperor, an Imperial Secretary, or Another Official" (Zhacheng neishi dengguan); 362, "Court Attendants Who Falsely Claim to Be Charged with a Private Mission" (Jinshi zhacheng sixing); 363, "Fraudulently Inventing a Good Omen" (Zhawei ruiying); 364, "Feigning Sickness, Death, or Injury to Avoid Tasks" (Zha bingsishang bishi); and 365, "Craftily Enticing Another to Commit an Offence" (Zha jiaoyouren fanfa).[8]

Several common threads run through this list. The key term and basic unifying concept is *zha*, which appears prominently in all but two (Articles 358, 359) of the eleven article headings. The treatise on punishment and law in the standard history of the Jin dynasty (266–316) defines *zha* as "treachery and cunning" (*beixin cangqiao*). Wang Kentang cites this definition in his commentary on *The Ming Code*, and the late-Qing official and legal scholar Xue Yunsheng reproduced it in his *Combined Edition of the Tang and Ming Codes* (Tang Ming lü hebian).[9] The commentary on Article 368 of *The Tang Code*

("Not Reporting the True Circumstances in Replying to an Imperial Decree or in Submitting Documents to the Emperor") defines *zha* more specifically as "knowing something and concealing it to cheat another person, or wanting to get or avoid something."[10]

This is helpful, but the *zhawei* section of both the Ming and Qing *Codes* was narrower in scope than its Tang ancestor. Comparing the Tang and Ming *Codes*, Xue Yunsheng complained that "the Tang Code totals twenty-seven articles, all matters of deception, regardless of what is falsified or who the criminal is, all lined up together in one place. The Ming Code has only one-third [of this number], the others separately appearing in various other statutes. How can it be that these few articles are *zhawei* and the other articles are not *zhawei*?"[11] This was a rhetorical question, reminding the reader that there were other crimes of deception scattered throughout *The Ming Code* (and its nearly identical Qing successor) and implying that, on this point, *The Tang Code* made more sense. We can take Xue's bemusement as a useful starting point, however, and revisit the question in its literal sense: "How can it be that these few articles are *zhawei* and other articles are not *zhawei*?" Why were these particular offenses grouped together in a special section?

The answer is that each article describes a form of misrepresentation that has some connection to the state. Three involve false pretense to official authority, five involve falsifying tools or symbols of state authority, and at least three involve deceiving officials or the throne. Even Article 365, "Craftily Enticing Another to Commit an Offense," falls into this category; its statutes emphasize luring an innocent person into crime and then reporting him to the authorities, bringing the wrath of the state down on the victim's head. In short, these statutes concern the fraudulent use of state authority and its instruments.

Shen Zhiqi's Commentary on The Great Qing Code

The clearest indication of the seriousness the state attached to a crime is the punishment prescribed for it in the *Code*. Eight of the eleven *zhawei* articles, and twelve of the thirty-five statutes they contain, prescribe a death sentence for the most serious offenses.[12] Article 355, "Counterfeiting an Imperial Written Order," is also listed under "Ten Abominations" (Shi e), heinous crimes calling for an irreducible sentence of death by slicing.[13]

The influential private commentary of Shen Zhiqi explains why these crimes incurred such harsh punishments—why, that is, they were so important. First published in 1715, Shen's commentary was included in part or in its entirety in most subsequent commentaries right up to the end of the Qing period.[14] It provides illuminating notes on the reasoning behind many of the statutes. The commentary on Article 355, "Counterfeiting an Imperial Written Order," for example, reads: "When *zhawei* reaches [the level of] an imperial written order, then it infringes on the authority of the Son of Heaven. Therefore, when it has already been carried out, all offenders are sentenced to decapitation, and when it has not been carried out, the principals are sentenced to strangulation, regardless of the seriousness of the circumstances."[15]

On the related crime of falsely transmitting an oral expression of the imperial will (Article 356), Shen went beyond "infringement" to suggest more concrete damage: "These [various commands] are all ones that ministers and people should receive obediently. If there is false transmission, then there must be selfish action and undermining of government. This is a great crime of deception and rashness [*qiwang*], and therefore the principals are sentenced to decapitation and strangulation, and accessories to a hundred strokes of the heavy bamboo and exile to three thousand *li*."[16]

The same principle applies in the commentary on Article 358, "Counterfeiting Seals, Almanacs, and the Like": "Seals, almanacs, delivery orders in the form of tallies, copper night-patrol tags, and tea or salt licenses—these five things are all bestowed by the Court and accepted as authentication by all under Heaven. They are extremely important, and therefore for forgery the principals are [sentenced] to decapitation."[17]

Article 359, "Privately Casting Copper Cash," is especially revealing. Although both copper coins and precious metals were instruments of market exchange, it was forgery of the less valuable coins that brought the greater punishment: strangulation after the assizes, as opposed to one hundred strokes with the heavy bamboo and three years of penal servitude for counterfeiting silver and gold. Shen explains the disparity in terms of political authority: "That the punishment for privately casting [copper cash] is heavy is probably because authority in the law of money comes from above. Privately casting then breaks prohibitions and violates the law, so the law is severe. The production of gold and silver comes from the earth; forgers are merely deceiving people to obtain profit, and so the law is light."[18] The Ming era commentator Lei Menglin makes the point more succinctly: "The authority to mint money resides with the Emperor (Shang), [and the law] detests the infringement of the imperial prerogative."[19]

Finally, Shen's commentary on Article 361, "Falsely Claiming to Be One in Close Attendance on the Emperor, an Imperial Secretary, or Another Official," reads in part: "those who, villainous and discontent, dare to claim to be one in close attendance on the emperor or an official . . . and invent the pretext of investigating matters outside the capital so as to deceive officials and delude the people, shall be beheaded. Villainous deceit to this point corrupts government and harms the people. The implications are not minor, and therefore the law is extremely severe."[20]

In short, Shen Zhiqi's commentaries explain the severity of the *zhawei* sentences in terms of the political implications and consequences of the crimes. *Zhawei* offenses "infringe on the authority of the Son of Heaven," "undermine government," and "corrupt government and harm the people." That is why the *Code* contained this category, and why we have case records to speak for it today.

Recognizing the Petty

Its strong political orientation notwithstanding, the *Code* did recognize that some crimes were less serious than others. This is obvious in the structure of the statutes, which prescribe successively lighter punishments for lesser variations of a given crime. Under Article 361, "Falsely Claiming to Be One in Close Attendance on the Emperor, an Imperial Secretary, or Another Official," for example, the punishment was beheading with delay for those who pretended to be on investigative missions and "deceived government offices and aroused the people." Those who claimed to be special envoys only for the purpose of gaining access to official courier stations, however, incurred a lighter sentence of exile to three thousand *li*. As Shen Zhiqi reasoned, the former was far more serious than the latter, in which "what is demanded is merely boats and horses."[21]

Such distinctions became more explicit in the eighteenth century with the promulgation of several new substatutes. An edict of 1727 introduced a clear distinction between serious political offenses and lesser crimes that involved only a small sum of money. The new substatute arose over the case of three men who forged the official seal of Maoming district, Guangdong, and stamped it on "rice tickets" (*mipiao*), which they then sold for profit. The Board of Punishments initially recommended immediate beheading, following a 1723 substatute that had increased the sentences for a host of forgery offenses. Instead of approving the recommendation, however, the Yongzheng emperor called for a revised sentence and a new law:

> The three of them shared 3,100 *wen* in cash, not a large amount and not comparable to using a fake seal to obtain an official post, which is a great transgression of the law. In the past, [the Board of Punishments] has only

deliberated and settled on the provision that counterfeiting a seal be punished with immediate beheading. As to the scale of the impropriety and the relative seriousness of the offense committed, these have not been carefully distinguished. This is not yet appropriate.[22]

The result was a revised substatute that retained the heavy punishments of the 1723 version for major transgressions involving military matters, government monies obtained under false pretenses, or impersonation of an official. At the same time, however, it introduced a distinction: If the crime involved only scheming to defraud for money and did not touch on one of these special areas, then the lighter, pre-1723 punishment, of beheading with delay, applied when large sums (more than ten taels or ten strings of cash) were involved; for lesser sums, the punishment would be lighter still (one hundred strokes of the heavy bamboo and exile to a distance of three thousand *li*).[23]

Thus, the new substatute contained a key innovation. While retaining harsh penalties for especially serious crimes, it reduced the punishments for simple schemes involving small sums of money. For counterfeits falling between these two extremes—that is, counterfeits that were not simple money scams but did not reach the newly defined high level of seriousness—the punishments prescribed in the original statute applied. As before, all of the crimes involved falsifying official seals, but the new standards explicitly recognized that within this broad category there was a distinction to be made between politically damaging offenses and petty economic ones.

This substatute was the basis for another, promulgated in 1740, that specifically addressed counterfeit calendars. In cosmo-political theory, an accurate calendar was a key factor in the reigning dynasty's ability to regulate the social order and thereby perpetuate its ruling mandate. The calendar was therefore an extremely important document, and through most of Chinese history, successive dynasties had attempted to enforce a monopoly on its production.[24] Political implications were the obvious if unstated reason for the inclusion of calendar forgery in the *zhawei* section of the Ming and Qing *Codes*.

Sometime in the mid-1730s, the court official Tang Suizu, citing the new substatute of 1727, proposed a reduction in the punishment for certain almanac forgeries.[25] Tang observed that, due to the insufficient supply of official almanacs in remote areas, "ignorant people" often copied the official editions and sold them for little more than ten taels apiece. Fearing that it would be difficult to deceive people without the official seal, they used yellow pigment (suggesting imperial provenance) to paint its likeness on the cover—but without the characters. With the seals neither carved nor traced,

Tang suggested, the crime perfectly matched that of "forging the seals of the various yamen but only intending to swindle money or property, the amount obtained not great, less than ten taels." He argued that the sentence handed out to almanac counterfeiters, decapitation, was therefore excessive.[26]

The Codification Office concurred, and the Qianlong emperor approved the change in 1740. The new substatute read: "In cases in which small-time merchants seek profit by copying almanacs in the official format and selling them, using yellow lead [*huangdan*] to draw the likeness of the official seal but without tracing the characters, they shall be variously punished in accord with the substatute 'In cases of counterfeiting the official seals of various yamen but only intending to swindle money, with the amount obtained not great. . . . '"[27]

Two substatutes of 1759 similarly modified Article 360, "Falsely Impersonating an Official." One reduced by one degree the sentences for criminals who assumed the name of a specific living and active official but did not forge an "identification certificate" (*pingzha*) and only planned a single deception of a solitary victim. The other prescribed reduced sentences for lesser crimes of those who wore official hat-buttons and falsely claimed to be officials, *shengyuan*, or *jiansheng* but were only scheming for "local glory" (*xiangli guangrong*), did not attempt to commit extortion, and used no identification certificate.[28]

The Limits of Depoliticization

Taken together, the new substatutes of 1727, 1740, and 1759 reflect an increasing willingness to distinguish between greater and lesser deceptions. This tendency had its limits, however. The tension between the petty and the political is evident in the discourse on counterfeit almanacs. The above-mentioned substatute of 1740 (providing lighter punishments for merchants who sold cheap replicas of the official calendar that bore only a crude representation of the Directorate of Astronomy's seal) was abolished just four years later, following the Board of Punishments' recommendation on two grounds. First, the Yongzheng emperor had in 1729 already authorized copying and sale of exact replicas of the official calendar in the provinces. The later substatute was therefore superfluous.[29] This certainly followed the principle that some forgeries did not merit overly harsh penalties. The board's second point of argument, however, reasserted the original principle that illegitimate almanacs—those that were not exact copies of the official calendar—could not be tolerated:

> The calendar is [the means by which] the heavenly king respectfully delivers the seasons to the people on the first day of the new year. If it is coun-

terfeited ... there is no greater irreverence than this. That is why the law is so heavy. If those who copy almanacs in the official format and use yellow lead to draw the likeness of the official seal are all sentenced to [mere] exile, this is sentencing without regard to whether the criminal has committed forgery, but only with regard to whether or not he has carved the seal of the Directorate of Astronomy.... We request that henceforward if there is a forged almanac that is completely different from the text of the original, judgment still be passed in accordance with the statute.[30]

The emperor agreed, and the substatute was repealed.[31] This marked a reaffirmation of the *Code*'s fundamental political orientation. While not rejecting the principle that in some cases forgery for paltry economic gain should be subject to lighter punishments (the sweeping forgery substatute of 1727 remained in effect), the state was insisting that certain crimes—petty economic motivation notwithstanding—were politically intolerable and therefore required extreme penalties. Private almanac production, as opposed to faithful copying of the official calendar, was first and foremost a political offense.

Taking these developments on seal and almanac forgery together, we can see a gradual clarification of the forgery statutes (Article 358) in the eighteenth century. At the same time that it introduced a new principle of relative leniency for obviously petty economic crimes, the state also increased punishments for crimes that compromised its authority or interfered with the smooth operation of government administration.

CRIME MEETS *CODE*: IMPLICIT NARRATIVE AND THE DEFUSING OF POLITICAL CRIMES

In the Ming and Qing *Codes*, *zhawei* was a fundamentally political and state-centered category, but statutory changes in the middle Qing partially depoliticized some of these offenses. What did all this mean for practice, in the official investigation, interpretation, and representation of actual criminal cases?

Bureaucratic Scripting: Code, Interrogation, and Reporting

Brian McKnight has written that *The Tang Code* contains "implicit rules of judicial procedure."[32] Case records suggest that this was also true of *The Qing Code*, its distinctions among and gradations of various crimes and punishments translating into procedural guidelines for interrogation, reporting, sentencing, and review. This is most obvious in routine memorials compiled at the capital in the later stages of a case, but the logic of the statutes and substatutes is also evident in confessions and other depositions appended to or cited in provincial memorials. Crime narratives tended to follow the *Code* in both general flow and particular details.

For example, the basic statutes of Article 358, "Counterfeiting Seals, Almanacs, and the Like," prescribed a sentence of beheading with delay for counterfeiting a yamen seal.[33] Substatutes addressed how much money the perpetrator(s) obtained; the aforementioned distinction between small-time offenses and major transgressions involving military matters and so on; and whether to treat the carver of a seal as principal or accessory (depending on whether the crime was his idea or someone hired him to do it).[34] In the report on the tax-remittance scam discussed above, the engraver Lin Asi's interrogation includes questions directly related to Article 358: "Why did you forge and use counterfeit seals and receipts, on what date did you do the carving, what seal did you forge, truly how many partners were there, how many receipts did you stamp, and how much silver did you swindle?"[35] Lin answered that he forged the district seal and that of the provincial administration commission so he could make money by pretending to remit people's tax payments for them. He admitted to making a profit of fifteen taels. The interrogators then pressed him as to how much money he and his accomplices "really" made, and whether he had used the seals to commit other abuses. Lin insisted he had told all. "It is only because I am poor and have nothing to live on [*pinqiong wu ke liaosheng*] that I thought of carving fake seals and stamping them on tax receipts, planning to swindle some silver to get by on. I didn't dare do anything else."

The acting district magistrate concluded, "Lin Asi carved a fake seal and deceitfully obtained silver in excess of ten taels. He should, in accordance with the substatute on the carver as principal . . . be sentenced to beheading with delay."[36] Thus, the interrogations and confessions (and the recommended sentence) clearly follow a design implicit in the *Code* itself, the only apparent departure being the chief criminal's declaration that he acted out of poverty.

Narrative Manipulations

The *Code* was, of course, subject to circumvention. In *zhawei* cases, the tension between economics (in criminal motivation) and politics (embodied in the *Code*) was conducive to certain kinds of rhetorical manipulation in official reporting. Judgments—and the depositions preceding them in a report—could alternately amplify or minimize a criminal's activities in order to channel the narrative toward a desired outcome. One such device was the rhetoric of indignation. Case records yield numerous instances of an official identifying a crime and noting its statutory punishment but protesting that said punishment is insufficient; the law was not stern enough.

For example, in 1765, Dong Zhengyu, an unsuccessful Yunnanese scholar turned farmer, was in debt. Hoping to impress acquaintances so that he could borrow money from them, he forged personal letters, a Peking gazette announcement, and ultimately an imperial decree—all to create the fiction that his long-lost brother had made good and been appointed a regional commander in northern China.[37] In their joint memorial on the case, the governor of Yunnan and the Yunnan-Guizhou governor-general concluded,

> Dong Zhengyu, scheming to swindle silver, forged an imperial decree and falsely claimed that his younger brother Dong Guozuo had become an official. He should, according to the statute . . . be sentenced to beheading with delay. However, the words he forged were wildly absurd and contemptuous of law and discipline. We therefore request a decree ordering the Board to enter the case under "circumstances deserving of capital punishment" at this year's autumn assizes, promptly executing him in order to [let his fate] serve as a warning.[38]

Just as a crime could be amplified, so, too, could it be minimized. The most direct way to achieve this was to change the facts of the case. In 1771, the acting governor of Hunan, Wudashan, received a report that a dismissed yamen underling had been arrested for forging the Anxiang district seal. The man had collected a landowner's tax payment and pretended to remit it on his behalf, stamping the phony seal on the official stub attached to the land deed.[39] In the interrogation record that district authorities forwarded to the provincial capital, the forger declared he had swindled only this one time, destroying the seal afterward. Wudashan was skeptical:

> Your minister finds that when the various departments and districts handle seal-forgery cases, they always allow the criminal to make a cunning confession, claiming either that the characters were incomplete after the carving, or that he had not been perpetrating the crime for very long and had not swindled much money. Some [reports] even falsely turn clerks into

commoners, scheming to avoid administrative sanctions and close the case lightly. Such abuse is widespread.

Now in this case, if Wang Xueyin only swindled some two thousand cash, how could he have been willing to violate the law? . . . We must thoroughly root out the truth as to really in what year the carving was done, how many receipts were used, whether the criminal was an official underling, and whether there were fellow conspirators; and then pass heavy sentences. Only this will suffice to punish knavery and block deception.

The governor had Wang interrogated again, and this time he confessed he had been swindling in this way since 1766, not 1770. On the basis of this revelation, he was sentenced to immediate execution.

In this instance, local officials had tried to minimize the crime by suppressing the facts of the case, characterizing the culprit as a one-time offender when in fact he had been plying his trade for years. The two conflicting narratives represented the interests of Wudashan on the one side (wanting to get to the bottom of the matter) and Wang and local officials on the other (Wang hoping for the lightest possible sentence, and district officials hoping to avoid punishment for their negligence in allowing him to go undetected for years on end).[40]

POVERTY AS A RHETORICAL DEVICE

This chapter began with the observation that in addition to obvious references to the culprit's desire for material gain, many *zhawei* case reports contain a direct statement that he acted out of poverty. In some memorials, this assertion comes in the criminal's deposition (e.g., "Because my family was poor and I had no way to make a living . . . " or "It is only because I am poor and have nothing to live on . . . "). In others, it appears in the official summary ("They began talking about how poor they all were"), while in still others, it can be found in both sections. What was the point of these assertions, and who put them there? One obvious possibility is that the culprits had indeed acted out of poverty and said as much in their confessions, and officials were simply relaying the facts in their reports. Another is that short poverty narratives appeared in the record simply to help explain how and why a criminal "got the idea" (*qiyi*) to act, identification of the mastermind and his motives being important factors in determining the appropriate punishment.

In his analysis of rhetorical questions in Qing law and literature, however, Robert Hegel makes a convincing argument that the criminal case report is a persuasive text carefully constructed to, first, represent an exhaustive investigation and proper judgment and, second, present the crime as an aberration in an otherwise harmonious and well-regulated society. Within this text, even seemingly authentic utterances of criminals and witnesses are best understood as rhetorical devices that serve the magistrate's overall purpose of precluding alternative interpretations and thereby protecting him from accusations of poor judgment or misconduct.[41] This approach does not require that we dismiss every statement in the case narrative as pure invention, but it does call for consciousness on the reader's part that each element of the text has been included and situated for a reason. It is useful to bring this understanding to the reading of *zhawei* cases. What was the rhetorical function of the poverty tale?

From the viewpoints of throne and provincial officialdom, a *zhawei* case was a potentially dangerous matter. Often, the first report to the capital was a short confidential memorial from a provincial governor, submitted when the culprit was still at large and yet to be identified or had just been arrested but had not yet been thoroughly interrogated. At this stage, it was an open question as to whether the imposture was relatively innocuous (a ne'er-do-well hoping to impress his relatives, a local troublemaker extorting a few cash) or something more serious. Repeated, systematic fraud could undermine the government's prestige. More worrisome still, the specter of treason loomed in the background; through much of Chinese history, rebels had gained recruits by conferring ranks and offices, an outright challenge to the ruling dynasty. The ideal outcome to a report of *zhawei*, for both the dynasty and local officials, was a speedy arrest followed by an investigation establishing that the crime was petty, the perpetrators few, and the damage minimal.

Students of Qing history learn to scan memorials for "documentary signposts," special terms that mark the flow of reports and instructions up, down, and across the official hierarchy.[42] One can picture another array of signposts comprising conventional expressions and rhetorical devices used to characterize people and events, guiding the reader toward certain conclusions.[43] Just as we use documentary signposts to follow the administrative process in legal case reports, so could we use rhetorical signposts to decode the crime-and-punishment narratives in the same documents.[44] The poverty clause ("Because I was poor . . . ," "Because he had no livelihood . . . ") may be such a signpost. Short, direct, and appearing near the beginning of a deposition or official crime summary, it suggests to the reader that the offense was based in personal economic distress and was not consciously political.[45] In other words, the poverty statement would have indicated to higher officials that the case

Poverty Tales and Statutory Politics 155

had been scrutinized for political intent and found to be safe. In this sense, it reflected the tension between competing characterizations of *zhawei* crimes as petty economic fraud and as grave political transgression. Having established (or wishing to establish) the absence of political intent, magistrates could use poverty to channel the case into the safe economic interpretation, defusing the ominous political import of the statutes. This characterization stood to shield the magistrate, reassure his superiors and the throne, and perhaps save the criminal from the full weight of the law.

CONCLUSION

I believe that the *zhawei* statutes served, or were intended to serve, two purposes. One was to defend the state's functional and symbolic integrity by punishing those who presumed to infringe on its prerogatives. The other was to screen all such infringements for overtly political intent, distinguishing mere greed and presumptuousness from lèse-majesté. To forge an official document was to misappropriate a basic tool of governance, and to present oneself to others as an official was to usurp prerogatives of the reigning dynasty and its appointed agents. In the rulers' eyes, both crimes were but a step away from treason, the appointment of officials and issue of various credentials and other documents being classic gestures of open opposition to the state. Any false pretense of official authority, however lowly, was at the least a symbolic usurpation, and anyone caught assuming the official facade would find his actions held up for special scrutiny. Investigation and sentencing involved ordering the facts of the case on a scale of political significance; the greater the misappropriation of official authority, the more serious the crime. Moreover, even when, as usually happened, officials became satisfied that there was no political intent in a case, the *Code* still required sentencing in terms of political content or effect. This was the larger political context in which even the humblest of petty frauds found himself when he made use of the state.

Case records indicate that most *zhawei* criminals—forgers of government documents and impersonators of officials and their underlings—were small-time operators, in it for the money or free travel. There are few signs of deeper motives, and statutory changes in the middle decades of the eighteenth century clearly reflected an official perception that some crimes did not merit the harsh punishments the *Code* prescribed. The Yongzheng emperor's edict on minor economic crimes, the debate over counterfeit calendars, and the 1759 substatutes on impersonators who did not go so far as to forge identity documents all suggest a partial softening in the official view of *zhawei* offenses.

In the repertoire of tropes and other narrative devices that officials could use when characterizing criminal activities, the poverty tale was well suited for the interpretive space between economic crime and political punishment.

NOTES

I am grateful for the comments and suggestions of two anonymous readers on an earlier version of this chapter; for those of my fellow conferees, especially Katherine Carlitz, Robert Hegel, Yasuhiko Karasawa, and Jonathan Ocko; and to Nancy Park, Allison Rottmann, Ling Shiao, and John Williams, who critiqued the first draft. Any errors and weaknesses are my responsibility.

1. My narrative of this case closely follows the confessions reproduced in a memorial submitted to the throne on January 18, 1807, and now housed in the First Historical Archive, Beijing. XKTB Qita (other), JQ 11, juan 217, JQ 11.12.10 (memorial of Dong Gao et al.).

2. The woman was his wife, who frequently crossed the river to visit her mother.

3. XKTB, Qita, QL 1, juan 307, QL 1.7.29 (memorial of Yang Yongbin).

4. LFZZ, QL, Falü, Qita, QL 25.5.11 (memorial of Feng Qian).

5. My chief sources are case records from the Qing archives in Beijing and Taipei and the fraud statutes of *The Great Qing Code*. The archival records comprise a sample of 227 criminal cases spanning the period 1720–1820. They include confidential "palace memorials" (*zhupi zouzhe*) or their "file copies" (*lufu zouzhe*) on 167 cases and routine memorials under the "violations of prohibitions" (*weijin*) and "other" (*qita*) categories of the Grand Secretariat's Punishments Office of Scrutiny (*Neige xingke tiben, XKTB*) on 60 more. Even for such relatively uncommon crimes (compared to the likes of murder, theft, adultery, and land disputes), the size of the XKTB collection precluded a year-by-year search; I screened it at five-year intervals.

6. *The Qing Code* comprised 436 articles in seven major divisions, one titled "Names and General Rules" and the others named for the Six Boards of central government administration (Personnel, Revenue, Rites, War, Punishments, and Works). For English equivalents of Chinese legal terms, I generally follow Jones, *The Great Qing Code*. I also consulted Bodde and Morris, *Law in Imperial China*; and Johnson, *The T'ang Code*.

7. See, respectively, Staunton, *Ta Tsing Leu Lee*, 392; Bodde and Morris, *Law in Imperial China*, 209; Johnson, *The T'ang Code*, vol. 1, 286, and vol. 2, 419; and Jones, *The Great Qing Code*, 339.

8. Jones, *The Great Qing Code*, xxvi–xxvii; *DLTY*, vol. 1, 115–22.

9. Qiu Hanping, *Lidai xingfazhi*, vol. 1, 160; Xue Yunsheng, *Tang Ming lü hebian*, 668, citing Wang Kentang's *Lüli jianshi*.

10. Changsun Wuji, *Tanglü shuyi*, 576, *juan* 25; Johnson, *The T'ang Code*, vol. 2, 419 n. 1, 429. The subcommentary explains that "wanting to get or avoid something refers to such things as wrongly seeking a reward or avoiding punishment."

11. Xue Yunsheng, *Tang Ming lü hebian*, 681.

12. By comparison, the *Collected Statutes* of 1899 estimates that 20 percent of the offenses in the Code (813 of a total of 3,987) were punishable by death. *Qinding Da Qing huidian*, 54, 1a–b, cited in Bodde and Morris, *Law in Imperial China*, 103–4.

13. Article 2 of the *Code*. The crime falls under the sixth abomination, "Great Lack of Respect" (or, in Wallace Johnson's rendition, "great irreverence" [*da bujing*]). *DLCY*, vol. 2, 17; Jones, *The Great Qing Code*, 35; Johnson, *The T'ang Code*, vol. 1, 69.

14. See Fu-mei Chang Chen, "Influence of Shen Chih-chi," and the collators' preface to Shen Zhiqi, *"Da Qing lü" jizhu*.

15. Shen Zhiqi, *"Da Qing lü" jizhu*, 889 (upper commentary).

16. Ibid., 891 (general commentary).

17. Ibid., 895 (general commentary).

18. Ibid., 899 (upper commentary).

19. Lei Menglin, *Dulü suoyan*, 439.

20. Shen Zhiqi, *"Da Qing lü" jizhu*, 904 (general commentary).

21. Jones, *The Great Qing Code*, 344–45; Shen Zhiqi, *"Da Qing lü" jizhu*, 905 (upper commentary).

22. *Qinding da Qing huidian shili (Jiaqing chao)*, 61:3188–89, *juan* 639: 6b–7. See chapter 5, by Thomas Buoye, in this volume for a discussion of the Chinese legal system's general (but also limited) predilection for leniency in the adjudication of capital cases.

23. Wu Tan, *"Da Qing lüli" tongkao*, 929; *Qinding da Qing huidian shili (Jiaqing chao)*, 61:3184–85, *juan* 639: 4b–5.

24. Richard J. Smith, *Chinese Almanacs*, 1–10.

25. Tang (d. 1753) was vice minister in the Court of Imperial Sacrifices from 1733 to July 21, 1738. Wu Tan, *"Da Qing lüli" tongkao*, 931, 932 n.17.

26. Wu Tan, *"Da Qing lüli" tongkao*, 931. See Pengsheng Chiu's chapter in this volume for a nuanced discussion of growing official sympathy for merchant interests, evident in mid-Qing legal discourse on insolvency and negligence.

27. Ibid.; *Qinding da Qing huidian shili (Jiaqing chao)*, 61:3187, *juan* 639: 6.

28. Wu Tan, *"Da Qing lüli" tongkao*, 943; *DLCY*, vol. 5, 1070, substatute 360-

06. The two substatutes were combined into one in 1809. *Shengyuan* and *jiansheng*, commonly denoting lower gentrymen, more specifically designated government students (or anyone eligible to sit for prefectural examinations) and Imperial Academy students, respectively. Hucker, *Dictionary of Official Titles*, entries 5193, 856.

29. Wu Tan, "Da Qing lüli" tongkao, 931.

30. Ibid. The phrase "respectfully delivers the seasons to the people" (*jing shou renshi*), a conventional expression for distributing the official calendar, comes from the *Classic of History* (Shujing), Book of Tang, Canon of Yao. *Hanyu da cidian*, vol. 5, 488. This English rendering is from Legge, *Chinese Classics*, vol. 3, 18.

31. Ibid.

32. McKnight, "T'ang Law and Later Law," 410–12, 420.

33. Jones, *The Great Qing Code*, 342; DLCY, vol. 5, 1056, *juan* 42.

34. Huang Zhangjian, *Mingdai lüli huibian*, 919–20; Shen Zhiqi, "Da Qing lü" jizhu, 896–97; Wu Tan, "Da Qing lüli" tongkao, 929–31; *Qinding da Qing huidian shili (Jiaqing chao)*, 61:3183–89, *juan* 639: 4–7; DLCY, vol. 5, 1056–60.

35. XKTB, Qita, QL 1, *juan* 307, QL 1.7.29 (Yang Yongbin).

36. Ibid. Fortunately for Lin and his partners, the crimes fell under the general amnesties of October and December 1735, and the final recommendation was that their sentences be suspended.

37. *Gongzhongdang Qianlongchao zouzhe* 25: 14-17, QL 30.5.18 (memorial of Liu Cao and Changyun).

38. *Gongzhongdang Qianlongchao zouzhe* 25: 15–16. The emperor had the report forwarded to the Board of Punishments for review.

39. The following paragraphs are based on LFZZ, QL, *Falü*, undated memorial of QL 40 (Wudashan). QL 40 (1775) is probably an archival error; Wudashan's known dates of tenure (and death in 1771), combined with internal evidence from the memorial itself, suggest a date sometime in the second or third month of QL 36 (1771).

40. See Jonathan Ocko's discussion of "dueling interpretive communities" in chapter 12 in this volume.

41. See Robert Hegel's discussion in chapter 4 in this volume.

42. Fairbank, *Ch'ing Documents*, 41.

43. See the discussion of "routinization of reporting" in Qing homicide cases in Buoye, "Suddenly Murderous Intent," 66–67.

44. Collectively, the chapters in this volume consider a broad range of such devices, many of them denoting particular character types and social ideals. See, for example, Maram Epstein on "sympathetic characterizations" of male defendants in homicide cases, in chapter 1; Janet Theiss on the shrew, in chapter 2;

Yasuhiko Karasawa on dissolute Buddhist monks, in chapter 3; Robert Hegel on harmonious neighborhoods, in chapter 4; Thomas Buoye on filial felons, in chapter 5; and Pengsheng Chiu on "merchants far away from home," in chapter 6.

45. Similarly, in chapter 5 in this volume, Thomas Buoye argues that magistrates routinely portrayed capital criminals as "otherwise decent people who inadvertently caused a death under duress in extraordinary circumstances."

8 Indictment Rituals and the Judicial Continuum in Late Imperial China

PAUL R. KATZ

Ritual played an integral role in the construction of legal culture in late imperial China. Evidence indicates that people of all social classes attempted to obtain justice by performing ritual supplications addressed to the gods of the underworld, especially the City God (Chenghuang), the Emperor of the Eastern Peak (Dongyue Dadi), and the Bodhisattva Dizang (Dizangwang Pusa). Such rites, which constitute judicial rituals (*shenpan yishi*, lit. "rites of divine judgment"), were generally performed in temples to the deities mentioned above, or at least in front of their statues. Late imperial judicial rituals were many and varied, but the most common appear to have been "oaths" (*lishi*); "oaths or curses accompanied by the beheading of a chicken" (*zhan jitou*); and "filing indictments" (*fanggao* or *gao yinzhuang*).[1]

This chapter considers what indictment rituals reveal about late imperial Chinese ideas of divine justice as well as how ritual fit into the larger context of Chinese legal practices. While a growing body of research has begun to consider the social history of Chinese law, including the importance of private mediation, relatively little work has been done on ritual remedies for disputes.[2] Preliminary research indicates that dispute resolution in late imperial China involved a wide range of practices, including private mediation, filing plaints at the magistrate's yamen, and performing rituals. These practices could be done in succession or, in some cases, in tandem. Moreover, even some late imperial officials did not hesitate to make offerings to judicial deities when dealing with seemingly insoluble cases and, on occasion, even moved trials to their temples.

Some might argue that since the rites to be described here do not fully adhere to official legal practices, they might better be termed "quasi-judicial." Judicial rites clearly were religious events and, like all other rituals in China, involved burning incense and making offerings to the gods. However, these rites were held by people who identified themselves as plaintiffs, defendants, or witnesses and were staged in temples; they were addressed to bureaucratic deities that were often arranged to resemble a magistrate's yamen and featured standardized plaints often referred to as "petitions" (*cheng*).

Regrettably, very few firsthand accounts of indictment rituals exist, and because plaints filed with the gods were burned, precious few texts survive. Thus, primary sources for this study range from more conventionally historiographical sources written by local officials and other commentators on legal administration, through eyewitness reports by nineteenth-century foreigner observers, to more recent field research. Other important sources include "gazetteers on local customs" (*fengsu zhi*) compiled during the late imperial and modern eras and works of fiction, especially *biji xiaoshuo*, or informal writings. The pursuit of justice is also a common theme in courtroom dramas, Mulian operas, and crime tales from the late Ming and late Qing.[3] Inasmuch as indictment rituals have a long history dating back to ancient times, other sources include data from ethnographic accounts, including the results of ongoing field research at the Dizang Abbey (Dizang An), a popular temple located in the city of Xinzhuang (Hsin-chuang) just south of Taipei dedicated to the Bodhisattva Dizang and a controller of unruly ghosts known as the Lord of the Hordes (Dazhong Ye).

Attempting to make any generalizations based on such a diverse body of data is admittedly highly risky, particularly since the sources mentioned above were written for different purposes and with different audiences in mind and underwent diverse processes of transmission and reception. We also should not assume that all the accounts described below are of equal validity in reflecting actual judicial ritual. Works of fiction might best be viewed as a means of corroborating findings in historical and ethnographic sources and as evidence that these practices were commonly known and were elaborated on and/or parodied in fictional texts by literati. While accounts of indictment rituals in works of fiction could be manipulated to serve artistic, political, and entertainment ends, it might not be wise to assume their pure "fictionality," as many literati did believe in the unseen world and the inevitability of divine retribution.[4] The diversity of all these texts should not prevent us from acknowledging one seemingly undisputable fact, however: people at all social levels over long periods of time saw the imperial judicial system as having a parallel in the divine realm, and they believed that both systems were interwoven and interacting.[5]

COMPARING LEGAL AND RITUAL INDICTMENTS

Before considering different representations of indictment rituals, it may be fruitful to consider the overlap between such rites and the actual filing of petitions or plaints, which were usually referred to as *cheng* (counterplaints were known as *su*).[6] In late imperial China, people could file five types of petitions. The first type encompassed plaints about matters some might compare to Western "civil law," including marriage, divorce, and disputes about commercial transactions or property.[7] Known as "fixed-date petitions" (*qicheng*), these documents could be submitted only on certain days of each lunar month, usually the third, eighth, thirteenth, eighteenth, twenty-third, and twenty-eighth. The second type, plaints about criminal cases such as those involving robbery or murder, were known as "summoning petitions" (*chuancheng*); in contrast to fixed-date petitions, they could be submitted at any time. The third type of petition, plaints submitted directly to local officials in the street, were known as "stopping the sedan chair" (*lanyu*) or "blocking the palanquin to express a grievance" (*lanjiao shenyuan*). There were formal prohibitions against this practice, and violators could be punished, but it persisted nevertheless. Fourth, verbal plaints known as "crying-out petitions" (*hancheng*) could be made at an official's yamen by an individual who had just witnessed a serious crime such as homicide. The fifth, petitions urging the magistrate's court to act on a particular case, were known as "prompting petitions" (*cuicheng*); these are the most common form of petition found in local archives. Petitions were filed on standardized forms, which had spaces for entering names of parties involved in a case, a grid for writing the petition, a preprinted entry detailing the name and rank of the official who was to review the case, a blank space where the official could write his endorsement of the petition and any additional comments, space for year-month-day entries that could be filled in with dates of earlier or subsequent actions related to the case, and finally a list of procedural rules for submitting a petition.[8]

Available evidence reveals some key similarities between performing indictment rituals and filing plaints at an official's yamen. For example, the texts used in both practices were often referred to using the Chinese term *cheng*, while another term (*fanggao*) was used to refer to both filing a fixed-date petition and performing an indictment ritual on a prearranged date, usually during the festival of an underworld deity. Moreover, indictment rites performed just after one had suffered an act of wrongdoing also appear somewhat similar to the summoning petitions and crying-out petitions mentioned above. Some individuals or lineage groups chose indictment rituals after a dispute had dragged on for a considerable period of time, a practice that resembles that of filing prompting petitions. Finally, aggrieved individuals did not hesitate to block palanquins of both officials and deities in order to state their cases. More evidence on actual legal and ritual practices will have to be collected before any definitive conclusions can be made, but at the very least, these similarities provide a basis for further explorations into the nature of the interaction between ritual and the law in the late imperial judicial continuum.

However, there is no denying the many important differences between actually filing an indictment at a yamen and performing an indictment ritual at a temple. Preliminary analysis identifies the following distinctions, many of which indicate that people may have found it easier to approach and seek justice from the gods rather than from earthly officials. Plaints used in indictment rituals tend to be shorter, less detailed, and confined to the basic facts of a particular case, compared to the petitions scholars have found in local archives. Plaints filed with the gods did not have to be based on actual law and were not necessarily rejected if they did not concur with the letter of the law, unlike petitions.[9] Ritual plaints could be composed by the plaintiffs themselves, although illiterate people had to hire specialists to write them out; in some cases, the plaint could be presented orally. Ritual plaints dealt with a wider range of issues than did petitions filed in earthly courts. While some indictment rituals were staged during festivals, most could be held anytime, regardless of the nature of the dispute. In theory, anyone could file a plaint, including the living, the dead, and other spiritual beings. Ritual plaints could be used to challenge the authority of the state or members of the local elite. Some ritual plaints could be accompanied by a blood sacrifice, including the beheading of a chicken, perhaps in order to redirect acts of violence away from the parties involved in the dispute and toward a helpless animal. Plaints were rarely rejected or acted upon immediately; instead, the process allowed for a waiting period in order to see if divine justice would occur.

Perhaps the most important difference is the last: regardless of the circumstances underlying their performance, many of the rites seem to have included a cooling-off period for the parties embroiled in a dispute.[10] While the gods invoked during such rites were not necessarily obliged to execute their grim judgments immediately, people did scrutinize what happened to the participants in the hours and days thereafter. Thus, it seems that while indictment rituals placed the issue of guilt in high relief, the performance of such a rite, and the period of waiting for divine judgment, may have allowed for tempers to cool and the entire matter to be brought to a peaceful resolution by more mundane means.

INDICTMENT RITUALS AMONG THE LIVING

Indictment rituals whereby people accused each other of crimes were almost invariably performed before underworld deities and involved the use of a plaint written on yellow paper. Some people recited their plaints aloud so that all could hear, while others preferred to read them sotto voce. We may also distinguish between indictment rituals in terms of whether or not they named the allegedly guilty party. In some cases, people entangled in legal disputes knew the alleged wrongdoer's identity and included his or her name in the text of the plaint. In others, people who had been victimized but could not identify the alleged criminal (a common occurrence in cases of theft) asked the gods to both track down and punish the guilty party.

Perhaps the most extensively studied example of public indictment rites involves those held in Wenzhou, Zhejiang, during the annual festival in honor of the plague-quelling deity Marshal Wen (Wen Yuanshuai).[11] According to an early-twentieth-century description of the ritual, the local rite of filing indictments was held at the "military drill grounds" (*jiaochang*) in the western suburbs during the procession to prevent outbreaks of epidemic. A placard was posted calling on all who were victims of unjust charges or who "harbored grievances" (*hanyuan yinhen*, lit. "held wrongs or had drunk resentment") to come forward and file indictments. Members of the temple committee, including an individual dressed as Wen's senior runner, helped supervise these rites. When all was ready, a runner would cry out that Marshal Wen was ready to preside over his "court" (*shengtang*, the same term used for civil officials when they ascended the bench). This was followed by the summoning of all men and women who were attempting to atone for their misdeeds by dressing as "criminals" (*fanren*) and "sinners" (*zuiren*) during the procession. Finally, the plaintiffs were allowed to enter. Each individual who chose to file an indictment had to dress in mourning and leave his or her hair in disarray.[12] Holding sticks of incense and carrying an "indictment" (*zhuang*) written on yellow paper, he or she would cry out: "Injustice [*yuanwang*]! Lord of the Eastern Peak [Marshal Wen], I implore you to right this wrong!" The plaintiff was initially driven back by men dressed as "judges" (*panguan*) and was allowed to approach Wen only after making three attempts to do so. Then, the plaintiff kneeled down and offered the indictment, crying continuously. Following this, the senior runner burned the indictment in an incense burner (in order to transmit it to the gods) and advised the plaintiff to retire.[13]

While some accounts state that those whom Marshal Wen deemed guilty would eventually suffer misfortune, or even death, it appears that the immediate administration of justice was not the purpose of such rites. It might make more sense to consider such ritual events as performative texts that featured reflexive processes of negotiation by which context-sensitive meanings and conflicting ideologies were brought into the open to be critically examined and interpreted by both the audience and the performers themselves.[14] Such performances also resembled official legal procedure, which, as Robert Hegel points out in his introduction to this volume, "was a spectacle designed to demonstrate the power of the state and to apply the authority of the cosmic moral order vested in the magistrate by his imperial appointment."[15] Thus, public indictment rites like those staged in late imperial Wenzhou confirm the presence of a judicial continuum featuring the interpenetration and even isomorphism of the earthly and spirit worlds. On a broader level, this may also be related to one key facet of Chinese cosmology—the idea that divine or spiritual power is not situated outside of or beyond the natural world (in other words, there was no idea of the "supernatural" in traditional China). Chinese of this time did not conceive of ritual as being outside of or beyond the law, thus blurring the boundary between ritual *in* legal practice and ritual *as* legal practice.

Similar indictment rites could be staged throughout other parts of southern Zhejiang but did not have to correspond to festivals. In Suichang county, indictments could be filed in the county seat's City God temple on the first and fifteenth days of each lunar month. As in the case of Wenzhou, such rites closely resembled dramatic performances, with people dressed up as yamen runners and clerks guiding plaintiffs through the different phases of each indictment ritual. Hundreds of people crowded into the temple to witness these rites.[16] We also have a number of accounts about indictment rites performed during the annual festival to the plague deities known as the Five Emperors (Wudi), which was held in the northern Fujian city of Fuzhou.[17] Perhaps the most striking aspect of these rituals is their close resemblance to actual trials in the magistrate's yamen. According to the 1871 edition of the *Fujian Provincial Gazetteer* (Fujian tongzhi), "When the officials make decisions, [the people] don't believe and don't obey, but rather must call the Five Emperors as witnesses and only then submit. The documents and ceremonies of their Heavenly Fairy Palace are majestic and upheld together with those of the officials."[18] This text shows that neither official nor ritual practices could command authority on their own; they coexisted with and were integrated by people of all classes into the late imperial judicial continuum. Fuzhou residents also staged trials in the presence of the Earth God or other tutelary deities, with the managers of these temples often serving as judges.[19]

In Taiwan today, public indictment rites performed during plague festivals have almost disappeared, apparently due to fears that they might provoke or exacerbate disputes. For example, in the southern Taiwan town of Xigang (Hsi-kang, in Tainan county), every three years, during the Royal Lords' Offering (*Wangjiao*), a plague boat expulsion festival, members of the local temple committee place a placard reading "filing indictments" (*fanggao*) outside the temple's main gate but then immediately remove it so as to prevent anyone from actually taking such action.[20] However, groups of people who feel they have been wronged may file indictments during processions by blocking the palanquins of local deities until they are allowed to state their cases.[21] People also do not hesitate to make impromptu pleas to elected officials who are visiting their constituents, and if the complaint is about a loved one who died wrongfully, family members often dress in mourning and bring the coffin of the deceased with them.

The performance of indictment rituals against the living did not necessarily have to coincide with large-scale festivals, however. Commoners and members of the elite also held indictment rituals in temples as a public means of engaging in symbolic or real acts of resistance to authority, when those accused of wrongdoing included landlords, members of the gentry, and even local magistrates. For example, during a 1640 uprising against the gentry in Wuxi county, Jiangsu, protesters compiled a list of seventeen grievances and presented them to the City God. Later, in 1740, when Suzhou weavers staged a protest because they felt they had been wronged by local officials, they prepared paper money and a yellow cloth containing a "list of grievances" (*yuandan*), with which they filed an indictment at the local City God temple. When the ritual was completed, they burned the paper money and yellow cloth in front of the official's home. Public indictment rites have also been performed during protracted disputes, including those that had entered the courts.[22]

The most common form of indictment ritual could be held in temples at any time as a response to real or perceived grievances. Witnesses and written texts were not required for such rituals, which were performed at least as early as the Song dynasty. According to one account preserved in the *Record of the Listener and Recorder* (Yijian zhi), by Hong Mai (1123–1201), a corrupt official and his son-in-law embezzled public funds and framed an innocent soldier in the process. Convicted of a crime that he had not committed, the soldier was beaten and forced to pay restitution. Overcome with resentment and anger, the soldier filed an indictment at a "branch temple" (*xinggong*) of the Emperor of the Eastern Peak, burning one copy of the plaint and keeping a second tied around his waist. He then killed himself outside the temple gates but continued his suit in the underworld, eventually gaining permission to haunt the official and son-in-law to their deaths.[23] Another account in Zheng Zhongkui's Ming dynasty work *Hearsay* (Erxin) is particularly noteworthy because no written text of the indictment is mentioned and because the apparent thief lost his mind as a result of the ritual. As discussed below, madness was often considered to be the result of an indictment ritual.

In southern Fujian and Taiwan, indictment rites often featured public cursing and the beheading of a chicken. A detailed account is found in the writings of the British Presbyterian missionary John Macgowan, a member of the London Missionary Society. Macgowan journeyed in 1863 to Amoy (modern-day Xiamen), where he preached for more than fifty years. Macgowan tells of an apprentice who had been accused of theft and decided to file an indictment against his coworker. The plaintiff prepared a white cockerel and an indictment written on yellow paper, which he took to Amoy's City God temple. There, in the presence of a large throng of witnesses, he hurled all manner of curses at the defendant, culminating in the wish for him to die like the cockerel, which the plaintiff promptly beheaded on the spot. Just two weeks later, the accused man's sister drowned and his family's fields were washed away in a flood. Eventually, the poor fellow went mad, wandering the streets aimlessly and muttering about ghosts (sent by the City God?) chasing him. Finally, his distraught father somehow produced the stolen amount, and the apprentice who had filed the indictment submitted a petition to the City God in which he dropped the charges. The guilty party recovered shortly thereafter.[24]

Numerous other references to indictment rituals, while lacking the detail of the accounts presented above, testify to the popularity of such rites. Consider a case discussed by Philip A. Kuhn in his study of "soulstealing" (*jiaohun*) panics in eighteenth-century Jiangnan. Archival sources reveal that Shen, a native of Renhe county in Zhejiang, fled his home after being tormented and cheated by the sons of his deceased older half-brother; he did not go to the authorities but filed an indictment against his relatives by burning a plaint written on yellow paper in a temple dedicated to the Bodhisattva

Ksitigarbha.[25] Indictment rituals were also performed in parts of northern China, Jiangsu, and Sichuan.[26] In his study of Chinese chthonic deities, Ma Shutian reports that during the late imperial era, Guangdong residents burned indictments in the presence of the City God in a rite popularly known as *shao wang'gao* (burning indictments [filed with] the king). Zheng Tuyou and Wang Xiansen describe similar rites, while also noting that *shao wang'-gao* could be referred to as *gao yinzhuang*, or "filing indictments."[27] Scholars of the commercial history of late imperial China have found numerous cases of members of guilds and other commercial organizations filing indictments before statues of their patron deities and asking the gods to judge their cases when disputes occurred.[28]

Because the texts of plaints used in indictment rituals are supposed to be burned, such documents are rare. Fortunately, Chinese ethnographers preserved a plaint filed during an 1885 indictment ritual in Yining county, Guilin prefecture, in Guangxi, concerning an ongoing land dispute between two brothers of the Liao family. The younger brother, who apparently lacked the money to file a plaint at the local yamen, chose to express his grievances to the spirits of Heaven and Earth at the local Earth God temple (dedicated to the Great King of Vast Blessings, Guangfu Dawang).[29] The younger Liao prepared a cockerel (whether or not it was beheaded is unclear), a bowl of oil, and a written indictment in which he asked the gods to send a "numinous official" (*lingguan*), probably Wang Lingguan, to investigate the dispute and arrest his older brother. He also stated that if he were lying, he would willingly accept any form of punishment the gods saw fit to inflict, including having his home burned down, being struck by lightning, being attacked by tigers and poisonous snakes, and being infected with contagious diseases.[30] Zhang Guanzi's detailed study of justice and judicial rituals in the non-Han communities of southern China reveals that members of the Miao people who felt they had been wronged could also file "documents of grievance" (*yuanwen*) before local deities.[31]

Additional examples of indictment ritual texts come from colonial-era Taiwan (1895–1945), where such rites were frequently performed at temples to the City God or the Lord of the Hordes. Perhaps the most famous involved members of the northern Taiwan elite. The plaintiff was the head of Xinzhuang's leading Zhang family, while the defendant was the head of the powerful Ye family of Taipei. Between 1913 and 1914, Zhang's grandfather failed in a business venture, and in order to hide his remaining assets from creditors, he listed them under the name of his son-in-law Ye. After the grandfather's death, Ye refused to return control of these assets to the Zhangs and apparently used the grandfather's chop to conduct the Ye family's business affairs. The Zhangs filed a lawsuit, but Ye proved a formidable adversary, having made a fortune in the canning industry and amassing assets of well over ¥100,000. The suit languished in the courts for years, until Zhang and Ye agreed to participate in an indictment ritual to be held on the morning of May 10, 1933, which also involved the beheading of chickens. Contemporary accounts reproduce the series of charges the Zhangs had filed against the Yes, culminating in the following malediction: "If the above facts are true, and the defendant [Ye] refuses to admit this, may his entire family—male and female, young and old—perish and may his ancestors be demoted to Dukes of Response [Youying Gong, lit. "Hungry Ghosts"]. If the above facts are false, and the plaintiff has filed a false plaint, may his entire family suffer the same fate, and his ancestors be demoted to Lords of Response."

Shortly after the completion of this rite—which appears to have turned out unfavorably for Ye—his wife, son, and daughter-in-law filed a document with the Taipei District Court declaring their refusal to recognize its efficacy because it was "superstitious" (*mixin*) as well as a "debased custom" (*louxi*). The impact (if any) of the chicken-beheading ritual on actual legal proceedings is as yet unknown, but in August 1934, the Zhangs won their case in court.[32]

The practice of filing indictments against the living continues to this day in Taiwan, particularly at temples to judges of the underworld, and the indictment ritual remains highly popular at the Dizang Abbey. People who wish to hold such a rite first ask the temple's "scribe" (*bisheng*), Lai Ming-hsien, to write out the text of their plaints (referred to as *diewen* or *suzhuang*) on lined yellow paper. The standard format is to record the plaintiff's name and address, followed by a summary of the grievances leading up to the plaint. The document concludes with pleas for intercession to the Lord of the Hordes and other underworld deities at his command. The plaintiff then makes offerings to the Lord of the Hordes and his chthonic minions, after which the Abbey's Taoist master recites the indictment sotto voce. The ritual concludes with the plaintiff burning the indictment outside the temple. The entire rite costs NT$400 (approximately US$13).[33] Perhaps the most renowned indictment filed at the Dizang Abbey was presented by the television actress Bai Bingbing (Pai Ping-ping) following the kidnapping and brutal murder of her teenage daughter Bai Xiaoyan (Pai Hsiao-yen) by three local gangsters. Members of the temple committee followed the case with intense interest and crossed out photos of each man on a police wanted poster as he was captured or killed. However, most plaints involve more mundane matters, such as recovery of stolen objects (particularly motor vehicles), resolution of court cases, and settlement of disputes over property.³⁴ Lai writes between ten and forty plaints on a given day and averages a total of nearly four thousand per year, more, as he has said, than most courts of law.

Qing dynasty texts of varying degrees of self-conscious fictionality describe similar practices. They served a range of purposes, from ostensibly didactic to more clearly entertainment-oriented reading. Those written in terse classical style range from reportage of perceived reality, through embroidered anecdotes about real people, to self-conscious fictional creation. Most classical-language tales were collected and circulated for the amusement of the highly educated elite. Vernacular texts were more self-consciously fictional, but these commercially popular stories were also produced by highly educated writers, even if their readership was somewhat broader.

A number of valuable accounts may be found in Xu Qing's *Accounts of Proof of Divine Retribution* (Xinzheng lu). This classical-language *biji xiaoshuo* collection is similar to the better-known Song dynasty collection *Record of the Listener and Recorder* in being very specific about places and dates and in identifying the informant for each account. One story describes a group of minters (counterfeiters) from Jiaxing prefecture, Zhejiang, whose number included a wealthy member of the local elite. In 1692, another member of the elite wanted a piece of the action but was turned down. He then filed an indictment with the Xiushui county magistrate, but the wealthy man bribed the magistrate into taking no action. When the plaintiff filed a second indictment, the wealthy man lodged a countersuit. The plaintiff then filed a suit with the Zhejiang provincial governor, but this official also deferred to the wishes of the wealthy (and apparently extremely well-connected) man. Finally, in a fit of "extreme anger and resentment" (*huiji*), the plaintiff filed an indictment at the Hangzhou City God temple. After a brief respite, all parties had their cases tried in the god's infernal court, with each and all receiving just punishments for their actions.³⁵

Another story in *Accounts of Proof of Divine Retribution* concerns two residents of Shijiazhuang, Hebei, named Zhong and Lao. In 1687, Lao apparently cheated Zhong out of a considerable sum of money. Zhong initially thought of taking his case to the local yamen but balked when he realized that Lao had close friends among the yamen's clerical staff. Instead, he prepared a "dark indictment" (*yinzhuang*) at the local City God temple. After a few days, Lao was on a boat bound for Jiaxing when the Earth God summoned him to the underworld. When Zhong heard of this, he told his wife, "My indictment has been approved, and I am going to die [in order to attend the underworld trial]. However, I estimate that my crimes will not result in capital punishment, so do not prepare my body for burial." The trial was held in the Earth God temple, with the god serving as presiding judge. In the end, both men revived, but Lao developed a leg ailment and was lame for the rest of his life. Other Qing works also contain stories describing unscrupulous litigation masters getting their just deserts as a result of divine retribution.[36]

The important Qing dynasty *biji* text *What the Master Did Not Speak About* (Zibuyu), by Yuan Mei (1716–1797), tells of a Suzhou man, Wu Sanfu, who failed to prevent his distraught father from hanging himself in 1764. Wu's acquaintance Gu Xinyi took advantage of Wu's guilty feelings by "setting up an altar for a fake spirit-writing cult" (*wei she jixian wei*) to summon what he claimed was the ghost of Wu's father. The ghost ordered Wu to use his remaining savings to pay Gu for performing rituals on the Wu family's behalf. When Wu realized he had been cheated, he tried three times to plead his case at the magistrate's yamen, but his case was turned down each time because he had failed to keep any written record of his financial transactions with Gu. Wu then filed an indictment with the Suzhou City God. After three days, he passed away, and Gu died three days later. Both were summoned to the City God's court, although the result of the trial is not clear.[37]

What the Master Did Not Speak About also contains didactic tales that feature descriptions of indictment rituals. One relates how a shrewish wife made life miserable for her husband's family, particularly her mother-in-law.[38] Desperate to be a filial son and resolve the situation, the husband filed an indictment with the City God, going so far as to ask the deity to kill his wife for his mother's sake. That night, the husband had a dream in which he was summoned to the City God's court and reprimanded for his inability to control his wife. The City God also told him that he was fated to have only one wife and that she would bear him two sons. In the end, the City God summoned the wife to the underworld and showed her the torments that awaited her should she persist in her shrewish behavior. Cowed, she promptly changed her ways.[39] The text also contains the story of an elite youth who filed a frivolous indictment with the gods. As a result, he was summoned to the underworld and scolded both for his audaciousness and for the miserable quality of his prose. He was allowed to come back to life but died three years later.[40]

Late imperial Chinese vernacular fiction also depicts indictment rituals. Short works, generally known as *huaben xiaoshuo*, often recast earlier tales from a variety of sources in order to emphasize the central character or a pivotal event. Story 38 of Feng Menglong's *Clear Words to Instruct the World* (*Yushi mingyan*) tells of a Hangzhou man, Ren Gui, who is being cuckolded.

Enraged, he purchases a knife and a white cockerel, as well as incense, candles, and paper money, and performs an indictment ritual at a temple dedicated to a local water god known as Duke Yan (Yan Gong). During the ritual, he curses his wife and her lover while beheading the cockerel.[41] In this account, Ren does not use a written document, suggesting that he states his case orally. The beheading also has a divinatory element, as Ren states that he intends to kill a number of people equal to the number of times the cockerel jumps during its death throes. The bird jumps five times, and Ren ends up killing five people.[42] Chapter 7 of the court case novel *The Chart of Good and Evil* (*Shan e tu*) describes another fictional indictment rite in which the villain, a local strongman named Li Lei (ironically nicknamed "The Living King of Hell," or *Huo Yanluo*), attempts to abduct and rape the wife of Nanjing resident Lin Kongzhao. Members of Lin's family tell him to inform the Stove God, but instead Lin heads to the City God temple. There, in front of the god and his chthonic minions, Lin burns incense and states his grievances, after which he picks up a sheet of yellow paper and writes out a formal indictment against Li.[43]

RITUALS PERFORMED AS COUNTERMEASURES AGAINST INDICTMENTS FILED BY SPIRITS

Anna Seidel and other scholars have found that even before Buddhism spread throughout Chinese society, people believed there was extensive overlap between earthly and underworld judicial systems.[44] The gods of the underworld courts could not only pass judgment on the deceased but also summon the living to appear as witnesses or even as defendants. Such beliefs were also widespread during the late imperial era, with numerous fictional texts describing men and women being summoned to a deity's underworld court during an illness or in a dream.[45]

There was a darker side to such beliefs, however, as people dreaded the suffering or death that could occur after being indicted in the courts of the underworld. Texts such as *What the Master Did Not Speak About* are full of stories of the living being indicted by the dead (particularly the ghosts of wronged women) and depict the ways in which the underworld bureaucracy deals with their plaints. Deceased plaintiffs usually filed indictments with the City God, but they did not hesitate to appeal to the Emperor of the Eastern Peak if they were unhappy with the results of the judicial process. Some ghosts presented their complaints directly to a living local magistrate, while in other cases, magistrates were summoned by the City God to witness the legal proceedings.⁴⁶ In chapter 35 of *The Chart of Good and Evil*, a magistrate named Tang dreams of visiting the City God temple where Lin Kongzhao had filed the indictment mentioned above and ends up viewing the ghosts of Li Lei's victims filing indictments in the deity's presence.⁴⁷

Some Qing dynasty accounts suggest that people feared the consequences of being the target of a sepulchral plaint. In a story in the early-nineteenth-century *biji* collection *Collected Discourses while Rambling in the Garden* (Lüyuan conghua), a young scholar goes to his teacher in tears, claiming that his deceased mother appeared in a dream to warn him: "Something has happened pertaining to your case of three generations ago. Tomorrow, officials from the underworld will arrest and interrogate you." His teacher scolds him for believing in such things, but that very night, the student passes away and is summoned to the court of the Emperor of the Eastern Peak. There, he and a female ghost argue their cases before netherworld officials, with the female ghost accusing the student of having an affair with her when she was newly widowed. After being restored to life, the student engages in charitable deeds in order to make up for the effects of his previous wrongdoings.⁴⁸

Other Qing sources indicate that behavior culturally defined as abnormal could be viewed as the result of being indicted by the soul of a person who had been wronged. In order to cope with such an indictment, as well as to resolve the issues that had prompted its filing in the first place, the afflicted individual was put on trial in the presence of underworld deities in a rite known as "trials of the insane" (*shen fengzi*). Zheng Tuyou and Wang Xiansen have found that City God temples in Qing China were frequently the sites for such rites, which involved recitations of scriptures, statements of penance, pleas for the plaintiff spirit to leave, and threats of divine punishment should it fail to do so.⁴⁹ Similar rites were also performed in Hangzhou at temples to the Emperor of the Eastern Peak as well as in parts of rural northern Zhejiang at the homes of those deemed insane.⁵⁰

Another practice that may be linked to the fear of spirit indictment is the attempt to atone for misdeeds by "dressing up as criminals" (*ban fanren*) in the processions that accompanied many festivals, particularly those involving underworld judges. Such acts, dating back to at least the Song dynasty, are broadly penitential in nature, yet their performance represents a very real fear of divine retribution, including that resulting from an underworld indictment. Many people in Taiwan who dress up as criminals believe that their sufferings are the result of their wrongdoing in this or a previous lifetime, while some Taiwanese who participate in this practice also submit "petitions of penance" (*shuzui zhuang*) in order to atone for all manner of misdeeds.⁵¹

In Taiwan today, people who fear that a ghost has indicted or unjustly haunted them go to temples such as Xinzhuang's Dizang Abbey and file petitions asking the temple's deities to resolve their cases. In an interesting division of labor, the Bodhisattva Dizang is usually viewed as dealing with plaints filed by the dead, while the Lord of the Hordes and his chthonic minions can intervene in disputes among the living, as explained above. Some plaintiffs also make offerings to the haunting spirit, who is usually conceived of as an ancestor or someone they have wronged in this life or in a previous existence; the term most commonly used is "wronged relatives and creditors" (*yuanqin zhaizhu*).[52] Reflecting the increase in abortions in Taiwan during the past two decades, some women who have had abortions and subsequently fear being indicted or otherwise haunted by "infant spirits" (*yingling*) go to the Dizang Abbey and file petitions designed to both placate these wronged spirits and cope with their own feelings of guilt. Marc Moskowitz's recent study of fetus-ghost cults in Taiwan describes a so-called red contract, prepared at the Dragon Lake Temple (Longhu Gong) in Miaoli county, which contains an admission of guilt, an apology from the woman who had the abortion, and a promise to appease the fetus ghost for a period of three years.[53]

INDICTMENTS FILED BY THE LIVING AGAINST SPIRITS

While there are numerous anecdotes about spirits filing plaints against the living, people could occasionally turn the tables and indict spiritual beings. One story describing this practice is preserved in Yuan Mei's *biji* anecdote collection *What the Master Did Not Speak About*. It recounts the tale of a young woman living in Taizhou, Zhejiang, who is repeatedly haunted by an ugly man dressed in red who tries to force her to marry him. The unfortunate woman moves to her relatives' home to escape, but to no avail. Finally, her parents and relatives file a plaint with the City God. That night, the god's subordinates summon the woman to the City God temple to witness the offending ghost's trial. It turns out that he is named Ma and was a palanquin-bearer. Ma is sentenced to forty blows and ordered to wear a cangue. However, the next night, Ma's deceased wife attacks the young woman and tries to gouge out her eyes. Once again, her parents and relatives file a plaint with the City God, and once again the young woman is summoned to the trial that same evening. The City God sentences Ma to be cut in two at the waist, and his wife is commanded to perform forced labor for demons.[54]

Ghosts were not the sole spiritual beings who could be indicted, however. Xiaofei Kang's recent research on the fox cult has shown that both officials and commoners did not hesitate to file plaints with the City God or other deities in the Register of Sacrifices (Sidian), such as Guandi, in order to stop hauntings by fox spirits. For example, one story in the collection of anecdotes by Xu Changzuo (fl. 1602), *Complete Records of Yanshan* (Yanshan conglu), describes a district magistrate in Zhangqiu, Shandong, filing a complaint with the City God on behalf of a husband whose wife is being possessed by a fox. In order to avoid being entangled in a lawsuit, the fox ceases its actions. The collection also contains a story of a military official serving in a frontier district of northern Hubei who forces a fox to leave by filing plaints in temples to the deities Guandi and Zhenwu. An anonymous *biji* collection titled *Record of Trivial Things Heard* (Zhiwen lu) (1843 preface) contains a detailed account of the Lu gentry family of Wenshang, Shandong, who suffer frequent hauntings by a fox, and the fox will not cease unless the family makes sacrifices to it. The family head tries to file a plaint at the local City God temple, only to be deceived by the fox, who disguises itself as the deity. When the magistrate hears of this, he tells Lu to set up a shrine to the fox. The magistrate then fasts and bathes and, on the very next day, files a plaint with the City God, following which he proceeds to "arrest" the fox by confiscating and burning its spirit tablet.[55]

USING JUDICIAL RITUALS IN OFFICIAL LEGAL PROCEDURES

Judicial rituals could also play a role in the state legal system. Officials sometimes attempted to contact spirits, as in the case of a Ming dynasty official, Cheng Deliang, who hired a "female shaman" (*nüwu*) to help him catch a thief.[56] Other officials did not hesitate to combine the practices of the official and religious realms. For example, renowned Qing dynasty magistrates such as Wang Huizu (1730–1807), Lan Dingyuan (1680–1733), and Huang Liuhong (1633–1693) held trials in City God temples or forced suspects to take oaths in front of this deity in order to induce them to confess.[57] One account in the 1872 edition of the *Shanghai County Gazetteer* (Shanghai xianzhi) describes a local official who investigated a murder case involving disputes over fishing rights. The official conducted an exhaustive criminal investigation, which included interviews with suspects and witnesses and a thorough examination of wounds on the victim's corpse. However, when he failed to crack the case, he decided to interrogate the prime suspect in front of the City God. This tactic proved effective, as the man broke down and confessed.[58]

Lest we think that such behavior was characteristic of the "traditional" or "premodern" era, we might also consider the many cases of Japanese policemen and judges who took part in oath and indictment rituals in colonial Taiwan.[59] Similar practices continue at temples like the Dizang Abbey, where police and prosecutors have been known to burn incense and/or file indictments when working on difficult criminal cases.[60] More recently, police investigating the murder and postmortem beheading of a woman in northern Taiwan during the month of February 2005 performed a divination ritual in the famous Xinzhu (Hsin-chu) City God temple and credited the deity with helping them apprehend the culprit. In another fascinating example just two months later, the spirit of a policeman who had been stabbed to death in the line of duty was said to have possessed one of his colleagues and appeared in a dream to one of his high school classmates, all for the purpose of guiding the authorities to the murderers, who were soon caught. Finally, Hong Kong policemen still sacrifice to Guan Gong for protection and assistance.[61]

Numerous late imperial *biji* also contain stories of officials who sought out the assistance of the City God or other judicial deities. One of the most striking, contained in *Record of Trivial Things Heard*, is titled "The Prefects of the Underworld and Earthly (Bureaucracies)" (Yinyang taishou). In this account, a new prefect meets the City God from his jurisdiction while traveling there by boat and relies on the god's help in solving a number of difficult cases.[62] *Compilation during the Gengsi Year* (Gengsi bian), by Lu Can (1494–1551), describes a Suzhou official who served as prefect for Gunzhou, Shandong. One night after taking up his post, he goes to offer incense in the local temple to the Emperor of the Eastern Peak. There, five deities from the temple's underworld bureaucracy come out to welcome him.[63] Other stories describe officials trusting dreams sent by judicial deities to help the officials fulfill their legal duties.[64]

Another example of officials relying on divine aid may be found in *What the Master Did Not Speak About*. The story concerns an Imperial Academy student, or *jiansheng*, from Putian named Wang who forges a land contract in order to acquire an old woman's property and then bribes the county magistrate to accept the text as authentic. When the old woman goes to the student's home to protest, he has her killed and then sends for her son to retrieve the corpse. He ties up the son, drags him to the county yamen, and accuses him of committing the murder. Some of Wang's friends bear false witness, and under torture, the young man confesses to the murder; the magistrate recommends death by slicing. However, the governor-general is not convinced and orders the prefects of Fuzhou and Quanzhou to try the case in the provincial City God temple.[65] The two prefects also recommend the death penalty, whereupon the son cries out: "City God, City God, our family has been wronged and you have completely failed to be efficacious! How do you still have the face to accept people's offerings?" As the son is led away, two statues of the City God's lictors suddenly lean forward and bar the way with their staffs. The two terrified prefects hastily retry the case, acquit the son, and find Wang guilty of murder.[66]

Even Chinese judicial deities were not exempt from the rigors of the underworld legal system. Valerie Hansen and others have concluded that, in theory at least, even China's underworld deities were subject to the legalistic restrictions on their behavior promulgated in the "celestial codes" (tianlü). Such texts reveal that the judges of the underworld could face demotion, forced labor, and even death for a wide range of offenses, such as using bureaucratic forms incorrectly, holding the accused beyond a specified time period without trial, accepting bribes, deciding excessive punishments, willfully adding or deducting from people's life spans, and so on.[67] In addition, Qing period texts such as the *What the Master Did Not Speak About* and *Sequel to "What the Master Did Not Speak About"* (Xu Zibuyu), also by Yuan Mei, contain numerous accounts of corrupt or incompetent judicial deities being punished for their wrongdoings.[68] Furthermore, these works reveal that the underworld judicial system could also punish earthly officials for similar flaws.[69] All of these diverse texts reflect a widespread sense that neither the earthly nor the underworld judicial system was ideal, but the latter functioned more effectively in terms of providing justice. This is not to deny that these accounts had entertainment and didactic value, but one might also consider the possibility that literati composed so many stories about their peers because they believed in the underworld bureaucracy and feared retribution for errors performed on the job.

CONCLUSION

The historical and ethnographic data presented here highlight the importance of indictment rituals in the legal, social, and cultural history of China and Taiwan. Indictment rituals were performed for centuries by people from all levels of Chinese society, which points to the problematic nature of analytical dichotomies such as "traditional" versus "modern" or "elite" versus "popular." Perhaps most important, despite the fact that some literary works portray the underworld bureaucracy as corrupt, the rituals described above were clearly predicated on the notion that the underworld system provided decisions that were more impartial. The atmosphere at temples to underworld deities inspired fear and awe as well as a sense of the inevitability of divine justice. According to one account of Suzhou's temple to the Emperor of the Eastern Peak, in the Belvedere of Mysterious Wonders (Xuanmiao Guan), "[t]he statues of the gods were fierce and terrifying [*ningzheng*], while ghostly beings entered and left [the temple]. Even people who went to the temple during the day would break out in a [cold] sweat."[70] Similar sentiments were expressed by many informants at the Dizang Abbey.

The prevalence of indictment rituals suggests that understanding of judicial procedures and conceptions of law in late imperial China cannot possibly be considered complete until historians regard such rites to be worthy of their attention. Unfortunately, however, most scholars have largely failed to appreciate this situation. As William P. Alford points out in his evaluation of the Chinese legal history field, we should pay closer attention to the disjunction between law and practice as well as to the need for conceptualizing law as a "contested dynamic" intimately intertwined with the functioning of local society.[71] One could take Alford's argument a step further by exploring the role of judicial rituals in this dynamic at the local level. A similar problem occurs in Jérôme Bourgon's recent critiques of attempts by some scholars (most notably Philip Huang and Liang Zhiping) to posit the existence of civil law in premodern China.[72] Conventional wisdom has long held that traditional China possessed a form of legal practice similar to civil law but known as "customary law" (*xiguan fa*), which was embodied in the rules enforced by lineages and local communities; it is also well known that scholars and legal experts relied in part on this customary law to supplement the Chinese civil code when it was promulgated in 1930. Bourgon argues that the idea was imported from the West and constituted an "invented tradition," concluding that "Western notions such as civil law or customary law are of no help in describing the connection between local popular practices and the imperial legal system."[73] His point has much merit, but some scholars' use of incorrect terms to describe customs such as judicial rituals should not discourage us from exploring their importance in late imperial legal practice.

Bourgon also maintains that the late imperial state bureaucracy managed social practices from the top down, and that while officials could and did take an interest in and occasionally utilize local customs, their underlying motivation in doing so was to "rectify such customs" (*zheng fengsu*), not use them to rule the people.[74] Again, Bourgon's point is well taken, yet it tends to overlook the extent to which legal practice was shaped not simply from the top down but also from the bottom up, as well as the extent to which officials viewed ritual as part of the late imperial judicial continuum. One example may be found in a collection of three hundred "legal judgments" (*pandu*) titled

Summaries of Judgments from Hubei and Hunan (Hu Xiang yan lue). The author of this text, Qian Chun, who served as a censorial official from 1612 to 1614 in the Huguang region (which included Hubei and Hunan), did not hesitate to state his conviction that gods and ghosts could become involved in administering earthly justice.[75] In another example of such sentiments, the *Sequel to "What the Master Did Not Speak About"* contains the story of a shop assistant who, while offering incense in a temple to Marshal Wen, screamed that he was being beaten and then confessed to having stolen money from his master. The Renhe county magistrate who witnessed these events is reported to have said: "This is the law of the netherworld [*mingfa*], not official law [*guanfa*]. Wait until he calms down and then take him to the yamen."[76] This acceptance of the overlap of the two legal systems worked both ways, as temple patrons accepted the importance of legal decisions by the state in settling disputes over temple properties.[77]

All these pieces of evidence suggest that the late imperial judicial continuum covered both legal and ritual realms, with considerable interaction occurring between the two. This continuum clearly included the conduct of criminal and civil procedures in the courts and in the temples of late imperial China. The judicial continuum was represented in a great variety of narrative texts, ranging from ethnography, through historical and religious writings, to the self-consciously literary texts produced by members of the elite in both classical and vernacular literary styles. At every stage, writing based on familiarity with a common body of beliefs and practices was central to conceptions of the pursuit of justice. The data thus far remain scattered and varied, and further research will be necessary before any definitive conclusions can be drawn. At the very least, however, we may begin to reconsider the nature of legal practice in late imperial China and the integral role that ritual played for plaintiffs, defendants, and the officials who judged their cases.

NOTES

1. For an overview of these rituals, see Katz, "Hanren shehui de shenpan" and "Divine Justice."

2. On private mediation, see, for example, Allee, *Law and Local Society*; Bernhardt and Huang, *Civil Law*; Philip C. C. Huang, "'Public Sphere'/'Civil Society,'" *Civil Justice in China*, and *Code, Custom, and Legal Practice*; Karasawa,

"Composing the Narrative"; Macauley, *Social Power and Legal Culture*; and Reed, *Talons and Teeth*.

3. For more on these texts, see Hansen, *Negotiating Daily Life*, 216–218; Hayden, *Crime and Punishment*; Johnson, *Ritual Opera, Operatic Ritual*; Kinkley, *Chinese Justice, the Fiction*; Y. W. Ma, "Textual Tradition"; and Waltner, "From Casebook to Fiction."

4. I am grateful to Robert Hegel for his guidance in considering these methodological issues. My understanding of fictional accounts of the spirit world has also been shaped by the work of scholars, including Campany, *Strange Writing*; Chan, *Discourse on Foxes and Ghosts*; Dudbridge, *Religious Experience*; Huntington, *Alien Kind*; Kang, *Power on the Margins*; and Zeitlin, *Historian of the Strange*. See also, in this volume, chapter 9, by James St. André; chapter 11, by Katherine Carlitz; and chapter 10, by Daniel M. Youd.

5. Jeffrey C. Kinkley, in his study of justice in modern Chinese fiction, *Chinese Justice*, 101–69, points out that fiction and legal codes appear to have mutually influenced each other, and that novels that portray officials righting wrongs (including by means of judicial rituals) have enjoyed widespread popularity during both the late imperial and modern eras.

6. This problem is also discussed in Zhang Guanzi, *Lun fa de chengzhang*, 487–89. For more on plaints and their function in legal procedures, see, in this volume, chapter 5, by Thomas Buoye; chapter 6, by Pengsheng Chiu; chapter 4, by Robert E. Hegel; chapter 7, by Mark McNicholas; and chapter 12, by Jonathan Ocko.

7. An important analysis of the problematic nature of the term "civil law" in the study of late imperial Chinese law may be found in recent publications by Jérôme Bourgon (see nn. 75–77 below).

8. Allee, *Law and Local Society*, 148–61; Ch'ü, *Local Government*, 118–19; and Philip C. C. Huang, *Civil Justice in China*, 111–22, 190–92, 210–14.

9. This is in marked contrast to Jonathan Ocko's observation, in chapter 12 in this volume, that the plaint writer "needed to demonstrate the wrong inflicted on his client and to do it in a way that *implicitly defined a matter of law* on which the magistrate could hang his decision to accept the case" (italics added). For more on this issue, see chapter 1, by Maram Epstein; chapter 4, by Robert E. Hegel; and chapter 3, by Yasuhiko Karasawa.

10. For more on these issues, see Katz, "Fowl Play."

11. While Marshal Wen was renowned as a plague-quelling deity, he also served in the chthonic bureaucracy headed by the Emperor of the Eastern Peak. For more on his cult, see Katz, *Demon Hordes*.

12. As opposed to being tied neatly in a queue. The loose hair, as well as mourning clothes, indicated the plaintiff's liminal status.

13. Katz, *Demon Hordes*, 200–201.

14. For more on these issues, see Bauman and Briggs, "Poetics and Performance." I am grateful to James Wilkerson for bringing this and other important theoretical perspectives to my attention.

15. Ho, "Butchering Fish and Executing Criminals," makes a similar point about executions and convincingly demonstrates that such acts of violence may be viewed as sacrificial dramas portraying archetypal meanings, particularly the inevitability of retribution for those who engaged in acts of unsanctioned violence that challenged the established political order and ethical norms.

16. Wu Zhen, "Suichang miaosi kaoxi," 24.

17. Xu Xiaowang, *Fujian minjian xinyang yuanliu*, 86–101. For more on the history and significance of this cult, see Szonyi, "Illusion of Standardizing."

18. Szonyi, *Practicing Kinship*, 283 n. 60.

19. Ibid., 190; *Houguan xian xiangtu zhi*, vol. 1, 29b–30a. For similar data from northern China, see Duara, *Culture, Power*, 138.

20. Liu Chih-wan, *Taiwan minjian xinyang lunji*, 365–66.

21. This action appears to be similar to the late imperial practice of blocking an official's palanquin to express a grievance; see Allee, *Law and Local Society*, 149, 150, 155.

22. For more on these practices, see Peng, *Zhongguo jindai shougongyeshi ziliao*, 94–95; ter Haar, "Local Society," 35–36, 37; Wu Jen-shu, "Jieqing, xinyang, yu kangzheng," 33, 34; *Yongzheng chao*, 29, 87–88.

23. *Yijian zhi*, vol. 3, 1024–25. See also vol. 1, 156–57, 168–69; vol. 2, 655–56.

24. John Macgowan, *Chinese Folklore Tales*, 140–45.

25. Kuhn, *Soulstealers*, 3.

26. For data from North China, see Arkush and Dong, *Huabei minjian wenhua*, 32–33; for Jiangsu, see Hu, *Zhonghua quanguo fengsu zhi*, 27; for Sichuan, see *Baxian zhi, juan* 23.

27. Ma, *Zhongguo mingjie zhushen*, 160; Zheng and Wang, *Zhongguo chenghuang xinyang*, 177.

28. Goodman, *Native Place*, 87; Macgowan, "Chinese Guilds," 140.

29. The term "Dawang" most likely refers to the Earth God.

30. Xia, *Shenpan*, 26; Zhang, *Lun fa de chengzhang*, 498–99.

31. Zhang, *Lun fa de chengzhang*, 484–86; see also Sutton, "Violence and Ethnicity."

32. Masuda, *Minzoku shinkyō o chūshin toshite*, 88–97.

33. Katz, "Xinzhuang Dizang An," 147; Katz, "Local Elites," 213–14. Lai has worked as the abbey's scribe since 1980. I am deeply grateful to him for taking

the time to explain the significance of the indictment rituals performed at the Abbey as well as the texts that he writes for such occasions.

34. The unruly dead also appear to have a talent for recovering lost or stolen items. In the central Taiwan town of Zhushan, Nantou county, stands a temple to a Qing dynasty yamen runner who was murdered by bandits. Now referred to as the Lord of the Red Banner (Hongqi Gong), he is renowned for his efficacy in these matters.

35. *Xinzheng lu*, 23a–b; for more on this text, see Chien, "Zongjiao yu sifa."

36. *Xinzheng lu*, 21a–22a; Yuan, *Zibuyu*, 3.47–48; *Qingdai biji xiaoshuo leibian*, 53–58, 151–52.

37. Yuan, *Zibuyu*, 5.85–86; see also Ling, "Taiwan Chenghuang xinyang." A similar story may be found in Ji, *Yuewei caotang biji*, 8.140–41.

38. For more on images of shrewish wives in late imperial China, as well as relevant gender issues, see Sommer, *Sex, Law, and Society*, and Yenna Wu, *Chinese Virago*.

39. Yuan, *Zibuyu*, 5.84–85. See also chapter 2, by Janet Theiss, in this volume as well as her recent book, *Disgraceful Matters*.

40. Yuan, *Zibuyu*, 9.171–73.

41. The practice of cursing while performing a blood sacrifice may originate in the oaths, "blood covenants" (*xuemeng*), and "maledictions" (*zu*) of ancient China. Although these rites are best known for their links to alliances, scattered evidence indicates that such rites could also be performed to resolve legal disputes. One oft-cited passage from the *Rites of Zhou* (Zhouli) states that if legal disputes occurred, the parties were to publicly perform covenant and malediction rituals using victims supplied by their neighbors; see Lewis, *Sanctioned Violence*, 46–48; and Yongping Liu, *Origins of Chinese Law*, 151–52.

42. Feng, *Yushi mingyan*, 616–17. For a story of using divination blocks to determine one's guilt or innocence, see Yuan, *Zibuyu*, 2.33.

43. *Shan e tu*, 135–36.

44. See, for example, Eberhard, *Guilt and Sin*; Sawada, *Jigoku hen*; Seidel, "Traces of Han Religion"; and Teiser, *Scripture on the Ten Kings*.

45. For stories of such occurrences, see Yuan, *Zibuyu*, 17.331–32; Yuan, *Xu "Zibuyu,"* 10.170–72; and *Jiandeng xinhua*, 3.22–23.

46. See, for example, Yuan, *Zibuyu*, 3.47–48, 10.198–99, 15.280–81, 22.436–37, 22.440–42; and Yuan, *Xu "Zibuyu,"* 5.85.

47. *Shan e tu*, 716–18, 725–26.

48. *Lüyuan conghua*, 17.459–60.

49. Zheng and Wang, *Zhongguo chenghuang xinyang*, 177.

50. Lin and Zhang, *Lao Dongyue*, 8–11; Xu, "Tongxiang shenge gaishu," 199; Yuan, *Zibuyu*, 10.199–200. Such practices, particularly their emphasis on spending money on rituals and burning spirit money, may reflect what Hill Gates terms the "political economy of the underworld"; see Gates, *China's Motor*, 162–76.

51. Katz, *Demon Hordes and Burning Boats*, 191–93; Katz, *Taiwan de wangye xinyang*, 159–60; Katz, "Xinzhuang Dizang An," 144; and Ling, "Taiwan Chenghuang xinyang," 34, 62–63, 73, 102, 182, 195–96.

52. Katz, "Xinzhuang Dizang An," 147.

53. Moskowitz, *The Haunting Fetus*, 104–5, 171–73; see also LaFleur, *Liquid Life*.

54. Yuan, *Zibuyu*, 3.61–62. See also Ma Shutian, *Zhongguo mingjie zhushen*, 155–56; and Zheng and Wang, *Zhongguo chenghuang xinyang*, 131.

55. For more on these stories, see Kang, *Power on the Margins*, 170–74.

56. *Bailian pan ji*, 6.12b–13a.

57. For an overview of this phenomenon, see Waley-Cohen, "Politics and the Supernatural." See also Ch'ü, *Local Government*, 212–13; Hao Tiechuan, *Zhongguo faxi yanjiu*, 139–40; and Zheng and Wang, *Zhongguo chenghuang xinyang*, 175. The case for which Huang Liuhong invoked the City God's help was none other than the "Death of Woman Wang"; see *Fuhui quan shu*, 28, 343–51, esp. 347. Spence also provides a fascinating account of this case in *Death of Woman Wang*.

58. *Shanghai xianzhi*, juan 32.

59. Kubo, "Taiwan no jōkōshin shinkō," 323; Kubo, "Taiwan chū, hokubu ni okeru jōkōshin shinkō," 173–75; Masuda, *Minzoku shinkyō o chūshin toshite*, 46–50, 56–58, 74, 83–85.

60. Katz, "Xinzhuang Dizang An," 147–48.

61. Li Huiyun, "Xianggang jingcha de Guandi chongbai."

62. See *Qingdai biji xiaoshuo leibian*, 216–20. Similar stories may be found in ibid., 105–9, 192–96, 270–72, 290–92.

63. *Gengsi bian*, 1.7.

64. See, for example, Yuan, *Zibuyu*, 12.233.

65. It is unclear why the prefect of Quanzhou became involved in a case from Fuzhou.

66. Yuan, *Zibuyu*, juan 9.168–69; see also Hao, *Zhongguo faxi yanjiu*, 148–49. For a story of how an official in Amoy resolved a difficult inheritance case by staging a trial at the City God temple, see John Macgowan, *Chinese Folklore Tales*, 140–42.

67. Hansen, *Negotiating Daily Life*, 219–21. Such beliefs date back to at least the medieval era. See Dudbridge, *Religious Experience and Lay Society*, 109–13, as well as 51–53, 186, 208, 209–10. See also Gjertson, *Miraculous Retribution*, 136, 251–55.

68. Yuan, *Zibuyu*, 9.170–71, 22.434–35; Yuan, *Xu "Zibuyu,"* 1.6, 2.19–20,

69. See, for example, an account in *Lüyuan conghua*, 22.594–95, which shows the City God punishing an official in the wake of his brutal suppression of a Miao rebellion. Another striking case may be found in *Huizui bian*, by Yu Yue (1821–1906), *juan* 18: the underworld judicial system saves the reputation of a murdered chaste widow after it had been besmirched by a corrupt official and aids an honest official in catching the criminals involved. For other examples, see *Lüyuan conghua*, 17.450–51; and *Yongxian zhai biji*, 2.46–47.

70. *Xiqiao yeji*, 2.606.

71. Alford, "Law, Law, What Law?"

72. Bourgon, "Uncivil Dialogue" and "Rights, Freedoms, and Customs."

73. Bourgon, "Uncivil Dialogue," 53. Similar processes also occurred in colonial Taiwan; see Bourgon, "Rights, Freedoms, and Customs," 85, 93–95; Wang Tay-sheng, *Legal Reform*.

74. Bourgon, "Uncivil Dialogue," 50, 68–72, 81, 84–85.

75. I am grateful to Chien Shuo-ch'eng for bringing this source to my attention.

76. Yuan, *Xu "Zibuyu,"* 4.59–60. Other *xiaoshuo* accounts that portray the parallels between earthly and underworld bureaucracies include Yuan, *Zibuyu*, 3.47–48, 6.109–10, 9.176–77; and Yuan, *Xu "Zibuyu,"* 1.5–6. See in particular the account of an earthly official doing his duties by day while serving in the chthonic bureaucracy at night, in Yuan, *Zibuyu*, 16.311–12.

77. Brook, *Praying for Power*, 170, 174; Goossaert, "Gestion des temples chinois," 13–15; and Katz, *Images of the Immortal*, 111–16.

PART III *Literature and Legal Procedure*

9 Reading Court Cases from the Song and the Ming
Fact and Fiction, Law and Literature

JAMES ST. ANDRÉ

The Southern Song dynasty *Collection of Enlightened Judgments by Famous Officials* (Minggong shupan qingming ji), attributed to Zhan Yanfu, contains 475 judgments by dozens of officials, mainly on the local level.[1] It follows in the wake of several earlier collections of cases but differs from them in being actual judgments written by presiding officials, rather than case summaries or anecdotes culled from history books.[2] Unlike the earlier collections, *Enlightened Judgments*, although published as an anthology, presumably for instruction, can still be considered as legal writing (law as literature). By contrast, the earlier collections are not copies of official court documents but rather secondhand accounts that seem more like fiction. Indeed, the earlier collections were a major inspiration for Ming court-case fiction, in terms of both form and content.[3] One such late Ming collection, *One Hundred Court Cases Adjudicated by Bao Longtu, Completely Supplemented* (Quan bu Bao Longtu pan baijia gong'an), contains stories that are quite obviously fiction, all purported to be solved by one official, Bao Longtu (given name Bao Zheng, usually referred to as Bao Gong or Lord Bao in the stories).[4]

These two very different compilations of "court cases"—one historical, one fictional—fall into the category of law and literature, but on different sides of the "law as literature and law in literature" divide discussed by Robert Hegel in the introduction to this volume. This chapter compares law *as* literature and law *in* literature to see what we can learn about various discourses concerning law in late imperial Chinese culture.

STRUCTURE AND ORGANIZATION OF THE TWO COLLECTIONS

Enlightened Judgments contains 475 cases, which tend to be shorter than those in *One Hundred Court Cases*, partly because they are written in terse classical Chinese. Formally, the greatest difference between the two collections is that *Enlightened Judgments* consists of judgments only, with no added background or narrative of the case under consideration, while *One Hundred Court Cases* almost invariably sets forth, sometimes in rich detail, the events leading up to the case and the trial itself (sometimes followed by a judgment) and occasionally concludes with a few words concerning the eventual fate of certain characters and/or a moral by the narrator. Written in a mixture of colloquial and simple classical Chinese and published in an inexpensive and popular illustrated format, its potential audience must have been much wider, compared to *Enlightened Judgments*, which would have been restricted mainly to the literati. In place of the formal judgment, many stories substitute a narrative of the judge's decision and describe the meting out of any punishment, so that there may be no verbatim legal passages whatsoever in the story. In this respect, *One Hundred Court Cases* is actually closer to earlier collections of court cases, such as *Parallel Cases from under the Pear-tree* (Tang yin bi shi), by Gui Wanrong, and draws on material from that collection.[5]

Because the cases in *Enlightened Judgments* necessarily end before punishment and provide no information concerning the eventual fate of the people involved, the collection has an open-ended feel; Brian McKnight and James T. C. Liu note this feature when they speculate on what eventually happened in certain cases.[6] In contrast, *One Hundred Court Cases* invariably gives the reader a strong sense of closure by describing the punishment and sometimes the later fate of the characters, a traditional characteristic of narrative fiction.

There are also important differences in organization. The editor of *Enlightened Judgments* arranged the cases loosely by legal categories, according to the type of law used to decide the case. The extant *Song Penal Code* (Song xing tong) is arranged in twelve sections, as shown in table 9.1. It begins with a general overview, continues with matters related to imperial and administrative affairs (mainly the conduct of officials), moves to matters concerning commoners and taxes, and finally, in the second half, addresses what today we would mainly consider criminal law—robbery, assault, fraud, arrest, and imprisonment. In general, there is a movement from general to specific, and from upper-class to lower-class matters. Each division is further broken down into subheadings, under which specific statutes are listed.

Enlightened Judgments follows a similar movement but is divided into fewer

TABLE 9.1. Sections in *The Song Penal Code*

	Section	Number of Statutes
1. Ming li	General Principles	24
2. Wei jin	Imperial Guard and Prohibitions	14
3. Zhi zhi	Administrative Regulations	72
4. Hu hun	The Household and Marriage	25
5. Jiu ku	Public Stables and Warehouses	11
6. Shan xing	Unauthorized Levies	9
7. Zei dao	Violence and Robbery	24
8. Dou song	Assaults and Accusations	26
9. Zha wei	Fraud and Counterfeit	10
10. Za	Miscellaneous Articles	26
11. Bu wang	Arrest and Flight	5
12. Duan yü	Judgment and Prison	17

NOTE: Dou Yi et al., *Song xing tong* (The Song penal code), 7. The English translations of the twelve divisions are taken from Johnson, *T'ang Code*, table of contents. (The Tang and Song section headings are identical.)

sections, as shown in table 9.2. Each section is also divided into a number of subsections, under which individual cases are grouped. The first section begins with a subsection titled "Admonitions" (Shen jing), which contains three pieces by one circuit commissioner, Zhen Xishan, who outlines for his subordinates the four tasks and ten things to avoid; in other words, these are not cases but rather general administrative directives similar to the "General Principles" section of *The Song Penal Code*.[7] The collection thus moves from considerations of officials, to taxes and academic affairs (including the maintenance of state schools), and then to households and marriage (the largest section, iden-

TABLE 9.2. Sections in the *Collection of Enlightened Judgments by Famous Officials*

	Section	Case No.	Number of Cases
1. Guan li	Officials	1–64	64
2. Fu yi	Taxes and Services	65–92	28
3. Wen shi	Academic Affairs	93–100	8
4. Hu hun	Households and Marriage	101–287	187
5. Ren lun	Human Relationships	288–330	43
6. Ren pin	Categories of Persons	331–74	44
7. Cheng e	Chastising Evil	375–475	101

NOTE: Zhan Yanfu (attributed), *Minggong shupan qingming ji* (Collection of enlightened judgments by famous officials).

tical in name to a section in the *Code*). After two brief sections concerning cases that involve kinship and special groups of people (for example, imperial clansmen, clergy, clerks), the collection groups the entire second half of the *Code* (sections 7–12) under the general category "Chastising Evil." The collection does not aim to be comprehensive or to mirror the *Code*; there are no stories, for example, regarding imperial guardsmen and prohibitions (section 2 of *The Song Penal Code*). The second half of the *Code*, lumped together under one category, is represented by far fewer stories compared to the sections of the first half, especially "Households and Marriage." Counting simply individual statutes and individual cases, "Households and Marriage" accounts for only 12 percent of *The Song Penal Code* but nearly 40 percent of *Enlightened Judgments*, while the last six sections of *The Song Penal Code* account for 51 percent of the statutes but only 21 percent of the cases in *Enlightened Judgments*.[8]

Nevertheless, *Enlightened Judgments* roughly follows the *Code*. By contrast, the earlier *Collection of Doubtful Cases* (Yi yu ji), by He Ning and He Meng, is arranged chronologically.[9] *Parallel Cases from under the Pear-tree* is organized in pairs of cases that share some common feature, but these pairs are not arranged according to any system of sections or subsections. *One Hundred*

Court Cases goes even further in this direction; its cases are in no discernible order. Patrick Hanan has argued convincingly that an earlier, shorter collection of stories about Bao Zheng was organized roughly in chronological order and that a later editor expanded the collection and mixed up the order.[10] These stories were, in turn, based on earlier plays and chantefables, some of which are still extant and detail Bao Zheng's birth and early life and the way he gradually became a famous official.[11] Hanan deplores this move, but the destruction of chronological order can be seen as a deliberate ploy to move Bao from historical to mythological status; the escape from chronology achieves a timeless present.[12] Nevertheless, this order is radically different from the taxonomic legal order of *Enlightened Judgments*, and it is consciously fictive, with the narrator drawing attention to a discrepancy between the official biography and the fictional narrative of his youth.[13]

Thus, *Enlightened Judgments* is still very much a legal text, both in terms of the structure of individual cases and in the organization of the anthology, whereas *One Hundred Court Cases* seems to have completely broken from the textual legal tradition as well as historiographical chronology in order to become self-conscious fiction.

THEMATIC CONCERNS

Unquestionably, the most important topic in *Enlightened Judgments* is property, whereas in *One Hundred Court Cases*, it is sex. There are astonishingly few cases relating to sexual misconduct in *Enlightened Judgments*—at least, it is astonishing for someone who has been reading Ming court-case fiction. There are even cases in which allegations of sexual impropriety are angrily rejected by the official in charge. For example, case 309 concerns a woman who sues for divorce, claiming that her husband is an idiot and her father-in-law has tried to seduce her. The magistrate rejects her claim without investigation, calling her accusation "extremely perverse."[14] In another (case 311) in the same section, a man who accuses his wife of adultery and theft is seen by the magistrate as having invented the charges as a pretext; he is beaten for slandering his wife, and she is granted a divorce. There are ten cases in which allegations of sexual misconduct turn out to be false, and such allegations seem to be substantiated in only twenty-five cases.[15] In two of these, the magistrate seems reluctant to deal with the accusation (cases 274, 322); in two others, it is merely a side issue (cases 415, 418).

The style of *One Hundred Court Cases* could not be further from that of *Enlightened Judgments*. In *One Hundred Court Cases*, plaints may turn out to be false, or judges are first mistaken in their views, but any accusation of sexual misconduct is sure to be all too true, and in forty-eight of the cases, sex is not just an issue but the mainspring of the plot.[16] In *One Hundred Court Cases*, an ape copulates with a widow right in Bao's yamen (case 2), a woman sleeps with her pet dog while her husband is away (case 17), and various fox spirits, flower spirits, and demons bewitch young men (cases 3, 4, 7, 29), making the father-in-law who attempts to seduce his daughter-in-law, case 309 in *Enlightened Judgments*, almost too commonplace to be worth mentioning. Case 18 does feature an old man seducing the widow of one of his young relatives, but Bao is at first reluctant to believe the accusation, not because of the outrageousness of the offense but because of the man's age. These are some of the more sensational cases, but sex drives the plot in dozens of others.

It is tempting to view these two collections as subscribing to two opposing views of the root of all crime: one identifies greed, and the other, lust. This is not to say that either collection totally lacks both types of story. In *Enlightened Judgments*, "Categories of Persons" has the subsection "Clerks" (Gongli), which contains several salacious tales, and "Chastising Evil" opens with the subsection "Adultery and Obscenity" (Jian hui). Tellingly, however, these and a few other subsections account for almost all cases involving sexual misconduct in the collection; sex is thus a relatively isolated issue, whereas cases involving disputes over land or some other form of greed are found in all seven sections. There are also numerous cases in which the official writing up the judgment cites greed as the root of all court cases (for example, cases 292, 293, 297, 305); none of the cases involving sexual misconduct makes such generalizations regarding sex.

There are also certainly many stories involving property in *One Hundred Court Cases*. However, unlike the cases in *Enlightened Judgments*, which are concerned mainly with landed property or the division of a family estate (which might be a mix of land and liquid assets), the disputes in *One Hundred Court Cases* usually involve liquid assets or trade goods belonging to merchants.[17] Thus, theft or robbery is much more prominent in *One Hundred Court Cases*, and very few cases relate to land. Case 65 in *One Hundred Court Cases* is the exception that proves the rule. It begins by telling of a lawsuit over property between He Da and his paternal cousin He Long. In *Enlightened Judgments*, such a case typically would begin with a long disquisition on the family tree, trace the ancestry of the two men back to a great-grandfather who had owned the land, and then lay out the lines of descent and proportions of shares due to each claimant. The case would probably include a complaint by the magistrate that the two sides had been squabbling for years and would then conclude with a decision as to who should get what. Rather than going into the details of the suit, however, the narrative in *One Hundred Court Cases* tells how He Da decides to take a trip with one of his maternal cousins, Shi Guifang, to escape from the case. Shi Guifang has an amorous encounter and disappears; when He Long hears of this, he accuses He Da of murdering Shi Guifang and bribes the officials to secure a conviction. Luckily, Bao Zheng tracks down Shi Guifang (who has been bewitched by spirits, as traveling young men tend to be), and all is set right. The property dispute is thus pushed aside by, or serves as an excuse for, the tale of travel, amorous adventure, and false accusation of violence. We never learn the outcome of the land dispute.

The ploy of linking sex to cases involving greed is often used in *One Hundred Court Cases*. So, for example, in case 8, Ye Guang returns after a modest nine years away from home on business, and his wife's lover overhears Ye talking about where he has hidden his profits and steals them. In this particular case, the wife is not involved directly in the theft (although Ye and Bao assume so), but clearly it is the man's status as her lover that allows him to learn the silver's hiding place. Just as clearly, adultery is the main crime of which he is guilty, while the theft is merely opportunistic. In other cases, sexual misconduct leads directly to other types of crimes. A wife plots with her lover to rob and murder her husband (case 8); husbands plot to get rid of first or second wives (cases 24, 26); and lascivious men either kidnap the beautiful wife of another man and destroy his family as a result (case 48) or kidnap a man's fiancée and cause the lovers to commit double suicide (case 5). All these cases posit a "slippery slope," in that a lustful thought leads to sexual longing, and the attempt to obtain the object of desire leads to the commission of ever more serious crimes.

There are several possible explanations for the radical difference in content between the two collections. On the one hand, the author of *Enlightened Judgments* may have considered cases of sexual misconduct less interesting from a technical point of view, whereas those involving the disposition of property might have been more complex and therefore merited more attention. Indeed, the average length of property-related cases is longer than any other type,[18] and many dragged on for years, even decades.[19] For the author of *One Hundred Court Cases*, on the other hand, such detailed legal reasoning might make for an intricate plot, but intricate plots relying on the technical details of inheritance laws may have been seen as boring.[20] In the late Ming, editors and publishers may have been pitching the book to an audience that expected sex, especially the illicit variety, to form a large part of its attraction; the rise of sexually explicit and pornographic fiction in both classical and vernacular Chinese at this time is well documented.[21] Certainly, the number of extant editions of court-case fiction from the late Ming seems to attest to its one-time popularity.[22] This was a profit-driven undertaking, which is almost certainly not true of *Enlightened Judgments*. Alternatively, it is possible that adultery, whether or not it was common, seldom came to trial in the Song for various reasons, although the number of statutes in the *Code* covering such crimes argues against this explanation. Finally, editorial predilection or prudery cannot be dismissed as a possible factor. Unlike the editor of *One Hundred Court Cases*, who was writing to entertain and may have wanted to play up the sensational as a selling point, the editor of *Enlightened Judgments* may have deliberately chosen to play down such elements in a work that was supposed to be instructional, not titillating.

The frequency of violent crime is another factor related to the prevalence of sex in *One Hundred Court Cases*. Murder and sex are the two most common crimes; if sex is the root, violence is the fruit, as in most modern Anglo-American crime fiction.[23] Again, this shows the logic of the slippery slope at work. *Enlightened Judgments* conspicuously lacks such cases. Physical violence of any kind is rare, occurring in thirty-one cases, of which only five lead to one or more deaths by suicide, accident, or murderous intent.[24] As with cases of sexual impropriety, there are also a substantial number of *accusations* of violence (fourteen), which turn out to be false, although one spectacular case records thirteen deaths in a fight between two boat-racing teams (case 468).[25] Coupled with the small number of sex-related crimes and the general underrepresentation of cases that would have fallen under the last six sections of the *Code*, however, the absence of such cases seems to reflect the editor's bias.

THE LITIGANTS

In *Enlightened Judgments*, the majority of cases involve family members and neighbors. This is natural given the nature of the cases; disputes over landed property or family matters normally involve people who are related or who know one another. Perhaps this is why the editor of *Enlightened Judgments* decided that cases involving the five relations merited a separate section over and above "Households and Marriage."

By contrast, the criminal and the victim are unrelated or unknown to each other in a large number of cases in *One Hundred Court Cases*. This is not surprising for cases in which a student ventures to the capital for examinations or a merchant is robbed or killed; as they traveled about from city to city and town to town, students and merchants necessarily came into contact with large numbers of strangers, even though students no doubt took advantage of the social networks available to them as holders of the second degree, and merchants must have built up contacts in the towns they visited. In *One Hundred Court Cases*, there are two instances of a servant killing his master on the road; in one (case 50), the servant harbors a grudge against his master from an earlier incident, and in the other (case 53), the servant is having an affair with the wife and kills the husband on the road in order to take his place at home. (In neither case is greed the root cause, although in both, the murderer stands to benefit financially.) More common, however, is a case such as case 32, in which two brothers meet another merchant by chance on the road, travel a distance together, and then rob and kill him.[26] Even when it might be logical for the criminal and the victim to know each other, *One Hundred Court Cases* often arranges for them to be strangers. So in case 9, the lover pretends to be a friend of the husband's, but in fact they do not know each other, although the text specifies that the lover lived nearby.[27] And in cases featuring skeleton demons, fox spirits, and other such phantasms, these forces are all portrayed as being foreign to the community; in case 14, for example, a snake demon takes over a temple from a local god and begins to demand human sacrifices.

When the criminal and victim do know each other in *One Hundred Court Cases*, they are more likely to covet their neighbors' wives than their neighbors' property. In case 53, Zhang Wan and Huang Gui, two butchers, are on friendly terms until Huang, who is unmarried, sees Zhang's wife and is overcome with desire. He lures Zhang out into the middle of nowhere, kills him, and then plays the sympathetic friend to the widow, whom he successfully woos. At no point is there any suggestion of an economic motive.[28]

On the surface, this division would seem to suggest that the cases in *Enlightened Judgments* arose in a rural, agricultural society, where population migration is minimal and everyone knows everyone else (as well as everyone else's business). Getting away with adultery is thus difficult, and violence is perhaps limited to brawls that are resolved without recourse to the magistrate. By contrast, *One Hundred Court Cases* portrays an urban and highly mobile society, where neighbors do not necessarily know one another despite their high-density housing, and people travel frequently. In such a situation, women are more visible and thus more desired, adultery is easier to arrange (especially if a husband is gone for nine years!), and opportunities for preying on strangers are frequent and tempting.

However, this dichotomy based upon modern ideas concerning urban and rural life deconstructs itself upon more careful examination of the individual cases. In the one case from *Enlightened Judgments* involving merchants (case 342), we catch a glimpse of a highly developed system of commerce with specialized roles. In this case, as in so many of the later cases in *One Hundred Court Cases*, a traveling merchant is victimized by a "broker" (*ya ren*), and the official displays sympathy with the merchant's plight.[29] In case 29 of *One Hundred Court Cases*, we learn that Ye Guang and his wife live alone, and their house is isolated from others. It is this isolation in the country, not the crowded anonymity of the city, that allows her to carry on an affair for eight years.

We should be cautious, then, about taking either collection of cases as an accurate reflection of contemporary social reality, and we may well want to look for some alternative understanding of these texts' relation to their times.

THE OFFICIALS

When we turn from the litigants to the officials involved in or responsible for solving the cases, we find a sharp dichotomy. *Enlightened Judgments* shows us enlightened, rational, compassionate bureaucrats who are forced to deal with an endless stream of quarrels arising among ignorant and recalcitrant locals; these officials must also keep in check the greed of clerks, who, it must be remembered, are also drawn from the local population. In *One Hundred Court Cases*, by contrast, approximately one-quarter of the cases feature corrupt and incompetent officials who cover up their own misdeeds, accept bribes to cover up the misdeeds of rich local bullies, or are simply inept.[30]

The different portrayals of the magistrate are most obvious in three areas: the use of torture, the number of incorrectly adjudicated cases, and the way in which cases are resolved. There are almost no references to the use of torture in *Enlightened Judgments*. In a very few cases, there are indirect or passing references, such as "upon examination in jail, X confessed in his own hand,"[31] but even this type of reference is rare.[32] As with allegations of sexual and violent crimes, the claim of torture is rejected in some cases: in case 271, the official examines the back of the person who claims to have been tortured and finds no scars, and in case 385, the claim of torture is deemed to have been lodged to muddy the waters of another case. In five (cases 344, 345, 364, 366, 394), torture is said to have been performed illegally, sometimes by local bullies, not officials (these could thus be classified as violent crimes, not torture). Once again, the almost complete absence of torture may be due to the type of cases selected for inclusion: torture would presumably be used more frequently in rape and murder cases, and most of its illegal use is linked to these cases and to a case of false accusations. Since violent crimes are rare in *Enlightened Judgments*, it should not surprise us that torture is rare; family squabbles would probably not be serious enough to merit such treatment.

By contrast, torture is frequently applied by many different officials, including Bao Zheng, in *One Hundred Court Cases*; Bao or some other magistrate uses torture to extract a confession in twenty-six cases.[33] Again, since this work was written as entertainment, the allure of the lurid torture scene may have been a consideration. A distinction is drawn, however, between Bao Zheng and all other officials. In the hands of Bao Zheng, torture is merely one of many options available to the magistrate in trying to resolve a case. Generally, Bao succeeds in solving a case without the use of torture, either through his own sagacity or through supernatural intervention. Bao thinks of a clever plan to find the unknown guilty person;[34] manages to find incriminating physical evidence;[35] succeeds in tricking the suspect into revealing his or her guilt;[36] prays for or demands supernatural aid in catching a criminal;[37] or obtains information from the ghost of a victim of violent crime.[38] In several of these cases, Bao subsequently uses torture to extract a confession, but these plot devices and the structure of the cases ensure that the reader understands that Bao is completely convinced of guilt before he applies torture. There are no cases of Bao Zheng torturing an innocent party in a mistaken effort to extract a confession.[39] The torture he uses, then, is necessary because a bad man or woman is recalcitrant, and such characters are usually subsequently executed for murder or some other serious crime.

Yet *One Hundred Court Cases* does not display a simplistic view of judicial torture. There are at least five cases in which another official uses torture to extract a confession, and the result in each is a false confession from an innocent person. Worse, the decision to torture is sometimes based not simply on incompetence or mistaken zeal but on the official's conscious malfeasance. So in cases 23, 57, 65, and 78, magistrates accept bribes from litigants in order to reach a conviction, and in case 70, a magistrate has a grudge against the defendant and tries to revenge himself through a case brought by someone else.

Thus, misuse of torture is linked to the second area of contrast between *Enlightened Judgments* and *One Hundred Court Cases*: the number of unjust sentences. In twenty cases, Bao either overturns another official's verdict or solves a case that no other official was able to solve; an additional thirteen cases feature corrupt officials who either commit the crimes themselves or try to prevent Bao from solving the case. These corrupt or incompetent officials range from district magistrates to members of the empress's family (cases 48, 49). Moreover, very few officials besides Bao Zheng are portrayed in a positive light; even the historical Di Qing, a popular general from the Song, is fooled in case 4 by a flower spirit posing as a woman (Bao subsequently exposes her).

It should come as no surprise that in a collection of cases titled *Enlightened Judgments by Famous Officials*, unjust sentences are few and far between. In 6 percent of the *Enlightened Judgment* cases, an official in a superior position overturns or returns for reconsideration the decision of a lower official,[40] as opposed to 20 percent of the cases in *One Hundred Court Cases*. Moreover, in only two *Enlightened Judgments* cases does the superior act to impeach the lower official (cases 358, 364); most of the time, the lower official is merely given a warning or transferred to another post. There are cases in which higher officials exhort lower officials to do a better job, but many of these are statements of general principles, not specific cases in which a lower official is corrected or punished. Furthermore, the objects of such statements are often the yamen clerks, not officials appointed by the central government.

Instead of unjust sentences, *Enlightened Judgments* is filled with litigious commoners who insist upon bringing lawsuits for no good reason and making false accusations, which the official always sees through. As noted above, accusations of sexual misconduct, violent crimes, and torture often turn out to be false; in all, there are at least forty-seven such cases (10 percent).[41] In forty-eight cases in *Enlightened Judgments*, the official correctly decides the case the first time, but the stubborn common people refuse to listen and repeatedly press suits.[42] So, for example, in case 161, the official complains that the two sides have been suing and countersuing over a mere two hundred square yards (one *jiao*, one-quarter of a Chinese acre, or *mu*). In another (case 414), an exasperated official refuses to decide the case at hand but punishes both sides for disturbing his peace. Such cases often end with a warning that the litigants will face severe punishment if they dare lodge another plaint (case 154, for example).

In *One Hundred Court Cases*, corrupt and inept officials create numerous injustices, which the common people (or their spirits) must take to Bao for redress. More than once, Bao Zheng is depicted as reluctant to take up a case, and the plaintiff must plead insistently to convince him. In all such instances, there is a case that needs to be resolved, whereas in *Enlightened Judgments*, the official often complains that people are suing for no reason. Moreover, in *Enlightened Judgments*, there are forty cases in which a judge accuses a third party of inciting people to file lawsuits.[43] This figure of the litigation master or "pettifogger" is totally absent from *One Hundred Court Cases*; there is always a case, and therefore always need for a judgment from Bao Zheng. Thus, we come to the third major difference between the two collections, the way in which cases are resolved. Officials in *Enlightened Judgments* often try to reject cases for a variety of reasons, including the statute of limitations. Sometimes they claim that there is insufficient evidence (cases 114, 128); sometimes they urge reconciliation between the parties, as in case 221, in which the eldest son, who is adopted, is forced to bow and apologize to his mother in court while his younger brothers are forced to do the same to him.[44] More often, the official assigns a portion of the blame to all parties involved or merely threatens punishment if the offender persists in his or her errors.[45] When punishment is applied, it often is not severe; there are forty-five cases in which the phrase "apply the lightest" (*cong qing*) or something similar is used.[46] In sixteen cases, there is mention of intervening amnesty, which reduces or voids the application of punishment.[47] This reluctance to render judgment or punish severely is due partly due to the fact that the cases often are not clear-cut, and the official seems reluctant to apply punishment, especially when relatives are involved.

In *One Hundred Court Cases*, although a case may have been unresolved for years, once Bao Zheng arrives, the truth is quickly and clearly revealed. The ensuing punishment is frequently harsh, sometimes to an astonishing degree. In case 72, Bao Zheng orders a ferryman who overcharged Bao (and presumably many other passengers in the past) to be boiled alive. By contrast, in case 474 from *Enlightened Judgments*, a ferryman who has been stopping in midstream and demanding an additional "tip" is let off lightly with a beating, even though the official notes that this behavior is equivalent to armed robbery (which could carry the death penalty) and the man resisted arrest. In case 79 of *One Hundred Court Cases*, Bao orders the immediate execution of a criminal, rather than referring the case up to the capital, over the objections of his yamen employees, who point out that this is illegal; however, his action causes crime to drop, and the people are thus able to live in peace. Moreover, in the next two entries (cases 80, 81), the official who threatens to censure Bao is caught with his luggage full of bribes and booty and is himself reported and demoted. In *Enlightened Judgments*, there are several cases in which low-level officials send up cases with tentative recommendations for punishment and higher-level officials send cases back down to lower-level officials, asking them to consider matters again before deciding. Case 153, for example, which had been dragging on for four years, was sent back down to the magistrate with instructions to examine all the documents carefully once more. *Enlightened Judgments* also has examples of magistrates who claim to have brought peace to their districts, not by deciding cases, but by discouraging people from filing suits altogether (cases 223, 294, 330).

Again by contrast, in case 47 of *One Hundred Court Cases*, Bao has an evil man tortured to death; far from having to answer for this, Bao is promoted as a result. In case 84, Bao orders the only son of an elderly man to perform frontier army duty, despite the old man's plea for mercy. Bao refuses to be swayed, and again "the people" are happy, because the son was a local bully. By contrast, in case 425 of *Enlightened Judgments*, a man's claim that he has an elderly parent to look after succeeds in substantially reducing his sentence. In case 49 of *One Hundred Court Cases*, Bao deliberately ignores an imperial amnesty for all criminals in the capital and executes the younger brother of the empress; later, the elder brother is spared only when the emperor issues an amnesty covering the entire country.

CONTRASTING WIEWS OF CRIME AND CRIMINALITY

Table 9.3 lists some of the contrasts between *Enlightened Judgments* and *One Hundred Court Cases*. These contrasts do not suggest that the two collections express essential differences between Song and Ming historical reality; however true or false such differences may be, reading these two texts does not provide conclusive evidence. Instead, the discrepancies reveal radically different points of view of the legal system.[48] These two briefs also represent different interest groups.

Enlightened Judgments represents the scholar-official's point of view. It was compiled by an official, and all of its judgments were written by members of this group. Zhan Yanfu chose cases by a large number of different jurists, which means that the cases represent to some extent a spectrum of opinions and the collection is more representative of a group than an individual. Even if one were to argue that the choice of cases represents Zhan's personal views, the fact that he could support his view with cases decided by so many different jurists indicates that his outlook was widely held among this group. In this collection, we hear the voice of the magistrate, who judges.

Written more than three hundred years later in a very different social setting, print culture, and literary milieu, *One Hundred Court Cases* seems to present the view of those facing the judge, both the victims, who demand justice, and those falsely accused, who demand redress. Though the collection was obviously composed by someone with the basics of a Confucian education, the poor quality of the illustrations, numerous typographical errors, and amount of borrowing from popular sources indicate that *One Hundred Court Cases* was a product of hacks and underemployed literati, not the work of an official qualified to be a judge. The protagonists include a wide

TABLE 9.3. Contrasts between *Enlightened Judgments* and *One Hundred Court Cases*

Enlightened Judgments	*One Hundred Court Cases*
Property	Sex
Landed property	Liquid assets or goods
Nonviolent crime	Violent crime
Torture is absent	Torture is standard practice
Ties between criminal and victim	Criminal and victim often strangers
All officials are basically good	All officials are corrupt or incompetent (except Bao Zheng)
Stupid or litigious people	Wronged or oppressed people
No supernatural intervention	Frequent supernatural intervention
Lenient sentencing	Harsh or excessive punishment

spectrum of the general populace, with perhaps a bias toward the merchant/artisan class: thirty-two cases involve merchants or traders,[49] eighteen involve commoners,[50] and sixteen involve protagonists of unclear status but who definitely are not upper class.[51] A sizable portion, twenty-three cases, involve students and officials,[52] but only eight feature landlords or farmers.[53]

In thinking about the issue of corruption, the antagonism between the judge and the judged becomes even more obvious in both works. In *Enlightened Judgments*, clerks are often labeled as the source of all corruption in the system. One of the ten things to avoid, as set out in the general principles at the beginning of the text, is the sending of clerks into the countryside on official business of any kind, because it is assumed (and demonstrated in later cases) that all yamen workers take every opportunity to extort, harass, and terrify the populace. Consequently, they are treated harshly when they are caught. Who are these rapacious clerks, and where do they come from? They are local, they are permanent, and in some cases, they are actually convicted criminals.⁵⁴ In other words, they belong either to the local population or to the criminal class. The scholar-official narrators in these cases often emphasize that they, by contrast, are not local, and they are rarely implicated in corruption. In *One Hundred Court Cases*, however, corruption is primarily a problem of such officials, not their clerks.

Enlightened Judgments and *One Hundred Court Cases* represent two fundamentally different views of the origins of crime, which helps explain several other differences between the two collections. In *Enlightened Judgments*, crime and litigation arise because of conflicts within society; these conflicts are often attributed to a lack of virtue on the part of both defendant and plaintiff. In case 161, discussed above, the two neighbors have been wrangling for years over a tiny plot of land not worth the money they have spent on the dispute. In case 162, the official complains: "Whenever something is to be gained, even if it is very small, people inevitably fight over it. Such a mentality drove Zhu Anli, without scruple, to insert forgeries in the contracts. It also made Zhang Qisi pretend without shame that he was the son of someone else. If such misconduct is not uprooted, how can the government expect to transform bad social customs into better ones?"⁵⁵ People commonly forge or alter land deeds in an attempt to fool the court, although many officials express contempt at their amateur efforts to do so.⁵⁶ In case 429, the official notes that people will often go so far as to inflict injuries on themselves in order to get revenge by suing their enemies for assault.⁵⁷ In short, there is nothing to which they will not stoop.

In *One Hundred Court Cases*, however, crime is portrayed as an extraordinary event that often strikes from outside. Ye Guang's wife is patiently reeling silk and keeping the house in readiness for her husband's return when her world is suddenly invaded by a stranger who seduces her and ultimately robs her husband (case 29). A god starts asking for human sacrifice because it is *not* the local god but an outside demon that has taken over (case 14). Strangers on the highway are more dangerous than acquaintances, unless there is an underlying motive of revenge or sexual desire (cases 11, 16, 21, 32, 50, 53).⁵⁸

A striking feature of this dichotomy is that *Enlightened Judgments* shows the magistrate, an outsider to his district, perceiving crime as a locally produced phenomenon. Many cases open with a general statement on the vices of the local population, which give rise to lawsuits:

> It is customary in Jiangdong [along the southern bank of the Yangzi River] for people to make use of sick or disabled relatives to accuse others fraudulently, as a device for getting revenge or as a form of blackmail.⁵⁹

Or again:

> To begin with, getting involved in plaints and lawsuits is not at all desirable. It leads to neglect of one's occupation, damages family property, lets the clerks make insatiable demands, causes humiliation at the hands of guards, entails tiring trips on the road, and may even lead to confinement in prison. A lawsuit against fellow clan members hurts the grace of kinship groups; a lawsuit against someone else in the community injures cordial relations. If someone is fortunate enough to win, much else has already been lost; if someone is unfortunate enough to lose, it is then too late for regrets.[60]

To the official looking down over his bench, both the actors in a lawsuit often begin to look guilty: one of having committed a crime, the other of bothering the magistrate with a petty squabble that the litigants should have resolved among themselves. Because the official sees that lawsuits arise among relatives and neighbors, he tries to avoid using the law to say that one party is right and the other is wrong (and therefore guilty). Because the magistrate is an outsider, he also is able to believe in his impartiality in administering the law. At the same time, the law and the legal system are shown as adequate to the task set before them; magistrates seem fairly confident in their judgments and go out of their way to assert their authority when necessary. Although there are frequent discussions of the relation between "law" (*fa*), "principle" (*li*), "righteousness" (*yi*), and "feelings" (*renqing*), the right of law to participate in this pantheon of sometimes conflicting values is never questioned. What is more, the absence of torture points both to the officials' love for the people and to their ability to solve cases without recourse to extreme measures; the light punishments, again, show a paternal forbearance.[61] Any problems that remain arise from the two sides in the case, who refuse to listen to the magistrate's admonitions to respect the five relationships and the four virtues.[62] Therefore, in case 133, "to end disputes in the future, the parties are required to submit statements for the file of this case."[63] Here and in many other cases, officials are worried that the fractious populace will be back in court at a later date disputing the same property.

By contrast, the stories in *One Hundred Court Cases*, which view crime and criminal activity as usually coming from outside the community, focus instead on the victim and his or her place in local society. This perspective is achieved by beginning the stories before the arrival of Bao Zheng, thereby introducing the characters, explaining their families and their plans, hopes, and aspirations, and then describing their victimization by unsympathetically portrayed criminals. For example, in case 8, the narrator describes one Mei Jing, his failure in the examinations, his filial piety, his decision to become a merchant, the dangers he faces on his trip back home, and his escape from death before depicting Mei's arrest for the murder of his wife. *Enlightened Judgments*, however, often concentrates on the judge, and neither the plaintiff nor the defendant is portrayed in a very positive light. The criminals in *One Hundred Court Cases*, then, are a different group of people from the victims, with whom we sympathize, while in *Enlightened Judgments* it is often not easy to distinguish between the two. Greed may be a factor in *One Hundred Court Cases*, but sexual attraction is more important. The criminal activity portrayed in these stories is also more extreme than that found in *Enlightened Judgments* and often features violence; this may reflect either reality or the fears and prejudices of the general population, or it may simply be that such stories had more entertainment value. Moreover, the cases are clear-cut, partly because of the omniscient narrator, so Bao's judgment is always accurate.

For all these reasons, *One Hundred Court Cases* expresses a strong desire for harsh punishment. If the criminal is an outside threat, it is easy for merchants and other victims to hope for the maximum penalty, both as a deterrent to other criminals and as a way of eliminating as many individual criminals as possible. Conversely, if the criminal is a neighbor with whom you have been quarreling over property boundaries, or is your paternal cousin, it is harder to reach such a conclusion for two reasons: pressure from other members of the family or community and the logical possibility that some day you may, in turn, be the accused in a different case.

IMPLICATIONS

These opposing viewpoints on crime should not appear strange to a modern audience. Is it the stranger, the outsider, who brutally stabs a man to death on the Orient Express, or is it a carefully planned and executed murder by the community?[64] If Boston's commuter rail is extended to Hingham, will this affluent suburb experience an increase in crime when riffraff journey from the inner city on inexpensive and convenient public transport? Such questions are also linked to the issue of whether crime arises from social circumstances or is a pathological condition of certain individuals or groups. Are serial killers born or created? In *Enlightened Judgments* and *One Hundred Court Cases*, the authors grapple with similar issues and reach conflicting answers. In *One Hundred Court Cases*, for example, the widow in case 2 is virtuous until she is contaminated after watching a romantic play; here, crime is something that is caught, like a disease. In *Enlightened Judgments*, however, virtue is taught, as in a lesson. For example, case 223 opens:

> Many people in Hunan and in the Xiang River valley like to resort to lawsuits. [The people of] Shaoyang district [the present Shaoyang in Hunan], although the region is remote and humble, have not been backward in displaying this penchant for writing litigation documents. However, since my arrival at this post, I have always used reason in providing explanations and the law in making decisions. Many who were known to be daring and aggressive in lawsuits have wholly submitted, withdrawn, and complied with my decisions. None has ever returned to resubmit a lawsuit.[65]

In other words, the people are living in a natural state of vice, from which the official as culture hero must rescue them.[66] Far from agreeing with Mencius's dictum that human nature is basically good, *Enlightened Judgments* sees the normal human condition as one of greed and vice; the official (who has undergone training and indoctrination) must in turn spread virtue by reason, example, and law. In this respect, *Enlightened Judgments* seems to reflect the continued influence of "legalist" (*fa jia*) views despite the supposed dominance of Confucianism.

The two collections also diverge in their views on the efficacy of the legal system. On the one hand, the magistrate as an outsider in *Enlightened Judgments* brings with him the legal code, which he attempts to impose locally in order to maintain order and justice for the local community. The sometimes impatient tone of the magistrate, annoyed that people simply will not go away and leave him alone, provides indirect evidence of dissatisfaction on the part of litigants, but the magistrate as master narrator seems to believe that the legal system he uses is fundamentally just. On the other hand, *One Hundred Court Cases* manifests a deep dissatisfaction with the legal system and the officials responsible for implementing it. Virtually every official except for Bao is either corrupt or incompetent, injustices abound, and, in four cases, the parties involved linger in jail for a year or more before their cases are resolved (cases 16, 67, 70, 71). In another (case 67), the author makes a point of saying that more than one of the parties died while imprisoned and awaiting the outcome of a trial. In these stories, the legal system is portrayed as routinely venal and ineffective. Although there are stories of corruption in *Enlightened Judgments*, nearly all such corruption is blamed on the clerks and other yamen employees, not on the officials.

In a situation like this, the figure of Bao Zheng is an anomaly; he is the perfect judge who always solves the case. Moreover, he often does so at the expense of and against the interests of other scholar-officials. In many cases, Bao comes into direct conflict with other officials both beneath and above him on the bureaucratic ladder, but in no case is he intimidated or swayed by their rank. In case 82, when Bao learns that his own nephew is corrupt, he immediately demands that the nephew be punished and that he himself be demoted, although the emperor recommends clemency. He even admonishes the emperor on more than one occasion. Bao thus should not be viewed as a representative of the scholar-officials; rather, he represents the desire of the general populace for justice, which it often does not receive from those who are supposed to administer the law impartially.[67] In several cases in *Enlightened Judgments*, scholar-officials receive favorable treatment from their peers and superiors. In case 52, a magistrate is implicated in corruption but everyone except the magistrate is punished. A magistrate who is both corrupt and lascivious is transferred to a new post and given a chance to reform in case 43.[68] Indeed, there is a whole category of such cases, "Exchange of posts" (*Dui yi*), with seven examples (cases 55–61) of corrupt officials being moved to new posts rather than facing impeachment. The possibility of a lower-ranking official impeaching a superior never even arises.

Bao's portrayal as one who disregards the law in certain cases is thus important. In *One Hundred Court Cases*, the law is portrayed as incapable of attaining the ideal of justice for everyone in society; rather, it all too often becomes a tool with which the rich and powerful oppress others. If the law and the legal system can be twisted, there is a gap between law and justice, a gap that does not exist in *Enlightened Judgments*. Into that breach steps an almost mythical figure who proposes to restore justice and, consequently, social harmony. Bao transgresses the bounds of legal punishments, and "the people" applaud. Bao mercilessly tortures recalcitrant criminal types and then sentences them to harsh punishments, and everyone praises him for his sagacity (one or two sentences to this effect are often added to the end of a case). Bao admonishes the emperor and roots out corruption at all levels of government, often to save or avenge victims of rapacious and lustful officers. In celebrating Bao Zheng's perfection, the stories actually give us a view of the legal system as deeply flawed and propose a model of ideal justice above and beyond the human legal system. This ideal system is sometimes referred to as the "will of Heaven" (*tianli*) and sometimes as "retribution" (*baoying*).

This ideal of justice is linked to religious beliefs, most especially Buddhism. Men or women who are kind to animals are miraculously saved from murderous attacks (case 59) or avenged through the agency of the animals they have saved (case 60), or their devotion to the gods is rewarded (cases 39, 64).[69] The stories are not exclusively Buddhist, however. There are also many cases in which Buddhist monks or priests are identified as culprits; in case 26, for example, a nephew who is wronged by his uncle asks Bao Zheng to spare his uncle from punishment out of filial feelings, and Bao is so moved that he petitions the emperor to give the nephew a job. There are also many cases in which the ghost of a murder victim returns to demand retribution, unable to rest until justice has been carried out. These stories are not related to Buddhism.

Bao Zheng is portrayed as straddling the human and spirit realms. The cover illustration caption reads: "By day, he decides cases in the world of light; among the living people there are none who do not benefit from his mercy. By night, he judges over the world of darkness; the ghosts of the dead all have their grievances washed clean." Indeed, Bao goes to the land of spirits more than once, seeking either aid or knowledge. In case 100, he can see entities from the other world following two unsuspecting men who have stolen unburned spirit money that was promised to the ghosts; in case 97, he sees a black cloud hanging over a pond where the corpse of a concubine who was beaten to death is concealed; and in several earlier cases, he is the only one who sees other such signs. He is, in short, the personification of a notion of ideal justice based on the concept of the will of Heaven and retribution. The punishment of being boiled in oil, in case 72, cited above, can be understood as the application to this world of a standard punishment from the realm of spirits. By contrast, *Enlightened Judgments* remains firmly rooted in the justice of this world, messy though that process may seem at times. Only six cases in *Enlightened Judgments* (cases 127, 308, 409, 414, 453, 468) make reference to such concepts as the will of Heaven, and none offers examples of anything approaching what we would call the supernatural.

CONCLUSION

Although the study of law and literature has been mainly an Anglo-American phenomenon to date, certain insights can be applied to the study of legal and literary traditions in other cultures and other time periods. In particular, the distinction between law as literature and law in literature, as well as the insight that legal writings are inescapably textual and therefore share certain traits with literature, including rhetorical strategies, seem just as valid in imperial China as in nineteenth- and twentieth-century England and the United States.

Reading Chinese historical and fictional cases together can aid our understanding of what each type may mean. Yet caution is necessary when reading historical collections of court cases as straightforward representations of their time. *Enlightened Judgments* is an anthology, not a court's unsifted filing cabinet, and thus reflects the editor's prejudices and agenda. In many cases, the individual officials who wrote the judgments also took a stand, made sweeping statements, and sought to persuade the reader, which includes those involved in the case, higher officials, and posterity. Likewise, reading *One Hundred Court Cases* alongside real case decisions shows just how fictionalized and idealized a figure Bao Zheng had become by the late Ming.

NOTES

1. McKnight and Liu translate roughly 40 percent of the cases in their *Enlightened Judgments*, the source of all quotations here unless otherwise noted, with Wade-Giles romanization modified to pinyin. It would be cumbersome to use the title of each case, especially since I often list large groups of cases, so I refer to the cases by number, based on the modern edition. When two or more judgments concerning the same case are grouped together and are given a single page reference in the table of contents, I have treated them as one long case.

2. The three most famous such collections are *Yi yu ji* (Collection of doubtful cases), by He Ning (907–960) and his son He Meng (951–995); *Zhe yu gui jian* (Magic mirror for solving cases), by Zheng Ke (d. 1133); and *Tang yin bi shi* (Parallel cases from under the pear-tree), by Gui Wanrong (*jinshi* degree 1196).

3. Hawes, "Reinterpreting Law," 26, cites two studies that trace the influence of Song court-case collections on later fiction: Bishop, Review; and Dunham-Stewart, "Sung Magistrate."

4. Because there are several editions, all with different pagination, and the chapters are generally quite short, I cite chapters rather than page numbers. All translations are my own.

5. Van Gulik, *T'ang-yin-pi-shih*.

6. McKnight and Liu, *The Enlightened Judgments*, 308, 411 (discussing cases 236 and 367).

7. There are several other such directives in the first section and a few more scattered throughout the rest of the collection.

8. In the earlier *Tang Code*, the "Households and Marriage" section represents only 9 percent of statutes, even lower than in the *Song Code*.

9. Van Gulik, *T'ang-yin-pi-shih*, 5, 29–35.

10. Hanan, "*Judge Bao's Hundred Cases* Reconstructed," 301–23.

11. For a description and a translation of some of the extant Yuan plays, see Hayden, *Crime and Punishment*. For a study of the chantefables, see McLaren, *Chinese Popular Culture*.

12. St. André, "History, Mystery, Myth," 173–78.

13. The fictional "Detailed Account of How Edict Attendant Bao First Became an Official" is placed immediately after the official biography.

14. McKnight and Liu, *The Enlightened Judgments*, 369.

15. Cases 157, 171, 180, 309, 311, 320, 321, 338, 431, and 436 involve false allegations of sexual misconduct. Cases 274, 296, 322, 323, 343, 344, 348, 349, 362, 367, 375–83, 385, 395, 399, 415, 418, and 438 involve unsubstantiated allegations of sexual misconduct, including that of a monk improperly confining someone's wife inside a monastery (case 379); no actual plaint of sexual misconduct was filed although the allegation is implied.

16. Cases 2–5, 7–10, 13, 17, 18, 20, 22–25, 28–30, 33, 36, 39, 44, 45, 47–49, 51–54, 56–58, 64–66, 69, 76–78, 85, 88, 90, 92–94, 99.

17. At least 208 cases in *Enlightened Judgments* involve agricultural property. By contrast, only 24 cases are about mercantile goods, pawnshops, family valuables (silver, an ox), and restaurants or teahouses—some of which could actually be classed as landed property (cases 47, 191, 198, 205, 224, 256, 269–72, 288, 331, 334, 335, 342, 375, 376, 387, 426, 436–38, 447, 452).

18. In the modern edition, cases in the "Households and Marriage" section average 1.3 pages versus 1.15 in "Chastising Evil," 1.1 in "Taxes and Services," and less than 1 for the rest.

19. Case 156 discusses events that cover more than one hundred years, and thirteen other cases cite the statute of limitations, generally twenty years for certain types of conditional sales of property (see cases 105, 109, 114, 119, 130, 133, 145, 146, 185, 251, 256, 258, 303).

20. Caution must be used in making such sweeping statements, however; Charles Dickens often relied on complex inheritance cases to structure his plots.

21. See Stone, *Fountainhead*; and Richard G. Wang, "Creating Artifacts."

22. There are at least fourteen editions of eight different collections of court-case fiction from the late Ming.

23. Including cases in which crimes of violence are not successful, there are fifty, or exactly half the total number of cases, that feature some sort of violent

crime: cases 5, 6, 8, 10, 13, 17, 20–23, 28–31, 33, 36, 37, 39, 40, 42, 45–47, 49, 50, 52, 53, 55, 57, 60, 61, 63, 64, 66–69, 71, 76–78, 87, 89, 90, 92–94, 96–98.

24. Cases 5, 11, 166, 196, 210, 260, 265, 331, 332, 335, 344, 350, 389, 392, 393, 395, 399, 411, 414, 416, 420, 423, 435, 438, 439, 446, 468, 471–73, 475.

25. Cases 221, 271, 273, 292, 412, 415–19, 421, 424, 429, and 432 are about accusations of violence.

26. In case 11, a merchant staying at an inn is robbed by a local thief and blames the landlord; in case 16, two rogues follow a traveling merchant to an inn and rob him; in case 21, a trader is murdered on the road by two highwaymen; and in case 87, a rich merchant on a journey is killed in his sleep by two strangers.

27. In case 15, a man trades horses with a stranger, who then steals his, it being the better horse; the stranger lives close enough for Bao to track him by letting the stranger's horse go free and then following it. In case 62, a local thief is unknown to the local victim.

28. See also case 64.

29. This is an early, isolated example of the theme, which is explored in this volume in chapter 6, by Pengsheng Chiu.

30. There are twenty-six such cases: 5, 23, 30, 33, 48, 49, 54, 55, 57, 59, 61, 65, 67, 68, 70, 71, 73–75, 78, 80–83, 85, 86.

31. Case 197; McKnight and Liu, *The Enlightened Judgments*, 269, translation slightly modified.

32. See also cases 230, 339, and 383.

33. Cases 8, 10, 18, 19, 21, 22, 24, 36, 42, 45–49, 52, 53, 59, 65, 66, 68, 70, 78, 85, 87, 90, 97.

34. Cases 11, 15, 36, 42, 51, 66, 73, 84, 91.

35. Cases 11, 16, 19, 64.

36. Cases 2, 34, 46, 47, 59, 61, 74, 75, 78.

37. Cases 1, 7, 12, 13, 17, 20–23, 32, 33, 40, 44, 57, 58, 63, 67, 70, 89, 90, 96.

38. Cases 6, 10, 13, 17, 20, 21, 27, 30, 37, 45, 46, 49, 50, 52, 57, 69, 87, 97, 98.

39. In case 11, he orders two litigants beaten for bringing an insoluble case to him, and in case 86, he orders a man beaten for assaulting his brother after Bao himself had told the man to do it. However, in both cases, these are punishments, not torture, and at least in the latter case, it is possible to argue that there is good reason for the beating.

40. Cases 5, 11, 15, 121, 150, 153, 159, 191, 199, 208, 212, 216, 237, 253, 258, 264, 270, 288, 319, 341, 347, 350, 358, 364, 382, 385, 435, 439.

41. Cases 38, 82, 84, 102, 122, 140, 153, 161, 179, 180, 187, 194, 196, 197, 201, 216, 223, 229, 231, 233, 250, 251, 267, 277, 385, 412, 415, 416, 420–37, 442.

42. Cases 102, 114, 120, 122, 124, 150, 153–55, 161–63, 168, 170, 176, 178, 183,

184, 188, 206, 209, 223, 229, 236, 238, 240, 251–54, 261, 285, 319, 336, 341, 344, 352, 383, 406, 414, 415, 420, 421, 423, 430, 435–37.

43. Cases 122, 147, 171, 178, 179, 185, 188, 190, 195, 206, 222, 229, 234, 250, 251, 253, 261, 277, 283, 307, 322, 329, 364, 379, 400–413, 436, 442.

44. See also cases 103, 145, 220, 288, 382, 290, and 300.

45. The official assigns blame to all parties involved in cases 101, 106, 111, 127, 129, 131, 139, 153, 162, 171, 257, 283, 290, 292, 298, 381, 414, 428, and 445. Case 101 is a good example, with the official saying: "The heedless Wu Hsi, the covetous Wu Su, and the tricky Wu Meng, all three have been equally at fault." McKnight and Liu, *The Enlightened Judgments*, 147. The official reserves punishment for a subsequent offense in cases 16, 23, 82, 102, 112, 142, 154, 162, 169, 176, 184, 191, 193, 194, 200, 217, 232, 234, 251, 252, 254, 257, 260, 273, 290, 293–95, 298, 305, 307, 325, 327, 347, 362, 405, 427, 430, 453, and 463.

46. Cases 155, 157, 193, 198, 254–56, 260, 271, 284, 285, 290, 293–95, 298, 304, 314, 318, 319, 325, 334–37, 339, 348, 353, 356, 359, 362, 365, 371, 372, 376, 388, 405, 406, 412, 419, 425, 426, 464, 472, 474.

47. Cases 135, 165, 202, 208, 216, 230, 239, 265, 281, 341, 377, 381, 421, 435, 438, 468. In cases 226, 240, 386, 453, the official either ignores an amnesty or says that the crime is not or should not be covered.

48. Here, the word "brief" is used in the legal sense.

49. Cases 3, 5, 6, 8, 9, 11, 13, 16, 17, 19, 21, 28, 32, 36, 37, 38, 39, 46, 47, 48, 52, 53, 55, 60, 62, 63, 66, 71, 87, 88, 96, 99.

50. Cases 1, 2, 14, 30, 31, 33, 34, 45, 72, 73, 76, 77, 83, 85, 86, 89, 90, 100.

51. Cases 18, 20, 22, 23, 29, 41, 50, 56, 59, 64, 67, 68, 79, 93, 94, 98.

52. Cases 4, 7, 10, 24, 25, 26, 40, 44, 49, 51, 54, 57, 58, 69, 70, 74, 75, 78, 80, 81, 82, 84, 92.

53. Cases 12, 15, 27, 42, 61, 65, 91, 97. Case 95 features a magician, and two cases feature animals (a bird in case 35, and a frog in case 43) as the main protagonists.

54. See case 347 for an example of convicts being used as clerks.

55. McKnight and Liu, *The Enlightened Judgments*, 205.

56. See case 268, in which the attempt of a "mean person" (*xiao ren*) to forge a document is said to be transparent to the official.

57. In this case, the plaintiff has driven a nail through his own leg.

58. See chapter 6, by Pengsheng Chiu, in this volume.

59. Case 433; McKnight and Liu, *The Enlightened Judgments*, 462.

60. Case 122; McKnight and Liu, *The Enlightened Judgments*, 155.

61. In this volume, see chapter 5, by Thomas Buoye; and chapter 1, by Maram Epstein, who shows that this forbearance was too often limited to male defendants.

62. The five relationships are those between ruler and subject, father and son, elder and younger brothers, husband and wife, and friend and friend. The four virtues are loyalty, filial piety, female chastity, and integrity.

63. McKnight and Liu, *The Enlightened Judgments*, 169.

64. Christie, *Murder on the Orient Express*. These are the two solutions proposed by Poirot.

65. McKnight and Liu, *The Enlightened Judgments*, 288.

66. See also case 294, in which the official not only takes credit for the spread of virtue in his district but also takes the blame when a lawsuit is filed.

67. In chapter 11 in this volume, Katherine Carlitz uses the term "justice hero" to describe Bao's function.

68. See also cases 334–37.

69. Also cases 44, 58, and 63. See note 39 above for a list.

10   Beyond *Bao*

Moral Ambiguity and the Law

in Late Imperial Chinese Narrative Literature

DANIEL M. YOUD

In recent years, scholars have become increasingly aware of the extent to which the "literary" permeated the processes of seeking and administering justice at all levels in late imperial China. In this volume alone, numerous essays emphasize how plaintiffs, magistrates, and emperors themselves relied, whether consciously or not, on diverse rhetorical strategies and literary tropes to achieve "culturally plausible" stories, thereby investing narrative with the power of eliciting comprehensibility—if not always order—from the chaos and violence of crime.

The magistrates' artfully worked narratives represent the culmination of a complex synthesis, whereby the pertinent facts of a case were simultaneously ascertained and constructed through forensic investigation, the critical reading of petitions, the give-and-take of interrogation, the assessment of courtroom testimony, and the like. It is crucial to remember, therefore, that however decisive a role magistrates played in the process of legal storytelling, the master narratives of case memorials often grew out of a mélange of sources, many of which were already rhetorically modeled to achieve maximum persuasive effect.[1] The point here is not merely that litigation in late imperial China was to a significant degree "conducted by constructing, delivering, and interpreting stories,"[2] but that such stories could themselves offer competing visions of justice, of human character and motivation, and of the function of law in ordering society and the cosmos.[3]

But what of legal storytelling that was neither necessitated by nor directly related to the litigation process? As is well known, stories of crime, detection, and punishment occupy an important position in the history of Chinese literature. How, then, did vernacular fiction, theater, classical-language tales, and "anecdotal jottings" (*biji xiaoshuo*), to name only some of the most obvious sources, frame legal themes and subject matter? Compared to the kinds of stories told in official court records, did these texts use literary tropes to shape crime narratives in similar, or at least similarly complex, ways?

LITERARY LEGAL FICTIONS

This reassessment must begin by noting a basic dissimilarity between legal storytelling as it occurred within the system and beyond.[4] On the one hand, legal storytelling within the system was motivated by the unique pressures of the litigation process, as plaintiffs, defendants, and magistrates sought to guide case developments to serve their own often incommensurate ends. On the other hand, insofar as literary texts—a variety of legal storytelling outside the system—were written for the enjoyment and edification of the reading public (as well as, quite often, for the profit of publishers and authors), they met the needs of markedly different "interpretive communities."

To be sure, there was significant interpenetration between these communities. To provide just two examples: Li Yu (1610/11–1680), one of the most important early Qing vernacular authors and dramatists, compiled three collections of legal cases; and Li Lüyuan (1707–1790), the author of the mid-Qing novel *A Lantern for the Crossroads* (Qilu deng), actually served for one year as county magistrate in Yinjiang county, Guizhou.[5] Likewise, the anonymous author of *Marriage Bonds to Awaken the World* (Xingshi yinyuan zhuan), written in the mid-to-late seventeenth century, must have had at least more than a passing familiarity with the late imperial legal system, given the high level of largely convincing detail that occurs in this work's many courtroom scenes.[6] But beyond any direct connections, either attested or supposed, the self-conscious, highly literate style of much Ming and Qing dynasty drama and vernacular fiction reveals the deep affinities of these genres with the broader elite culture of the day.[7] Participants in this culture were educated for service in the imperial bureaucracy, one function of which was the administration of justice. Not surprisingly, even at the level of isolated rhetorical figures such as rhetorical questions, one can observe a consonance between case memorials and various literary texts.[8]

Nevertheless, important differences between literary and nonliterary sources remain. Most notably, two great areas of thematic concern, largely absent from inside-the-system legal storytelling, dominate literary representations of the law and lend a misleading sense of homogeneity to these texts. The first is the concept of *bao* (requital); the second is the notion of the "justice hero," usually, but certainly not always, Judge Bao.[9] Superficially, both ideas appear to impose rather simplistic structures on crime narratives: *bao*, by reinforcing the belief that human beings live in a "morally active universe," in which all acts entail appropriate consequences, and the justice hero, by assuring audiences that even if the system fails, there will always be a "clear-sky" (*qing tian*) official to intervene on their behalf to see justice done.[10]

On closer analysis, however, narratives that rely on notions of requital, or justice heroism, or a combination of the two, often exhibit both great flexibility and nuance.[11] As Karl Kao has argued, narratives that premise "moral order" on the "'inevitability' of coincidence" remain themselves inevitably ambiguous—even to those who told and retold them.[12] In his insightful analysis of the Ming short story "Fifteen Strings of Cash" (Shiwu guan xiyan cheng qiaohuo), Kao asserts that one of the reasons for this work's abiding interest is the blatant arbitrariness of its narrative, which self-consciously exposes a fundamental uneasiness with its own ideological structure.[13]

Andrew Plaks takes this argument further in his reading of *Marriage Bonds to Awaken the World*, noting that this novel's author continually chafes against and seeks to problematize, if not undermine completely, the retributive scheme of his own narrative.[14] Indeed, the narrator at one point interjects: "If later generations are made to go on suffering harsh retribution for the sins of their fathers, regardless of whether they are good or evil in their own right, then the whole idea of retribution is unfair."[15]

Ostensibly, this comment explains the good fortune of a character who is the son of morally reprehensible parents. The parents, a certain Ma Congwu and his wife, disown Ma's patrons and adoptive parents after Ma achieves success in the civil service examinations and is given an official posting. Turned away from the gates of Ma's official residence, the adoptive parents die in penury at a roadside inn. Their spirits return, however, to possess the bodies of both Ma and his wife, causing them to rip out their hair, poke out their eyes, and drive iron fire pokers into their ears. Bleeding from their "seven apertures," husband and wife die gruesome deaths. But their son survives unharmed; in fact, he prospers. Here, the narrator finds it necessary to explain that on the basis of their behavior alone, Ma Congwu and his wife "ought never to have had a son." Yet, since the son displayed the depth of his own moral character by remonstrating with his parents to do right by his father's benefactors, "Heaven and Earth had other plans [for him]."[16]

In this context, the narrator's above-cited interjection seems less a "cry of indignation" (as Plaks reads it) and more a spirited defense of the fairness of the Heavenly ordained system of retributive justice.[17] What the story of Ma Congwu and his son appears to demonstrate, in fact, is the *untruth* of the idea that the "sins of the fathers are visited upon their sons and grandsons" (*bao zai er sun*).[18] Yet, as soon as the narrator brings the Ma Congwu episode to its dénouement, he immediately turns his attention to events that sharply contradict his reassuring conclusions, thereby confirming Plaks's larger point that the novel is profoundly ambivalent toward its retribution theme and narrative framework.

At issue again is the problem of cross-generational retribution: Yan Liexing, a licentiate of low morals, shoots arrows at the statue of a local tutelary deity, but he does not pay directly for his impiety; rather, each of his sons dies shortly after delivery. The first, born without an anus, dies because he cannot move his bowels. The second, similarly afflicted, also dies, but only after his parents undertake the drastic measure of cutting an opening where his anus should be. Finally, a third son is born without the odd deformity of his two deceased older brothers; his body, unfortunately, is riddled with innumerable holes—just like the arrow-pierced statue of the temple god—out of which his blood and his life drain away.[19] With the image of these misshapen and mutilated infant corpses before our eyes, it seems almost impossible to read these events as anything but a devastatingly ironic response to the narrator's bland assurances of the fairness and justice of cosmic *bao*.

BEYOND *BAO*

The ironic treatment of the justice theme in *Marriage Bonds to Awaken the World* points to another body of texts—those that, eschewing the narrative and moral logic of requital altogether, sought alternate ways of representing crime, punishment, and the working of the law. Although not many, these works remain significant for the ways in which they further complicate the dominant *bao*-based mode of figuring meaning in late imperial narrative literature. Beyond *bao*, however, where might meaning lie?

To the authors of the seventeenth and eighteenth centuries, the answer to this question was not at all apparent. Consider the following entry from Shen Defu's (1578–1642) *Anecdotes from the Wanli Period* (Wanli yehuo bian), a collection of anecdotal jottings from the late Ming:

In the reign of the Jiajing emperor, a resident of the capital, Zhang Fu by name, wanted to incriminate his neighbor, a certain Zhang Zhu. [Zhang Fu] thus murdered his own mother and put the blame for the crime on [Zhang] Zhu. But upon investigation, the actual state of affairs [*qing*] was ascertained; moreover, [Zhang] Fu's elder sister gave evidence against him. Nevertheless, His Majesty said this could not possibly be so [*bi bu ran*]. The case was thoroughly reinvestigated, with the result that the judge resubmitted his original findings unaltered. Still, His Majesty would not believe [the facts], whereupon he sentenced [Zhang] Zhu to death. His Majesty is reported to have claimed that within all the world there exists no one who would kill his own mother.[20]

Like the quintessential justice hero, Judge Bao, who adjudicated in the human world during the day and in the underworld at night, the emperor, by virtue of his position, was believed to link the spheres of earthly and cosmic justice. It was his role, in theory, to ensure that the moral imperatives of the cosmic order were realized in the system of human-administered justice. Even more than the examples from *Marriage Bonds* discussed earlier, then, this anecdote is deeply subversive of the coherence of a belief in *bao*.

As its title "Sagely Filial Piety" (Sheng xiao) implies, this brief and allegedly truthful report is framed as an exemplum: its purpose, to illustrate the emperor's profound virtue. To wit, His Majesty is so innocent of reality, so filial himself, that he is simply unable to contemplate the existence of "one who would kill his own mother." This so-called sageliness, however, condemns an innocent man to death. Ironically, then, this account of imperial incompetence inverts the narrative trajectory of a typical tale of justice heroism, figuring the emperor as what we might term a "justice antihero." The inversion of the justice-hero plot is so neat, in fact, that whereas normally the justice hero intervenes in the legal process to redress wrongs perpetrated by the actions of corrupt or negligent officials, in this instance the emperor performs the opposite function, ensuring that the careful and correct findings of his judge are overturned.

That is not to say that the emperor, as depicted here, is either corrupt or negligent. On the contrary, the issue is his incorruptibility, that is, his inability to incorporate *qing*—"the actual state of affairs"—into his vision of the world; his tragic error is that he confuses what "ought not to be but is" (*bu dang ran er ran*) with what "cannot possibly be" (*bi bu ran*). In this way, the anecdote cleverly undercuts the emperor's qualifications to preside over a legal system that demanded of its representatives the ability to function in two

Beyond Bao: Moral Ambiguity and the Law   219

"coexisting realities," one defined by the idealistic "moralism" that was encoded into official representations of the system, the other defined by a "pragmatic approach to the real problems of government."[21]

Lack of faith in the idealistic moralism of the late imperial system is particularly pronounced in a remarkable text, in rather free translation, *A New Book for Aid in Eliminating Deceptions as Based on What Has Been Experienced and Witnessed in the Great Wide World* (Jiang hu lilan du pian xinshu), by Zhang Yingyu.[22] This work's preface, dated Wanli 45 (1617), captures its author's jaundiced view of the world:

> The current age is far removed from antiquity; our ways have become decadent, and those who are deceitful grow stronger in number by the day ... [Thus, the author] has culled through what he has seen and heard and hunted for material both far away and close at hand in order to give a full account of the lives of the people and to make known, as plainly as pointing to the palm of one's hand, what has been concealed. He offers readers a complete account of evil thoughts and criminal deeds, which he has investigated thoroughly so that they may appear in their entirety before your very eyes.[23]

Composed of a series of crime stories, *New Book for Aid in Eliminating Deceptions* appeared during a boom period in the publication of "court-case" (*gong'an*) fiction.[24] For reasons discussed below, we may ultimately wish to treat *New Book for Aid in Eliminating Deceptions* as a sui generis work. Nevertheless, there are suggestive connections between it and late Ming court-case fiction. For instance, this work shares its rather artless "half classical, half vernacular" (*ban wen ban bai*) idiom with other court-case story collections. What is more, a certain Chen Huaixuan, about whom no biographical information is available, was involved in the publication not only of *New Book for Aid in Eliminating Deceptions* but also of a more typical collection of court-case stories, *Court Cases Examined in Detail* (Xiangqing gong'an).[25] Given this connection, it seems not entirely unreasonable to assume that Zhang Yingyu was influenced by court-case fiction collections such as *Court Cases Examined in Detail* and that his own work was intended to appeal to a similar audience.

Many examples of late Ming court-case fiction, including *Court Cases Examined in Detail*, arrange their stories of crime and punishment under headings that bear a certain relationship to those of the official legal code, thus highlighting the role of "fiction" (*xiaoshuo*) in the popularization of legal knowledge. This was especially so among residents of the economically advanced urban centers of Jiangnan and along China's southeastern coast where such works were published. Zhang Yingyu's *New Book for Aid in Eliminating Deceptions* is similarly organized. As all of Zhang's material is more narrowly focused on crimes of fraud and "deception" (*pian*), however, he departs from the broader categories of court-case collections, administrative handbooks, and the legal code in order to create a much more finely calibrated taxonomy of criminal behavior. Whereas other collections of court-case stories may devote but a single chapter to tales of scams and swindles, Zhang's contains twenty-four. The eighty-three brief stories of *New Book for Aid in Eliminating Deceptions* are divided into chapters with headings such as "Deceptions Involving Changing Silver" (Huan yin pian), "Deceptions Involving False Friends" (Wei jiao pian), "Marriage Deceptions" (Hunqu pian), and "Deceptions Involving Women" (Furen pian).

The editorial comments at the end of every story are also a staple of late Ming court-case literature. While each rudimentary narrative implicitly engineers its own interpretation, the addition of the editorial voice represents a far more direct and forceful approach to the task of ordering the events of a crime into a meaningful whole. More often than not, the editor's remarks confirm the conclusions—the moral judgments—that we as readers have already drawn. In a small number of cases, however, the editor's comments propose moral interpretations of events, which, if left to stand on their own, might be otherwise construed. We are told, for example, of a man who is robbed of some silver while showing off its high quality to his traveling companions on a boat. Where one might expect sympathy for the victim of this crime, the editor's comments are far from understanding: "All responsibility lies with Student Fei [the man from whom the silver was stolen]. By bragging and showing off, he was asking for it to be taken."[26]

This story and its editorial comment bring into focus a major theme of this collection of crime stories: personal responsibility. Time and again, the editorial slant of *New Book for Aid in Eliminating Deceptions* places an onus on the individual to avoid being swindled. As a result, its stories seem less interested in the workings of justice, whether human or divine, compared to more typical court-case fictions. On trial in these stories is the victim, not the perpetrator. That is to say, the message of this work appears to be that victims of crimes cannot depend on external forces—either the legal system or cosmic *bao*—to intervene to right the wrongs committed against them. Instead, they are encouraged to examine their own complicity, even guilt, in the misfortunes that befall them.

Consider, for example, the woodblock print that serves as the frontispiece to the second fascicule (fig. 1, opposite) in *New Book for Aid in Eliminating Deceptions*. The iconography of this illustration suggests that the official behind the desk may be King Yama, lord of the underworld, using his preternatural mirror to look into the heart of a recently deceased woman. Although there is no way to know for sure the identity of the figure at the lower left, in the context of these stories, she is as likely to be a victim of a crime as she is to be a criminal herself. Indeed, her dramatic gesture of soul-baring represents precisely the attitude of moral self-examination the text encourages its readers to adopt as a means of avoiding sundry calamities. The illustration's implication seems to be that if one takes proper precautions—that is, guards against the duplicity of others and makes sure one is not duplicitous oneself—the dangers of an immoral world can be held at bay.

DEPARTURES FROM THE COURT-CASE MODEL

Just as there are certain similarities between *New Book for Aid in Eliminating Deceptions* and the late Ming court-case collections, so, too, there are significant differences. In addition to the editorial summations just discussed, Ming dynasty court-case stories regularly include accounts of courtroom testimony and various "transcriptions" of legal documents such as accusations brought by "plaintiffs" (*zhuangci*), responses filed by "defendants" (*suci*), and rulings delivered by "judges" (*panci*). The center of gravity in these stories is the courtroom. They are concerned not only with crime but with the ways in which the judicial system deals with crime. Not surprisingly, justice heroes feature prominently in this literature.

In stark contrast, the legal system and its representatives are largely absent from *New Book for Aid in Eliminating Deceptions*. The reason for this is simple, if somewhat unsettling to the idea that a just and moral order prevails in the cosmos: Rather than being caught and punished, most of the malefactors and con artists in this collection of crime narratives escape (often with sizable sums of cash or other valuables), leaving their victims with little more to do than regret their own gullibility.

When judges do appear, moreover, their powers to see justice done are much reduced. Consider the following example. Chen Qing, a man from Jiangxi, goes to Nanjing to sell a horse, as he has often done in the past. Along comes a man holding a fine parasol and dressed in stylish clothes. He desires to buy the horse but wants to conclude the transaction at his home. Chen Qing agrees. Along the way, the man stops outside a shop that sells silk. He asks Chen to wait for him outside the shop while he goes in to buy several

Frontispiece in Dupian xinshu, *1617 edition, juan 2, reprinted in* Zhongguo gudai xiaoshuo banhua jicheng *(Shanghai: Hanyu da cidian chubanshe, 2002), vol. 3, p. 904.*

bolts of material. Again, Chen agrees. In the shop, the man haggles with the storekeeper over the price of the silk and explains that he would like to show it to a friend who will be able to verify its quality. Pointing outside the shop to Chen and the horse, the man says, "There are my horse and my companion. What reason could you possibly have to be concerned?" Thus reassured, the shopkeeper allows the man to leave the shop with the silk. The man never returns.

Meanwhile, Chen, waits outside the silk shop for some time. But when the man who wanted to buy his horse does not reappear, Chen determines that he is wasting his time and sets off in the direction of his lodgings. Seeing this, the shopkeeper emerges from his shop and demands to know where Chen's companion has gone with the silk. Naturally, Chen denies being the man's companion. "I don't know who that devil was, or where he is from," he protests. But the shopkeeper is not convinced and accuses Chen of conspiring with the mystery man to steal his goods.

The dispute between Chen and the shopkeeper ends up in court. After hearing both sides of the case, the judge employs his detective skills to get to the bottom of the matter. Relying on testimony from the keeper of the inn in which Chen regularly stays when doing business in Nanjing, the judge becomes convinced of Chen's honesty. He correctly concludes that Chen was merely an unwilling and unknowing participant in the rogue's scheme to steal the silk. When the shopkeeper objects to this finding, the judge replies: "This [thief] was a real rogue indeed. It is as if, 'In order to attack the state of Guo, he contrived first to pass through the territory of the state of Yu.' He feigned interest in buying Chen's horse and duped Chen into standing surety for him, so that he might steal your silk. Now, it is you who has been swindled. Why place the blame on Chen?"[27]

On the one hand, the judge in this story acquits himself admirably. He gives careful consideration to the case that comes before him, and he sees it to a fitting conclusion. For this reason, the editorial comment attached to the story praises the judge for his intelligent "investigative practices" (*mingcha*). On the other hand, in the larger narrative context, the legal dispute between Chen and the shopkeeper is only of secondary importance. Addressing this point, the editor notes: "Although Chen Qing did not end up mistakenly bound in the chains of a criminal, the silk merchant was nevertheless diabolically deceived and robbed in broad daylight." Ultimately, then, this is a story that seems to be about the realistic limits of what can be accomplished by recourse to the law and the courts. In the wake of a brazen crime, a conscientious judge intervenes to pick up the pieces. He successfully solves a dispute between the crime's two victims, but the criminal himself gets off scot-free. Justice has been served, but only to a degree.

In another example of criminal behavior going unpunished, a young landlord is gulled into trespassing on the virtue of the wife of one of his tenants. As planned by the tenant, his mother, and his wife, when the landlord's shameful behavior is "discovered," he must not only forgive the tenant three years' back rent but also give the tenant title to two parcels of land valued at twenty ounces of silver. Then, in a bizarre twist, the tenant's mother arranges for her daughter-in-law to sleep with the landlord a second time—just so the landlord will not think he has gotten too bad a deal. The story ends by simply noting: "The landlord was thus deceived. He slept with the woman for only one more night and then left. Nothing else happened."[28]

Such an ending is unthinkable in the more typical sort of court-case literature, in which the tenant, the mother-in-law, the wife, and the landlord would surely be called to answer for their behavior, whether in a magistrate's courtroom or by means of some form of divine justice. In *New Book for Aid in Eliminating Deceptions*, however, events unfold in a world that is indifferent to moral concerns, where justice is uncertain and recompense rare.

QING AND LI

Tracing the significance of this work's rather cynical view of a morally uncaring universe well into the eighteenth century reveals the relationship between this isolated and obscure work of late Ming narrative prose and some broader trends in Chinese intellectual and literary history. Like the entry from Shen Defu's *Anecdotes from the Wanli Period*, discussed earlier, the stories in *New Book for Aid in Eliminating Deceptions* achieve their ironic effect by exploiting a basic tension between the "real" and the "ideal"—between the world as it ought to be and the world as it is in the current age. From this perspective, *New Book for Aid in Eliminating Deceptions* can be seen as an early manifestation of a set of values central to the rise, from the late Ming to the mid-Qing, of a genre known to modern literary scholars as *renqing xiaoshuo* (the fiction of human relations and sentiments). Characteristic of this fiction is a fundamental respect for *qing*, or "the actual state of affairs," as *Anecdotes from the Wanli Period* expresses it, over and above a commitment to abstract, ideal *li* (moral principle).

The two key terms *qing* and *li* delineate this tension between real and ideal in scholarly discourse post Zhu Xi (1130–1200). *Qing*, translated above as "the actual state of affairs," possesses a truly remarkable semantic range. Accord-

Beyond Bao: Moral Ambiguity and the Law 225

ing to William Rowe's useful overview, possible translations (depending on context) include "circumstances," "genuineness," "reality," "affection," and "desire."[29] As Rowe also points out, the notion of *qing* was closely allied to that of *renqing*, a term with a similarly complex array of meanings, including "human emotions," "empathy," "reciprocal obligation," "romantic attachment," "common sense," "popular attitudes," and "public opinion."[30]

Regularly characterized as what "ought to be so" (*dang ran*) and/or what "must be so" (*bi ran*), *li* was not necessarily antithetical to either *qing* or *renqing*. Philosophers (in particular, those active in the seventeenth and eighteenth centuries) were especially eager to reconcile *qing* with *li* by arguing that human affections constituted the fount of the moral life and were thereby coterminous with natural principle. Such arguments, however, had the tendency to be derailed by human affective energies themselves, insofar as they regularly exceeded the bounds of what ought to be so.[31]

The importance of *qing*, *li*, and related terms radiated outward from the realm of moral philosophy, impacting both literary and legal discourses. Thus, writing of the Ming novel *The Plum in the Golden Vase* (Jin ping mei), the literary critic Zhang Zhupo (1670–1698) accounted for its greatness by arguing that its author had achieved, through the depiction of the novel's characters and the construction of its plot, a remarkable level of fidelity to the complexity of human life. In his own words, *Plum in the Golden Vase* "gives full consideration to both *renqing* [human sentiment] and *tianli* [i.e., the natural, moral order of the universe]."[32] About forty-five years later, in a preface (dated 1740) to one of the periodic revisions of *The Qing Penal Code*, the Qianlong emperor (1711–1799) extolled the virtues of his empire's laws with recourse to the exact same terminology, noting that the editing of the *Code* was guided by a dual process of "calculating *tianli* and taking full account of *renqing*."[33]

Although there is no evidence to suggest that either emperor or literary critic sought to establish a link between the fashioning of literary narratives and the complex tradition of juridical thinking (of which *The Qing Code* may be seen as a culmination), the observations of both men nevertheless suggest that the legal and literary traditions of the late imperial period shared a conceptual vocabulary that lent to each a sophisticated means of discussing the potential gaps between the real and the ideal. What is more, in certain literary texts, notably a number of short stories and novels dating from the late Ming to the mid-Qing, concern with the notions of *qing* and *li* opened up a space for legal storytelling, in which *bao* was only a peripheral factor, if it was relevant at all.

"Receiving Good News in Prison" (Tong guita jianxin denghuo), by Ling

Mengchu (1580–1644), provides a good example of this phenomenon. Essentially a romance, this vernacular short story involves two young people who enter into a clandestine relationship and are caught in flagrante delicto. The young girl's family initiates legal proceedings against the young man, Zhang Youqian, who is remanded into custody. While awaiting the adjudication of his case, Zhang receives news that he has passed high in the imperial civil service examinations. Impressed by this accomplishment, the magistrate releases Zhang and proposes a marriage between the young couple in order to legitimize their affair. Unfortunately, the young girl has already been betrothed to another young man. This young man's family appeals the case to the magistrate's superior, arguing: "Zhang Youqian debauched a young woman and was thus imprisoned. Relying on his own authority and acting out of favoritism [*wei qing*], the county magistrate did not properly pursue the case. Indeed, he is a corrupt official [*wang fa*]!"[34]

Crucial here is the semantic slippage of the term *qing*. From the complainant's perspective, "acting out of favoritism" is nothing more than evidence of corruption. Deeply invested in the fulfillment of the young couple's "romantic affection" (*qing*), however, the narrative treats the county magistrate's desire to balance the requirements of the law against the "prompting of his heart" (another possible translation for *wei qing*) as a positive gesture, even though the magistrate himself must admit that the complainant is "justified" (*lizhi*) in appealing the case. This tolerance of moral ambiguities is a key feature of the mature style of late imperial *renqing xiaoshuo*.

RENQING AND JUSTICE IN *A LANTERN FOR THE CROSSROADS*

Especially illustrative of just how far realistic *renqing* fiction from the seventeenth and eighteenth centuries could stray from the ironclad certainties of the *bao* plot are a number of episodes from *A Lantern for the Crossroads* (Qilu deng). This mid-Qing novel tells the story of Tan Shaowen, a young man from a good family, who becomes addicted to gambling and nearly loses his family fortune before reforming his errant ways. Written between 1748 and 1777 by Li Lüyuan, *Lantern for the Crossroads* appears at first sight to have very little to do with *New Book for Aid in Eliminating Deceptions*, a work that predates Li's novel by some 150 years. The didactic authority of *Lantern for the Crossroads*, however, derives from a similar rhetoric of experience. Just as the preface of *New Book for Aid in Eliminating Deceptions* promises a certain insight into the decadent ways of humankind, so, too, the narrator of *Lantern for the Crossroads* presumes to guide readers away from the worldly temptations that lead Tan Shaowen astray. Both works, moreover, preach an ethic of self-mastery and control.

But the similarities between Li's *Lantern for the Crossroads* and *New Book for Aid in Eliminating Deceptions* run even deeper, as the plot of the landlord gulled into trespassing on the virtue of his tenant's wife reappears in Li's novel, this time with Tan Shaowen as the luckless landlord. As is well known, Ming and Qing novelists drew from a wide variety of sources in the creation of their various narrative episodes and plots: other works of fiction, the theater, classical tales, joke books, personal experience, and what they claim to have overheard in conversation with friends, neighbors, and acquaintances. There is thus no reason to assume any direct connection between the two works just because they share common narrative material. For the purposes of this study, it is sufficient to recognize this plot as part of what we might call a "cultural imaginary"—a repository of images, ideas, and stories from which people constructed their interpretations of the world.

In this regard, we would do well to consider how or whether the landlord-tenant story changes from one telling to the next. As we might expect, the treatment of the same basic plot in *Lantern for the Crossroads* and *New Book for Aid in Eliminating Deceptions* entails certain differences. In the latter, the story is an isolated anecdote told primarily to illustrate the kind of shamelessness to which people will stoop in order to make a profit. The anecdotal character of the story is reflected in the lifeless half-classical, half-vernacular language in which it is told, an idiom used throughout *New Book for Aid in Eliminating Deceptions*. In the former, however, this subplot serves a greater purpose. The minor family crisis occasioned by the discovery of Tan's dalliance with the tenant's wife provides Li Lüyuan with a means of addressing the thematic core of his novel: the emotional ties and moral commitments—in other words, *renqing*—that constitute the bedrock of family and social life. Thus, whereas the landlord, the tenant, and the tenant's wife in *New Book for Aid in Eliminating Deceptions* are basically characterless ciphers, in *Lantern for the Crossroads*, readers see Tan Shaowen tremble, cry, and beg for his mother's forgiveness.

At a certain level of abstraction, however, there are clear similarities between the two versions. Neither author is interested in seeing the malefactors brought to justice. In both anecdotes, the tenant and his wife go unpunished, simply disappearing into the night. Both authors are significantly interested, moreover, in describing the depravity—what might be called the deficiency of *renqing*—that defines this and all other examples of criminal behavior. From this perspective, victims quite often share responsibility for the crimes that are committed against them, insofar as lack of self-restraint has allowed them to become easy targets for criminals, rogues, and con men of all stripes.

Certainly, Li Lüyuan favors this approach to making sense out of crime in *Lantern for the Crossroads*. Consider, for example, the way in which the wronged tenant upbraids Tan Shaowen: "Uncle Tan, woe is me! My wife and I have left our native village. When we were at home, we trusted in our parents to nurture us, but we are abroad now and must look to you, our landlord and master, for protection. Since you have read both Confucius and Mencius, you must be aware of the rituals of the Duke of Zhou. Why, then, do you take advantage of us and oppress us so?"[35] Although deeply ironic, this speech nevertheless hits its mark; Tan's actions have indeed trampled on the human sentiment that in theory ought to bind a landlord to his tenants. What is perhaps even more significant is the etiology of Tan's bad behavior: Identified by the narrator as stemming from "unsettled blood and *qi*" (*xie qi bu ding*), Tan's sexual interest in the tenant's wife is thus tied to deficient moral self-cultivation, through which a young man might be expected to control his unruly desires

Obviously, the focus on issues of *renqing* in the example above is not necessarily opposed to the kinds of considerations that come into play when crime narratives center on the reciprocal justice of *bao*. In fact, we can see a clear kinship between both kinds of narratives—crime narratives that focus on *renqing* and crime narratives that focus on the workings of *bao*—insofar as each is concerned with a sense of balance. Thus, even though not all wrongdoers receive the punishment they deserve in the landlord-tenant episode from *Lantern for the Crossroads*, Tan Shaowen's predicament illustrates, however imperfectly, a kind of *bao*, because the narrative clearly implies that Shaowen's own misdeeds set him up to be victimized.

Unlike narratives that illustrate the straightforward application of *bao* as a structuring and ideological principle, however, legal fictions that prioritize issues of *renqing* often involve a far greater tolerance of moral ambiguity. Recall, for example, how the landlord-tenant plot in *New Book for Aid in Eliminating Deceptions* concludes with the victimized landlord allowed one additional night of dalliance as a means of assuaging his offended sentiments. If readers are expecting the absolute justice inherent in a *bao*-based narrative, this solution cannot help but be highly unsatisfactory. As a narrative concerned with balancing *renqing*, however, the conclusion is far more comprehensible, however perverse it may be.

CONCLUSION

To conclude, I would like to turn to the way the discourse of *renqing* influenced the actual representation of legal proceedings in vernacular fiction. In one final episode from *Lantern for the Crossroads*, the novel's protagonist benefits from a miscarriage of justice that is never remedied. The facts of the case are as follows: Tan Shaowen is a participant in a game of dice in which another young man, Dou Yougui, loses a considerable sum of money. In despair, Dou kills himself, exposing Shaowen to legal prosecution as an accessory to suicide. The bereaved father lodges a complaint with the court. Through the connections of family friends, Shaowen hastily arranges to become the student of the magistrate who will judge the matter. In exchange for accepting Shaowen as his student, the magistrate also accepts a large and hastily assembled collection of gifts from his new disciple. Tellingly, the gifts/bribes are referred to throughout the episode as *renqing*, the term rendered here as "human sentiment." When the magistrate hears the case, he does indeed take due consideration of *renqing* and refuses to allow Shaowen's name to be mentioned in court. The one defendant who does is brutally beaten.[36]

That this miscarriage of justice works to the advantage of the novel's protagonist highlights the uneasy linguistic and narrative collusion between bribery and sentiment in a fictional world that is far removed from the moral calculus of *bao*, as represented in the more standard fictional accounts of courtroom procedure. This episode also appears to expose the negative aspects of the injunction that magistrates accord appropriate consideration to *renqing* as it affected abstract legal or moral principle (*li*). Of course, a certain narrative and emotional justice is served by allowing Shaowen to escape the punishment others receive in his stead. At the same time, one cannot help but feel bribed—that is, forced to consider *renqing*—to the extent that pity for Shaowen hinges on the connection we feel with him as the protagonist of the novel.

Ultimately, the consideration of *renqing* in judicial deliberations may be interpreted simultaneously as either the worst kind of corruption or the greatest kind of compassion. Episodes such as this one remind us that certain kinds of legal storytelling in late imperial China—whether within the system or without—were quite sophisticated as well as considerably tolerant of moral ambiguity. Pushing our understanding of crime, punishment, and vernacular fiction beyond *bao*, moreover, leads us to understand that not all late imperial fictional accounts of legal matters relied for their meaning on a single ideological-aesthetic structure. As powerful and as flexible a notion as *bao* was, it remained susceptible to critique. Indeed, dissatisfaction with its explanatory power was strong enough to compel a significant minority of authors to explore alternate ways of narrating stories of crime, criminality, and justice (or the lack thereof). A common thread running through all the crime narratives addressed here is that meaning must be found in the uncertain task of negotiating the contingencies of a legal system shaped by both the ideals *and* the imperfections of the humans who lived within it.

NOTES

1. Jonathan Ocko makes this point in chapter 12 in this volume. He explains: "Parties to conflicts first shaped . . . dueling narratives to make cogent cases to potential mediators. Then, if necessary, as plaintiffs or defendants, the parties revised their narratives in an effort to persuade the magistrate to hear or dismiss the case and to obtain the result they sought."

2. Korobkin, *Criminal Conversations*, 11.

3. See Ocko, chapter 12, in this volume.

4. To borrow a distinction made by Jonathan Ocko, in chapter 12 in this volume.

5. Li Yu's three collections are *A New Aid to Administration* (Zizhi xinshu), "*A New Aid to Administration,*" Second Collection (Zizhi xinshu erji), and *Preserving Life* (Qiu sheng lu). These texts are discussed in Hanan, *Invention of Li Yu*, 25–26. On Li Lüyuan, see Yinjiang County Gazetteer (Yinjiang xianzhi), ed. Zheng Shifan (1837), as quoted in Luan, "*Qilu deng" yanjiu ziliao*, 21.

6. See Ocko, chapter 12 in this volume.

7. On the connection of vernacular fiction with literati culture, see Plaks, *Four Masterworks*, 3–52.

8. See chapter 4, by Robert Hegel, in this volume.

9. The term "justice hero" is from Katherine Carlitz, chapter 11, in this volume.

10. On the morally active universe, see Hanan, *Chinese Vernacular Story*, 26–27.

11. Carlitz also demonstrates how the notion of justice shifted over time in successive retellings of one *bao*-based tale; see chapter 11 in this volume.

12. Kao, "Bao and Baoying," 135.

13. Ibid., 133–36. "Fifteen Strings of Cash" is in Feng Menglong, *Xing shi heng*

yan, 724–40. The plot of the story may be divided into two parts. In the first, a series of tragic coincidences leads to the death of three people, two by execution for a crime they did not commit. In part two, another series of coincidences (which unfortunately include the death of an old man) leads to the punishment of the actual criminal and the belated rectification of judicial mistakes.

14. Plaks, "After the Fall," 575–79.

15. Xingshi yinyuan zhuan, vol. 1, 402. Translated in Plaks, "After the Fall," 576.

16. Xingshi yinyuan zhuan, vol. 1, 402.

17. When exacting revenge on Ma and his wife, Ma's adoptive parents claim to be acting on Heaven's behalf. Just how the parallel systems of cosmic and human justice ought to interact, however, was a contested issue in the late imperial period, as this very incident from Marriage Bonds to Awaken the World demonstrates. When the spirits of Ma's adoptive parents first inhabit the bodies of Ma and his wife, they are banished by an exorcist who censures them thus: "Humans and ghosts have separate dominions. If you have a grievance, you ought to make your complaint in the underworld court. Why have you chosen to vex the mortal world with such spectral mischief? [Cosmic] law cannot easily countenance your confounding of the distinction between yin and yang!" Thus, when the adoptive parents' spirits return to re-possess the bodies of Ma Congwu and his wife, they make sure this time to offer evidence of the legitimacy of their actions in the form of a "Heavenly tally" (tian fu). See Xingshi yinyuan zhuan, vol. 1, 401–2.

18. Ibid., 402.

19. Ibid., 403.

20. Shen Defu, Wanli yehuo bian, 6.

21. Philip C. C. Huang, Civil Justice in China, 203.

22. In addition to his name, all that is known of this individual is that he hailed from Kuizhong in Zhejiang.

23. This preface is not found in the Naikaku Bunko edition of Zhang Yingyu, Du pian xinshu. According to the editors of Rare and Scarce Editions of Classical Chinese Novels (Zhongguo gudai zhenxiben xiaoshuo), the preface exists in an edition of Du pian xinshu in the collection of the Tōkyō Daigaku Tōkyō Bunka Kenkyūjo. These same editors have included a partial transcription of this preface in Zhongguo gudai zhenxiben xiaoshuo, vol. 5, 4.

24. From 1594, the date of the publication of the earliest extant edition of Judge Bao's Hundred Cases (Bao Longtu pan baijia gong'an), to the end of the Ming dynasty, at least eleven collections of court-case stories were published; these shared common themes, a literary style, and the verbatim copying of material from one collection to another. For a list of these titles, see Qi, Mingdai xiaoshuo shi, 219–27; for a detailed textual study, see Hanan, "Judge Bao's Hundred Cases

Reconstructed," 301–23; and for discussion of the textual borrowings among court-case collections, see Y. W. Ma, "The Textual Tradition," 190–220.

25. The title page of *New Book for Aid in Eliminating Deceptions* indicates Chen as the publisher of the work; the exact wording is "Printed by Chen Huaixuan of the Cunren Tang [Publishing House]." The title page of *Court Cases Examined in Detail* has a similar notation. I have been unable to find out any information about the Cunren Tang, but Wang Qingyuan, Mou Renlong, and Han Xiduo, *Xiaoshuo shufang lu*, give Chen's formal name as Chen Junjing.

26. Zhang Yingyu, *Du pian xinshu*, 25a.

27. Ibid., 6a–8b.

28. Ibid., 146a–49a.

29. Rowe, *Saving the World*, 103.

30. Ibid., 103.

31. For extensive discussion of this issue, see Martin W. Huang, *Desire and Fictional Narrative*, 23–56.

32. Zhang Zhupo, "Piping diyi qishu *Jin Ping Mei* dufa," 45.

33. Quoted in Rowe, *Saving the World*, 103.

34. Ling Mengchu, *Pai'an jingqi*, vol. 2, 519.

35. Li Lüyuan, *Qilu deng*, vol. 1, 269.

36. Ibid., vol. 2, 469–90.

11   Genre and Justice in Late Qing China
     Wu Woyao's Strange Case of Nine Murders
     and Its Antecedents

KATHERINE CARLITZ

How much law did late imperial Chinese people know, and what did they expect from it? What can we learn from the fiction they created about law? The works examined here, whose audiences ranged from intellectuals to the illiterate, suggest that they may have had quite an accurate understanding of their legal system. Their idea of real justice, however, might involve personal and cosmic demands better met by literature, with its unlimited capacity to right wrongs and avenge the innocent, or by the rituals, described by Paul Katz in chapter 8, whose practitioners could try to influence Heaven itself. Nevertheless, the works discussed here all tell a tale of vindication through the *courts*. Why did this tale remain attractive, and how did the language and shaping effect of literature provide audiences the justice they demanded?

The core story is best known to modern audiences from the late Qing novel *The Strange Case of Nine Murders* (Jiuming qiyuan), by Wu Woyao (1866–1910).[1] Wu's plot derives from an eighteenth-century property dispute in Panyu county, Guangdong, which is said to have resulted in the wholesale slaughter of one family by another. The sole survivor takes his appeal for justice all the way to the emperor, arguing his case at the county, prefectural, provincial, and capital levels, in a startlingly accurate representation of the late imperial appeals route. Frustrated at every turn by the machinations of his enemies, he is finally vindicated by high officials who have the emperor's confidence.

This case had been fictionalized at least twice before Wu wrote, and the story was still widely known by the mid-twentieth century. Three late Qing printed versions are analyzed here: the traditional novel *A New Warning about Wealth* (Jing fu xin shu), from 1809; an anonymous *nanyin*, a form of narrative song popular since at least the Ming dynasty, *Liang Tianlai Brings His Complaint to the Emperor* (Liang Tianlai gao yu zhuang), from 1904; and Wu Woyao's modern novel *The Strange Case of Nine Murders*, from 1907.[2]

Spanning a century, these three versions were produced in very different social and judicial contexts, in which the same tale could have very different resonances. The earliest, *New Warning*, is a traditional vernacular novel, in which a cumulative, linear narrative progression works to create a sense of cosmic inevitability. A century later, in Wu Woyao's *Nine Murders*, a fractured narrative pattern expresses the breakdown of faith in cosmic justice—at least on the part of intellectuals in the late Qing. The late Qing *nanyin*, whose certainties are underscored by repeated refrains and the sense of coherence engendered by rhyme, remind us that vast numbers of Chinese retained the faith in cosmic requital that Wu Woyao rejects. Important for us, however, is that throughout the nineteenth century and into the twentieth, a tale of a quest for justice through an accurately represented legal system remained persistently popular. Fiction could do what law could not: actual cases led jurists deeper and deeper into complexity, while literary form allowed for simpler, comprehensive solutions. But the paradigm of law—punishment of the guilty and vindication of the innocent—was ideally suited to those comprehensive literary solutions.

CODE, COSMOLOGY, AND FICTION

This paradigm of law was understood by most Chinese in late imperial times as a matter of cosmic as well as earthly justice. By the end of the Qing dynasty, however, modernizers were questioning this traditional belief. Thus, the works examined here express radically different ideas about humanity and Heaven. Understanding these differences and their historical significance requires some background on late imperial views of justice.

First, though cosmic and earthly justice were intertwined in ways that are discussed below, law was promulgated by the imperial dynasties and small states that preceded them. It was never understood as the gift of a deity, or even a gift from the semidivine culture heroes who had tamed the primordial floods and given humanity agriculture and writing.[3] But while the laws of empire remained basically secular, serving the state by regulating administration and punishment, these laws never exhausted the category of judgment in the general understanding. Paralleling the evolution of secular law was that of an all-encompassing vision of the cosmos, now seen as interconnected by numerous overlapping classification systems: *yin* and *yang*, the Five Phases, correlations with the planets and constellations, and many more. The Han dynasty (206 B.C.E.–220 C.E.) saw a monumental and long-lasting synthesis of these correlations, linking natural phenomena to human ethics and actions such that any deed had the power to reinforce or disturb cosmic harmony. In the sixteenth century, for example, officials regularly petitioned the emperor to reduce taxes in order to avert droughts, and cosmic correlations published in today's East Asian almanacs are still used to calculate appropriate times to marry, build, or encoffin.[4]

Developments in religious and judicial thought worked to deepen a sense of congruence between the earthly and the divine.[5] Texts antedating Confucius saw Heaven as lengthening or shortening lives in response to virtue or vice, and Chinese over the next two millennia developed an ever more detailed understanding of celestial and infernal bureaucracies, seen as completely congruent with officialdom on earth.[6] (As Katz shows in chapter 8 in this volume, judicial procedure was the same on earth and in the underworld.) By the Song dynasty (960–1279), the state claimed a monopoly over relations with the spirit bureaucracy, creating registers of recognized deities and forbidding the worship of those not on the lists.[7] One result was increasing mistrust of individuals who claimed independent ability to discern or influence divine judgment, and this is amply demonstrated in the treatment of the geomancer Semi-Immortal Ma in the texts discussed below.

The systematization of the spirit world paralleled that of the earthly judiciary. Song judicial practice was increasingly standardized, as seen from the widespread adoption of China's great forensic manual *The Washing Away of Wrongs* (Xi yuan lu).[8] Song dynasty plaintiffs faced magistrates, prefects, and provincial officials whose status was greatly enhanced.[9] Not surprisingly, then, the Song is the dynasty in which imaginative literature about earthly courts began to appear. Initially, this literature centered on the figure of the judge himself. (As imperial China had no independent judiciary, this judge would have been a county magistrate, a prefect, a censor, or a provincial official.) These fictional judges were soon endowed with semidivine power: a Song dynasty prefect named Bao Zheng (999–1062) developed into a figure of mythic proportions, uniting the earthly and underworld realms, judging Earth by day and Hell by night. As James St. André explains in chapter 9, Judge Bao and his ilk play fast and loose with actual law, but by the nineteenth and early twentieth centuries, the nine murders texts had become vastly more faithful to actual judicial practice. Nevertheless, two of the three works studied here express firm belief in the interpenetration of human and divine justice.

APPEALING A CAPITAL VERDICT IN QING DYNASTY LAW

In his introduction to this volume, Robert E. Hegel describes the painstaking review process required under Qing dynasty law for judging capital crimes. The county magistrate took direct testimony from all parties concerned and recommended an appropriate sentence, but this sentence could not be executed until officials at the prefectural, provincial, and capital levels had reexamined the defendant and the evidence (and sometimes relevant witnesses as well) and seen to it that the case record was free of procedural errors. Only after this multistage review was the case given to the emperor for his concurrence, and even then, it would be examined once more by provincial and capital authorities before the sentence was carried out.

Two seminal articles show that plaintiffs and defendants also used these stages to appeal unfavorable judgments. Jonathan Ocko surveys Qing regulations and archival materials and demonstrates that a flood of such appeals threatened to overwhelm the system by the early nineteenth century.[10] Professional plaint-writers who helped with these appeals were the bane of officialdom, contributing as they did to the backlog. But in fiction, the appeals process could be experienced as a powerful way to clear one's name, and the skillful plaint-writer could be seen as a Heaven-sent friend.[11]

This is not to say, however, that appeals always, or even typically, proceeded swiftly along the path prescribed by regulation. William P. Alford chronicles a murder case that made its way upward through the Qing appeals process in the 1890s.[12] Yang Naiwu, unjustly accused of murdering his landlord's wife "Little Cabbage" (Xiao Baicai), was convicted at the county, prefectural, and provincial levels. He filed two appeals directly at the capital level and was finally released when forensic evidence was reexamined. Significantly, however, the appeals process came perilously close to failing him. Only through the efforts of a peripherally involved censor was the case retrieved from the archives, and only through the demands of eighteen scandalized officials was the evidence found to be tainted and Yang Naiwu (after two more reviews) released.[13] In such a case, can the system itself be trusted, or must the accused hope for a "justice hero" to come to his aid and make the laws function as they should? The three works discussed here incline to the latter view. In all of them, however, transcendental schemata ensure that a justice hero will appear, to rehabilitate the legal system by linking it either to divine reward and punishment or to the expectation that modernizing rationality will sweep corruption away.

A NEW WARNING ABOUT WEALTH

The forty-chapter *A New Warning about Wealth* was published in or shortly after 1809, by the Hanxuan Lou, probably of Guangdong. It is a vernacular novel in chapters, with typical late Qing generic features: parallel-prose chapter-title couplets, a simulated storyteller context (the narrator tells readers to "listen" to the tale to come), and ample use of interlinear commentary. The preface, by the otherwise unidentified Minzhai Jushi (Resident Scholar of Sagacity Studio), names a similarly pseudonymous Anhe Xiansheng (Master of Peace and Harmony) as the author. This 1809 edition is illustrated and clearly printed, but the illustrations are fairly crude, and the text is riddled with nonstandard characters. *New Warning* does not seem to be self-consciously directed at an elite audience, though it presumes considerable literacy.

The earliest extant record of the case itself is a narrative dating from 1794, which was quickly followed by *New Warning*.[14] Only in 1871 did the Panyu county gazetteer include a brief mention of the hero, the villain, and the "seven corpses and eight deaths" that would become a byword for the crime itself.[15] Whatever the historicity of the case, the story of the case was firmly established by the time of *New Warning*. Certain key events (outrages committed by the hero's enemies, instances of devotion by the hero's friends) are repeated in all versions, though they are not interpreted uniformly. The alternate titles to *New Warning* and *Liang Tianlai's Complaint* allude to age-old connotations of the word *xue* (snow), namely, avenging wrongs to clear one's name.

New Warning begins, like much of late imperial Chinese fiction and drama, with a poem advocating detachment from the struggle for fortune and fame:

> Is it not comfortable, to be idle and without cares?
> The red sun in your eastern window finds you still asleep.
> Peaceful contemplation shows you the self-contained world,
> The pleasures of the four seasons the same as those of men.
> Throughout Heaven and Earth, the Way exists in a formless state,
> Loose your thoughts into wind and clouds, and transformation will hit the mark.
> Rich and famous without excess, humble but nonetheless happy,
> He who reaches this point becomes a hero indeed.[16]

The next sentence reminds us that "we Confucians" (*wu ru*) contain within our own breasts the secret of true happiness, with no need of wealth or rank, and advises readers not to venture above their station. The story to come, says the narrator, is a tale of a wealthy scion who did not heed this advice, causing contention and Heavenly wrath.

After this brief prologue, the story introduces the protagonists Liang Tianlai and Ling Guixing, the sons of two deceased merchants who had been devoted friends. (The two families are also connected by marriage, Liang Tianlai's father having taken a wife from the Ling family.) Liang Tianlai, who runs a candy store, is happy to continue in the path of small commerce. But the Ling family has become wealthy, and Ling Guixing aches to satisfy his one remaining desire by becoming an official. However, he has repeatedly failed the civil service examination. Not even a bribe to the provincial examiner produces the desired result. His evil uncle Zongkong suggests calling in a *fengshui* master with the intriguing name of Semi-Immortal Ma (Ma Banxian) to ascertain the cause. Semi-Immortal Ma tells them that Liang Tianlai's stone house (built by Tianlai's father, and the pride of the Liang family) is an obstacle to the proper flow of *qi*, or vital energy, around the Ling family tombs. He assures the Ling uncle and nephew that if they manage to raze the stone house, their family is bound to produce examination winners.

Here, a litany of evil deeds begins. When the astonished Liang Tianlai refuses to accommodate them, the Lings carry out a series of attacks that culminate in setting fire to the stone house, producing seven corpses and eight deaths. (Tianlai's brother's pregnant wife dies, and her unborn child is the eighth death.) The ninth death occurs when the virtuous beggar Zhang Feng, who has overheard the plot and tried to warn the Liang family, serves as their witness in court and is tortured to death by bribed officials.

Liang Tianlai begins the trek from county to prefecture to province in search of justice, aided by a devoted friend, Shi Zhibo, who writes the necessary legal complaints for him. At each level, officials are initially persuaded, and Tianlai appears poised to achieve justice—until the Ling family uses its wealth to subvert the process. Shi Zhibo dies of exhaustion and despair, and the steadfast beggar Zhang Feng succumbs to his third round of torture.

Finally, however, Tianlai finds his justice hero. Shi Zhibo, on his deathbed, counsels Tianlai to seek out the monk Donglai, who writes a new plaint in the form of a song. They plant this song in a Buddhist temple that the provincial governor-general Kong Dapeng is expected to pass. Kong finds the song and is intrigued, whereupon Tianlai throws himself at Kong's feet. Kong quickly takes charge of the case, has Ling Guixing, Ling Zongkong, and their band of thugs thrown in jail, and promises to finish up with an execution as soon as he has managed to get the Yellow River under control. (Kong Dapeng is modeled on an actual governor-general, Kong Yuxun, who administered Guangdong and Guangxi during the Yongzheng era.[17])

Here, a second quest begins. With Kong absent, the Ling family use their wealth to have the prisoners released, and Liang Tianlai is once again in danger. The first half of the book is a journey through the legal system; the second is a journey through China itself, as Tianlai proceeds to Beijing to plead for justice from the emperor. Guixing pays thugs to patrol all roads and passes leading to Beijing, but virtue attracts virtue, and Tianlai is aided by one new friend after another. At a particularly dangerous pass, where customs inspections are being carried out by a local warlord, he crosses hidden in a box supplied by a wealthy merchant. (In this ordeal, his breathing holes are plugged up in part by his own feces, and he almost dies.) Tianlai reaches the capital with letters to powerful officials from his new friends, and the officials bring Kong Dapeng back into the case.

At this point, legal procedure works against Liang Tianlai. Since the case had been decided against him at the provincial level, the emperor is reluctant to intervene and rejects Tianlai's plaint on procedural grounds. But he is persuaded to relent, and the case is once again remanded to Kong Dapeng.

Now the criminals have no recourse. Kong rounds them up and has the wives enslaved and the Ling family goods confiscated.[18] Ling Guixing's young son is to be beheaded. Guixing himself is sentenced to death by slow slicing, the most severe punishment in both *The Ming Code* and *The Qing Code*. In front of the families of the victims, he is pierced, stabbed, gouged, and finally dismembered, a confession having been extracted by torture. But the fate of Guixing's son is more than Liang Tianlai can bear: he cries out that as a Ling family relative by marriage, he cannot let them lose their only male heir. He covers the boy's body with his own and insists on offering his own head. Kong Dapeng is moved to mercy, and the novel ends with praise for the laws of the land, the virtue of Liang Tianlai, and the compassion of Kong Dapeng. Later, in the Qianlong era, says the narrator, the villains will be reborn as slaves, and Liang Tianlai as a man of high standing.

New Warning presents legal procedure and legal materials with scrupulous accuracy. Tianlai brings his petition to the Panyu county magistrate, the Guangzhou prefect, and, at the provincial level, to the Guangdong provincial surveillance commissioner, the provincial governor, and the governor-general. (His case thus follows the rules more strictly than does the actual case described by Alford.) Coroners are shown at work in chapter 13, carrying out tests like those prescribed in *The Washing Away of Wrongs*. (Hot vinegar is applied to the stomach of Tianlai's brother's dead wife, and an image of a male baby appears, thus establishing the sex of the fetus.) We are reminded in chapter 38, as various court officials discuss Tianlai's case, that the Board of Punishments does not take new cases at the end of the year. Standard legal terms are used—*mousha* for the intentional homicide with which Guixing will finally be charged, and *pi* for the rescript in which the magistrate, prefect, or surveillance commissioner hands down his judgment. Tianlai's various advisers impress upon him and the beggar Zhang Feng that a witness is crucial to his success in court, and the emperor himself is a stickler for correct procedure. In chapter 40, officials deliberating Guixing's fate adduce a 1701 capital case as precedent. Legal writing and legal knowledge are clearly salient: Tianlai's friends write legal plaints for him, letters are used to give Tianlai entrée to important people, and the emperor's willingness to hear Tianlai's case hinges on the procedure for presenting written case narratives. The plaint that Shi Zhibo first crafts in chapter 14, while extreme in the events it describes, is formally indistinguishable from those in the case records quoted throughout this volume:

> *Petitioner*: Liang Tianlai
> *Subject of plaint*: The matter of tigerlike overbearing power being used repeatedly to devour, rob, and murder, resulting in seven corpses and eight lost lives.
>
> [I humble as an] ant, tragically alone in the world, live in close proximity to Ling Guixing and his uncle. [Uncle and nephew] wrongly listened to the counsel of a geomancer, and pressed me to tear down my house in order to improve their *fengshui*. Considering that what a father has built, a son should not dismantle, I refused, whereupon we became enemies, and I was repeatedly harassed by them. They dug up the grave of my grandfather Tiangang and cut down the pine trees around it. They set up a white tiger [image] facing my hall and tore down our back wall. They ruined my fishponds, plundered my gardens, ambushed me at the ferry, beat me and stole my money, dug up my taro from the hillside, pulled up my young shoots, stole my white jade flowerpots and pear-wood tables and chairs,[19] repeatedly devouring my substance, and in all things casting me aside. I desired to prepare an accusation, but because of my mother's injunction that rich and poor should cleave to one another, and pebbles refrain from contending, I had no choice but to endure [these wrongs]. Who could have known that ten evil actions would give rise to one thousand woes! The

eighteenth night of the seventh month of the *wu shen* year [1728] was my mother's birthday, and they knew that my brother and I would return home. They gathered a band of ruffians and led them to burn down my house, asphyxiating seven corpses and extinguishing eight lives. I hope to receive the favor of a careful examination by your honor. Zhang Feng saw it all and heard it all, and he desires to testify. Given such a great wrong as this, the blood that has been shed cries out to Heaven. I implore Your Honor to examine this case, and give me immediate relief.[20]

Ling Guixing responds in kind, with a formally appropriate counterplaint, bringing before the court a false claim of a Liang family debt to his father and completely reversing the story of the fight at the ferry. Plaint and counterplaint function, in the context of this vernacular novel, to convey a sense of mythic structure. We read Tianlai's plaint four times: at the county, the prefecture, the provincial surveillance commission, and the provincial governor's yamen. We read Guixing's counterplaint twice, at the county and the prefecture. This steady rise through levels of judgment brings us closer and closer to Heaven's representative on earth, the emperor. That Heaven will see to correct judgment is adumbrated throughout the novel: the commentator remarks in chapter 11 that "Creation is not the work of man." Warning bells ring mysteriously when wrong judgments are handed down in chapter 15. In chapter 28, winds spring up and dash Guixing's evil minions into a ravine when they attempt to open the box in which Liang Tianlai is being spirited through the customs station. And Heaven's hand is evident as the novel concludes with appropriate reincarnations. The legal documents in *New Warning* reinforce these mythic ends: *New Warning* is firmly in the tradition of fiction whose "moral grammar" is the paradigm of *bao*, or requital, the fates of the protagonists ultimately governed by a "morally active universe."[21] As Daniel Youd shows in chapter 10, *bao* did not govern all of late imperial fiction, but in *New Warning*, a justice hero sees to it that law and justice are one. Legal documents function in *New Warning* as instruments of *bao*, enriching the narrative texture by adding the authority of legal process to the authority of the cosmos.[22]

But what of Liang Tianlai's judicial setbacks? Shi Zhibo embellishes his plaint at each level, but the rescripts of denial become increasingly angry, until the provincial governor threatens Liang Tianlai with death if he tries to sue again. The courts seem to be failing Tianlai altogether, ultimately driving him out to a temple to find his protector. Each of Ling Guixing's successful bribes, however, serves in the long run only to magnify his villainy and increase our sense of Tianlai's wronged innocence. And in the end, the paradigm of law is upheld. Only because he follows the appeals route to the letter does Tianlai find his protector and gain access to the emperor. Semi-Immortal Ma, Ling Guixing, and all of Ling's relatives and confederates are given sentences that accord reasonably with *The Qing Code*. Judgment fails, in fact, only at the systemic level: none of the bribed officials is punished, a point to which we return below.

The very diction of *New Warning* works to convey a sense of certainty and predictability. While the plaints are written in elevated classical language, the rhythm of their four-, six-, and seven-character phrases is quite similar to that of the conventional, stylized vernacular of the narrative. The following passage, in which Guixing's sister attempts to reason with him, suggests the cadences of this novel: "'Brother, you surely know that blood and flesh make us close. How then is Tianlai distant? How could you dig up his hillside, cut down his trees, and demolish his wall? Why are you clear about me, but confused about him?' Guixing answered: 'If he sees me as kin, how can he ruin my *fengshui*, and deny me a post?'"[23] The lull of these parallel constructions and familiar rhythms tends to be associated with a whole range of familiar expectations, and the rhythms of *New Warning* work together with those of legal language to make justice seem all the more inevitable. In the great masterpieces of traditional vernacular fiction, these familiar rhythms and expectations are often manipulated to produce startling ironies, but *New Warning*, a modest work, reinforces rather than questions our faith in requital.

Finally, the conventions of illustration and page layout in the 1809 edition of *New Warning* reinforce the reader's expectation of judgment. Before the text begins, the reader is presented with twelve full-page illustrations, beginning with Semi-Immortal Ma, the *fengshui* master whose divination sets the Lings on their nefarious course, and concluding with Provincial Surveillance Commissioner Kong Dapeng, who has Ma beaten and banished, and "washes away" the wrong done to Liang Tianlai by executing Ling Guixing. Captions to the illustrations leave no doubt that we are proceeding from evil to good. And in chapter 39, when Liang Tianlai actually meets the emperor, the orthographic conventions that require words denoting the emperor to be printed at the top of a column cause the reader, who now joins Tianlai in the presence of the ruler, to respond with awe. The totalizing rhetoric of *New Warning* leaves readers no space in which to consider alternatives: moralizing poems stud the text, and interlinear commentary, in reduced-size double columns interpolated into many pages, creates the illusion of learned teachers who reinforce the book's certainties.

LIANG TIANLAI BRINGS HIS COMPLAINT TO THE EMPEROR

Like the poem that opens *New Warning*, the opening poem to the *nanyin Liang Tianlai Brings His Complaint to the Emperor* invokes cosmic cycles and advises readers to stay in their stations. Added to this, however, is a warning against the abuse of power:

> Worldly affairs that swirl like snow should always be curtailed;
> Holding fast to one's lot in life serves to reduce one's woes.
> Careful, cautious, I rely on my virtuous nature,
> While my enemy and his henchmen presume on unscrupulous might.
> But wealth redoubled through hidden vice gives rise to villainous ways,
> And law will bring bad deeds to light, vanquishing greed and guile.
> Realize that the tyrant's might is no more than a dream,
> And only then will you understand the cycles of Heaven and Earth.

This 1904 *nanyin* streamlines the story and makes it even more clearly a tale of reward and punishment, with earthly law inseparable from supernatural judgment.

This *nanyin* version testifies to the widespread currency of the nine murders tale. *Nanyin* is one of a family of genres, including the *tanci* of central and northern China, in which stories are sung in seven-character lines, with brief interpolations of spoken prose. (*Nanyin* can run to the length of a short novel and were doubtless performed over many sessions.) *Nanyin* are best preserved today in Fujian, Taiwan, and Guangdong, where they are sung in local dialects. In Guangdong, *nanyin* are traditionally identified with itinerant blind singers. An early-twentieth-century vogue for printing inexpensive *nanyin* texts probably stabilized these oral versions, as was the case with the printing of vernacular literature during the Ming and Qing dynasties.[24]

The extant *Liang Tianlai's Complaint*, a *nanyin* in six *juan*, or sections, shows clear evidence of oral development independent of or divergent from the text of the novel *New Warning*. Here, Guixing's name is written with the character *gui* (cassia) rather than the character *gui* (honorable, costly) of both novels. Moreover, Guixing and Zongkong trade names in this version: Guixing is the uncle, and Zongkong the nephew who pines for an official post.

Nonetheless, and despite plot differences detailed below, *Liang Tianlai's Complaint* is faithful to the core story in *New Warning*. Here, too, we follow the case through each level of an accurately represented Qing dynasty appeals route. At each level, plaint and counterplaint are reproduced, transformed to fit the seven-character *nanyin* line. Thus, at the prefecture, uncle and nephew are indignant about the charges filed against them:

> May Heaven's bright mirror hear our words,
> In the bandit raid we took no part!
> This has to do with our father's wealth:
> He lent the Liangs three thousand taels.
> Years passed; no interest did they pay,
> Thus wealth created enmity.[25]

Uncle and nephew continue with their version of the fight at the ferry, but Tianlai pleads with the prefect to see their true part in the murders:

> Zongkong and Guixing, with evil hearts,
> Led a bandit troupe to do me harm!
> They toppled my walls, destroyed my ponds,
> Pulled up my crops, and cursed my hall.
> At the ferry, they stole my cash receipts;
> At my family tombs, destroyed our graves.
> Heartlessly, they all made off
> With my tables, chairs, and flowerpots!
> Who knew they would compound their crime
> And target my brother's life and mine!
> Mother's birthday they calculated,
> And stealthily by our gates they waited.
> That beggar warned me, and none too soon—
> We ran off guided by stars and moon,
> Leaving my mother, wife, and maid,
> And my brother's wife, within our gates.
> All ran to the room they thought was safe:
> They thought that thus they'd saved their lives.
> But Guixing, Zongkong, and all their gang
> A night of wickedness had planned.
> In through the cracks swept smoke and fire,
> Claiming seven corpses and eight lives.[26]

Within the constraints of the *nanyin* form, these stanzas function as legal documents: Tianlai "asks a legal expert to write him a document" (*qing lüshi zuo zhi*), introduces his plaint with the locution *bing*, standard for introducing legal

Genre and Justice in Late Qing China 245

testimony, and speaks of himself as "bringing suit" (*gao zhuang*). As far as the *nanyin* is concerned, this is simply legal language in verse, though an actual legal document is used to render judgment against the criminals at the end of the text.

Where *Liang Tianlai's Complaint* differs from *New Warning*, the effect is to focus our attention on the Lings as villains and Tianlai as victim, paring away side plots that might divert our attention. The Ling uncle and nephew, concerned that the family has no successful examination candidates, call in Semi-Immortal Ma and learn that *fengshui* is indeed to blame. But the bribery of the examination official, and Guixing's and Zongkong's disappointment, are not in the *nanyin* at all. And instead of asking Tianlai to sell his house, nephew and uncle simply begin the series of depredations designed to drive him out. Tianlai's complaints to the authorities omit all mention of the *fengshui* master, plunging immediately into a recital of the Ling family's evil deeds. Kong Dapeng does not find Tianlai's plaint in a Buddhist temple; rather, Tianlai stops Kong's carriage and hands him the document. And while new friends help Tianlai on his way to Beijing, *Liang Tianlai's Complaint* omits the most affecting friendship in *New Warning*, namely that of Shi Zhibo, who willingly martyrs himself in the service of Tianlai's cause. In *Liang Tianlai's Complaint*, Tianlai simply has an unidentified practitioner draw up his complaint.

The most radical differences between *nanyin* and novel, however, are found in their concluding episodes. *New Warning* adumbrated a link between earthly and supernatural justice, but in *Liang Tianlai's Complaint*, that link is made explicit. Storms arise and bells ring as in *New Warning*, but *Liang Tianlai's Complaint* goes further. Once jailed, Guixing and Zongkong are executed, not by the state, but by the spirits of those they have wronged:

> Our agonies of torment and floods of tears,
> Resentment like the sea and high as Heaven,
> Caused the Lord of the Underworld to give us leave
> To apprehend you in the world of light!
> Whirling, swirling in the flux of Hell,
> Our bellies sliced by stabs of pain,
> He saw the suffering of us piteous souls,
> Our undried tears, our death in vain;
> No weapon to wield except our grief,
> Our tearstained eyes gazing high and low,
> Unrighteous Guixing caused us rage
> By his vicious assault on our house and home,

>   The endless list of his evil deeds,
>   The fire that took eight innocent lives!²⁷

The spirits then pour into the jail where Guixing and Zongkong are sleeping and beat them mercilessly until they sicken, confess their guilt, and die.

But far from supplanting earthly justice, their deaths energize the presiding supervising censor to convene court and order the beheading of their confederates. As in *New Warning*, Tianlai pleads successfully to have the nephew's son spared, and the account of justice concludes with the authority of a case report rendered in standard legal language:

> In the matter of the capital case previously decided by Governor-General Kong of Guangdong and Guangxi, and subsequently reinvestigated by Supervising Censor E in the seventh month of the year Yongzheng 9. Confession has been obtained to the effect that Ling Zongkong ordered his servant Yuanxiang to contract for illegal services, promising payment of two taels of silver to each [member] of a gang of ruffians, by a stipulated date. His trusted friend Xu Wanchang assembled a gang of seventeen, and on the second day of the ninth month of Yongzheng 5, the gang gathered at Songzai Ridge. Ling Yuanxiang then pointed out Liang Tianlai's dwelling to them, and they set the fire that resulted in seven corpses and [the loss of] eight lives. So determined on this date in the tenth month.²⁸

The *nanyin* ends with a true comic resolution, a realization of the promised cycles of Heaven and Earth: once the case is resolved, Tianlai's friends send for a matchmaker, who finds a bride for Tianlai. *Liang Tianlai's Complaint* concludes with society (in the form of Tianlai's family) fully restored. His mother is still at his side, his brother is also remarried, their children and grandchildren will marry as well, and Tianlai's family members will all live past the age of ninety. Reward and punishment are seen as the theme of the tale:

>   One who fails to repay favor is not a true gentleman;
>   One who fails to avenge wrongs cannot be considered human.²⁹

THE STRANGE CASE OF NINE MURDERS

This cosmic certainty evaporates when we turn to Wu Woyao. Wu left Guangdong at the age of twenty to work as a journalist in Shanghai, and he served

Genre and Justice in Late Qing China 247

his literary apprenticeship under the satirist Li Baojia (1867–1906). Both men published fiction in the Shanghai periodical press, and Wu followed Li in producing biting social critique. As a young turn-of-the-century intellectual, Wu Woyao was enraged over Western incursions into China, even as he devoured the translations of Western literature that were easily available in Shanghai. He was simultaneously a rebel and a conservative: true to a number of traditional Chinese ideals (filial piety, heroic chastity) but a declared enemy of superstition and corruption, the two evils that he felt had caused China to lose ground in its struggle with the West.[30]

Intellectuals such as Wu Woyao worked to modernize the novel in accordance with a program enunciated by the reformer Liang Qichao, in his 1898 "Preface to the Printing of Political Novels in Translation" (Yi yin zhengzhi xiaoshuo xu). Liang explicitly called upon the novel to be a means of strengthening China by reforming both society and subjectivity. As Theodore Huters has shown, Liang's call was issued in the atmosphere of "crisis and utopian hope" following China's defeat by Japan in 1895.[31] Liang saw the vernacular novel as an ideal instrument for reaching mass audiences, but only if it could be thoroughly reformed: no longer must it be allowed to lead readers to crime, as did *Water Margin* (Shuihu zhuan), or to lust, as did *The Story of the Stone* (Shitou ji). Readers should, instead, be led to a new vision of modern civic participation. Endemic corruption in the old society was a given; the progressive political novel would lay this corruption bare and produce self-strengthening social reform.

Wu Woyao responded to the 1903 founding of Liang's journal *New Fiction* (Xin xiaoshuo) with a burst of creativity. Between 1903 and his death in 1910, he produced short stories, half a dozen novels, a body of detective fiction, and adaptations of modern Japanese novels of the sort that Liang admired.[32] In an extended analysis of Wu's most ambitious work, *Strange Events Eyewitnessed over Twenty Years* (Ershi nian mudu zhiguai xianzhuang), Huters demonstrates the near-impossibility of making the new novel do all that Liang demanded of it, but shows that *Strange Events* is nevertheless a powerful and moving evocation of the difficulties China faced in attempting to shake off the past.[33] In this context, we can easily understand Wu Woyao's seizing upon the well-known Guangdong tale of nine murders and turning it to his modernizing purposes. The tale is filled with corruption, which he could label as a hallmark of the old order, and in the figure of Semi-Immortal Ma, Wu could deploy the new intellectual label of *mixin* (superstition), a category recently invented to characterize traditional religiosity. Law, in the traditional versions of the tale, vanquishes the evildoers but only in conjunction with cosmic forces in which Wu put no stock. The tale was ripe for recasting in a new mode of rational, psychological, and politically engaged realism.

Formally, *Nine Murders* does not represent a clean break from the traditional vernacular novel. Direct quotation of legal language shows that Wu was working with the text of *New Warning* rather than with *Liang Tianlai's Complaint* or other versions of the tale,[34] and *Nine Murders* and *New Warning* share certain traditional features such as chapter titles in parallel couplets and chapter conclusions adjuring the reader to "listen to the next session." But in language, structure, plot, and appearance on the page, *Nine Murders* exhibits striking new features.[35] Liang Qichao's magazine *New Fiction* was a self-consciously modern publication, following the newspapers of the day in using movable metal type and setting itself apart from traditional woodblock books.[36] Wu's new approach is evident from the opening lines of the novel. Readers were accustomed to some sort of brief, sometimes ironic prologue that set the coming narrative in a cosmic, geographic, and social context. *Nine Murders*, by contrast, starts by plunging us directly into a shouting match for which the Chinese novel had barely developed typographical conventions:

> "Hey! Fellows! It's at the end of the field! Look, the gates are closed tight. How can we break through them?"
>
> "You fool! Can't you break down two pairs of wooden gates? Come on. Bring me my iron hammers."
>
> Bang! Bang! What a noise!
>
> "Good, good. The outer gates are broken. . . . What's this! The inner gates are made of iron! What can we do with them?"
>
> "Okay, okay . . . This must be Brother Lin."
>
> "Brother Lin, we can't break through these iron gates."
>
> "Well, I've traveled about for more than ten years, and I've never found iron gates that can't be broken. Let me take a look. What! This is trivial! Bring me some oil and straw. We'll set them afire. They'll become soft when they get hot."
>
> "Let's set them on fire!"
>
> "Straw won't work! Bring charcoal!"[37]

Once the criminals set the fire and depart, Wu speaks to us directly.[38] He attacks the idealized view of the Yongzheng emperor, in whose reign the crime occurred, noting sarcastically that despite Yongzheng's supposedly superhuman discernment, his reign saw corruption in Guangdong that "rendered Earth as dark as the underworld." No longer simply a contest between good and evil, *Nine Murders* is now an indictment of Manchu rule, and a call for a new sort of individual and society to replace it. This interest in subjectivity affected the shape of the narrative itself, greatly dilating some episodes and suppressing others.

Semi-Immortal Ma, for instance, first appears in *New Warning* when Zongkong accosts him on the road and brings him to the house. But in *Nine Murders*, we are introduced to Semi-Immortal Ma through Guixing's gaze, as Guixing happens upon Ma's shop on his way home from the division of paternal property. Through Ma's open doorway, Guixing sees an elegantly dressed, sophisticated figure smoking a tobacco pipe (and blowing smoke rings!), languidly folding and unfolding his fan, his eyes glittering behind a pair of spectacles. Ma, in his turn, sees a pampered young man dressed in luxurious garments, and he immediately conceives a plan. When Guixing asks to have his fortune told, Ma launches into a monologue unmatched in either of the earlier sources:

> Your "eight characters" show that you've got fame and fortune coming. I've been telling people's fortunes all through the rivers and lakes for twenty-some years now, and I've hardly ever seen "eight characters" like these! I still remember fifteen years ago, once when I was in Beijing, someone brought me a set of eight characters and asked for a prediction. As I saw it, this person not only was going to achieve fame and wealth, but he'd be a success in the civil service and the military too! He'd have only one man above him, and ten thousand below. But there was just one funny thing. In his old age, he was going to run up against seven malignant influences. My calculations showed that in the course of two years, he'd hit a whole set of bad constellations: the "lose your household," the "wear mourning," the "spirit of death," the "white tiger," the "explosive defeat," the "Heavenly dog," the "Heavenly tears," and plenty of others! There was no way he'd meet a good end, and he'd die beneath the knife. But I just made my predictions according to the manual, and when I got to the bad luck, I said it looked as though he might run into a bit of trouble later on, so he might want to be extra-careful. You'd think that with a speech like that from an experienced professional like me, he'd take to his heels! But at that time I actually had no idea whose fortune I was telling. Only later did someone tell me that it was General Nian Gengyao! I didn't believe it myself. How was it possible that someone as rich and famous as he was would have his head cut off? I thought I must have made a mistake and my skills were not up to the job. Who could have known that once the Kangxi emperor passed

away and our Venerable Yongzheng took the throne, he'd waste no time in putting General Nian to death! I really thought well of myself after that. I decided I couldn't go wrong. And now, looking at *your* eight characters, I see all kinds of honors and wealth. Even if you don't get as high up as General Nian, still—and this isn't empty talk!—you're not going to be able to escape coming in first in the exams, or being prime minister, or a noble lord, and the older you get the better off you'll be. The stars are lined up just right, and you don't have to worry about the future. Looking at it from this angle, I'd say your fortune is ten times as good as General Nian's![39]

Nian Gengyao (d. 1726) was a member of the Chinese Bordered Yellow Banner. He ran afoul of the partisans of the Yongzheng emperor during the Kangxi-Yongzheng transition and was condemned to death by the Yongzheng emperor. Wu Woyao has the facts slightly wrong: Nian was allowed to commit suicide rather than being beheaded, though his eldest son Nian Fu was not so fortunate.[40] This monologue can certainly be read as an additional implicit criticism of the Yongzheng reign, skillfully delivered through Semi-Immortal Ma's charismatically explosive impact upon Ling Guixing.

Other episodes are similarly re-crafted. The corruption of the examination official requires 240 characters in *New Warning*, but 1,200 characters in *Nine Murders*, in which the intermediary is a scam artist who takes Guixing's money (and that of a number of other young men) and disappears, with no hint that the examination official has been paid at all. The scene in which Guixing waits in vain for news of the successful examination candidates, and falls asleep in despair, provides a depth of psychological motivation that *New Warning* never matches. By such scenes as this, Wu Woyao constructs a new kind of rational reader, more likely to be swayed by psychological realism and evidence of corruption than by traditional moralizing.

Law thus operates in a new context in *Nine Murders*, which lends it a different weight. No longer the arm of cosmic judgment, law is presented as an appropriate instrument of punishment when wielded by rational, disinterested individuals. Liang Tianlai's progress through the courts is unchanged; this core story was clearly too well known to be altered. Liang Tianlai's and Ling Guixing's plaint and counterplaint are barely changed. But we read them only once: we no longer experience their rhythmic repetition as we rise toward the emperor. The quest motif that structured the second half of *New Warning* also disappears: we learn in a line or two that Tianlai goes to Beijing, but we hear nothing of his ordeals along the way, or the friendships that that forged a new community for him in *New Warning*. We see corruption in a purely secular setting, as a set of behaviors that Wu wants to eradicate.

By contrast with his negative portrayal of Manchu officialdom, Wu gives us through the justice hero Kong Dapeng not only a new vision of human potential but also the systemic reform that was missing in *New Warning*. In *Nine Murders*, Kong Dapeng uses arguments about justice to win over one of Guixing's collaborators, who becomes Tianlai's friend and thus conveys the message that men of good sense can work together. Rather than showing us Guixing's grisly execution (we are simply told that the sentence was carried out as the law required), Wu details for us the military exile of the magistrate, prefect, and surveillance commissioner who have abused their authority. Zhang Feng refuses payment for his testimony because he knows that working through the courts will bring more bandits to justice, and Shi Zhibo, who refused money for his services in *New Warning* because "a hero's word is worth a thousand pieces of gold," refuses it for reasons of abstract justice in *Nine Murders*: "I have never taken money for writing plaints, because I am moved solely by the desire to right wrongs."

This new vision of human potential means that Wu is more concerned with changing behavior than with punishment per se. Law itself has less rhetorical force in *Nine Murders* than it does in *New Warning* or *Liang Tianlai's Complaint*, in which the paradigm of judgment on earth was intertwined with the larger all-enveloping paradigm of cosmic judgment. In Wu's thoroughgoing reinterpretation of the story, *Nine Murders* is less a tale of Liang Tianlai avenged than a tale of Ling Guixing undone by forces rampant in a China desperately in need of renewal. "How sad," writes Wu in the final paragraph of the novel, "that Ling Guixing, a wealthy man of the region, came to such an end. This was all because of the word *mixin* [superstition]." And after listing the sentences meted out to the various bribed officials, he continues: "This was all because of the one word *tan* [greed]." Greed and superstition must be rooted out before law can be fully effective. Law in *Nine Murders* is at best an adjunct to the radical shift in consciousness that Wu and other reformers called for.

Nevertheless, the standard legal appeals route, which Wu reproduces meticulously, serves his purpose well. This legal framework, which created mythic resonances in *New Warning* and *Liang Tianlai's Complaint*, here serves the different but equally transcendent ideology of modernization. Use of the appeals route enables Wu to demonstrate corruption at each level of government, showing that the whole system needs to be rationalized and reformed.

CONCLUSION: WRITING, FICTION, AND SOCIAL MEANING

Thomas Buoye identifies phenomena that may have served as nuclei for the stories discussed in this chapter—whether or not the Liangs and the Lings ever actually fought for possession of a stone house. Foremost was the growing tension over land disputes in the eighteenth century. Buoye points out that with population growth and increasing pressure on land, two opposing conceptions of landownership were developing: the view of land as "inviolable patrimony" versus a view of land as an "alienable commodity."[41] This opposition is visible in the Guangdong texts considered here: Tianlai repeatedly tells Guixing that it would be unfilial to sell the house that his (Tianlai's) father built. Tianlai does see the house as his "inviolable patrimony"; Guixing sees it as alienable and wants to buy it.

This line of argument should not be taken too far. As Buoye demonstrates, while parts of Guangdong displayed a very high incidence of interlineage violence, Panyu county had one of the lowest rates. Still, there is much in these narratives that ties them to Guangdong. The mix of taro cultivation, aquaculture (Guixing destroys Tianlai's ponds), and small commerce was characteristic of the region, and we can perhaps even detect a regional flavor to the way the story is structured: Y. W. Ma shows that *New Warning* was not characteristic of crime-case fiction by the late eighteenth and early nineteenth centuries, by which time the genre favored knight-errant plots, with the judge as justice hero no longer prominent.[42] This suggests that we are looking at a Guangdong phenomenon—a Guangdong crime with its own narrative tradition.

However, historicizing the text in this way does not exhaust its literary or social meaning. We still want to ask: why was it fictionalized, why was it written down, why was it published? And what added satisfactions came from casting this interlineage feud as *legal* fiction?

We can answer the last question by observing that, whatever its deficiencies, three millennia of tradition made law the accepted mechanism for punishing the guilty, exonerating the innocent, and thus containing the tensions Buoye describes. And where the law fell short, fiction and ritual could harness it to transcendent forces and compel it, at least in the imaginary or ritual realms, to provide satisfying outcomes. Legal fiction puts into our hands the power of the state: authors use legal language, with its aura of authority, to prove the guilt or innocence of their protagonists; and readers, who bring their own passions to the text, participate in judgment. The multiple versions of the nine murders tale, all of which retain the same legal structure and the same final judgment, suggest that Guangdong itself became the sort of interpretive community that Jonathan Ocko describes in chapter 12, creating and consuming a tale that gave the public power over otherwise unmanageable events.

The nine murders texts also fit what we know about the accessibility of legal knowledge in the Ming and the Qing. Both the Ming and Qing *Codes* were published and apparently were not difficult to obtain; bibliophiles in the late Ming whose catalogs have been published tended to own copies of the *Code* and anthologies of famous cases.[43] Works with as much law in them as the nine murders tales would have been popular only with a public to whom law was in some degree familiar. Moreover, the fact that the nine murders texts represented law accurately was surely a factor in their popularity: as well as confirming what people knew, these books taught them more, creating at least an impression of usefulness. It should be noted that in its *New Warning* version, the story "teaches" about other topics as well: chapter 28, in which Tianlai crosses the pass in his airless box, is a mini-textbook of customs regulation; chapter 34 functions as travel literature, when a knowledgeable friend explains to Tianlai the cultural significance of steles and pavilions they pass on their way; and chapter 35 exposes the secrets of a text on weather prediction. (We see the same provision of useful knowledge in Zhang Yingyu's *A New Book for Aid in Eliminating Deceptions as Based on Strange Accounts from the Great Wide World* (Jiang hu lilan du pian xinshu), analyzed by Daniel Youd in chapter 10; the two works disagree on the efficacy of *bao*, but they are clearly in the same intellectual and social universe.)

Ultimately, the nine murders texts considered here blur the boundary between law *in* literature and law *as* literature, a staple distinction in Law and Literature analyses in the West. As we have seen, plausible legal documents move the plot forward in all three versions of the nine murders tale. A key feature of the Ming and Qing legal systems, namely the systems' openness to individual plaints at all levels, allows the characters to voice their deepest feelings through these documents. The Judge Bao tales discussed by James St. André in chapter 9 generally bypass this option, letting the judge operate through righteous instinct. The *renqing* tales analyzed by Youd are as ambivalent about the law as they are about the inevitability of requital. But the nine murders tales, linking law to the pathos and drama of individual lives, on the one hand, and to metalegal narratives of requital, recompense, or modernization, on the other, realize the implicit narrative of the law itself, the unfolding of authoritative, final judgment to which law always aspires but never quite reaches in ordinary life.

NOTES

1. Wu was also known by his style-name Wu Jianren.

2. *New Warning* has the alternate title *A New Warning to the World in a Handful of Snow* (Yi peng xue jing shi xin shu) printed on the flyleaf of the facsimile edition listed in the bibliography. Similarly, *Liang Tianlai* has the alternate title *Xin ke zheng zi chang shuo yi peng xue* (Newly engraved and character-corrected chantefable of the handful of snow) printed on the first inner page.

3. See Yongping Liu, *Origins of Chinese Law*.

4. See, for example, Graham, *Disputers of the Tao*, 315–69, for a summary of these correlative schemata.

5. Hsu, "Crime and Cosmic Order," 111, argues that Western scholars have been mistaken in assuming that Chinese law regards crime "primarily as a disturbance of the cosmic order." I agree with Hsu that imperial Chinese law was fundamentally secular; however, I argue here that whatever the intent with which law was promulgated, it was largely experienced as having supernatural resonances.

6. On the long history of Chinese bureaucratization of the underworld, see Campany, *To Live as Long*, 47–61; Nickerson, "Great Petition"; Robinet, *Taoism*, 53–77; and Teiser, "Growth of Purgatory."

7. Hansen, *Changing Gods*.

8. See Song Ci (Sung Tz'u), *Washing Away of Wrongs*. This text, repeatedly revised, was in continuous use throughout Ming and Qing China.

9. McKnight, *Law and Order*.

10. See Ocko, "I'll Take It All the Way."

11. See Macauley, *Social Power and Legal Culture*, for the social role of these plaint-writers.

12. Alford, "Of Arsenic and Old Laws."

13. Like the nine murders tale, this case engendered numerous imaginative treatments, from fiction to opera. See Dong, "Communities and Communication"; Fang, *Scholar and the Serving Maid*; Waltner, "From Casebook to Fiction"; and *Yang Naiwu yu Xiao Baicai*.

14. This 1794 narrative is described in Li Mengsheng's modern preface to the facsimile edition of *New Warning*.

15. See *Panyu xianzhi*, 854, juan 54. The preface to the modern facsimile edition of *New Warning* observes that the absence of any mention of the case in standard Qing dynasty sources raised doubts about its historicity, but claims that Professor Luo Ergang has established its historicity through documents from the Qing Qianlong era (1736–95) archives.

16. Translated by Wu Xiaolong and Katherine Carlitz.

17. Y. W. Ma, "*Kung-an* Fiction," 253. See *Panyu xianzhi*, 571, *juan* 54, for an entry on Kong Yuxun, which does not, however, mention this case.

18. As Ling Guixing's wife, concubine, and sister have already committed suicide to protest his course of action, they are not included in the punishment.

19. In all three versions, Guixing sends men to overpower Tianlai and steal the jade flowerpots that went to Tianlai at the division of their fathers' property. This theft highlights Guixing's perversion of filial piety.

20. *Jing fu xin shu*, chapter 14, 13b–14a (82–83).

21. Hanan, "Chinese Vernacular Fiction," 26–27, points out that this is not the only paradigm and that much Qing fiction despairs at the apparent indifference of the cosmos. But there is a long unbroken tradition of *bao* fiction, and a relatively modest work such as *New Warning* does not problematize it. See also Kao, "*Bao* and *Baoying*," for the centrality of *bao* to the motivation of characters in Ming and Qing vernacular fiction.

22. This was characteristic of long vernacular fiction. Most of the major novels include plausible legal or ritual documents. Y. W. Ma's view, in "*Kung-an* Fiction," 252–54, that legal documents interrupt the narrative of *New Warning* appears to miss their narrative function in this novel.

23. *Jing fu xin shu*, chapter 6, 19a (37).

24. Numerous texts of *nanyin* and other Guangdong popular literary genres have been collected in the Hong Kong Wuguitang library of popular literature.

25. This somewhat free translation is an attempt to suggest the flexible rhymes and rhythmic structure of the original. Four stresses per line in this English-language version have been chosen because of the frequent use of a four-syllable line in English nursery rhymes and folk poetry.

26. *Jing fu xin shu*, 3.21–22.

27. Ibid., 6.21.

28. Ibid., 6.23–24.

29. Ibid., final (unnumbered) page of *juan* 6.

30. See Peter Li's essay on Li Baojia in Nienhauser, *Indiana Companion*, 547–548, and Helmut Martin's essay on Wu Woyao in ibid., 905–7.

31. Huters, "Shattered Mirror," 282.

32. *Strange Events* and *Nine Murders* were both serialized in *New Fiction*; *Nine Murders* was published in book form in 1907.

33. Huters, "Shattered Mirror," 278.

34. Wu reproduces Liang Tianlai's plaint from *New Warning* in chapter 19 and Guixing's counterplaint in chapter 21; see Wu Woyao, *Jiuming qiyuan*, 85, 95.

35. A Ying, *Wan Qing xiaoshuo shi*, 178–85, discusses the contrast between *Nine*

Murders and *New Warning*. Like Y. W. Ma, A Ying considers *New Warning* far inferior to *Nine Murders*.

36. By the last years of the Qing, lithography and the use of movable metal type were more common than woodblock printing, but the woodblock look was preserved well into the 1930s for self-consciously "traditional" texts like gazetteers.

37. Wu Woyao, *Jiuming qiyuan*, 1. Fong, "Time in *Nine Murders*," discusses the rhetorical effects produced by this and other inversions.

38. Hanan, *Chinese Fiction*, discusses the narrator's voice in Wu Woyao's fiction in two essays: "The Narrator's Voice before the 'Fiction Revolution,'" 9–32; and "Wu Jianren and the Narrator," 162–81. Concentrating mainly on Wu's novel *Strange Events Eyewitnessed over Twenty Years*, he pays particular attention to Wu's employment of a "restricted narrator." This analysis is not, however, applicable to *Nine Murders*, which, like most of premodern vernacular fiction, employs an omniscient narrator's voice.

39. Wu Woyao, *Jiuming qiyuan*, 6–7.
40. See *ECCP*, 587–90.
41. Buoye, *Manslaughter, Markets*, 6.
42. Y. W. Ma, "*Kung-an* Fiction," 253.
43. See, for example, Gao Ru (fl. 1540), *Baichuan shu zhi*.

PART IV *Retrospectives*

12 Interpretive Communities
Legal Meaning in Qing Law

JONATHAN OCKO

The issues considered in this volume—the nature of the relationship between law and literature, complaints and counter-complaints as dueling narratives, the intertextuality of petitions, the interaction between legal practice and legal fiction, trials as didactic and subversive drama, the awareness of the power of rhetoric in the writing of legal documents—all revolve around the production and interpretation of texts. Moreover, many of these texts demonstrate that while the basic narrative form remained roughly constant as cases moved up and down the system, the documentary record was rephrased and restructured as various individual officials and groups of officials successively mapped the facts onto *The Qing Code*. One might make sense of these issues and processes through literary scholar Stanley Fish's concept of "interpretive communities," composed of "bundles of interests."

There is, of course, always some danger in appropriating another field's heuristic devices; one must use Fish's concept loosely rather than rigidly. Fish argues that the meaning of a text is produced by these communities rather than by the text itself or a single reader, and he defined these communities as being constituted by those "who share interpretive strategies not for reading but for writing texts."[1] Several chapters in this volume demonstrate that district magistrates who drafted the judgments in the courts of first instance fit Fish's description reasonably closely; however, his concept may be deployed more expansively in order to examine communities that engaged in both the reading and the writing of texts. Furthermore, this more elastic definition neither mandates that these communities be clearly defined by discrete values, understandings, and texts nor precludes separate interpretive communities, each with its own "bundle of interests," from sharing foundational texts or values.

Thus, eighteenth-century magistrates and defendants agreed that filiality was a cornerstone of a harmonious society, but cases centered on filiality produced texts that often generated antipodal meanings in the service of antithetical interests.[2] Similarly, even within a legal bureaucracy shaped by the hegemonic matrix of *The Qing Code*, magistrates seeking leniency and senior officials advocating the death penalty can be seen as constituting distinct interpretive communities. Certainly, all of these officials belonged to the same normative community, but the disputes that arose about applying their shared fundamental values to specific situations reveal how generating legal meaning can fragment as well as create interpretive communities.[3]

Indeed, this chapter explores the intertextual interactions within and among the congeries of interpretive communities. In the Qing system, as in most legal systems, these interactions were often complex, reflecting the multiplicity of "bundles of interests" and texts at play in any single legal action. The texts being read and written comprised operas, plays, novels, magistrates' handbooks, secret pettifogger handbooks, disciplinary regulations, the *Code*, the internal yamen rules of the magistrate's underlings, provincial regulations, and, of course, the plaintiffs' petitions and magistrates' judgments. However, despite our acknowledgment that the judicial system (from the clerks and runners at the bottom to the emperor at the top) was no more monolithic than were litigants and their communities, we treat them here as undifferentiated wholes: the inside and the outside of the system.

In this view, the system and the parties to a case are dueling interpretive communities, each trying to impose its own meaning on the text. By establishing access procedures, by (fruitlessly) requiring petitioners to use only their own words in complaints, by maintaining decorum and a sense of majesty in the courtroom, and by trying to control the setting and text of punishments, the system sought to ensure that trials and punishments served its particular didactic purposes. Conversely, the parties and defendants, often aided (illegally) by litigation masters, attempted to use courtrooms and execution grounds to construct their own interpretations.[4] They may have been using the legal process not simply to redress grievances, determine right from wrong, or end a relationship but rather to readjust relationships that they fully intended to preserve. Moreover, they may have been "reading" what took place in courts and on execution grounds not as doing justice or as an awesome "spectacle of suffering,"[5] but rather as divertissement or entertainment. Indeed, that is why the family divisions, marriage and inheritance disputes, business quarrels, adulteries, beatings, murders, and punishments imposed by the legal system were incorporated into the stuff of literature.[6] And it was then that the producers of this literature became an additional—albeit outsider—interpretive community whose public and conventional points of view may well in turn have been absorbed by those on the inside.

The effect of these imbricated communities on the legal system can be loosely analogized to the *tiaokuai* structure that characterizes the criss-crossing bureaucratic jurisdictions of vertical bureaucracies in the People's Republic of China: vertical lines, or *tiao*, and horizontal coordinating bodies, or *kuai* (pieces).[7] For our purposes, the legal system, from intake to final processing of a case, is the vertical *tiao*, while the internal and external interpretive communities at various levels are the horizontal *kuai*. In this chapter, we explore the *tiaokuai* relationships of Qing law and judicial procedure.

OUTSIDE THE SYSTEM

From the moment people perceive that someone has injured their reputations, their property rights, their families, or their own persons, they have a decision at hand. Should they seek redress, and if so, how? In late imperial China, the first step in this thought process had to be to determine whether their positions in the hierarchical status structures (gender, character, age, and familial relationship) even permitted them to file complaints against the alleged offenders. Presuming that they were not formally precluded or socially discouraged from airing their grievance, their next step would be to consider the range of mechanisms: an apology or compensation sought through intermediaries; mediation by community leaders; filing a suit to force court-ordered mediation that mitigated the asymmetrical power relationships within the community; or filing a suit to obtain a judgment. Of course, this decision was made in the context of their own knowledge and understanding of the legal system as well as that of their families and friends. This understanding came from various sources: from the solicited (or unsolicited) advice of litigation masters;[8] from previous interactions with the legal system;[9] from observation of the legal system, as trials generally were open;[10] and from stories (both written and oral) and plays. In addition to the court-case literature and fictional accounts of injustice, a wide array of popular literature that would have been accessible to both the literate and illiterate also produced legal knowledge. Though there existed significant disparities in tone and theme not only within the court-case genre itself but also between court-case fiction and other genres, all of this literature still comprised some recurring themes that would have influenced readers.[11] Let us consider a few of the more prominent ones.[12]

Money and Status

The rich and influential can choose to have either more or less law. They may use it defensively, offensively, or even predatorily. They may avoid the law; as described in the eighteenth-century novel *Story of the Stone* (Honglou meng), the "mandarin's life preserver" (*huguanfu*) listed the names of the "richest and most influential people" a sensible magistrate should leave alone.[13] Or they may tendentiously deploy the law—forestalling a complaint by inducing a private settlement even in a homicide case;[14] buying a better scribe;[15] inducing a beating or eliciting leniency by having "a word with the judge"; improving custodial conditions;[16] or financing or derailing an appeal.[17] Money and status are so tied to the self-interested perversion of the law that the absence of bribery or influence peddling becomes a marker of innocence.[18] It would seem, then, that literature conveyed to readers the meaning that "status is what counts and always has"[19] and that "a heavy silver cover can conceal litigation even from Heaven."[20] Yet, as we all know, the villains who tilt the scales of justice can be balanced (albeit neither always nor perfectly) by heroes and "clear sky officials" (*qing tian guan*). The heroes' acts of requital are not without violence: Zhang Fei, a swordsman-hero in *The Three Kingdoms* (Sanguo zhi yanyi), is "straight and true. . . . He'll pay out everyone what he's due."[21] And in *Outlaws of the Marsh*, popularly known as *Water Margin* (Shuihu zhuan), choleric, ax-wielding Li Kui derisively warns: "The law. The law! If everyone obeyed the law, everything would be serene! I'm in favor of hitting . . . first and talking afterward. If he complains to the court, I'll hack him and the friggin' judge together!"[22] Even the deus ex machina righteous officials like the imperial commissioners in Wu Woyao's *The Strange Case of Nine Murders* (Jiuming qiyuan) and Judge Bao sometimes must be not only tough but also cruel in order to combat the influence of wealth and status.[23]

The Interconnectedness of Heaven and Earth

The interrelation of the temporal and spiritual worlds was a pervasive notion and hardly peculiar to literature. Indeed, as Paul Katz demonstrates in chapter 8, in late imperial China, people often pursued justice by way of parallel paths: through the actual courts and through judicial rituals by filing indictments with the gods. And not all literary representations of crime and punishment embodied "the narrative and moral logic of requital."[24] However, in much of literature, particularly in the court-case genre, the concept of a morally active universe in which *bao*, the principle of requital, operating together with the trope of clear-sky officials, provided a source of hope that injustices could be redressed. As the seventeenth-century author of *Marriage Bonds to Awaken the World* (Xingshi yinyuan zhuan) wrote: "Now this is a clear case of the operation of the justice of Heaven. It was the gods that caused the magistrate to pass by the Chao mansion that day. . . . If not for the work of the gods, Madame Chao would have found it difficult to bring her grievances to the attention of the magistrate and even more difficult to prove the justness of her cause."[25] Ghosts—whether in the Yuan dynasty play *Injustice to Dou E* (Dou E yuan), in *Outlaws of the Marsh* (in which Wu Song's brother's ghost tells him, "I died a cruel death"), or in the Judge Bao stories—serve as agents from the beyond, present in this world to ensure that justice is done.[26] Indeed, Y. W. Ma sees the Judge Bao stories in *One Hundred Cases Decided by Judge Bao* (Bao Longtu pan baijia gong'an) as "essentially a recast moral or religious tract."[27] There are, moreover, examples of villains who escape temporal justice and suffer in the afterlife or in a subsequent existence. Yet the messages about karma and karmic retribution do not always cut the same way. The novel *Journey to the West* (Xiyou ji), which can be read as a tale of redemption through faith and right conduct, portrays the sparing of life as a way of guaranteeing justice for oneself, but in *The Three Kingdoms*, Zhuge Liang (in language that prefigures that of the Qianlong emperor's edicts on the autumn assizes) sees excessive leniency as the path to failure.[28] "My Lord," he advises Liu Bei, "if you rule with womanish benevolence, this land will not long be yours."[29]

Statutory and Procedural Advice

A striking feature of late imperial popular literature is the frequency with which detailed, frequent, but not always accurate, references to law and courts occur. In texts about legal cases, such as *The Strange Case of Nine Murders*, this is no surprise, but in other novels, such references appear in passing, adding little to narrative vitality or coherence. In *Journey to the West*, we learn that the "ignorant" are not "held culpable," that a thieving demon could not be convicted, indeed should not have even been arrested, because he had not been caught with the loot on him, and that highwaymen who did not use violence would not be sentenced to death.[30] Arguably, when Tripitaka imparts this knowledge in the course of his corrective disciplining of Monkey, it underscores Monkey's rash, unenlightened, violent character, but that point is after all one of the central threads of the novel, and a naive monk seems an odd choice as the vehicle for legal advice. There are also instances in which characters' discussions of the law are narratively necessary, such as Gold Star's warning to Monkey that pursuing a suit against Devaraja could cost Tripitaka his life because "one day's litigation can take ten days to settle."[31] And in *Outlaws of the Marsh*, Wu Song's murderous sister-in-law learns that Wu Song cannot impede her remarriage—"parents pick the first husband, widows choose the second, a brother-in-law can't interfere."[32] At the same time, Wu Song decides to take matters into his own hands only after he learns that the magistrate lacks the requisite evidentiary elements to launch an investigation into the murder.[33]

The Importance of Well-Drafted Petitions

Though a person considering a business deal would probably prefer the contract forms available in almanacs and freestanding sets, literature provided no shortage of examples of other sorts of documents—from brotherhood oaths, to family division agreements, to adoption and marriage contracts. However, what may have most excited reader interest were the petitions, for the key to opening the door of the legal system was the properly delivered, cogent, well-crafted plaint that persuaded a magistrate to accept a case for hearing. The law prescribed that plaintiffs present their cases in clear, unadorned language, written down either by the plaintiff or by a licensed scribe who recorded an oral complaint, but fictional accounts did not always echo that message. In the works discussed by Katherine Carlitz in chapter 11, the victimized protagonist Liang Tianlai has to rely on litigation masters in order to have his case heard and justice done.[34] Moreover, Liang's petition writer advises him on how to prevent officials from discovering that he himself had not authored his own complaint. "Brother Liang, read this thoroughly, inscribe it in your heart. When you're in court, be able to answer a question as soon as it's asked. There can be no mistakes."[35]

Marriage Bonds to Awaken the World also offers considerable advice on petitions but in a slightly different vein. In addition to instructing its readers that a woman submitting a petition without a proxy has little chance of being heard, that anyone who entrusts the writing assignment to an inexperienced scribe unfamiliar with the required form is sure to antagonize the magistrate,[36] and that it is best to file a complaint quickly after an injury, the text further admonishes that victims (indeed all who have reason on their side) could best serve their interests by stating the facts simply, without embellishment or falsehood.[37] Indeed, early in the novel, when the narrative is driven by the conflict and litigation between Ji Du and his son-in-law, Chao Yuan, it is Ji Du's exemplary, straightforward complaint that explains the conflict's etiology to readers.[38] By contrast, Chao Yuan's counter-complaint, filed at the suggestion of the runners sent to summon him, and portrayed as having been drafted without apparent involvement by litigation masters, is rife with harsh counter-charges and unflattering characterizations.[39] These statements comprise many of the standard elements that would have been necessary to grab an actual magistrate's favorable attention. Chao's father was an official, and he was a filial son burdened with a shrewish wife who had tried to kill him and thus deserved the death her suicide brought about.[40] This account and others suggest that in literature, at least, the lying and guilty are signified not only by bribery but also by heated, hyperbolic, tendentious petitions.

Given Robert Hegel's intriguing observation that in archival records, the "rhetorically persuasive characters were conventionally coded as morally upright," one is tempted to infer chicanery and guilt from the tone of actual petitions.[41] However, it is a temptation best resisted. Rarely does one find a complete record with a final judgment that cogently demarcates right and wrong, and, as in Wang Huizu's proverb, "a plaint without exaggeration will not work." Indeed, as Yasuhiko Karasawa argues in chapter 3, it was common practice in Qing complaints to "describe the accused in terms we would have to call slanderous." And unless one is fortunate enough to discover relevant testimony, the case record, unlike fiction, provides no markers to tell us whether we are hearing the voice of the plaintiff or a petition writer. Still, the fictional complaint and counter-complaint in *Marriage Bonds to Awaken the World* comprise tropes that are strikingly similar to those in the actual complaints considered in this volume. Ji's petition raises the issues of poverty and the morality of monks, while Chao's invokes filiality and a morally restrained husband dealing with a termagant wife. Clearly, then, if not at the level of specific phrases, at least at the level of tropes and attitudes, there was an intertextual and mutually constructive conversation at work.[42]

In sum, consumers of fiction would have been exposed to a variety of information (of indeterminate accuracy) about legal provisions, which they may or may not have understood properly, and to the message that the rich get more law but a hero, a good magistrate, or karmic retribution might balance the scales. They would also have been treated to examples of winning and losing petitions. The novelists, storytellers, and dramatists who created this content had more than one strategy for producing their texts, but collectively they generated a conventional wisdom about the legal system.

INSIDE THE SYSTEM

The officials, clerks, and runners who operated the legal system were aware to varying degrees of the "meanings" produced by fiction, but for them the more important interpretive communities were those framed by the *Code*, magistrates' handbooks and casebooks, circulars from the Board of Punishments, memorials in the *Peking Gazette*, "disciplinary administrative regulations" (*chufen zeli*), the expertise of legal secretaries, the institutional memories and internal rules of yamen staffs, and, of course, the text of the complaints they received.

The Petition

As noted above, the petition was the key that opened the door to the system. If the magistrate "accepted it" (*zhun*) for a hearing, the plaintiff was in—thus the attraction of professionally drafted petitions and the legal system's effort to filter them out. Petitions lacking claims of physical injury could be received only on certain days and had no presumption of being heard. However, a charge of physical injury left the magistrate no choice but to accept the complaint and conduct an initial investigation to determine whether there had been an injury. Thus, numerous cases of property, business, and family disputes gained a hearing not simply by exaggerating the deviousness or harmfulness of the defendant's action but also by claiming that the defendant had struck the plaintiff. Plaintiffs who are allegedly hurt so badly that they cannot rise from their beds or eat or drink are as much a staple in case archives as is the swooning maiden in an Anglo-American historical romance. However, as the following petitions indicate, charges of failure to abide by previous judgments or of unfiliality were also likely to get a hearing.

On Tongzhi 3.10.19 (November 9, 1864), using her cousin as a proxy, Mrs. Ding née Ma, age fifty-two, filed a complaint with the magistrate of Ba county, Sichuan.

> In re. the matter of disobedience, deception, and expulsion. After I became Ding Qishao's concubine, we adopted the third branch's Ding Chuanmo

as our son. At the time he was young, and I raised him to adulthood and arranged his marriage. Later my husband died, and his son Chuanmo, who is a runner in the prefectural yamen, forcibly occupied land and buildings worth several thousand. He destroyed proper moral relations [*mielun*] and tried unsuccessfully to force me to remarry. In Xianfeng 10, he incited my husband's wife, née Lei, to falsely accuse me of being recalcitrant and disruptive. Your predecessor investigated and ordered Ding Chuanmo to care for me with monthly payments of xx,[43] but he violated the judgment by only pretending to implement it. He gave me only one year of support and cheated me out of the rest. Consequently, I have nothing to eat and nowhere to live. I learned that this disobedient character has a tenant relinquishing his lease, so this fall, I moved into that house. But then my husband's younger brother, Ding Songning, stirred his family to force me to move out. I petitioned the head of the *tuan*, who judged that I could stay, but Chuanmo again ignored the instruction, and, under a different name, Ding Fuxing, falsely charged me with conspiring to seize the house. In that case, I am accused as Ding née Song.[44]

The references in this petition to a previous case record and to other petitions are important. They underscore that in the interpretive community constituted by the parties to a case, the magistrate, and the yamen underlings, there is a significant amount of intertextual exchange as all of the authors seek to shape the judgment that will for the moment stand as the definitive meaning that they collectively have produced. Even if petitions were not posted publicly, defendants did not frame their responses in a vacuum because in some jurisdictions at least the magistrate appears to have provided them with a copy of the accusation, and a summons or warrant in any case always included a summary of the charge.[45]

On Tongzhi 3.11.12 (December 10, 1864), using her co-respondent Ding Chuanmo as proxy, Mrs. Ding née Lei, age sixty-one, filed her counter-complaint.

> In re. a pettifogger inciting. My husband, Ding Qishao, took Ms. Song as his concubine, but she bore no children. After my husband's death, this disobedient concubine did not observe the wifely way [*bushou fudao*]. In Xianfeng 9 [1859], I filed a complaint with your predecessor, and after investigating, he ordered that her nephew, Ding Chuanshi, be beaten and that my son, Ding Chuanmo, give Ms. Song fifty taels and remarry her out of the family. The case record is on file in the criminal matters section [*xingke*] and can be checked. In the eighth month, the litigation monger Ma Jie,

also known as Ma Wenzhai, established a sibling relationship with Ms. Song in order to take advantage of her status as a widow and try to seize the house for which I had a tenant. My son Ding Fuxing accused them of conspiring to seize the property, the case was accepted for hearing, and warrants were issued for Ding Chuanshi and Ma Wenzhai, who wolfishly incited Ms. Song to violate the previous judgment. Under her new name, Ding née Ma, she filed her complaint regarding disobedience, deception, and forced remarriage. The case has now been accepted and summonses issued. I ask that Ding Chuanshi and Ma Wenzhai be added for cross-examination so as to prevent further harm.

This petition's tone and content suggest that it was written either by Ding Chuanmo or by a scribe with whom he was friendly through his work as chief runner for the prefecture. It plays all the right notes and reveals a detailed knowledge of the yamen's workings. As a concubine brought in to bear sons, the plaintiff had failed to deliver and then, by establishing a "sworn sibling" relationship—with a litigation monger, of all people—had failed to act as a widow ought. And if the magistrate had doubts about the prior judgments, he could find the case not simply "in the records," as the plaintiff had indicated, but in the punishments section, an assertion only someone with inside knowledge could make.[46]

There were several more exchanges in this case, which appears to conclude two years later, in late Tongzhi 5 (early 1867). First, the plaintiff's brother-in-law submits a petition asserting that he is a hardworking member of the staff of the gentry bureau and has been unfairly implicated in this case by his brother's widowed concubine, Ding née Ma. She in turn bypasses the magistrate (*yuesong*) and makes a complaint to the prefect, which she says is necessitated by the magistrate's runners trying to force her out of her home. She asserts that she invested the money saved from her previous marriage in her second husband's business, managed the family's finances, and raised, educated, and arranged marriages for the children, yet when left a widow, she was abused because she refused to lend money to Ding Chuanmo, who was using the family's assets for his personal benefit. When she asked her brother-in-law to sanction Chuanmo, the brother-in-law demanded money to resolve the problem and then laid accusations against her. The prefect returned the case to Ba county, only to have Ding née Ma submit another complaint to him without waiting for the magistrate's decision. When she acknowledged the error of her ways, he did not impose the required beating, and the case seemed settled, with Ding née Lei and her son Chuanmo providing a house and a stipend to Ding née Ma, and both sides agreeing to have no further contact with each other. But in Tongzhi 5.12 (January 1867), another exchange of petitions occurred, with Ding née Ma complaining that she is being cheated of her stipend and variously abused, and Ding Chuanmo and his brother charging that she is once again simply extorting money from them.

The Magistrate

What was the magistrate's reading of these petitions? Would fictional accounts have impinged on it? It is difficult to answer the first question, though we can safely say that in this case, the magistrate's relatively no-fault decision suggests that neither side monopolized the production of meaning. It is even more difficult to answer the second question because, although magistrates probably read the great Ming novels, we know little beyond that assumption, and there are few if any hints of magistrates' reading tastes in either public or private editions of their decisions. Still, it is intriguing to read the petitions as if they were in novels. For example, the plaintiff elicits our sympathy by situating herself as the good mother betrayed and victimized by unfilial adoptive sons who use their influence as yamen runners to manipulate the law against her. The counter-complaints, in turn, try to prejudice the reader against the plaintiff by underscoring that she had been married before coming into the Ding family, that she had produced no sons, that she lacked propriety, and that she was in league with pettifoggers and greedy to boot.

It is important to remember, though, that long before the magistrate saw a case, the various interpretive communities of plaint writers, notaries, and yamen underlings would have already framed it.[47] The yamen underlings' reading of a case had particular importance because it determined which section within the yamen handled the case and, consequently, which group of runners would serve any summonses or warrants that the magistrate issued. Moreover, clerks could clearly exercise considerable discretion over the order in which a magistrate read petitions and determine which to accept and which to reject, thereby shaping the context of each case.[48]

Once a complaint arrived on the magistrate's desk, he became involved in constructing a narrative for himself. As he parsed the petitions, he would identify the lacunae that needed to be filled through witness testimony, inquests, and examination and cross-examination of the parties. The process was hardly peculiar to the Qing legal system, but for Qing magistrates, this building project, especially in criminal cases, had to be tightly framed by the particularistic *Qing*

Code. Not only did a magistrate have to determine the facts, but he also had to position them firmly and precisely in the *Code*'s myriad categorical cubbyholes. His first step would be to determine whether any sort of mourning or other critical hierarchical relationship existed that would determine the nature of the crime. Was a couple actually married or merely betrothed? Had the betrothal been properly conducted? Was a worker engaged in one-time paid labor or a long-term commitment that made him a member of the household? How old were the perpetrator and the victim? These questions would shape the magistrate's decision. If the violence had occurred between two ordinary people with none of the aggravating or mitigating hierarchical factors, a magistrate had much greater latitude in making sense of events.

Indeed, the magistrate's role in constructing case narrative is at the heart of many of the chapters in this volume. Robert Hegel, in chapter 4, sees magistrates as producing texts that portray only the perpetrator as having acted "antisocially," while depicting the magistrate himself and the perpetrator's neighbors as all without moral flaw. Thomas Buoye, Maram Epstein, Mark McNicholas, Janet Theiss, and, to a lesser extent, Pengsheng Chiu argue that magistrates intentionally shaped their reports to elicit sympathy or disgust for defendants in an effort to, in McNicholas's words, "channel" the narrative toward a "desired outcome." Building on his previous work, Buoye asserts a magisterial inclination for leniency, and Chiu describes how a magistrate in Hunan used references to Jiangsu and Zhejiang provincial regulations to create a sympathetic understanding of merchants' interests.[49] However, in the cases of fraud, discussed by McNicholas in chapter 7, and wife-killing, examined by Theiss in chapter 2, magistrates actively either minimized or aggravated a suspect's guilt. Indeed, McNicholas cites a case in which the narration's "rhetoric of indignation" caused a harsher punishment not only to be applied in the specific case but also to be instantiated as a new substatute in the *Code*.

We should note, though, that the production of narratives that minimized or aggravated guilt and channeled toward desired outcomes did not escape the notice of Qing legislators. Both *The Qing Code* and the *Administrative Disciplinary Regulations* (Chufen zeli) stipulated punishments for intentional as well as inadvertent diminution or "aggravation" (*churu*) of the seriousness of circumstances and, thus, of punishment.[50] Of particular interest here are two substatutes, one that prohibited trial officials from changing testimony and another that sanctioned trial officials for amending or emending the initial deposition and higher provincial officials for passing along the illegally revised document.[51] We need to consider these constraints in our accounts of Qing legal narratives. Did they affect magisterial inventiveness and tendentiousness? Did they have more of an impact at some times, in some cases, and in some places than in others? For the moment, the only evidence is the testimony of Xue Yunsheng, the late-nineteenth-century Board of Punishments official who compiled *Remaining Doubts after Reading the Substatutes* (Du li cunyi). Commenting on the second substatute, he dourly observes that despite its harsh penalties (ranging from dismissal from office to death, depending on the nature of the case), its pervasive violation had made it a dead letter. Rarely, he complains, does the deposition remain the same from the trial of first instance through the retrial. And how, Xue asks, could that happen without violations of the ostensibly proscribed editing of case records?[52]

Magistrates, then, are perhaps the best example of an interpretive community because they operated in a common framework and shared strategies for the production of texts. They produced not only judgments but judgments that were in many ways patterned on a matrix created by other magistrates (as well as legal secretaries) through their handbooks and casebooks.[53] Granted, no one has yet adduced any citations to demonstrate conclusively that their successors throughout the Qing drew explicitly on Huang Liuhong, Lan Dingyuan, Wang Huizu, Liu Heng, and the authors of myriad casebooks.[54] But because these were commercially circulating texts and not vanity publications, it seems reasonable to infer that magistrates relied on them for direction in much the same way that merchants used widely circulated guide and form books. Indeed, as the number of magistrate handbooks proliferated during the nineteenth century and some of their content was incorporated into statecraft collections, they became an enormous body of conventional wisdom. Though not every magistrate might have agreed with Lan Dingyuan's skeptical view that behind every ordinary person's capital crime complaint was a constable, and behind him a pettifogger, few would have taken issue with his other advice: in sensitive criminal investigations, clear the court to prevent word leaking to other suspects; limit the number of people who may be named in a single complaint; "implement the law fully and certainly so that the people will exercise self-control and not violate it"; and "the manner of the compassionate gentleman is to uphold the law strictly but use it with benevolence."[55]

REVIEWS AND APPEALS

First, it is important to note that the text of the case record underwent significant change as it moved up through the system.[56] The testimonies and judgments at the top were far from exact replicas of those heard in the courtroom.⁵⁷ The Qing legal system was hardly unique in this regard. Whether or not a legal system purports to retry the case at every level, as did the Qing, reviewing judges, even United States Supreme Court justices, who are supposed to deal only with questions of law, are inclined to retell the facts of the case in their own particular way so as to frame their legal interpretations.⁵⁸ Their inclusion or omission of narrative elements can have a powerful influence on the meaning produced by their recounting of a case. Qing appellate records summarize the facts of a case in such a highly formulaic way that one almost imagines clerks using computers to cut and paste those sections. However, once the packaged summary had been presented, an appellate official could begin to unpack it to suit his interpretive ends.

Second, in the Qing, as in many systems, reviews or appeals, even in mundane cases, were likely to elicit contestation by multiple interpretive communities and thus were highly susceptible to becoming vehicles for political as opposed to purely legal discourse. This was particularly true in the late Qing, when newspapers and novels as well as censors and quasi-formal official factions became players in the process.⁵⁹ *The Strange Case of Nine Murders* reads in part like a textbook on the appellate process as it details how a capital appeal is submitted, who must accept it, and how the imperial commissioners are selected and sent out to deal with a case. Indeed, the last forty years of the Qing may in some ways be a period of heightened intertextual interaction among interpretive communities. For there were not only many more avenues for the production of texts but a plethora of high-profile cases and officials to provide the stuff of commentary. The case of Yang Naiwu was well known, but the "Three Great Cases" of Dongxiang (in Sichuan), Wang Shuwen, and Sanpailou also attracted considerable attention in officialdom, in the young Chinese-language newspaper *Shenbao*, and in contemporaneous literature.⁶⁰ Chapters 10–14 in Li Boyuan's *The Bureaucrats: A Revelation* (Guanchang xianxing ji) track the Dongxiang case very closely, and the mockery of pointlessly harsh magistrates expressed in Liu E's *The Travels of Lao Can* (Laocan youji) almost certainly is directed at the well-known Manchu legal official Gang Yi.

Third, at least twice along their way, reviews and appeals passed through the hands of people who were legal specialists and brought a professional rather than an amateur eye to their reading of cases and production of recommendations: once at the Judicial Bureau of the Provincial Judicial Commissioner, the office charged specifically with handling appeals, and once at the Board of Punishments, where cases were the stuff of potential revisions to or new substatutes in the *Code*. The impetus for a new, harsher law or, conversely, a new, sympathetic reading of an existing statute might have come from below.[61] Yet in the end, at the top of the system, alone, were interpretive communities that saw themselves as charged with producing definitive meanings. One of these was the group of officials charged with reviewing what Buoye refers to as "revisable" death sentences, or what are more generally known as sentences of death "after the assizes."[62]

EXECUTION AFTER THE ASSIZES

In chapter 5, Buoye suggestively describes an interpretive community comprising officials from the county magistrate to the metropolitan officials of the Three Judicial Offices whose case report texts promoted consideration of leniency in certain kinds of cases. Arguably, this tendency to weave threads of extenuation through the narratives was shaped at all levels both by the knowledge that negligent aggravation of sentences resulted in harsher administrative sanctions than did negligent diminution of sentences and by the belief that one acquired the hidden virtue of good karma by seeking life rather than death. Yet, these texts often failed to persuade their most important audience, the emperor, who held the ultimate discretionary power of life and death. After the assizes regularly overturned eighteenth-century governors' recommendations for reprieves, the Qianlong emperor mocked their "womanly compassion" and reminded them that since the final decision was his, "it was more fitting with the political structure for the judicial officials in the provinces to stick to the law strictly and have the metropolitan officials reverse, or have the metropolitan officials be strict and the emperor reverse."[63] Between 1740 and 1780, the Qianlong emperor employed a variety of devices to rein in the governors. Admonitions were followed by discipline for excessive reversals and finally by the *Rules of Comparison* (Qiushen bijiao tiaokuan), 185 articles grouped by type of case, which the Board of Punishments issued in 1784. Over the next century, in a process that exemplifies the creation of an interpretive community, this revised version of an earlier, shorter text became the basis for a series of unofficial commentaries by board officials and the private legal secretaries of provincial officials. Most of these commentaries appeared after the 1820s, a period marked as well by the growth of statecraft literature and the proliferation of magistrates' handbooks and casebooks. Some versions state the black letter rule and then list by date the factual situations of a run of cases as well as indicate how each case was finally categorized. Others supplemented the rule with a discursive analysis of the elements weighed in making decisions.

These proliferating heuristic tools unsurprisingly failed to engender consistency. Even within a community based on the rules, honest disagreement over how to balance principle, or *li*, against circumstances, or *qing*, was inevitable. It was more likely still between an interpretive community centered on the *Code* and death and one centered on the *Rules of Comparison* and life. This tension appeared not only between the governors and the emperor but among the interpretive communities of metropolitan officials who participated each fall in the final assize decisions. Although one might expect the Board of Punishments to produce texts that emphasized the statutes, in distinguishing cases, it often gave greater weight to circumstances, an approach that tended toward leniency. Often on the other side were moralist officials from the Censorate who focused on statutory explication in order to leave little room for extenuation. Each interpretive community's production of meanings is a function of its sense of the state of society, of the law's inherent fairness and ability to deliver justice, and of the law's role and efficacy in maintaining social order. Perhaps the interpretive community represented by the Board of Punishments developed a contextualized spectrum or matrix onto which it placed the range of violence it encountered. It reserved harshness for the truly egregious case. Conversely, for the other officials, the truly egregious case was simply the particular aberrant behavior before them.

CONCLUSION

The texts produced by the external and internal communities of interpretations that intersected the Qing legal system not only provided the data the system processed but also influenced the legal sensibility with which those texts were read and new ones created. Taken as a whole, the interactions among these communities involved a circulation and exchange of texts that were never exclusively hierarchical. However, as one moved from extramural communities into and up through the system's intramural communities, the nature of the communities changed from open, inchoate, and multivocal to more closed, structured, and univocal.

Outside the walls of the magistrate's yamen lay a complex of communities of interpretation, driven by disparate motivations that produced distinctive texts. Parties to conflicts first shaped their dueling narratives in order to make cogent cases to potential mediators. Then, if necessary, plaintiffs and defendants revised their narratives in an effort to persuade the magistrate to hear or dismiss the case and to obtain the result they sought. Strikingly, by using the same tools and tropes to make their respective cases, the adversarial parties effectively cooperated in creating the text put before the magistrate. Yet, because petitioners could not make a legal argument and were restricted to a simple statement of the "facts," the narration alone had to persuade the magistrate that the matter of law involved warranted his time and attention. Here lay the opportunity for the complaint writer or, in more serious, complex, or appellate cases, for the litigation master. Since litigation masters and their clients both sought a win, their interests briefly aligned, but the complaint writer sought to produce more than a simple statement of facts. He needed to demonstrate the wrong inflicted on his client and to do it in a way that implicitly defined a matter of law on which the magistrate could hang his decision to accept the case. Yet unlike petitioners, who had to appear in court and ostensibly use their own words, the complaint writer's success and survival depended on producing texts that hid his own hand from magistrates while revealing it to potential clients. Litigation masters could enjoy only such hidden triumphs because publicity meant ignominy and harsh punishment. Unlike French lawyers in the last years of the old regime, litigation masters could not aspire to celebrity, salon invitations, and electoral victories by writing briefs that turned private scandal into critiques of the body politic.[64]

Indeed, in the Qing, before the appearance of newspapers and exposé literature in the last quarter of the nineteenth century, no extramural communities of interpretation took the risk of turning a cause célèbre into a systematic critique. Within the system, a censor might dare; however, on the outside, storytellers, playwrights, and novelists drew on their shared, amorphous body of "story stuff" primarily to entertain their readers.[65] Still, though these readers would willingly suspend their disbelief for the sake of seeing Judge Bao ensure that justice was done, they were also sufficiently familiar with the law and the legal system, as well as with the corruption, inconsistencies, and incompetence of the system, to expect a reasonable degree of verisimilitude in their fiction. Thus, for example, notwithstanding their different authors, tones, and perspectives, all three versions of the Liang Tianlai story discussed by Katherine Carlitz in chapter 11 offer fairly accurate accounts of legal procedures. However, little, if any, Qing fiction displays the same mastery of the language, logic, and arcana of the law of its time as do Shakespeare's plays.[66] Nor did Qing authors appear to have, like Shakespeare, either a theory of law or an interest in changing society. Yet, unlike actual parties to a case or litigation masters, this community of interpretation was perhaps the only one outside the system that could make arguments about the law.

By contrast, within the system, once the facts had been established, the law and its application became the heart of the matter. All decisions had to be based on and cite specific provisions of *The Qing Code*. In matters of property, contract, and inheritance that did not involve violence and could be settled on their own authority without automatic review, magistrates appear to have rarely invoked the *Code*.[67] Yet these decisions formed what was in some ways the magisterial community of interpretation's most important product and consumable. For magistrates, these constituted the core content of their casebooks, which provided their contemporaries and later magistrates with models for analysis and judgment. Some of these casebooks, as well as other handbooks, also guided magistrates on how to prepare draft judgments for reviewable cases, specifically, how to map their decisions onto the proper forms and statutory provisions. Significantly, as the other chapters in this volume demonstrate, regardless of the subsequent, repeated reshapings of the case narrative, magistrates left an indelible if not dispositive imprint on a case, perhaps one that at some level embodied the interpretive meanings of the external communities adjacent to that of the magistrates. Moreover, even if it was revised or rejected, the magistrate's original interpretation had a disproportionately large effect because his decision reached two audiences: an extramural one composed of the people in his district as well as the intramural one made up of his bureaucratic superiors. In contrast, until the last quarter of the nineteenth century, the magistrate's superiors faced only inward and largely upward.

In capital cases, the autumn assizes represented an even more closed community. Its debates were internal and based on the *Code* as well as on a matrix of a clear, but narrow set of interpretive rules, and it produced texts for an audience of one, the emperor. In turn, the emperor, an interpretive community of one, produced the final text, and the explanation of the decision to execute provided a libretto for the performance. The cycle of interpretation then began again as the witnesses to the execution drew their own conclusions about the meaning of the text and how, if necessary, to incorporate it into their own.

As the late legal historian Robert Cover wrote, "rules and principles of justice" are only a small part of the story. "No set of legal institutions or prescriptions exists apart from the narratives that locate it and give it meaning. . . . Once understood in the context of the narratives that give it meaning, law becomes not merely a system of rules to be observed, but a world in which we live."[68]

The "nomos" or "normative universe" of right and wrong that we create, continued Cover, "is held together by the force of interpretive commitments—some small and private, others immense and public. These commitments—of officials and others—do determine what law means and what law shall be."[69] What is striking about the Qing is that although the overlapping communities of interpretation produced substantial differences in their narratives and meanings, they all shared a common way of imagining how the world fit together, of how legitimate authority was defined, namely in terms of rules, procedures, and processes.[70] None of them was in any significant way iconoclastic.

NOTE

1. Fish, *Is There a Text?* 14.
2. See chapter 1, by Maram Epstein, and chapter 5, by Thomas Buoye.
3. See Cover, "Nomos and Narrative."
4. For a comprehensive study of litigation masters, key players in the legal system, see Macauley, *Social Power and Legal Culture*.
5. The term is Spierenberg's, in *Spectacle of Suffering*.
6. Hanan, *Vernacular Story*, 25, notes the frequency of law cases in vernacular literature because they allowed "the resolution of a socially significant conflict."
7. For a cogent explanation of this terminology, see Lieberthal, *Governing China*, 169–70.
8. Macauley, *Social Power and Legal Culture*, 19, argues that over the three centuries from 1500 to 1800, attitudes had hardened so that any facilitation of litigation might be construed as "litigation mongering."
9. Some Huizhou merchant families retained copies of judgments from every case in which they were involved, and others compiled their own records of cases—some woodblock printed, some hand-copied—including copies of petitions from all parties to the case as well the magistrates' comments. Tian Tao of China University of Political Science and Law and Shanghai University has recently collected numerous examples of this type of document, some of which were distributed to all members of a lineage. They are currently being repaired, summarized, and readied for publication.
10. Janet Theiss, in chapter 2 in this volume, notes that courtroom readings of judgments constituted "public morality tales."
11. Hanan, "*Judge Bao's Hundred Cases* Reconstructed," 301, 312, notes variations within the court-case genre and observes that Judge Bao stories cannot be characterized as a cycle because they "do not share a single broad conception of

his mind and character"; while the earlier chantefables reflect the oral tradition's "bold irreverence toward authority," the later cases focus on criminal acts of private citizens. On differences between court-case fiction and other genres, see, for example, chapter 10, by Daniel Youd, in this volume.

12. Many relatively common themes are not discussed here:, such as the importance of knowing one's place as a way of avoiding trouble (*Journey to the West*) and of avoiding litigation by writing good contracts and maintaining betrothals, even to impoverished sons-in-law.

13. *Huguanfu*, literally, "the officials' protective charm." See Cao, *"Honglou meng" bashihui jiaoben*, vol. 1, 37; and Cao, *Story of the Stone*, vol. 1, 111.

14. *Xingshi yinyuan zhuan*, 1143–44.

15. Cao, *"Honglou meng" bashihui jiaoben*, vol. 3, 56–57; Cao, *Story of the Stone*, vol. 4, 134; *Xingshi yinyuan zhuan*, 1161.

16. Cao, *"Honglou meng" bashihui jiaoben*, vol. 3, 56–57; Cao, *Story of the Stone*, vol. 4, 134; *Xingshi yinyuan zhuan*, 1167–70.

17. Cao, *"Honglou meng" bashihui jiaoben*, vol. 3, 59; Cao, *Story of the Stone*, vol. 4, 138; Wu Woyao, *Jiuming qiyuan*.

18. Liu E, *Lao Can youji*, 181; Liu T'ieh-yün, *Travels of Lao Ts'an*, 171.

19. *Sanguo yanyi huipingben*, vol. 1, 11; Luo, *Three Kingdoms*, 13.

20. *Xingshi yinyuan zhuan*, 139.

21. *Sanguo yanyi huipingben*, 11; Luo, *Three Kingdoms*, 13.

22. *"Shuihu zhuan" huipingben*, 953; Shapiro, *Outlaws of the Marsh*, vol. 2, 838–39.

23. See chapter 11, by Katherine Carlitz, and chapter 9, by James St. André, in this volume.

24. Youd, chapter 10, in this volume. For more on this argument, see chapter 10, by Youd, and chapter 11, by Carlitz. Carlitz's comparison of two fictionalizations of the same crime a century apart shows a progression from an earlier belief in cosmic retribution to a later, secular grounding in human motivation.

25. This passage is from the end of chapter 20; translation by Chi-chen Wang in Ts'un-yan Liu, *Chinese Middlebrow Fiction*, 94.

26. Guan, *Dou E yuan*, act 4; Shih, *Injustice to Tou O*, contains both the original text and a translation. *"Shuihu zhuan" huipingben*, vol. 1, 493; Shapiro, *Outlaws of the Marsh*, vol. 1, 413–14.

27. Y. W. Ma, "Themes and Characterization," 201.

28. See, for example, in chapter 9, the account of how Tripitaka's father's unjust death is redressed and life is restored to him by a fish, whose own life Tripitaka's father had saved and who was in fact the Dragon King. Wu Cheng'en, *Li Zhuowu ping ben "Xiyou ji"*; Yu, *Journey to the West*, vol. 1, 198–213, especially 202.

29. *Sanguo yanyi huipingben*, vol. 1, 808; Luo, *Three Kingdoms*, 500.

30. Wu Cheng'en, *Li Zhuowu ping ben "Xiyou ji,"* 178; Yu, *Journey to the West*, vol. 1, 307.

31. Wu Cheng'en, *Li Zhuowu ping ben "Xiyou ji,"* 1124; Yu, *Journey to the West*, vol. 4, 135. The original phrase is "Yiri guanshi shiri da."

32. *"Shuihu zhuan" huipingben*, vol. 1, 478; Shapiro, *Outlaws of the Marsh*, vol. 1, 402.

33. *"Shuihu zhuan" huipingben*, vol. 1, 499–500; Shapiro, *Outlaws of the Marsh*, vol. 1, 419.

34. See chapter 11, by Carlitz; Wu Woyao, *Jiuming qiyuan*, 83–84, 108–9.

35. Wu Woyao, *Jiuming qiyuan*, 84.

36. *Xingshi yinyuan zhuan*, 1056–57.

37. Ibid., 137, 1161.

38. Ibid., 138.

39. Ibid., 139.

40. *The Qing Code* stipulates that to bully someone into committing suicide is a capital crime (*DLCY*, vol. 4, 869–70 [299:00]), but in many instances of "murder," if the victim deserved death as a consequence of having committed a capital crime, then the offender's punishment was reduced. See, for example, the statutes on killing an escaped prisoner who has not resisted arrest (*DLCY*, vol. 5, 1124 [388:00(3)]) and on killing three people (none of whom is guilty of a capital offense) in a single family (*DLCY*, vol. 4, 815 [287:00]).

41. See chapter 4, by Robert Hegel, in this volume.

42. In chapter 1 in this volume, Epstein raises the question of whether the resurgence of filial themes in mid-eighteenth to early-nineteenth-century literati novels influenced the way in which the accused deployed the trope of filiality. On these elements, see also chapter 2, by Theiss; chapter 3, by Karasawa; and chapter 7, by McNicholas.

43. The characters for the amount are obscure in the original text.

44. This case is in *BXDA*, 6.5.3393.

45. The Huizhou merchant families' case records collected by Tian Tao contain both the plaint and the counterplaint as well as copies of summonses and decisions.

46. See Reed, *Talons and Teeth*, for a discussion of the assignment of cases to the different clerical sections within the yamen.

47. See the discussion of plaint writers' "narrative fashioning" in chapter 3, by Karasawa, in this volume.

48. See Reed, *Talons and Teeth*.

49. See in this volume, chapter 5, by Buoye, and chapter 6, by Chiu.

50. *DLCY*, vol. 5, 1229–35 (409:00-06).

51. The prohibition against changing testimony is in ibid., 1232 (409:01).

52. Ibid., 1233 (409:02, note).

53. Will, *Official Handbooks and Anthologies*, is the most comprehensive guide to magistrate handbooks. It would be a worthwhile project for legal and literary scholars to undertake a collaborative analysis of the handbooks.

54. Mark Allee is working on an analytic comparison of Liu Heng's casebooks and actual case decisions (in Ba county).

55. Lan Dingyuan, *Luzhou gong'an*, 70–74, 138, 143, 258.

56. For a more detailed discussion of the Qing appellate system, see Ocko, "I'll Take It All the Way."

57. See chapter 2, by Janet Theiss, in this volume.

58. U.S. Supreme Court cases on the death penalty are particularly revealing. See especially *Payne v. Tennessee* (501 U.S. 808), in which the court held that there was no constitutional bar to allowing victim impact statements to be presented to a capital sentencing jury as part of its deliberations.

59. See Polachek, *Inner Opium War*, for discussion of the informal but highly structured groups of officials who engaged in the "inner opium war."

60. On Yang Naiwu, see Alford, "Of Arsenic and Old Laws." The Dongxiang case concerned excessive use of military force in the suppression of a tax protest and its subsequent cover-up. Wang Shuwen was a Henan youth tricked into confessing to being ringleader of an armed robbery. Sanpailou is the site of a murder in Nanjing for which innocent people were convicted and executed. On the Dongxiang case, also see Zhou, "Illusion and Reality."

61. For examples of these respective phenomena, see, in this volume, chapter 7, by McNicholas, and chapter 6, by Chiu.

62. See chapter 5, by Buoye, in this volume. For more detailed discussions of the assizes, see Meijer, "Autumn Assizes"; *HDSL*, juan 844–50; *DLCY*, vol. 5, 1239–56 (411:01–34); and Gang Yi, *Qiuyan jiyao*.

63. *HDSL*, 846.3b.

64. On France, see Maza, *Private Lives*.

65. The term "story stuff" was suggested to me by Robert Hegel.

66. Not only have Shakespeare's plays provided apt quotes for judges; they are also extraordinarily rich in legal content and commentary and have accordingly drawn the attention of legal scholars. See, for example, Domnarski, "Shakespeare in the Law"; Peterson, "Bard and the Bench"; Kornstein, "Shakespeare the Unacknowledged Legislator" and *Kill All the Lawyers?*

67. For two views on magistrates' use of *The Qing Code* in such cases, see Allee, "Code, Culture, and Custom"; and Philip C. C. Huang, "Codified Law and Mag-

isterial Adjudication." On the influence of customary law on magistrates' decisions, see Liang Zhiping, *Qingdai xiguanfa*.

68. Cover, "Nomos and Narrative," 5.

69. Ibid., 7.

70. See ibid., 46, 53, on the conflict between the role of judges in controlling the proliferation of legal meaning, which conflicts with the state's desire to use law as means for social control.

Glossary

An neng tao Zhenzhi dongjian hu?
　安能逃朕之洞鑒乎
anchashi 按察使
Anchasi 按察司
Anhe Xiansheng 安和先生
Anxiang (county) 安鄉
Ba 巴
baguwen 八股文
Bai Bingbing 白冰冰
Bai Xiaoyan 白曉燕
Baixing zu, jun shuyu buzu.　百姓足
　君孰與不足
ban fanren 扮犯人
ban wen ban bai 半文半白
Ban'an yaolue 辦案要略
bao (requital) 報

bao zai er sun 報在兒孫
Bao Zheng 包拯
baofu 保富
baojia 保甲
baoying 報應
Baxian Archives 巴縣檔案
beixin cangqiao 背信藏巧
benkui huozhe 本虧貨折
bi bu ran 必不然
bi ran 必然
biji 筆記
biji xiaoshuo 筆記小說
bing 稟
Bing bushi youxin yao zhi si tade
　並不是有心要致死他的
bisheng 筆生

Boluo (county) 博羅
bu dang ran er ran 不當然而然
Bu shishuo jiu yao xingshen ni le! 不實說就要刑審你了
Bu wang 捕亡
Bu yi le hu? 不亦樂乎
Bu yi ren suojian wei wo suojian hu? 不以人所見為我所見乎
buliao 不料
buqi 不期
Bushi ta mouhai le shi shui? 不是他謀害了是誰
bushi ting fuqin zhuling 不是聽父親主令
bushou fudao 不守婦道
bushou qinggui siyou funü zaimiao jianyin 不守清規，私誘婦女，在廟姦淫
Cai Yunu biyu zhuang yinseng 蔡玉奴避雨撞淫僧
Changlin of the Gioro clan 覺羅長麟
Chaoyang (district) 朝楊
Chen Huaixian 陳懷軒 (Chen Junjing 君敬)
Chen Huizu 陳輝祖
cheng 呈
Cheng Deliang 程德良
Cheng e 懲惡

Chenghuang 城隍
chuancheng 傳呈
Chufen zeli 處分則例
chujia 出家
churu 出入
cong qing 從輕
cuicheng 催呈
Cunren Tang 存仁堂
da bujing 大不敬
da wang 大王
daishu gao 代書稿
daishu zuo 代書作
Dalisi 大理寺
Dan-Xin Archives 淡新檔案
dang ran 當然
Dang ri xiaode shi yin Ceng Nengchun oushang muqin qingji duotiao shishou zhi shang bing bushi youxin yao zhi si tade. 當日小的實因曾能春毆傷母親情急奪挑失手致傷並不是有心要致死他的
dang ri xiaofuren bing mei heling zhu ou de 當日小婦人並沒有喝令助毆的
dangpu 當鋪
Dazhong Ye 大眾爺
dengshi 登時
Di Qing 狄青
diandang 典當

dianshi 典史
diewen 牒文
Dizang An 地藏庵
Dizangwang Pusa 地藏王菩薩
Dongchang (prefecture) 東昌
Dongyue Dadi 東嶽大帝
Dou song 鬥訟
dou'ou 鬥毆
dou'ou sharen 鬥毆殺人
dousha 鬥殺
du yushi 都禦史
Duan yü 斷獄
Duchayuan 都察院
dui yi 對移
duizhi shangshu zha buyishi 對制上書詐不以實
dushu 讀書
e qi hanpo 惡其悍潑
Ernü yingxiong zhuan 兒女英兄傳
Ershi nian mudu zhiguai xianzhuang 二十年目睹之怪現狀
Ershisi xiao 二十四孝
fa (law) 法
fa jia 法家
fa poma 發潑罵
Fan Juqing jishu sisheng jiao 范巨卿雞黍死生交
fang ye tiaodao 防夜挑刀
fanggao 放告

fanren 犯人
fashang shengxi 發商生息
fazhi 法制
fengshui 風水
fengsu zhi 風俗志
fengyan buce ge ting tianming 風煙不測各聽天命
Fengzhen shi 封診式
fu (district, prefecture) 府
fu nai pinzhi mu 富乃貧之母
Fu qi jiu wei renxia zhe? 夫豈久為人下者
Fu yi 賦役
Fulehun 富勒渾
Fumu bei'ou lüwen 父母被毆律文
fuqin bing meiyou zhushi ouda de shi 父親並沒有主使毆打的事
Furen pian 婦人騙
Gao Jin 高晉
gao yinzhuang 告陰狀
gao zhuang 告狀
gong'an 公案
gong'an xiaoshuo 公案小說
Gongli 公吏
gongli zhi li 公利之利
gongsuo 公所
guan daishu 官代書
Guan Gong 關公
Guan li 官吏

Glossary 287

guanbuzhu 管不著
Guandi 關帝
guanfa 官法
Guangfu *dawang* 廣福大王
guanhua 官話
guanjiao 管教
guanya zhidu 官牙制度
gui (cassia) 桂
gui (honorable, costly) 貴
Gunzhou 袞州
guojia yuanqi 國家元氣
gusha 故殺
Hai gan hun gong qiu fu shishou de hua ma? 還敢混供救父失手的話麼
hancheng 喊呈
hanfu 悍婦
Hanxuan lou 翰選樓
hanyuan yinhen 含冤飲恨
haowu guojiu 毫無過咎
Hebi sheng zhi wei le, si zhi wei bei? 何必生之為樂死之為悲
hehao 和好
hexie 和諧
Hongqi gong 紅旗公
Hu hun 戶婚
Hu-Xiang yan lue 湖湘讞略
huaben 話本
huaben xiaoshuo 話本小說

Huan yin pian 換銀騙
Huan you ren sheng, pindao heneng jie? 幻由人生，貧道何能解
huangdan 黃丹
huanjue 緩決
huguanfu 護官符
Huguang 湖廣
huiguan 會館
huiji 恚極
Hunqu pian 婚娶騙
hunyin jianqing 婚姻姦情
Huzhou 湖州
ji lü yuan shang 羈旅遠商
Ji yi you yan, naihe zhong gai? 既已有言，奈何中改
jia pin wuji yingsheng 家貧無計營生
jian hui 姦穢
Jiang shishi mudu erhou xin hu? 將事事目睹而後信乎
Jiang Zhe liang sheng xianxing shengli 江浙兩省現行省例
jiangqi pinku 講起貧苦
jiansheng 監生
jiansuo 姦所
jianyin 姦淫
jianyin fanjie 姦淫犯戒
jiao 角

jiao jianhou qiu hou chujue 絞監侯秋後處決
jiaochang 校場
jiaohun 叫魂
Jiaxing 嘉興
jiazhong qiongku 家中窮苦
Jin ping mei 金瓶梅
Jin Yingdou 金應斗
Jinghua yuan 鏡花緣
jingji 經紀
jinshi (presented scholar) 進士
jinshi zhacheng sixing 近侍詐稱私行
jishi 即時
jiu ku 廄庫
Jiu qing 九卿
ju 詎
juan 卷
kanshu 看書
kejin 可矜
keqian 客欠
kong fuqin bei ou 恐父親被毆
kong muqin shang 恐母親傷
Kong Yuxun 孔毓珣
Korkun of the Gioro clan 覺羅科爾坤
kougong 口供
kuai 塊

kuishi funü 窺視婦女
Kuizhong (county) 夔衷
kuli 庫吏
Lai Ming-hsien 賴明賢
Lan Tingzhen 藍廷珍
lanjiao shenyuan 攔轎申冤
lanyu 攔輿
laowangba buru zao si 老忘八不如早死
li (principle) 理
li (substatute) 例
li (unit of distance) 里
Li Baojia 李寶嘉
Li Le 李樂
Li Mengsheng 李夢生
Li Ruzhen 李汝珍
Li Shirong 李世榮
Li Yu 李漁
liandan 聯單
liang (unit of weight) 兩
Liang Qichao 梁啟超
lianpiao 聯票
Liaocheng (county) 聊城
Liaozhai zhiyi 聊齋志異
Libu zeli 吏部則例
lijue 立決
Lin Hou qiu Guanyin qiyu 林侯求觀音祈雨

Ling Tao 凌燾
lingchi 淩遲
lingguan 靈官
lishi 立誓
liuyang 留養
lizhi 理直
Longhu gong 龍湖宮
louxi 陋習
lü (statute) 律
Lu Tingcong 盧廷琮
Lufeng (county) 陸豐
Lüli jianshi 律例箋釋
lunli 論理
Luo Ergang 羅爾綱
ma (curse) 罵
ma qi banghu 罵其幫護
Maoming (district) 茂名
Miao 苗
Miaoli 苗栗
mielun 滅倫
Ming li 名例
mingcha 明查
mingfa 冥法
Minzhai jushi 敏齋居士
mipiao 米票
mixin 迷信
mousha 謀殺
mu (unit of land) 畝
mu bian 木扁

mu qiang 木槍
Mulian 目連
muyou 幕友
na zhi 那知
nang ma 嚷罵
nanyin 南音
Neige daku 內閣大庫
Neige xingke tiben 內閣刑科題本
Neiwufu guandang 內務府官當
Nian Fu 年富
Nian Gengyao 年羹堯
nieseng 孽僧
nieseng qitiao 孽僧欺調
niesi 臬司
ningzheng 獰猙
nüwu 女巫
ouda shi xi shi zai weiji 毆打實係事在危急
pa fuqin bei ou 怕父親被毆
pa fuqin nian lao bei ta dashang yishi qingqie 怕父親年老被他打傷一時情切
panci 判詞
pandu 判牘
panguan 判官
Panyu (county) 番禺
pi 批
pian 騙
piaohao 票號

pingri bing wu xianyuan 平日並無嫌怨
pingri hehao 平日和好
pingzha 馮劄
pinqiong wu ke liaosheng 貧窮無可聊生
pofu 潑婦
Pu Songling 蒲松齡
Putian 莆田
qi 氣
Qi ken bieyou yinni de? 豈肯別有隱匿的
Qi neng du sheng ye? 豈能獨生耶
Qian Chun 錢春
qiangzui duma 強嘴毒罵
Qianshu 潛書
qianzhuang 錢莊
qicheng 期呈
qing (emotion or state of affairs) 情
qing lüshi zuo zhi 請律師做紙
qing tian 青天
qing tian guan 清天官
qingji 情急
Qingqie qiuhu 情切求護
qingshi 情史
qingshi 情實
Qingzhen 青鎮
qita 其他
qiu qin qingqie 救親情切

Qiu sheng lu 求生錄
Qiushen 秋審
Qiushen bijiao tiaokuan 秋審比較條款
qiwang 欺妄
qixing yuan zui buhao 氣性原最不好
qiyi 起意
Qiyou jinnian Gansheng du duozhi zhi li? 豈有今年甘省獨多之之理
Qiyou . . . zhi li?! 豈有 . . . 之理
Quanzhou 泉州
Qujiang (county) 曲江
Ren lun 人倫
Ren pin 人品
Renhe (county) 仁和
renqing 人情
renqing xiaoshuo 人情小說
riyong leishu 日用類書
Ruhe jiang hao yanyu yinzhu xiaofuren? 如何將好言語穩住小婦人
Rulin waishi 儒林外史
Sanfasi 三法司
sapo 撒婆
sapo fan ba xiaode chou ma 撒潑反把小的臭罵
sapo qilai 撒潑起來
sengpi 僧痞
Shan xing 擅興
Shang 上

shangshu 尚書
shao wang'gao 燒王告
Shei ken shele shenjia xingming ti wo yinji ne? 誰肯捨了身家性命替我隱寄呢
shemi 奢靡
shen fengzi 審瘋子
shen jing 申儆
Shen Xiaoxia xianghui Chushi biao 沈小霞相會出師表
Shen Zhiqi 沈之奇
Shenbao 申報
Sheng xiao 聖孝
shengqing pohan 生情潑悍
shengtang 升堂
Shengyu 聖諭
shengyuan 生員
shenpan yishi 神判儀式
shi e 十惡
Shijiazhuang 石家莊
Shitou ji 石頭記
Shiwu guan xiyan cheng qiaohuo 十五貫戲言成巧禍
shuaijiao 率教
shuang feiyan diaofa 雙飛燕吊法
Shui luo shi chu 水落石出
Shujing 書經
shuzui zhuang 贖罪狀

Si Mingwang suo yi wei Mingwang yu? 斯冥王所以為冥王歟
sidian 祀典
sihui niangjia 私回娘家
Siku quanshu 四庫全書
sizhu tongqian 私鑄銅錢
songgun 訟棍
Songjiang 松江
songshi 訟師
songshi miben 訟師秘本
su 訴
suci 訴詞
Suichang (county) 遂昌
Suining (county) 遂寧
sushou qinggui 素守清規
suxing hanpo 素性悍潑
suzhuang 訴狀
Taizhou (city) 台州
tan 貪
tanci 彈詞
Tang Suizu 唐綏祖
Tang Zhen 唐甄
ti fuqin chuqi 替父親出氣
Tian 天
tian fu 天符
Tian Tao 田濤
tianli 天理
tianlü 天律

tiao 條
tiaokuai 條塊
tiaoxi qiujian 調戲求姦
tie zui jian 鐵嘴尖
Tong guita jianxin denghuo 通罣罣堅心燈火
tongshang bianmin 通商便民
tongsu xiaoshuo 通俗小說
tongxiang gongzhi 通鄉共知
tongyangxi 童養媳
tuan 團
tuanyue 團約
Wang Ao 王鏊
Wang Danwang 王亶望
wang fa 枉法
Wang Huizu 汪輝祖
Wang Kentang 王肯堂
Wang Lingguan 王靈官
Wang Youhuai 王又槐
wang jiao 王醮
wei fu xie chi 為父洩恥
Wei jiao pian 偽交騙
Wei jin (Imperial Guard and Prohibitions) 衛禁
wei qing 為情
wei she jixian wei 偽設乩仙位
weijin (violations of prohibitions) 違禁

weizao yinxin shixianshu deng 偽造印信時憲書等
wen (copper coin) 文
Wen Kang 文康
Wen shi 文事
Wen Yuanshuai 溫元帥
Wenshang (county) 汶上
wenyan 文言
wenyin 紋銀
Wenzhou 溫州
Wu and Qing market towns 烏鎮青鎮
Wu Jianren 吳趼人
Wu Jingzi 吳敬梓
wu ru 吾儒
wu shen 戊申
Wudashan 吳達善
Wudi (Five Emperors) 五帝
Wuhuang bucheng zhuang. 無謊不成狀
Wuxi (county) 無錫
Wuzhen 烏鎮
Xi yuan lu 洗冤錄
Xia Jingqu 夏敬渠
Xiahai chenghuang miao 霞海城隍廟
Xiamen 廈門
xian li 縣吏

xiangli guangrong	鄉里光榮
Xiangqing gong'an	詳情公案
Xiangtan (district)	湘潭
xiangzhang	鄉長
xianxi	嫌隙
xianzhang	縣長
xiao ren	小人
Xiaode shishou dashang bing bushi youxin yao zhi si tade.	小的失手打傷並不是有心要致死他
Xiaode yin qiuhu fuqin qingqie yishi shishou ba ta dashang.	小的因救護父親情切一時失手把他打傷
xiaoshuo	小說
xie qi bu ding	血氣不定
xiefen	洩忿
Xigang	西港
xiguan fa	習慣法
Xin ke zheng zi chang shuo yi peng xue	新刻正字唱說一捧雪
Xin xiaoshuo	新小說
Xing'an huilan	刑案匯覽
Xingbu	刑部
xingbu daxueshi	刑部大學士
xinggong	行宮
xingjian	行姦
xingke	刑科
xingke tiben	刑科題本
xingqing buhao	性情不好
xingqing jueqiang	性情不好
xingzi diaoman yao shi qizhi xie	性子刁蠻要使氣質些
Xinzhu	新竹
Xinzhuang	新莊
Xiushui (county)	秀水
Xu Changzuo	徐昌作
Xu Ren	徐任
Xuanmiao Guan	玄妙觀
xue	雪
xuemeng	血盟
xunfu	巡撫
xunxin	尋釁
ya ren	牙人
yahang	牙行
yamen	衙門
Yan Youxi	嚴有禧
Yan Gong	晏公
Yanshan conglu	燕山叢錄
Ye Mengzhu	葉夢珠
Yesou puyan	野叟曝言
yi (righteousness)	義
Yi yi quzheng zhongkou hu?	抑以取證眾口乎
yiding zhi li	一定之理
yiji	義激
yinfu	淫婦
yingling	嬰靈
Yining (county)	義寧

Yinjiang (county) 印江
yinseng 淫僧
Yinyang taishou 陰陽太守
yinzhuang 陰狀
Yipeng xue jing shi xin shu 一捧雪警世新書
Yiri guanshi shiri da. 一日官事十日打
yishi qingji 一時情急
yishi qingqie 一時情切
Youying gong 有應公
Yu Jianwu 余健吾
yuandan 冤單
yuanqin zhaizhu 冤親債主
yuanwang 冤枉
yuanwen 冤文
yuesong 越訟
Yuewei caotang biji 閱微草堂筆記
Yunluo dian sixing 雲落店私刑
Za 雜
zai weiji 在危急
Zei dao 賊盜
Zeng Jing 曾靜
zha bingsishang bishi 詐病死傷避事
zha jiaguan 詐假官
zha jiaoyouren fanfa 詐教誘人犯法
zhacheng neishi dengguan 詐稱內使等官
zhachuan zhaozhi 詐傳詔旨

zhan jitou 斬雞頭
zhan lijue 斬立決
Zhang 張
Zhang Boxing 張伯行
Zhang jianseng juepei yuanfang 杖姦僧決配遠方
Zhang Yingyu 張應俞
Zhang Zhupo 張竹坡
zhangfang 賬房
zhanghui 章回
Zhangqiu (county) 章丘
Zhao Yi 趙翼
zhaozhuang 招狀
zhawei (Zha wei) 詐偽
zhawei ruiying 詐為瑞應
zhawei zhishu 詐為制書
Zhe ming shi ni fuqin hen ta niuou zhuling ni ba ta dashang shen side le. 這明是你父親恨他扭毆. 主令你把他打傷身死的了
Zhen Xishan 真西山
zheng dou 爭鬥
zheng fengsu 整風俗
Zheng zhe, zheng ye. Zi shuai yi zheng, shu gan buzheng? 政者正也子帥以正 孰敢不正
zhengnao 爭鬧
zhengyan zebei ta 正言責備他
zhengzai 正在

Zhenwu 真武
zhi ming 致命
zhi ou qiqin boshu shasi zhe 姪毆其親伯叔殺死者
zhi shi yin nüren bu xiaoshun 只是因女人不孝順
Zhi zhi 職制
zhifu 知府
zhipu 治譜
Zhiwen lu 咫文錄
zhixian 知縣
zizhi jiongpo 自致窘迫
zhong zhi zhu shi 踵至助勢
Zhou Jing 周經
Zhouli 周禮
zhu 主
zhu jian 竹尖
Zhu Yigui 朱一貴

zhuang 狀
zhuangci 狀詞
zhuangshi 狀式
zhuling 主令
zhun 准
Zhushan 竹山
Zi yu shan er min shan yi. 子欲善而民善矣
zihao 字號
zizhi jiongpo 自致窘迫
Zizhi xinshu 資治新書
Zizhi xinshu erji 資治新書二集
zongdu 總督
zu 詛
zuiming 罪名
zuiren 罪人
zunzhang yueshu 尊長約束
zuo renjia 作人家

Bibliography

PRIMARY SOURCES: TEXTS AND TRANSLATIONS

Bailian pan ji 白蓮沜集 (Collected writings of the White Lotus at the Water's Edge). Cheng Deliang 程德良 Wanli edition preserved at the Center for Chinese Studies, Taipei.

Bao Longtu pan baijia gong'an 包龍圖判百家公案 (Judge Bao's hundred cases). Wanli edition. In *Guben xiaoshuo congkan* 古本小說叢刊 (Collected old editions of novels). Beijing: Zhonghua Shuju, 1991.

Baxian dang'an 巴縣檔案 (Ba County Archives). In Sichuan Provincial Archives, Chengdu, Sichuan. Cited by serial number.

Baxian zhi 巴縣志 (Ba County Gazetteer). In *Xinxiu fangzhi congkan* 新修志叢刊, no. 6, *Sichuan fangzhi* 四川方志. 1939. Reprint, Taipei: Xuesheng Shuju, 1967.

BXDA. See *Baxian dang'an*.

Cao Xueqin 曹雪芹. *"Honglou meng" bashihui jiaoben* 紅樓夢八十回校本. (Eighty-chapter variorum edition of *Dream of red mansions*). Edited by Yu Pingbo 俞平伯. 4 vols. Beijing: Renmin Wenxue, 1958.

———. *The Story of the Stone*. Translated by David Hawkes. Vol. 1. Harmondsworth, England: Penguin, 1973.

Changsun Wuji 長孫無忌 et al. *Tanglü shuyi* 唐律疏義 (Tang code with commentaries). Edited by Liu Junwen 劉俊文. Beijing: Zhonghua Shuju, 1983.

Christie, Agatha. *Murder on the Orient Express*. London: Collins, 1934.

Confucius. *The Analects*. Translated by D. C. Lau. Hong Kong: Chinese University Press, 1983.

Da Qing huidian shili 大清會典實例 (Institutes of the Qing dynasty).

Dayi juemi lu 大義覺迷錄 (A record of how true virtue led to an awakening from delusion). Compiled by imperial command, 1730. Reprint, Taipei: Wenhai, 1970.

DLCY. See Xue Yunsheng, *Du li cunyi*.

Dou Yi 竇儀 et al., eds. *Song xing tong* 宋刑統 (The Song penal code). Edited by Wu Yiru 吳翊如. Beijing: Zhonghua Shuju, 1984.

Erxin 耳新 (Hearsay). Zheng Zhongkui 鄭仲夔. In *Congshu jicheng* 叢書集成 (A collection of collections), vol. 2946. Shanghai: Shangwu Yinshuguan, 1925.

Fabi jingtianlei: Xinke fabi jingtianlei 新刻法筆驚天雷 (Legal writing that startles heaven with thunder: A new edition). Qing edition in the Institute of Oriental Culture, University of Tokyo.

Fabi tianyou: Xinke fabi tianyou 新刻法筆天油 (Legal writing that induces the grace of heaven: A new edition). Qing edition in the Institute of Oriental Culture, University of Tokyo.

Fang, Ai. *The Scholar and the Serving Maid: A Qing Dynasty Mystery*. Translated by Yu Fangqin and Esther Samson. Beijing: Panda Books, 1980.

Feng Menglong 馮夢龍. *Gujin xiaoshuo* 古今小說 (Stories old and new). Edited by Xu Zhengyang 許正揚. Beijing: Renmin Wenxue, 1984.

———. *Stories Old and New: A Ming Dynasty Collection*. Translated by Shuhui Yang and Yunqin Yang. Seattle: University of Washington Press, 2000.

———. *Xing shi heng yan* 醒世恒言 (Constant words to awaken the world). Nanjing: Jiangsu Guji Chubanshe, 1991.

———. *Yushi mingyan* 喻世明言 (Clear words to instruct the world). Beijing: Renmin Wenxue Chubanshe, 1990.

Fengliu heshang 風流和尚 (Buddhist monks addicted to love). N.d. Reprint, Taipei: Shuangdi Guoji Chubanshe, 1995.

Gang Yi 剛毅. *Qiuyan jiyao* 秋讞輯要 (Essentials of the autumn assizes). Shanghai, 1889. Reprint in *Jindai Zhongguo shiliao congkan* 近代中國史料叢刊 (Collected historical materials on China), vol. 236. Taipei: Wenhai Chubanshe, 1968).

Gao Ru 高儒. *Baichuan shu zhi* 百川書志 (One hundred streams of bibliography). Beijing: Gudian Wenxue Chubanshe, 1957.

Gengsi bian 庚巳編 (Compilation during the *gengsi* year). Lu Can 陸粲 (1494–1551). Beijing: Zhonghua Shuju, 1985.

Gongzhongdang Qianlongchao zouzhe 宮中檔乾隆朝奏摺 (Secret palace memorials of the Qianlong reign). Guoli Gugong Bowuyuan 國立故宮博物院

(National Palace Museum). 75 vols. Taipei: Guoli Gugong Bowuyuan, 1982–89.

Guan Hanqing 関漢卿 Dou E yuan 竇娥冤 (Injustice to Dou E). In *Injustice to Tou O (Tou O yüan): A Study and Translation*, by Chung-wen Shih. Cambridge: Cambridge University Press, 1972.

Guanzhenshu jicheng 官箴書集成 (A collection of books on administration). Hefei: Huangshan Shushe, 1997.

Gui Wanrong 桂萬榮. *Tang yin bi shi* 棠陰比事 (Parallel cases from under the pear-tree). Zhibuzu Zhai 知不足齋 manuscript. Edited by Zhang Yuanji 張元濟. In *Sibu congkan, Xu ji zi bu* 四部叢刊續集子部, vol. 321. Shanghai: Shangwu, 1934.

Gujin lütiao gong'an 古今律條公案 (Old and new crime tales categorized by statute). Wanli edition. In *Guben xiaoshuo jicheng* (Collected old editions of novels). Shanghai: Shanghai Guji Chubanshe, 1992.

GZDQL. See *Gongzhongdang Qianlongchao zhouzhe*.

Hayden, George. *Crime and Punishment in Medieval Chinese Drama: Three Judge Pao Plays*. Cambridge, Mass.: Harvard University Council on East Asian Studies, 1978.

HDSL. See *Da Qing huidian shili*.

He Changling 賀長齡, comp. *Huangchao jingshi wenbian* 皇朝經世文編 (Statecraft compendium from the Qing dynasty). 1826. Reprint, Taipei: Guofeng, 1963.

He Ning 和凝 and He Meng 和蒙. *Yi yu ji* 疑獄集 (Collection of doubtful cases). Reprint in *Siku quanshu* 四庫全書, vol. 729. Taipei: Shangwu Chubanshe, 1983.

Houguan xian xiangtu zhi 侯官縣鄉土志 (Rural gazetteer from Houguan county). 1906. In *Zhongguo fangzhi congshu, Huanan difang, Fujian sheng* 中國方志叢書, 華南地方, 福建省 (Collectanea of Chinese gazetteers: South China region, Fujian province), no. 227. 2 vols. Taipei: Chengwen, 1974.

Huang Liuhong 黃六鴻. *Fuhui quan shu* 福惠全書 (Complete book concerning happiness and benevolence). Jinling (Nanjing): Lianxi Shuwu 濂溪書屋, 1699. Reprint in *Guanzhenshu jicheng* 官箴書集成 (A collection of books on administration), vol. 3, 211–592. Hefei: Huangshan Shushe, 1997.

Huang Liu-hung. *A Complete Book concerning Happiness and Benevolence: A Manual for Local Magistrates in Seventeenth-Century China*. Translated and edited by Djang Chu. Tucson: University of Arizona Press, 1984.

Huang Zhangjian 黃彰健. *Mingdai lüli huibian* 明代律例彙編 (Collated edition of Ming-era statutes and substatutes). 2 vols. Taipei: Zhongyang Yanjiuyuan Lishi Yuyan Yanjiusuo, 1979.

Huanxi yuanjia 歡喜冤家 (Lovers who cause both joy and pain). Xihu Yuyin Zhuren 西湖漁隱主人. Beijing: Beijing Shifan Daxue, 1992.

Huizui bian 薈蕞編 (Collection of concealed trivia). Yu Yue 俞樾. In *Biji xiaoshuo daguan* 筆記小說大觀 (Great collection of informal writings), 2nd series, no. 4. Taipei: Xinxing Shuju, 1988.

Hunan shengli cheng'an 湖南省例成案 (Hunan provincial statutes). Ca. 1820.

Ji Yun 紀昀. *Yuewei caotang biji* 閱微草堂筆記 (Random jottings at the Cottage of Close Scrutiny). Taipei: Da Zhongguo Tushu Gongsi, 1992.

Jiandeng xinhua 剪燈新話 (New stories to trim the lamp by). Qu You 瞿佑. In *Zheng Zhenduo shijie wenku* 鄭振鐸世界文庫, vols. 5, 6. Shijiazhuang: Hebei Renmin Chubanshe, 1991).

Jiang Yonglin, trans. *The Great Ming Code / Da Ming lü*. Seattle: University of Washington Press, 2004.

Jiaqing huidian shili. See *Qinding Da Qing huidian shili (Jiaqing chao)*.

Jingfu xin shu 警富新墊 (A new warning about wealth). By Anhe Xiansheng 安和先生. In *Guben xiaoshuo jicheng*, no. 83. Facsimile of Hanxuan Lou edition, 1809. Shanghai: Shanghai Guji, 1990.

Johnson, Wallace, trans. *The T'ang Code*. 2 vols. Princeton, N.J.: Princeton University Press, 1979–97.

Jones, William C., trans. *The Great Qing Code*. Oxford: Clarendon Press, 1994.

Lan Dingyuan 藍鼎元. *Luzhou gong'an* 鹿洲公案 (Legal cases from Luzhou). Beijing: Qunzhong Chubanshe, 1985.

Legge, James, trans. *The Chinese Classics*. Revised 2nd edition. 5 vols. Reprint, Taipei: SMC Publishing, 1991.

Lei Menglin 雷夢麟. *Dulü suoyan* 讀律瑣言 (Trifling words on reading the statutes). Collated by Huai Xiaofeng 懷效鋒 and Li Jun 李俊. Zhongguo lüxue congkan (Chinese legal studies reprints) series. Beijing: Falü Chubanshe, 1999.

LFZZ. See *Lufu zouzhe*.

Li Boyuan 李伯元. *Guanchang xianxing ji* 官場現記 (Officialdom unmasked). Hong Kong: Guangzhi Shuju, ca. 1970.

———. *Officialdom Unmasked*. Translated and abridged by T. L. Yang. Hong Kong: Hong Kong University Press, 2001.

Li Le 李樂. *Xu "Jianwen zaji"* 續見聞雜記 (Further *Random notes on matters seen and heard*). Wanli edition. Reprint, Shanghai: Shanghai Guji, 1986.

Li Lüyuan 李綠園. *Qilu deng* 歧路燈 (A lantern for the crossroads). 3 vols. Zhengzhou: Zhongzhou Shuhuashe, 1980.

Liang Tianlai gao yu zhuang 梁天來告御狀 (Liang Tianlai brings his complaint to the emperor). Hong Kong: Wu Gui Tang, 1904.

Ling Mengchu 凌濛初. *Pai'an jingqi* 拍案驚奇 (Striking the table in amazement). 2 vols. 1628. Reprint, Shanghai: Shanghai Guji, 1985.

Ling Zhu 凌燽. *Xijiang shinie jishi* 西江視臬紀事 (Memoirs of a Jiangxi provincial judge). 1743. Reprinted as no. 882 in *Xuxiu Siku quanshu* 續修四庫全書. Shanghai: Shanghai Guji, 1997.

Liu E 劉鶚. *Lao Can youji* 老殘遊記 (Travels of Lao Can). Beijing: Renmin Wenxue, 1957.

Liu T'ieh-yün. *The Travels of Lao Ts'an*. Translated by Harold Shadick. Ithaca, N.Y.: Cornell University Press, 1952.

Liu, Ts'un-yan, ed. *Chinese Middlebrow Fiction from the Ch'ing and Early Republican Eras*. Hong Kong: The Chinese University Press, 1984.

Lufu zouzhe 錄副奏摺 ([Grand Council] file copies of palace memorials). First Historical Archives, Beijing.

Luo Guanzhong. *Three Kingdoms*. Translated by Moss Roberts. Berkeley: University of California Press, 1991.

Lüyuan conghua 履園叢話 (Collected discourses while rambling in the garden). Qian Yong 錢泳. Beijing: Zhonghua Shuju, 1983.

McKnight, Brian, and James T. C. Liu, eds. and trans. *The Enlightened Judgments: Ch'ing Ming chi, The Sung Dynasty Collection*. Albany: State University of New York Press, 1999.

Ming Qing dang'an 明清檔案 (Ming and Qing archives). Comp. Chang Wejen 張偉仁. Projected 800 vols. Taipei: Lianjing Chubanshe, 1986–.

Ming Qing Suzhou gongshangye beike ji 明清蘇州工商業碑刻集 (Collection of stele inscriptions on industry and commerce in Suzhou during the Ming and Qing). Nanjing: Jiangsu Renmin, 1981.

Mingjing gong'an 明鏡公案 (Crime cases clearly resolved). Edited by Ge Tianmin 葛天民 and Wu Peiquan 吳沛泉. Late Ming edition. Reprinted in *Guben xiaoshuo jicheng* 古本小說集成 (Collected old editions of novels). Shanghai: Shanghai Guji, 1992.

Nanbu xian dang'an 南部縣 (Nanbu county archive). Held in Nanchong Municipal Archives 南充市檔案館.

Neige xingke tiben 內閣刑科題本 (Routine memorials of the Grand Secretariat's Punishments Office of Scrutiny, *XKTB*). First Historical Archives, Beijing.

Panyu xianzhi 番禺縣志 (Panyu county gazetteer). 1871. Modern typeset edition. Guangzhou: Guangdong Nanfang Ribao She, 1998.

Pili shoubi: Xinjuan dingbu shizhu Pili shoubi 新鐫訂補釋註霹靂手筆 (Thunderous writing abilities: A new edition, revised and annotated). Ming edition in the East Asian Library, University of California, Los Angeles.

Qinding Da Qing huidian 欽定大清會典 (Imperially collected statutes of the Great Qing). Edited by Kungang 崑岡 et al. 1899. Reprint, Taipei: Taiwan Zhongwen Shuju, 1963.

Qinding Da Qing huidian shili 欽定大清會典事例 (Imperially collected statutes and substatutes of the Great Qing). Comp. Kungang 崑岡 et al. Reprinted in *Xuxiu Siku quanshu* 續修四庫全書, nos. 798–814. Shanghai: Shanghai Guji, 1997.

Qinding Da Qing huidian shili (Jiaqing chao). 欽定大清會典事例 (嘉慶朝) (Imperially commissioned collected statutes and substatutes of the Great Qing [Jiaqing edition (1818)]). Comp. Tuojin 托津 et al. Reprinted 83 vols. in *Jindai Zhongguo shiliao congkan*, 3rd series, collections 65–70, vols. 641–90. Taipei Xian, Yonghe Shi: Wenhai, 1991–92.

Qingdai biji xiaoshuo leibian 清代筆記小說類編 (Stories from Qing-era *biji* organized by category). Hefei: Huangshan Shushe, 1994.

Qiu Hanping 丘漢平. *Lidai xingfa zhi* 歷代刑法志 (Penal laws of successive dynasties). 2 vols. Changsha: Commercial Press, 1938.

Quan bu Bao Longtu pan baijia gong'an 全補包龍圖判百家公案 (One hundred court cases adjudicated by Bao Longtu, completely supplemented). 1594.

Sanguo yanyi huipingben 三國演義會評本 (Romance of the Three Kingdoms, combined commentary edition). Edited by Chen Xizhong 陳曦鐘 et al. Beijing: Beijing Daxue, 1986.

Sengni niehai 僧尼孽海 (Monks and nuns in a sea of sin). Late Ming edition. Taipei: Shuangdi Guoji Chuban, 1995.

Shan e tu 善惡圖 (The chart of good and evil). In *Guben xiaoshuo jicheng* 古本小說集成 (Collected old editions of novels), series 2, vols. 140–41. Beijing: Zhonghua Shuju, 1990.

Shanghai xianzhi 上海縣志 (Shanghai county gazetteer), 1872. In *Zhongguo fangzhi congshu, Huazhong difang, Jiangsu sheng* 中國方志叢書, 華中地方, 江蘇省 (Collectanea of Chinese gazetteers, central China region, Jiangsu province), no. 169. Taipei: Chengwen Chubanshe, 1975.

Shapiro, Sidney, trans. *Outlaws of the Marsh*. 2 vols. Beijing: Foreign Languages Press, 1981.

Shen Defu 沈德符. *Wanli yehuo bian* 萬歷野獲編 (Anecdotes from the Wanli period). Beijing: Xueyuan Chubanshe, 2002.

Shen Jiaben. 沈家本. *Qiushen tiaokuan* 秋審條款 (Rules for the autumn assizes). Preface dated 1906.

Shen Zhiqi 沈之奇, ed. *"Da Qing lü" jizhu* 大清律輯註 (The Great Qing code with collected commentaries). Preface 1715. Collated by Huai Xiaofeng 懷效鋒 and Li Jun 李俊. 2 vols. Beijing: Falü Chubanshe, 1998, 2000.

Shi diantou 石點頭 (Even the rocks nod). Comp. Tianran Chisou 天然癡叟. 1957. Reprint, Shanghai: Shanghai Guji, 1985.

Shuihu zhuan huipingben 水滸傳會評本 (Outlaws of the marsh, combined commentary edition). Edited by Chen Xizhong 陳曦鐘, Hou Zhongyi 侯忠義, and Lu Yuchuan 魯玉川. 2 vols. Beijing: Beijing Daxue, 1981.

Shuntian fu dang'an 順天府檔案 (Shuntian prefecture archives). First Historical Archives, Beijing.

Song Ci (Sung Tz'u). *The Washing Away of Wrongs*. Translated by Brian McKnight. Ann Arbor: University of Michigan Center for Chinese Studies, 1981.

Stone, Charles, trans. and ed. *The Fountainhead of Chinese Erotica: The Lord of Perfect Satisfaction (Ruyijun zhuan), with a Translation and Critical Edition*. Honolulu: University of Hawai'i Press, 2003.

Tang Zhen 唐甄. *Qian shu* 潛書 (Writings after [Tao] Qian). Reprinted in *Xuxiu Siku quanshu* 續修四庫全書, no. 945. Shanghai: Shanghai Guji, 1997.

Wang Huizu 汪輝祖. "Lun qinmin" 論親民 (On being close to the people). In *Huangchao jingshi wenbian*, comp. He Changling.

———. *Shuangjietang yongxun* 雙節堂庸訓 (Simple precepts from the Hall Enshrining a Pair of Chaste Widows). 1794. Reprint, Taipei: Huawen Shuju, 1970.

———. *Xu Zuozhi yaoyan* 續佐治藥言 (Sequel to "Admonitions on assisting with governance"). 1786. In *Wang Longzhuang yishu* 汪龍莊遺書 (Last writings by Wang Longzhuang [Huizu]). 1889. Reprint, Taipei: Huawen Shuju, 1970.

———. *Xuezhi xushuo* 學治續說 (Further explanations for the study of administration). 1793. In *Wang Longzhuang yishu* 汪龍莊遺書 (Last writings by Wang Longzhuang [Huizu]). 1889. Reprint, Taipei: Huawen Shuju, 1970.

Wu Cheng'en 吳承恩. *Li Zhuowu ping ben "Xiyou ji"* 李卓吾評本西遊記 (Journey to the West: Li Zhouwu commentary edition). Edited by Chen Xianxing 陳先行 and Bao Yufei 包于飛. Shanghai: Shanghai Guji, 1994.

Wu Tan 吳壇. *"Da Qing lüli" tongkao* 大清律例通考 (Thorough examination of The Great Qing code). Draft, 1778; preface by Wu Chongshi 吳重熹, 1886. Reprinted as *"Da Qing lüli tongkao" jiaozhu* 大清律例通考校注 (Collated and annotated thorough examination of "The Great Qing code"), ed. Ma Jianshi 馬建石 and Yang Yutang 楊育棠. Beijing: Zhongguo Zhengfa Daxue, 1992.

Wu Woyao 吳沃堯. *Jiuming qiyuan* 九命奇冤 (The strange case of nine murders). Taipei: Shijie Shuju, 1962.

Xiao-Cao yibi: Xinke jiaozhengyin shici jiabianlan Xiao-Cao yibi 新刻校正音釋詞家便覽蕭曹遺筆 (The last writings of Xiao He and Cao Shen: A handy corrected edition for litigation specialists). 1614. In the East Asian Library, University of California, Los Angeles.

Xijiang shinie jishi 西江視臬紀事 (Memoirs of a Jiangxi provincial judge). By Ling Tao 凌燽. 1743. Reprinted in *Xuxiu Siku quanshu* 續修四庫全書, no. 882. Shanghai: Shanghai Guji, 1997.

Xijiang zhengyao 西江政要 (Jiangxi provincial statutes). Jiangxi Anchasi 按察司 (Provincial Judicial Commission) edition, ca. 1895.

Xingke tiben 刑科題本 (Board of Punishments routine memorials).

Xingshi yinyuan zhuan 醒世姻緣傳 (Marriage bonds to awaken the world). 3 vols. Shanghai: Shanghai Guji Chubanshe, 1981.

Xinjuan fajia toudan han 新鐫法家透膽寒 (Legal specialists' extremely frightening techniques: A new edition). Buxiangzi 補相子. Qing edition in the Institute of Oriental Culture, University of Tokyo.

Xinke fajia xinshu 新刻法家新書 (New handbook for legal specialists: A new edition). Wu Tianmin 吳天民 and Da Keqi 達可奇. 1862 edition in the Institute of Oriental Culture, University of Tokyo.

Xinke Tianxia simin bianlan Santai wanyong zhengzong 新刻天下四民便覽 三台萬用正宗 (Santai's all-purpose true teachings for the convenience of all people under Heaven, new edition). Edited by Yu Xiangdou. 余象斗. 1599.

Xinzheng lu 信徵錄 (Accounts of proof of divine retribution). Edited by Xu Qing 徐慶. In *Biji xiaoshuo daguan* 筆記小說大觀 (Great collection of informal writings), series 39, vol. 7. Taipei: Xinxin Shuju, 1990.

Xiqiao yeji 西樵野紀 (Records of the western woodsman in the wild). Hou Dian 侯甸 (Ming). In *Siku quanshu cunmu congshu* 四庫全書存目叢書, vol. 246. Based on the Wanli edition in the Beijing Library. Tainan: Zhuangyan Chubanshe, 1995.

XKTB. See *Xingke tiben*.

Xu *"Zhizhu tan"* 續隻塵譚 (Sequel to *Discussions of the lone deer*). Hu Chengpu 胡承譜. In *Congshu jicheng, chubian* 叢書集成, 初編 (A collection of collectanea, first edition), vol. 2968. Shanghai: Shangwu Yinshu Guan, 1936.

Xue Yunsheng 薛允升. *Du li cunyi* 讀例存疑 (Remaining doubts after reading the substatutes). 1905. Reprinted as *"Du li cun yi" chongkanben* 讀例存疑重刊本, *A Typeset Edition of the "Tu-li ts'un-i,"* ed. Huang Tsing-chia (Huang Jingjia) 黃靜嘉, comp. Hsüeh Yun-sheng. 5 vols. Taipei: Chengwen, 1970.

———. *Tang-Ming lü hebian* 唐明律合編 (Combined edition of the Tang and Ming codes). Edited by Huai Xiaofeng 懷效鋒 and Li Ming 李鳴. Beijing: Falü Chubanshe, 1999.

Xue'an mingyuanlü: Xinke fajia Xiao-Cao liangzao xue'an mingyuanlü 新刻法家蕭曹兩造雪案鳴冤律 (Clearing suspicions and pleading for vindication by Xiao He and Cao Shen: For the use of plaintiffs and defendants. A new edition for legal specialists). Qing edition in the private collection of Tian Tao.

Yang Naiwu yu Xiao Baicai 楊乃武與小白菜 (Yang Naiwu and "Little Cabbage"). Sound recording. Taipei: Ming Feng Chang Pian, 1970.

Ye Mengzhu 葉夢珠. *Yueshi bian* 閱世編 (Seeing the world). Taipei: Muduo, 1982.

Yijian zhi 夷堅志 (Record of the listener and recorder). Hong Mai 洪邁. 4 vols. 1157–1202. Reprint, Beijing: Zhonghua Shuju, 1981.

Yongxian zhai biji 庸閒齋筆記 (Random jottings from the Studio of Simplicity and Leisure). Chen Qiyuan 陳其元. Taipei: Guangwen Shuju, 1982.

Yongzheng chao Hanwen zhupi zouzhe ziliao huibian 雍正朝漢文朱批奏摺資料彙編 (Collection of materials from imperially rescripted memorials written in Chinese during the Yongzhen reign). 40 vols. Shanghai: Jiangsu Guji Chubanshe, 1989–91.

Yu, Anthony C., trans. and ed. *The Journey to the West*. 4 vols. Chicago: University of Chicago Press, 1977–83.

Yuan Mei 袁枚. *Xu "Zibuyu"* 續子不語 (Sequel to *What the master did not speak about*). In *Yuan Mei quanji* 袁枚全集 (The complete works of Yuan Mei), ed. Wang Zhiying 王志英. 8 vols. Shanghai: Jiangsu Guji, 1993.

———. *Zibuyu* 子不語 (What the master did not speak about). In *Yuan Mei quanji* 袁枚全集 (The complete works of Yuan Mei), ed. Wang Zhiying 王志英. 8 vols. Shanghai: Jiangsu Guji Chubanshe, 1993.

Zhan Yanfu 詹琰夫 (attributed). *Minggong shupan qingming ji* 名公書判清明集 (Collection of enlightened judgments by famous officials). 1261. 2 vols. Reprint, Beijing: Zhonghua Shuju, 1987.

Zhang Boxing 張伯行. *Zhengyitang ji* 正誼堂集 (Collected works of Zhengyitang [Zhang Boxing]). In *Sanxian zhengshu* 三賢政書 (Texts on administration by three worthies), ed. Wu Yuanbing 吳元炳. 1879. Reprint, Taipei: Xuesheng Shuju, 1976.

Zhang Yingyu 張應俞. *Du pian xinshu* 杜騙新書 (A new book for aid in eliminating deception). Microfilm copy of an edition in the Naikaku Bunko collection, Tokyo, 1617.

Zhang Zhupo 張竹坡. "Piping diyi qishu Jin Ping Mei dufa" 批評第一奇書金瓶梅讀法 (How to read the commentaries on *Jin Ping Mei*, the "First work of genius"). In *"Jin Ping Mei" ziliao huibian* 金瓶梅資料匯編 (Collected research materials on *Jin Ping Mei*), ed. Hou Zongyi 侯忠義 et al., 24–46. Beijing: Beijing Daxue Chubanshe, 1985.

Zhao Yi 趙翼. *Gaiyu congkao* 陔餘叢考 (Mourning period miscellaneous notes). 1790. Reprint, Taipei: Huashi, 1975.

Zheng Ke 鄭克. *Zhe yu gui jian* 折獄龜鑑 (Magic mirror for solving cases). Modern edition, *"Zhe yu gui jian" yi zhu* 折獄龜鑑譯注 (*Magic mirror for solving cases*, an annotated translation). Edited by Liu Junwen 劉俊文. Shanghai: Shanghai Guji Chubanshe, 1988.

Zhen'gao 真誥 (Declarations of the perfected). In *(Zhengtong) Daozang* 正統道藏 (Daoist canon of the Zhengtong reign). 1445. Reprint, Shanghai, 1923–26; Taipei: Xinwenfeng, 1983, 637–40. Also in *Concordance du Tao-tsang, titres des ouvrages*, ed. Kristofer M. Schipper, 1016. Paris: Publications de l'École Française d'Extrême-Orient, 1975.

Zheyu mingzhu: Xinke zhaixuan zengbu zhushi fajia yaolan zheyu mingzhu 新刻摘選增補注釋法家要覽折獄明珠 (Cases adjudicated as clear as a glittering pearl: A handy new compilation with annotations for legal specialists). 1602. In the East Asian Library, University of California, Los Angeles.

Zheyu qibian: Dingqie Jinling yuanban Anlü bianmin zheyu qibian 鼎鍥金陵原版按律便民折獄奇編 (A collection of unique adjudications categorized by statute to aid people: A definitive edition originally published in Nanjing). Edited by Letianzi 樂天子. Ming edition in the East Asian Library, University of California, Los Angeles.

Zhi Zhe chenggui 治浙成規 (Collected statutes of Nanzhili and Zhejiang). In *Guanzhenshu jicheng* 官箴書集成 (A collection of books on administration), vol. 6. Hefei: Huangshan Shushe, 1997.

Zhongguo gudai zhenxiben xiaoshuo 中國古代珍稀本小說. Ed. Hou Zhongyi 侯忠義, et al. Shenyang: Chunfeng wenyi, 1994. 10 vols.

Zhongyang yanjiuyuan Lishi yuyan yanjiu suo xiancun Qingdai Neige daku yuancang Ming Qing dang'an Zhupi zouzhe 中央研究院歷史語言研究所現存清代大庫原藏明清檔案要在硃批奏摺 (Imperially rescripted memorials from the Ming and Qing archives currently stored at the Academia Sinica Institute of History and Philology).

Zhupi zouzhe 硃批奏折 (Imperially rescripted memorials). First Historical Archives, Beijing.

"Zouyi dianshang shoudang huowu shihuo yanshao peishang zhangcheng" 奏議典商收當貨物失火延燒賠償章程 (A memorial on rules for compensation by pawnbrokers when pawned articles have been destroyed by fire). Submitted by Gao Jin 高晉, 1776. Reprint in *Zhongyang yanjiuyuan Lishi yuyan yanjiu suo xiancun Qingdai Neige daku yuancang Ming Qing dang'an* 中央研究院歷史語言研究所現存清代內閣大庫原藏明清檔案 (Ming and Qing archives from the storehouse of the Grand Secretariat currently stored at the Academia Sinica Institute of History and Philology), ed. Chang Wejen 張偉仁, vol. 227, 048–055. 1986–95.

ZPZZ. See *Zhupi zouzhe*.

SECONDARY MATERIALS

A Ying 阿英. *Wan Qing xiaoshuo shi* 晚清小說史 (History of late Qing fiction). Beijing: Dongfang Chubanshe, 1996.

Alabaster, Ernest, ed. *Notes and Commentaries on Chinese Criminal Law and Cognate Topics. With Special Relation to Ruling Cases. Together with a Brief Excursus on the Law of Property, Chiefly Founded on the Writings of the Late Sir Chaloner Alabaster, K.C.M.G., etc., Sometime H. B. M. Consul-General in China*. London, 1899. Reprint, Taipei: Ch'eng-Wen, 1968.

Alford, William P. "Law, Law, What Law? Why Western Scholars of Chinese History and Society Have Not Had More to Say about Its Law." *Modern China* 23.4 (1997), 398–419. Reprint in *The Limits of the Rule of Law in China*, ed. Karen G. Turner et al., 45–64. Seattle: University of Washington Press, 2000.

———. "Of Arsenic and Old Laws: Looking Anew at Criminal Justice in Late Imperial China." *California Law Review* 72.6 (1984), 1180–1256. Reprint in *Law, the State, and Society*, by Tahirih V. Lee, 2–72.

Allee, Mark A. "Code, Culture, and Custom: Foundations of Civil Case Verdicts in a Nineteenth-Century County Court." In *Civil Law in Qing and Republican China*, ed. Kathryn Bernhard and Philip C. C. Huang, 122–41. Stanford, Calif.: Stanford University Press, 1994.

———. *Law and Local Society in Late Imperial China: Northern Taiwan in the Nineteenth Century*. Stanford, Calif.: Stanford University Press, 1994.

Antony, Robert J. "Scourges on the People: Perceptions of Robbery, Snatching, and Theft in the Mid-Qing Period." *Late Imperial China* 16.2 (1995), 98–132.

Aristodemou, M. "Studies in Law and Literature: Directions and Concerns." *Anglo-American Law Review* 22 (1993), 157–93.

Arkush, R. David, and Dong Xiaoping 董曉萍. *Huabei minjian wenhua* 華北民間文化 (Popular culture in North China). Hebei: Hebei Jiaoyu Chubanshe, 1995.

Bartlett, Beatrice S. "An Archival Revival: The Ch'ing Central Government Archives in Beijing Today." *Ch'ing-shih wen-t'i* 4.6 (1981), 81–100.

Bauer, Wolfgang. "The Tradition of the 'Criminal Cases of Master Pao' *Pao-kung-an* (*Lung-t'u kung-an*)." *Oriens* 23–24 (1970–71), 433–49.

Bauman, Richard, and Charles L. Briggs. "Poetics and Performance as Critical Perspectives on Language and Social Life." *American Review of Anthropology*, 19 (1990), 59–88.

Bell, Christine. "Teaching Law as Kafkaesque." In *Tall Stories?*, ed. John Morison and Christine Bell, 11–38.

Bender, John. *Imagining the Penitentiary: Fiction and the Architecture of Mind in Eighteenth Century England*. Chicago: University of Chicago Press, 1987.

Bernhardt, Kathryn, and Philip C. C. Huang, eds. *Civil Law in Qing and Republican China*. Stanford, Calif.: Stanford University Press, 1994.

Binder, Guyora. "The Poetics of the Pragmatic: What *Literary Criticisms of Law* Offers Posner." *Stanford Law Review* 53 (2000–2001), 1509–39.

Binder, Guyora, and Robert Weisberg. "Cultural Criticism of Law." *Stanford Law Review* 49 (1997), 1149–1221.

———. *Literary Criticisms of Law*. Princeton, N.J.: Princeton University Press, 2000.

Bishop, John L. Review of Robert van Gulik's *Parallel Cases from Under the Peartree*. *Harvard Journal of Asiatic Studies* 20 (1957), 227–30.

Bodde, Derk, and Clarence Morris. *Law in Imperial China Exemplified by 190 Ch'ing Dynasty Cases (Translated from the* Hsing-an hui-lan 刑案匯覽*) with Historical, Social, and Juridical Commentaries*. Cambridge, Mass.: Harvard University Press, 1967.

Børdahl, Vibeke. "Narrative Voices in Yangzhou Storytelling." *CHINOPERL Papers* 18 (1995), 1–31.

Bourdieu, Pierre. *Language and Symbolic Power*. Translated by Gino Raymond and Matthew Adamson. Edited by John B. Thompson. Cambridge, Mass.: Harvard University Press, 1991.

Bourgon, Jérôme. "Rights, Freedoms, and Customs in the Making of Chinese Civil Law, 1900–1936." In *Realms of Freedom in Modern China*, ed. William C. Kirby, 84–112. Stanford, Calif.: Stanford University Press, 2004.

———. "Uncivil Dialogue: Law and Custom Did Not Merge into Civil Law under the Qing." *Late Imperial China*, 23.1 (2002), 50–90.

Brook, Timothy. "The Merchants' Network in Sixteenth-Century China: A Discussion and Translation of Chang Han's 'On Merchants.'" *Journal of the Economic and Social History of the Orient* 24.2 (1981), 165–214.

———. *Praying for Power: Buddhism and the Formation of Gentry Society in Late-Ming China*. Cambridge, Mass.: Harvard University Press, 1993.

Brooks, Peter. *Troubling Confessions: Speaking Guilt in Law and Literature*. Chicago: University of Chicago Press, 2000.

Brooks, Peter, and Paul Gewirtz, eds. *Law's Stories*. New Haven, Conn.: Yale University Press, 1996.

Buoye, Thomas. *Manslaughter, Markets, and Moral Economy: Violent Disputes over Property Rights in 18th-Century China*. New York: Cambridge University Press, 2000.

———. "Suddenly Murderous Intent Arose: Bureaucratization and Benevolence in Eighteenth-Century Homicide Reports." *Late Imperial China* 16.2 (1995), 62–97.

Campany, Robert Ford. *Strange Writing: Anomaly Accounts in Early Medieval China*. Albany: State University of New York Press, 1996.

———. *To Live as Long as Heaven and Earth: A Translation and Study of Ge Hong's Traditions of Divine Transcendents*. Berkeley: University of California Press, 2002.

Carlitz, Katherine. "Style and Suffering in Two Stories by 'Langxian.'" In *Culture and the State in Chinese History: Conventions, Accommodations, and Critiques*, ed. Theodore Huters, R. Bin Wong, and Pauline Yu, 207–35. Stanford, Calif.: Stanford University Press, 1997.

Certeau, Michel de. *The Writing of History*. Translated by Tom Conley. 1975; New York: Columbia University Press, 1988.

Chan, Leo Tak-hung. *The Discourse on Foxes and Ghosts: Ji Yun and Eighteenth-Century Literati Storytelling*. Hong Kong: Chinese University Press; Honolulu: University of Hawai'i Press, 1998.

Chang Wejen (Zhang Weiren 張偉仁). "Legal Education in Ch'ing China." In *Education and Society in Late Imperial China, 1600–1900*, ed. Benjamin A. Elman and Alexander Woodside, 292–339. Berkeley: University of California Press, 1994.

———. "Liangmu xunli Wang Huizu" 良幕循吏汪輝祖 (Conscientious secretary and honest official Wang Huizu). *Guoli Taiwan daxue faxue luncong* 國立臺灣大學法學論叢 19.1 (1990), 1–49; 19.2 (1990), 19–50.

———. *Qingdai fazhi yanjiu* 清代法制研究 (Studies of the Qing legal system). 3 vols. Taipei: Zhongyang Yanjiuyuan, 1983.

Chao Xiaohong 鈔曉紅. "Ming Qing ren de 'shemi' guannian ji yanbian—lizu yu difangzhi de kaocha" 明清人的「奢靡」觀念及其演變—立足於地方志的考察 (The concept of *shemi* [extravagance and waste] during the Ming and Qing dynasties and its evolution—An investigation based on local chronicles). *Lishi yanjiu* 歷史研究 (Beijing) 2002.4, 96–117.

Chao, Yuen Ren. "Chinese Language." In *Encyclopaedia Britannia*, vol. 5. London: Encyclopaedia Britannia, 1972.

Chen, Fu-mei, and Ramon H. Myers. "Coping with Transaction Costs: The

Case of Merchant Associations in the Ch'ing Period." In *The Second Conference on Modern Chinese Economic History*, 317–41. Taipei: The Institute of Economics, Academia Sinica, 1989.

Chen, Fu-mei Chang. "The Influence of Shen Chih-chi's *Chi-chu Commentary* upon Ch'ing Judicial Decisions." In *Essays on China's Legal Tradition*, ed. Jerome Alan Cohen, R. Randle Edwards, and Fu-mei Chang Chen. Princeton, N.J.: Princeton University Press, 1980.

Chen Kuo-tung 陳國棟. "You guan Lu Ji *Jinshe pan* zhi yanjiu suo sheji de xueli wenti—kua xuemen de yijian" 有關陸楫〈禁奢辨〉之研究所涉及的 學理問題—跨學門的意見 (A reconsideration of questions involved in Lu Ji's *Decisions on prohibited extravagance*—An interdisciplinary view). *Xin Shixue* 新史學 5.2 (1994): 159–79.

Chen Minjie 陳敏傑 and Ding Xiaochang 丁曉昌, eds. and annotators. *Anyu juan* 案獄卷 (Legal stories). In *Qingdai biji xiaoshuo leibian* 清代筆記小說類編 (Classified collection of fiction from Qing period "Random notes"), ed. Lu Lin 陸林. Hefei: Huangshan Shushe, 1994.

Chi Yün (Ji Yun). *Shadows in a Chinese Landscape*. Translated by David L. Keenan. Armonk, N.Y.: M. E. Sharpe, 1999.

Chien Shuo-ch'eng 簡朔成. "Zongjiao yu sifa—Ming-Qing 'shenpan' ziliao ju'ou" 宗教與司法—明清「神判」史料舉隅 (Religion and the law—Random examples of "Divine justice" from the Ming and Qing). Graduate seminar paper, National Central University, Taiwan, 2001.

Chiu Pengsheng 邱澎生. "Shiba shiji Dian tong shichang zhong de guanshang guanxi yu liyi guannian" 十八世紀滇銅市場中的官商關係與利益觀念 (Interests in economic organization: The shaping of the Yunnan copper market in eighteenth-century China). *Zhongyang yanjiuyuan Lishi yuyan yanjiu suo jikan* 中央研究院歷史語言研究所集刊 (The bulletin of the Institute of History and Philology, Academia Sinica) 72.1 (2001), 49–119.

———. "Yi fa wei ming—Songshi yu muyou dui Ming Qing falü zhixu de chongji" 以法為命—訟師與幕友對明清法律秩序的衝擊 (Taking law as mandate: The conflict over legal order between pettifoggers and legal assistants during the Ming and Qing). *Xin shixue* 新史學 15.4 (2004), 93–148.

———. "You shi lüli yanbian kan Ming Qing zhengfu dui shichang de falü guifan" 由市廛律例演變看明清政府對市場的法律規範 (The transformation of market regulations in the Ming and Qing codes). In *Shixue: Chuancheng yu bianqian xueshu yantaohui lunwen ji* 史學: 傳承與變遷學術研討會論文集 (Historiography: Papers presented at the conference on received and adapted scholarship), ed. National Taiwan University Department of History 國立台灣大學歷史系 291–334. Taipei: Guoli Taiwan Daxue Lishi Xi, 1998.

———. "You Suzhou jingshang chongtu shijian kan Qingdai qianqi de guanshang guanxi" 由蘇州經商衝突事件看清代前期的官商關係 (Mandarins and merchants: Contentions and judicial precedents regarding commerce in Suzhou during the early Qing period). *Wenshizhe xuebao* 文史哲學報 43 (1995), 37–92.

Ch'ü T'ung-tsu 瞿同祖. *Law and Society in Traditional China.* Paris: Mouton, 1961.

———. *Local Government in China Under the Ch'ing.* 1962. Reprint, Stanford, Calif.: Stanford University Press, 1969.

Coase, R. H. *The Firm, the Market and the Law.* Chicago: University of Chicago Press, 1988.

Cover, Robert. "Nomos and Narrative." *Harvard Law Review* 97.4 (1983), 4–68.

Davis, Natalie Z. *Fiction in the Archives: Pardon Tales and Their Tellers in Sixteenth-Century France.* Stanford, Calif.: Stanford University Press, 1987.

Dawson, Norma. "The Law of Literature: Folklore and the Law." In *Tall Stories?*, ed. John Morison and Christine Bell, 245–66.

Domnarski, William. "Shakespeare in the Law." *Connecticut Bar Journal* 67 (August 1993), 317–51.

Dong, Madeleine Yue. "Communities and Communication: A Study of the Case of Yang Naiwu." *Late Imperial China* 16.1 (1995), 79–119.

Duara, Prasenjit. *Culture, Power, and the State: Rural North China, 1900–1942.* Stanford, Calif.: Stanford University Press, 1988.

Dudbridge, Glen. *Religious Experience and Lay Society in T'ang China: A Reading of Tai Fu's Kuang-i chi.* Cambridge: Cambridge University Press, 1995.

Dunham-Stewart, Robert Lewis. "The Sung Magistrate and the Fundamental Importance of the 'Tang-ying-pi-shih' in Chinese Literary Evolution." Ph.D. diss., Georgetown University, 1990.

Dunstan, Helen. *Conflicting Counsels to Confuse the Age: A Documentary Study of Political Economy in Qing China, 1644–1840.* Ann Arbor: Center for Chinese Studies, University of Michigan, 1996.

Eberhard, Wolfram. *Guilt and Sin in Traditional China.* Berkeley: University of California Press, 1967.

Ebrey, Patricia Buckley. *Confucianism and Family Rituals in Imperial China: A Social History of Writing about Rites.* Princeton, N.J.: Princeton University Press, 1991.

ECCP. See *Eminent Chinese of the Ch'ing Period*.

Elman, Benjamin A. *A Cultural History of Civil Examinations in Late Imperial China*. Berkeley: University of California Press, 2000.

Eminent Chinese of the Ch'ing Period. Edited by Arthur W. Hummel. Washington, D.C.: U.S. Government Printing Office, 1943.

Epstein, Maram. *Competing Discourses: Orthodoxy, Authenticity and Engendered Meanings in Late Imperial Fiction*. Cambridge, Mass.: Harvard University Asia Center, 2001.

Fairbank, John K. *Ch'ing Documents, an Introductory Syllabus*. 3rd edition. Cambridge, Mass.: Harvard University East Asian Research Center, 1970.

Fan Jinmin 范金民. *Ming Qing Jiangnan shangye de fazhan* 明清江南商業的發展 (The development of commerce in Jiangnan during the Ming and Qing). Nanjing: Nanjing Daxue, 1998.

Farber, Daniel A., and Suzanna Sherry. "Telling Stories Out of School: An Essay on Legal Narratives." *Stanford Law Review* 45 (1993), 807–55.

Fish, Stanley. *Is There a Text in This Class? The Authority of Interpretive Communities*. Cambridge, Mass.: Harvard University Press, 1980.

———. "Rhetoric." In *Critical Terms for Literary Study*, ed. Frank Lentricchia and Thomas McLaughlin, 203–22. 2nd edition. Chicago: University of Chicago Press, 1995.

Fisher, William W., III. "Texts and Contexts: The Application to American Legal History of the Methodologies of Intellectual History." *Stanford Law Review* 49 (1997), 971–1019.

Fong, Gilbert. "Time in *Nine Murders*: Western Influence and Domestic Tradition." In *The Chinese Novel at the Turn of the Century*, ed. Milena Doleželová-Velingerová, 116–28. Toronto: University of Toronto Press, 1980).

Foucault, Michel. *Discipline and Punish: The Birth of the Prison*. Translated by Alan Sheridan. New York: Pantheon, 1977.

Fox, Marie. "Crime and Punishment: Representations of Female Killers in Law and Literature." In *Tall Stories?*, ed. John Morison and Christine Bell, 145–78.

Fu Chongju 傅崇矩. *Chengdu tonglan* 成都通覽 (A guide to Chengdu). Chengdu: Bashu Shushe, 1987.

Fuma Susumu 夫馬進. "Min-Shin jidai no shōshi to soshō seido" 明清時代の訟師と訴訟制度 (Pettifoggers and the system of filing complaints during the Ming and Qing periods). In *Chūgoku kinsei no hōsei to shakai* 中国近世の法制と社会 (Legal systems and society in modern China), ed. Umehara Kaoru 梅原郁, 437–83. Kyoto: Kyōto Daigaku Jinbun Kagaku Kenkyūjo, 1993).

———. "Shōshi hihon no sekai" 訟師秘本の世界 (The world of secret pettifogger manuals). In *Minmatsu Shinsho no shakai to bunka* 明末清初の社会と文化 (Society and culture in the late Ming–early Qing), ed. Ono Kazuko 小野和子, 189–238. Kyoto: Kyōto Daigaku Jinbun Kagaku Kenkyūjo, 1996.

———. "Shōshi hihon 'Shō-Sō ihitsu' no shutsugen" 訟師秘本'蕭曹遺筆'の出現 (The appearance of the secret pettifogger manual *Last writings of Su and Cao*). *Shirin* 77.2 (1994), 157–89.

Furth, Charlotte, Judith T. Zeitlin, and Ping-chen Hsiung, eds. *Thinking with Cases: Specialist Knowledge in Chinese Cultural History*. Honolulu: University of Hawai'i Press, 2007.

Gates, Hill. *China's Motor. A Thousand Years of Petty Capitalism*. Ithaca, N.Y.: Cornell University Press, 1996.

Getman, Jules G. "Colloquy: Human Voice in Legal Discourse." *Texas Law Review* 66 (1988), 577–88.

Gifis, Steven H. *Law Dictionary*. 3rd edition. New York: Barron's Educational Series, 1991.

Ginzburg, Carlo. *The Cheese and the Worms: The Cosmos of a Sixteenth-Century Miller*. Baltimore: Johns Hopkins University Press, 1976.

Gjertson, Daniel E. *Miraculous Retribution: A Study and Translation of T'ang Lin's "Ming-pao chi."* Berkeley, Calif.: Berkeley Buddhist Series, 1989.

Gong'an xiaoshuo yanjiu ziliao 公案小説研究資料 (Research materials on court case fiction). Vol. 322 of *Zhongguo gudian xiaoshuo yanjiu ziliao huibian* 中國古典小説研究資料彙編 (Collected research materials on Chinese classic fiction). Taipei: Tianyi, 1983.

Goodman, Bryna. *Native Place, City, and Nation: Regional Networks and Identities in Shanghai, 1853–1937*. Berkeley: University of California Press, 1995.

Goody, Jack. *The Domestication of the Savage Mind*. Cambridge: Cambridge University Press, 1977.

———. *The Interface between the Written and the Oral*. Cambridge: Cambridge University Press, 1987.

Goossaert, Vincent. "La gestion des temples chinois au XIXe siècle: Droit coutumier ou laissez-faire?" *Extrême-Orient, Extrême-Occident* 23 (2001), 11–24.

Gordon, Robert W. "Foreword: The Arrival of Critical Historicism." *Stanford Law Review* 49 (1997), 1023–29.

Graham, Angus Charles. *Disputers of the Tao: Philosophical Argument in Ancient China*. La Salle, Ill.: Open Court, 1989.

Han Dacheng 韓大成. "Mingdai de fu shang ju jia" 明代的富商巨賈 (The richest merchants of the Ming period). In *Mingdai shehui jingji chutan* 明代社會經濟初探 (Preliminary investigation of society and the economy of the Ming), 168–220. Beijing: Renmin, 1986.

Hanan, Patrick. *Chinese Fiction of the Nineteenth and Early Twentieth Centuries.* New York: Columbia University Press, 2004.

———. *The Chinese Vernacular Story.* Cambridge, Mass.: Harvard University Press, 1981.

———. *The Invention of Li Yu.* Cambridge, Mass.: Harvard University Press, 1988.

———. "*Judge Bao's Hundred Cases* Reconstructed." *Harvard Journal of Asiatic Studies* 40.2 (1980), 301–23.

Hansen, Valerie. *Changing Gods in Medieval China, 1127–1276.* Princeton, N.J.: Princeton University Press, 1990.

———. *Negotiating Daily Life in Traditional China: How Ordinary People Used Contracts, 600–1400.* New Haven, Conn.: Yale University Press, 1995.

Hanyu da cidian 漢語大詞典 (Great dictionary of the Chinese language). Edited by Luo Zhufeng 羅竹風 et al. 12 vols. plus index. Shanghai: Hanyu Da Cidian Chubanshe, 1990–94.

Hao Tiechuan 郝鐵川. *Zhongguo faxi yanjiu* 中國法系研究 (A history of Chinese legal systems). Shanghai: Fudan Daxue Chubanshe, 1997.

Hawes, Colin. "Reinterpreting Law in the Song: Zheng Ke's Commentary to the 'Magic Mirror for Deciding Cases.'" *Journal of Asian Legal History* 1 (2001), 23–68.

Hayden, George A. *Crime and Punishment in Medieval Chinese Drama: Three Judge Bao Plays.* Cambridge, Mass.: Harvard University Press, 1978.

Hegel, Robert E. "Images in Legal and Fictional Texts from Qing China." *Bulletin de l'École français d'Extrême-Orient* 89 (2002), 271–83.

———. "Imagined Violence: Representing Homicide in Late Imperial Crime Reports and Fiction." *Zhongguo wenzhe yanjiu jikan* 中國文哲研究季刊 (Bulletin of the Institute of Chinese Literature and Philosophy, Academia Sinica) 25 (2004), 61–89.

———. "Traditional Chinese Fiction: The State of the Field." *The Journal of Asian Studies* 53.2 (1994), 394–426.

Ho, Virgil Kit-yiu. "Butchering Fish and Executing Criminals: Public Executions and the Meanings of Violence in Late Imperial and Modern China." In *Meanings of Violence: A Cross Cultural Perspective*, ed. Göran Aijmer and Jos Abbink, 141–60. Oxford: Berg, 2000.

Hsiung Ping-chen 熊秉真. "Cong Tang Zhen kan geren jingyan dui jingshi sixiang yansheng de yingxiang" 從唐甄看個人經驗對經世思想衍生之影響 (The effect of personal experience on the development of administrative thinking from the perspective of Tang Zhen). *Zhongyang yanjiuyuan Jindai shi yanjiusuo jikan* 中央研究院近代史研究所集刊 14 (1985), 1–28.

Hsu, Daulin. "Crime and Cosmic Order." *Harvard Journal of Asiatic Studies* 30:1 (1970), 111–25.

Hu Pu'an 胡樸安. *Zhonghua quanguo fengsu zhi* 中華全國風俗誌 (A gazetteer of Chinese customs). 1923. Beijing: Zhongzhou Guji, 1990.

Huang, Martin W. *Desire and Fictional Narrative in Late Imperial China*. Cambridge, Mass.: Harvard University Asia Center, 2001.

Huang, Philip C. C. *Civil Justice in China*. Stanford, Calif.: Stanford University Press, 1996.

———. *Code, Custom, and Legal Practice in China: The Qing and Republic Compared*. Stanford, Calif.: Stanford University Press, 2001.

———. "Codified Law and Magisterial Adjudication in the Qing." In *Civil Law in Qing and Republican China*, ed. Kathryn Bernhard and Philip C. C. Huang, 142–86. Stanford, Calif.: Stanford University Press, 1994.

———. "'Public Sphere'/'Civil Society' in China? The Third Realm Between State and Society." *Modern China* 19.2 (1993), 216–40.

Hucker, Charles O. *A Dictionary of Official Titles in Imperial China*. Stanford, Calif.: Stanford University Press, 1985.

Huntington, Rania. *Alien Kind: Foxes and Late Imperial Chinese Narrative*. Cambridge, Mass.: Harvard University Asia Center, 2003.

Huters, Theodore. "The Shattered Mirror: Wu Jianren and the Reflection of Strange Events." In *Culture and the State in Chinese History: Conventions, Accommodations, and Critiques*, ed. Theodore Huters, R. Bin Wong, and Pauline Yu, 277–302. Stanford, Calif.: Stanford University Press, 1997.

Ingram, Peter. "Victorian Values: Law and Justice in the Novels of Trollop." In *Tall Stories?*, ed. John Morison and Christine Bell, 223–43.

Jiang Yonglin, trans. *The Great Ming Code / Da Ming lü*. Seattle: University of Washington Press, 2004.

Johnson, David, ed. *Ritual Opera, Operatic Ritual: "Mu-lien Rescues His Mother" in Chinese Popular Culture*. Berkeley, Calif.: Publications of the Chinese Popular Culture Project, Number 1, 1989.

Jones, William C., trans. *The Great Qing Code*. Oxford: Clarendon Press, 1994.

Kang Xiaofei. *Power on the Margins: The Cult of the Fox in Late Imperial and Modern North China*. New York: Columbia University Press, 2006.

Kao, Karl. "*Bao* and *Baoying*: Narrative Causality and External Motivations in Chinese Fiction." *Chinese Literature: Essays, Articles, Reviews* 11 (1989), 115–38.

Karasawa, Yasuhiko 唐澤靖彥. "Composing the Narrative: A Preliminary Study of Plaints in Qing Legal Cases." Paper presented at the Conference on Code and Practice in Qing and Republican Law, Los Angeles, 1993.

———. "Hanasu koto to kaku koto no wagemade—Shindai saiban bunsho ni okeru kyōjutsusho no tekusuto sei" 話ことと書くことのはげまで—清代裁判文書における供述書のてくすと性 (Composing speech and writing—The textual nature of oral testimony in Qing period judicial documents). *Chūgoku—shakai to bunka* 中國—社會と文化 10 (1995), 212–50.

———. "Orality, Textuality, and Reality: Legal Case Records in Nineteenth Century China." Ph.D. diss., University of California, Los Angeles, forthcoming.

———. "Rethinking Legal Case Records in the Context of Chinese Written Culture: The Written Records of Oral Testimony in Qing Legal Cases." In *Thinking Through Cases*, ed. Charlotte Furth and Judith Zeitlin.

———. "Shindai ni okeru sojō to sono sakuseisha" 清代における訴狀とその作成者 (Plaints and their authors during the Qing period). *Chūgoku—shakai to bunka* 中国—社会と文化 13 (1998), 306–30.

Katz, Paul R. *Demon Hordes and Burning Boats: The Cult of Marshal Wen in Late Imperial Chekiang*. Albany: State University of New York Press, 1995.

———. "Divine Justice in Late Imperial China: A Preliminary Study of Indictments, Oaths, and Ordeals." In *Religion and Chinese Society*, ed. John Lagerwey, 869–902. Hong Kong: The Chinese University Press, 2004.

———. "Fowl Play—Chicken-Beheading Rituals and Dispute Resolution in Taiwan." In *The Minor Arts of Daily Life: Popular Culture in Taiwan*, ed. David K. Jordan, Marc Moskowitz, and Andrew Morris, 35–49. Honolulu: University of Hawai'i Press, 2004.

———. "Hanren shehui de shenpan yishi chutan—Cong zhan jitou shuoqi" 漢人社會的神判儀式初探—從斬雞頭說起 (A preliminary study of judicial rituals in Han Chinese society based on chicken-beheadings). *Bulletin of the Institute of Ethnology, Academia Sinica* 88 (2000), 173–202.

———. *Images of the Immortal: The Cult of Lü Dongbin at the Palace of Eternal Joy*. Honolulu: University of Hawai'i Press, 1999.

———. "Local Elites and Sacred Sites in Hsin-Chuang—The Growth of the Ti-tsang An during the Japanese Occupation." In *Belief, Ritual, and Society: Papers from the Third International Conference on Sinology, Anthropology Section*, ed. Lin Mei-rong, 179–227. Nanking: Institute of Ethnology, Academia Sinica, 2003.

———. *Taiwan de wangye xinyang* 台灣的王爺信仰 (The cult of the Royal Lords in Taiwan); Taipei: Shang-ting Publishing Company, 1997.

———. "Xinzhuang Dizang An de dazhong ye chongbai" 新莊地藏庵的大眾爺崇拜 (The cult of the Lord of the Hordes at the Abbey of Ksitigarbha in Xinzhuang). *Journal of Humanities East/West*, 16 (1998), 123–59.

Kinkley, Jeffrey C. *Chinese Justice, the Fiction: Law and Literature in Modern China.* Stanford, Calif.: Stanford University Press, 2000.

Ko, Dorothy. *Teachers of the Inner Chambers: Women and Culture in Seventeenth-Century China.* Stanford, Calif.: Stanford University Press, 1994.

Koffler, Judith S. "Forged Alliance: Law and Literature." *Columbia Law Review* 89 (1989), 1374–93.

Kornstein, Daniel. *Kill All the Lawyers? Shakespeare's Legal Appeal.* Princeton, N.J.: Princeton University Press, 1994.

———. "Shakespeare the Unacknowledged Legislator." *New York State Bar Journal*, January 1994, 50–55.

Korobkin, Laura Hanft. *Criminal Conversations: Sentimentality and Nineteenth-Century Legal Stories of Adultery.* New York: Columbia University Press, 1998.

Kubo Noritada 窪德忠. "Taiwan chū, hokubu ni okeru jōkōshin shinkō" 臺灣中、北部における城隍神信仰 (The cult of the City God in central and northern Taiwan). In *Suzuki Shun Sensei koki kinen tōyōshi ronsō* 鈴木俊先生古稀記念東洋史 論叢 (Collection of essays on East Asian history in honor of Suzuki Shun's seventieth birthday), 165–80. Tokyo: Yamakawa shuppansha, 1975.

———. "Taiwan no jōkōshin shinkō" 臺灣の城隍神信仰 (The cult of the City God in Taiwan). In *Tōhō gakuhō sōritsu nijūgo shūnen kinen: Tōhōgaku ronshū* 東方學會創立二十五週年記念: 東方學論集 (Collection of essays on Oriental studies to commemorate the twenty-fifth anniversary of the founding of the Society for Oriental Studies), 311–26. Tokyo: Tōhō Gakuhō, 1972.

Kuhn, Philip A. *Soulstealers: The Chinese Sorcery Scare of 1768.* Cambridge, Mass.: Harvard University Press, 1990.

Kundera, Milan. *The Art of the Novel.* Translated by Linda Asher. New York: Harper and Row, 1988.

LaFleur, William R. *Liquid Life: Abortion and Buddhism in Japan.* Princeton, N.J.: Princeton University Press, 1992.

Lai Huimin 賴惠敏. "Qianlong chao Neiwufu de dangpu yu fashang shengxi" 乾隆朝內務府的當鋪與發商生息 (1736–1795)" (Imperial Household Department pawnshops and the production of commercial interest during the Qianlong period). *Zhongyang yanjiuyuan Jindai shi yanjiusuo jikan* 中央研究院近代史研究所集刊 28 (1997), 137–75.

Lan Dingyuan 藍鼎元. "Lan Lu-chow's Criminal Cases." In *Historic China and Other Sketches*, by Herbert A. Giles, 141–232. London: Thos. de la Rue, 1882.

———. "Lan Ting-yüan's Casebook." Translated by Lai Jeh-hang and Lily Hwa. In *Chinese Civilization and Society: A Sourcebook*, ed. Patricia Buckley Ebrey, 200–203. New York: Free Press, 1981.

———. *Luzhou gong'an* 鹿洲公案 (Legal cases from Luzhou). Edited by Kuang Minben 曠敏本. Ca. 1729. Reprinted as *Jindai Zhongguo shiliao congkan xubian* 近代中國史料叢刊續編, comp. Shen Yunlong 沈雲龍. Collection 41. Yonghe, Taipei: Wenhai, ca. 1976.

———. *Luzhou gong'an* 鹿洲公案 (Legal cases from Luzhou). Beijing: Qunzhong Chubanshe, 1985.

Lee, Leo O., and Andrew Nathan. "The Beginnings of Mass Culture." In *Popular Culture in Late Imperial China*, ed. David Johnson, Andrew J. Nathan, and Evelyn S. Rawski, 360–95. Berkeley: University of California Press, 1985.

Lee, Tahirih V. *Law, the State, and Society in China*. New York and London: Garland Publishing, 1997.

Lewis, Mark E. *Sanctioned Violence in Early China*. Albany: State University of New York Press, 1990.

Li Bozhong 李伯重. "Zhongguo quanguo shichang de xingcheng" 中國全國市場 的形成, 1500–1840 (The formation of national markets in China, 1500–1840). *Qinghua daxue xue bao* 清華大學學報 (哲學社會科 學版) 14.4 (1999), 48–54.

Li Huiyun 李慧筠. "Xianggang jingcha de Guandi chongbai" 香港警察的關帝崇拜 (The cult of Guangdi among the Hong Kong police). *Taiwan zongjiao yanjiu tongxun* 臺灣宗教研究通訊, 5 (2003), 223–36.

Liang Fanzhong 梁方仲. *Zhongguo lidai hukou, tiandi, tianfu tongji* 中國歷代戶口、田地、田賦統計 (Statistics on households, land, and land taxes in China through the ages). Shanghai: Shanghai Renmin, 1980.

Liang Zhiping 梁治平. *Qingdai xiguanfa: Shehui yu guojia* 清代習慣法: 社會與國家 (Qing customary law: Society and the state). Beijing: Zhongguo Zhengfa Daxue Chubanshe, 1996.

Lieberthal, Kenneth. *Governing China: From Revolution Through Reform*. New York: W.W. Norton, 1995.

Lin Liyue 林麗月. "Jianjiatang gao yu Lu Ji 'Fanjin she' sixiang zhi chuanyan" 《蒹葭堂 稿》與陸楫「反禁奢」思想之傳衍 (Manuscripts from Jianjiatang and the spread of Lu Ji's ideas about "Opposing extravagance"). *Ming ren wenji yu Mingdai yanjiu* 明人文集與明代研究 (Collected writings by Ming writers and research on the Ming period), 121–34. Taipei: Zhongguo Mingdai Yanjiu Xuehui, 2001.

———. "Lu Ji (1515–1552) chongshe sixiang zaitan—jianlun jinnian Ming Qing jingji sixiang shi yanjiu de jige wenti" 陸楫崇奢思想再探—兼 論近年明清經濟思想史研究的幾個問題 (Another look at Lu Ji's admiration for extravagance, and a reconsideration of several questions in the recent study of economic thought during the Ming and Qing). *Xin shixue* 新史學 5.1 (1994), 131–51.

Lin Yongzhong and Zhang Songshou 林用中, 章松壽. *Lao Dongyue: Miaohui diaocha baogao* 老東嶽: 廟會調查報告 (The Eastern Peak: A report on temple fairs). Hangzhou: Zhejiang Yinshuaju, 1936.

Ling Shuyuan 凌淑菀. "Taiwan Chenghuang xinyang de jianli yu fazhan (1683–1945)" 臺灣城隍信仰的建立與發展 (1683–1945) (The establishment and development of the cult of the City God in Taiwan [1683–1945]). M.A. thesis, National Chung Cheng University, 2003.

Liu Chih-wan 劉枝萬. *Taiwan minjian xinyang lunji* 台灣民間信仰論集 (Collected essays on Taiwan's popular beliefs). Taipei: Lianjing, 1983.

Liu Kuang-ching 劉廣京. "Chinese Merchant Guilds: An Historical Inquiry." *Pacific Historical Review* 57.1 (1988), 1–23.

———. "Houxu: Jinshi zhidu yu shangren" 後序: 近世制度 與商人 (Epilogue: Institutions and merchants in early modern China). In *Zhongguo Jinshi zongjiao lunli yu shangren jingshen* 中國 近世宗教倫理與商人精神 (Religious ethics in early modern China and the mercantile spirit), ed. Yu Ying-shih 余英時, 25–53. Taipei: Lianjing, 1987.

Liu, Yongping. *Origins of Chinese Law: Penal and Administrative Law in Its Early Development*. Hong Kong: Oxford University Press, 1998.

Long, Elizabeth. "Textual Interpretation as Collective Action." In *The Ethnography of Reading*, ed. Jonathan Boyarin, 180–211. Berkeley: University of California Press, 1993.

Luan Xing 欒星, ed. "*Qilu deng*" *yanjiu ziliao* 歧路燈研究資料 (Research materials for *Qilu deng*). Zhengzhou: Zhongzhou Shuhua She, 1982.

Ma Jianshi 馬建石 and Yang Yutang 楊育棠, eds. *Da Qing lüli tongkao jiaozhu* 大清律例通考校注 (Compendium of revisions to the Qing law code). Beijing: Zhongguo Zhengfa Daxue Chubanshe, 1992.

Ma Shutian 馬書田. *Zhongguo mingjie zhushen* 中國冥界諸神 (China's chthonic deities). Beijing: Tuanjie Chubanshe, 1998.

Ma, Y. W. (Yau-woon). "*Kung-an* Fiction: A Historical and Critical Introduction." *T'oung Pao* (Leiden) 65.4-5 (1979), 200–259.

———. "The Textual Tradition of Ming *Kung-an* 公案 Fiction: A Study of the *Lung-t'u kung-an* 龍圖公案." *Harvard Journal of Asiatic Studies* 35 (1975), 190–220.

———. "Themes and Characterization in the *Lung-t'u kung-an*." *T'oung Pao* 59 (1973), 179–202.

Macauley, Melissa. "Civil and Uncivil Disputes in Southeast Coastal China, 1723–

1820." In *Civil Law in Qing and Republican China*, ed. Kathryn Bernhardt and Philip C. C. Huang, 85–121. Stanford, Calif.: Stanford University Press, 1994.

———. *Social Power and Legal Culture: Litigation Masters in Late Imperial China*. Stanford, Calif.: Stanford University Press, 1998.

MacCormack, Geoffrey. "Cause, Status and Fault in the Traditional Chinese Law of Homicide." In *Critical Studies in Ancient Law, Comparative Law and Legal History*, ed. John W. Cairns, O. F. Robinson, and Alan Watson, 173–82. Portland, Ore.: Hart Publishing, 2001.

———. "The *Lü Hsing*: Problems of Legal Interpretation." *Monumenta Serica* 37 (1986–87), 35–47.

———. *The Spirit of Traditional Chinese Law*. Athens: University of Georgia Press, 1996.

———. *Traditional Chinese Penal Law*. Edinburgh, Scotland: University of Edinburgh Press, 1991.

Macgowan, D. J. "Chinese Guilds or Chambers of Commerce and Trades Unions." *Journal of the North China Branch of the Royal Asiatic Society* 21 (1886–87), 133–92.

Macgowan, John. *Chinese Folklore Tales*. London: Macmillan and Company, 1910.

Mair, Victor H. "Language and Ideology in the Written Popularizations of the Sacred Edict." In *Popular Culture in Late Imperial China*, ed. David Johnson, Andrew J. Nathan, and Evelyn Rawski, 325–59. Berkeley: University of California Press, 1985.

Mann, Susan. *Local Merchants and the Chinese Bureaucracy, 1750–1950*. Stanford, Calif.: Stanford University Press, 1987.

———. *Precious Records: Women in China's Long Eighteenth Century*. Stanford, Calif.: Stanford University Press, 1997.

Massaro, T. M. "Empathy, Legal Storytelling, and the Rule of Law: New Words, Old Wounds?" *Michigan Law Review* 87 (1988), 2099–2127.

Masuda Fukutaro 増田福太郎. *Minzoku shinkyō o chūshin toshite—Tōa hōchitsujo josetsu* 民族信仰中心として—東亞法制序說 (An introductory study of East Asian law centering on folk religion). 1942. Reprint, Taipei: Southern Materials Center, 1996.

Maza, Sarah. *Private Lives and Public Affairs: The Causes Célèbres of Prerevolutionary France*. Berkeley: University of California Press, 1993.

McDermott, Joseph P. "Family Financial Plans of the Southern Sung." *Asia Major* 4.2 (1991), 15–52.

McEvoy, Kieran. "Newspapers and Crime: Narrative and the Construction of Identity." In *Tall Stories?*, ed. John Morison and Christine Bell, 179–200.

McKnight, Brian E. *Law and Order in Sung China*. New York and Cambridge: Cambridge University Press, 1992.

———. "T'ang Law and Later Law: The Roots of Continuity." *Journal of the American Oriental Society* 115.3 (July–September 1995), 410–20.

McLaren, Anne E. *Chinese Popular Culture and Ming Chantefables*. Leiden, Netherlands: E. J. Brill, 1998.

McLeod, Katrina C. D., and Robin D. S. Yates. "Forms of Ch'in Law: An Annotated Translation of the *Feng-chen shih*." *Harvard Journal of Asiatic Studies* 41:1 (1981), 111–63.

McMahon, Keith. *Causality and Containment in Seventeenth-Century Chinese Fiction*. Leiden, Netherlands: Brill, 1988.

———. *Misers, Shrews, and Polygamists: Sexuality and Male-Female Relations in Eighteenth-Century Chinese Fiction*. Durham, N.C.: Duke University Press, 1995.

McNicholas, Mark. "Fraud and Social Order in Late Imperial China: Forgery, Impersonation, and the State, 1700–1820." Ph.D. diss., University of California, Berkeley, forthcoming.

Meijer, Marinus Johan. "The Autumn Assizes in Ch'ing Law." *T'oung Pao* 70 (1984), 1–17.

———. *Murder and Adultery in Late Imperial China: A Study of Law and Morality*. Leiden, Netherlands: Brill, 1991.

Metzger, Thomas A. "Foreword." In *Moral Behavior in Chinese Society*, ed. Richard Wilson, Sidney L. Greenblatt, and Amy Auerbacher Wilson. New York: Praeger, 1981.

Morison, John, and Christine Bell, eds. *Tall Stories? Reading Law and Literature*. Aldershot, England: Dartmouth, 1996.

Moskowitz, Marc L. *The Haunting Fetus: Abortion, Sexuality, and the Spirit World in Taiwan*. Honolulu: University of Hawai'i Press, 2001.

Murphy, Thérèse. "Bursting Binary Bubbles: Law, Literature and the Sexed Body." In *Tall Stories?*, ed. John Morison and Christine Bell, 57–82.

Myers, Ramon H. "Customary Law, Markets, and Resource Transactions in Late Imperial China." In *Explorations in the New Economic History: Essays in Honor of Douglass C. North*, ed. Roger L. Ransom, Richard Sutch, and Gary M. Walton, 273–98. New York: Academic Press, 1982.

Na, Silu 那思陸. *Qingdai zhongyang sifa shenban zhidu* 清代中央司法審判制度 (The Qing era central judicial trial system). Taipei: Wen Shi Zhe, 1992.

Ng, Vivien. "Sexual Abuse of Daughters-in-law in Qing China: Cases from *Xing'an Huilan*." *Feminist Studies* 20.2 (1994), 373–91.

Nichols, Stephen G. "Foreword." In *Fictional Truth*, by Michael Riffaterre, vi–x. Baltimore: Johns Hopkins University Press, 1990.

Nickerson, Peter. "The Great Petition for Sepulchral Plaints." In *Early Daoist Scriptures*, ed. Stephen R. Bokenkamp, 230–74. Berkeley: University of California Press, 1997.

Nienhauser, William H., et al., eds. *The Indiana Companion to Traditional Chinese Literature*. Volume 1. Bloomington: Indiana University Press, 1986.

Niida Noboru 仁井田陞. *Chūgoku hōseishi kenkyū: Hō to kanshū, hō to dōtoku* 中國法制史研究: 法と慣習,法と道德 (A study of Chinese legal history: Law and custom, law and morality). Tokyo: Tokyo Daigaku, 1964.

Ocko, Jonathan K. *Bureaucratic Reform in Provincial China: Ting Jih-ch'ang in Restoration Kiangsu, 1867–1870*. Cambridge, Mass.: Harvard Council on East Asian Studies, 1983.

———. "I'll Take It All the Way to Beijing: Capital Appeals in the Qing." *Journal of Asian Studies* 47.2 (1988), 291–315.

———. "The Missing Metaphor: Applying Western Legal Scholarship to the Study of Contract and Property in Early Modern China." In *Contract and Property in Early Modern China*, ed. Madeleine Zelin, Jonathan K. Ocko, and Robert Gardella, 178–205. Stanford, Calif.: Stanford University Press, 2004.

O'Donovan, Katherine. "Identification with Whom?" In *Tall Stories?*, ed. John Morison and Christine Bell.

Ong, Walter J. *Orality and Literacy: The Technologizing of the Word*. London and New York: Methuen, 1982.

Paderni, Paola. "An Appeal Case of Honor in Eighteenth Century China." In *Ming Qing yanjiu: Redazione a cura di Paolo Santangelo*, 81–90. Rome and Naples: Dipartimento di Studi Asiactici, Instituto Universitario Orientale, 1992.

Pan Ming-te 潘敏德. *Zhongguo jindai diandang ye yanjiu* 中國近代典當業研究, 1644–1937 (Studies of China's modern professional pawnshops, 1644–1937). Taipei: Guoli Shifan Daxue Lishi Yanjiusuo, 1985.

Park, Nancy, and Robert Antony. "Archival Research in Qing Legal History." *Late Imperial China* 14.1 (1993), 93–137.

Park, Nancy E. "Corruption in Eighteenth-Century China." *Journal of Asian Studies* 56.4 (1997), 967–1005.

Parry, Milman. *The Making of Homeric Verse: The Collected Papers of Milman Parry*. Edited by A. Parry. Oxford: Clarendon Press, 1971.

Peng Zeyi 澎澤益. *Zhongguo jindai shougongyeshi ziliao* 中國近代手工業史資料 (Materials on the history of the modern Chinese handicrafts industry). Beijing: Zhonghua Shuju, 1984.

Peterson, Robert. "The Bard and the Bench: An Opinion and Brief Writer's Guide to Shakespeare." *Santa Clara Law Review* 39 (1999), 789–807.

Plaks, Andrew. "After the Fall: *Hsing-shi yin-yüan chuan* and the Seventeenth-Century Novel." *Harvard Journal of Asiatic Studies* 45.2 (December 1985), 543–80.

———. *The Four Masterworks of the Ming Novel: Ssu ta ch'i-shu*. Princeton, N.J.: Princeton University Press, 1987.

Polachek, James M. *The Inner Opium War*. Cambridge, Mass.: Harvard Council on East Asian Studies, 1992.

Posner, Richard. *Law and Literature*. Revised edition. Cambridge, Mass.: Harvard University Press, 1998.

Propp, Vladimir. *The Morphology of the Folktale*. Translated by Laurence Scott. Austin: University of Texas Press, 1968.

Qi Yukun 齊裕焜. *Mingdai xiaoshuo shi* 明代小說史 (A history of Ming dynasty fiction). Hangzhou: Zhejiang Guji, 1997.

Reed, Bradly W. "Money and Justice: Clerks, Runners, and the Magistrate's Court in Late Imperial Sichuan." *Modern China* 21 (1995), 345–82.

———. *Talons and Teeth: County Clerks and Runners in the Qing Dynasty*. Stanford, Calif.: Stanford University Press, 2000.

Reid, John Phillip. "The Jurisprudence of Liberty: The Ancient Constitution in the Legal History of the Seventeenth and Eighteenth Centuries." In *The Roots of Liberty: Magna Carta, Ancient Constitution, and the Anglo-American Tradition of Rule of Law*, ed. Ellis Sandoz. Columbia: University of Missouri Press, 1993.

Robinet, Isabelle. *Taoism: Growth of a Religion*. Stanford, Calif.: Stanford University Press, 1997.

Robson, Peter. "Images of Law in the Fiction of John Grisham." In *Tall Stories?*, ed. John Morison and Christine Bell, 201–22.

Rouzer, Paul. *Articulated Ladies: Gender and the Male Community in Early Chinese Texts*. Cambridge, Mass.: Harvard University Asia Center, 2001.

Rowe, William T. *Saving the World: Chen Hongmou and Elite Consciousness in Eighteenth-Century China*. Stanford, Calif.: Stanford University Press, 2001.

———. "State and Market in Mid-Qing Economic Thought: The Career of Chen Hongmou, 1696–1771." *Études Chinoises* 12.1 (1993), 7–39.

Ruskola, Teemu. "Conceptualizing Corporations and Kinship: Comparative Law and Development Theory in a Chinese Perspective." *Stanford Law Review* 52 (1999–2000), 1599–1730.

———. "Legal Orientalism." *Michigan Law Review* 101 (2002–3), 179–234.

Sarat, Austin, Lawrence Douglas, and Martha Merrill Umphrey, eds. *Law on the Screen*. Stanford, Calif.: Stanford University Press, 2005.

Sawada Mizuho 澤田瑞穗. *Jigoku hen: Chūgoku no meikai setsu* 地獄變: 中國

の冥界説 (The story of purgatory: Tales of the underworld in China). Kyoto: Hozokan, 1968.

Scarry, Elaine. *The Body in Pain: The Making and Unmaking of the World.* New York: Oxford University Press, 1985.

Seidel, Anna. "Traces of Han Religion in Funerary Texts Found in Tombs." In *Dōkyō to shūkyō bunka* 道教と宗教文化 (Daoism and religious culture), ed. Akizuki Kanei 秋月觀暎, 21–57. Tokyo: Hirakawa, 1987.

Shang, Wei. "*Jin Ping Mei* and Late Ming Print Culture." In *Writing and Materiality in China: Essays in Honor of Patrick Hanan*, ed. Judith T. Zeitlin and Lydia H. Liu, 187–238. Cambridge, Mass.: Harvard University Asia Center, 2003.

Shapiro, Sidney, trans. *Outlaws of the Marsh.* 2 vols. Beijing: Foreign Languages Press, 1981.

Smith, Arthur H. *Chinese Characteristics.* New York and Chicago: Fleming H. Revell, 1894.

Smith, Richard J. *Chinese Almanacs.* Hong Kong: Oxford University Press, 1992.

Sommer, Matthew H. "The Penetrated Male in Late Imperial China: Judicial Constructions and Social Stigma." *Modern China* 23.2 (1997), 140–80.

———. *Sex, Law, and Society in Late Imperial China.* Stanford, Calif.: Stanford University Press, 2000.

Spence, Jonathan D. *The Death of Woman Wang.* New York: Viking, 1978.

———. *Treason by the Book.* New York: Viking, 2001.

Spierenberg, Petrus C. *The Spectacle of Suffering: Executions and the Evolution of Repression from a Preindustrial Metropolis to the European Experience.* Cambridge: Cambridge University Press, 1984.

Staunton, George Thomas, trans. *Ta Tsing Leu Lee, Being the Fundamental Laws, and a Section from the Supplementary Statues of the Penal Code of China Originally Printed and Published in Pekin, in Various Successive Editions, Under the Sanction, and by the Authority, of the Several Emperors of the Ta Tsing, or Present Dynasty.* London: T. Cadell and W. Davies, in the Strand, 1810; reprint, Taipei: Ch'eng Wen, 1966.

St. André, James. "History, Mystery, Myth: A Comparative Study of Narrative Strategies in the *Baijia gongan* and *The Complete Sherlock Holmes.*" Ph.D. diss., University of Chicago, 1998.

Sutton, Donald S. "Violence and Ethnicity on a Qing Colonial Frontier: Customary Statuary Law in the Eighteenth-Century Miao Pale." *Modern Asian Studies* 37.1 (2003), 41–80.

Szonyi, Michael. "The Illusion of Standardizing the Gods: The Cult of the Five

Emperors in Late Imperial China." *The Journal of Asian Studies* 56.1 (1997), 113–35.

——. *Practicing Kinship. Lineage and Descent in Late Imperial China.* Stanford, Calif.: Stanford University Press, 2002.

Teiser, Stephen F. "The Growth of Purgatory." In *Religion and Society in T'ang and Sung China*, ed. Patricia Buckley Ebrey and Peter N. Gregory, 115–45. Honolulu: University of Hawai'i Press, 1989.

——. *The Scripture on the Ten Kings and the Making of Purgatory in Medieval Chinese Buddhism.* Honolulu: Kuroda Institute, 1994.

Telford, Ted A., and Michael H. Finegan. "Qing Archival Materials from the Number One Historical Archives on Microfilm at the Genealogical Society of Utah." *Late Imperial China* 9.2 (1988), 86–114.

Ter Haar, Barend. "Local Society and the Organization of Cults in Early Modern China: A Preliminary Study." *Studies in Central and East Asian Religions* 8 (1995), 1–43.

Theiss, Janet M. *Disgraceful Matters: The Politics of Chastity in Eighteenth-Century China.* Berkeley: University of California Press, 2004.

Thomas, Brook. "Reflections on the Law and Literature Revival." *Critical Inquiry* 17 (1991), 510–39.

van der Sprenkel, Sybille. *Legal Institutions in Manchu China: A Sociological Analysis.* London: University of London Athlone Press, 1962.

van Gulik, R. H. *T'ang-yin-pi-shih,"Parallel Cases from under the Pear-tree," A 13th Century Manual of Jurisprudence and Detection, Translated from the Original Chinese with an Introduction and Notes.* Leiden, Netherlands: E. J. Brill, 1956.

Waley-Cohen, Joanna. "Politics and the Supernatural in Mid-Qing Legal Culture." *Modern China* 19.3 (1993), 330–53.

Waltner, Ann. "From Casebook to Fiction: *Kung-an* in Late Imperial China." *Journal of the American Oriental Society* 110.2 (1990), 281–89.

Wang Chunyu 王春瑜. "Fang pian qishu: *Du pian xinshu*" 防騙奇書:《杜騙新書》(A curious book about avoiding deceptions: *Dupian xinshu*). In *Jianghu qi wen du pian xinshu* 江湖七聞杜騙新書 (A new book for aid in eliminating deceptions as based on strange accounts from the great wide world), by Zhang Yingyu 張應俞, 1–4. Taiyuan: Shanxi Guji Chubanshe, 2003.

Wang Qingyuan 王清原, Mou Renlong 牟仁隆, and Han Xiduo 韓錫鐸, eds. *Xiaoshuo shufang lu* 小説書坊錄 (A catalog of fiction publishers). Beijing: Beijing Tushuguan, 2002.

Wang, Richard G. "Creating Artifacts: The Ming Erotic Novella in Cultural Practice." Ph.D. diss., University of Chicago, 1999.

Wang Tay-sheng. *Legal Reform in Taiwan under Japanese Colonial Rule, 1895-1945: The Reception of Western Law*. Seattle: University of Washington Press, 2000.

Wang Yeh-chien 王業鍵. "Qingdai jingji chulun" 清代經濟芻論 (Humble discussions of the Qing economy). *Shihuo fukan* 食貨復刊 2.11 (1973), 541-50.

Ward, Ian. "Law and Literature: A Feminist Perspective." *Feminist Legal Studies* 2 (1994), 133-58.

———. *Law and Literature: Possibilities and Perspectives*. Cambridge: Cambridge University Press, 1995.

Watt, John R. *The District Magistrate in Late Imperial China*. New York: Columbia University Press, 1972.

Weisberg, Richard. *Poethics and Other Strategies of Law and Literature*. New York: Columbia University Press, 1992.

West, Robin. "Communities, Texts and Law: Reflections on the Law and Literature Movement." *Yale Journal of Law and the Humanities* 1 (1988), 129-56.

———. *Narrative, Authority, and Law*. Ann Arbor: University of Michigan Press, 1993.

White, James Boyd. *The Legal Imagination*. Boston: Little, Brown, 1973.

Will, Pierre-Étienne. "Discussions about the Market-Place and the Market Principle in Eighteenth-Century Guangdong." In *Zhongguo haiyang fazhan shi lunwen ji* 中國海洋發展史論文集 (Essays on the history of China's maritime development), ed. Sun Yat-sen Institute of Social Sciences and Philosophy, vol. 7, 323-89. Taipei: Academia Sinica, 1999.

———. *Official Handbooks and Anthologies of Imperial China: A Descriptive and Critical Bibliography*. In preparation, manuscript dated October 2001.

Wolf, Arthur. "Gods, Ghosts, and Ancestors." In *Religion and Ritual in Chinese Society*, 131-82. Stanford, Calif.: Stanford University Press, 1974.

Wong, R. Bin. *China Transformed: Historical Change and the Limits of European Experience*. Ithaca, N.Y., and London: Cornell University Press, 1997.

Wong, R. Bin, Theodore Huters, and Pauline Yu. "Introduction: Shifting Paradigms of Political and Social Order." In *Culture and State in Chinese History: Conventions, Accommodations, and Critiques*, ed. Theodore Huters, R. Bin Wong, and Pauline Yu, 1-26. Stanford, Calif.: Stanford University Press, 1997.

Wu Chengming 吳承明. *Zhongguo zibenzhuyi yu guonei shichang* 中國資本主義與國內市場 (Capitalism and national markets in China). Beijing: Zhongguo Shehui Kexue, 1985.

Wu Huifang 吳蕙芳. *Wanbao quanshu: Ming Qing shiqi de minjian shenghuo shilu* 萬寶全書:明清時期的民間生活實錄 (The book of all treasures: A record of everyday life during Ming and Qing periods). Taipei: Guoli Zhengshi Daxue Lishixi, 2001.

Wu Jen-shu 巫仁恕. "Jieqing, xinyang, yu kangzheng—Ming-Qing chenghuang xinyang yu chengshi qunzhong de jiti kangyi xingwei" 節慶、信仰、與抗爭—明清城隍信仰與城市群眾的集體抗議行為 (Festivals, faith, and resistance—The cult of the City God and acts of collective resistance by the urban masses during the Ming and Qing). *Bulletin of the Institute of Modern History, Academia Sinica* 34 (2000), 145–210.

Wu Qiyen 吳奇衍. "Qingdai qianqi yahang zhi shishu" 清代前期牙行制試述 (A preliminary description of the brokerage system of the early Qing). *Qing shi luncong* 清史論叢 6 (1985), 26–52.

Wu, Yenna. *The Chinese Virago: A Literary Theme.* Cambridge, Mass.: Harvard University Press, 1995.

Wu Zhen 吳真. "Suichang miaosi kaoxi—Zhejiang xinan shanqu xinyang minsu diaocha zhi er" 遂昌廟祀考析—浙江西南山區信仰民俗調查之二 (An examination of temple sacrifices in Suichang: Part 2 of folklore investigations on beliefs in southwest Zhejiang's mountain regions). In *Zhongguo minjian wenhua* 中國民間文化 (Chinese folk culture), vol. 18, 8–32. Shanghai: Xuelin Chubanshe, 1995.

Xia Zhiqian 夏之乾. *Shenpan* 神判 (Divine justice). Shanghai: Sanlian Shudian, 1990.

———. *Shenyi caipan* 神意裁判 (Trial by divine will). Beijing: Tuanjie Chubanshe, 1993.

Xu Chunlei 徐春雷. "Tongxiang shenge gaishu" 桐鄉神歌概述 (A synopsis of divine songs in Tongxiang [Zhejiang]). In *Zhongguo minjian wenhua* 中國民間文化 (Chinese folk culture), vol. 14, 189–208. Shanghai: Xuelin Chubanshe, 1994.

Xu Dingxin 徐鼎新 and Wu Chengming 吳承明, eds. *Zhongguo zibenzhuyi de mengya* 中國資本主義的萌芽 (The "sprouts" of Chinese capitalism). Vol. 1 of *Zhongguo zibenzhuyi fazhan shi* 中國資本主義發展史 (A history of the development of Chinese capitalism). Beijing: Renmin, 1985.

Xu Xiaowang 徐曉望. *Fujian minjian xinyang yuanliu* 福建民間信仰源流 (The origins and development of popular beliefs in Fujian). Fuzhou: Fujian Jiaoyu Chubanshe, 1993.

Xue Yunsheng 薛允升. *Du li cunyi* 讀例存疑 (Remaining doubts after reading the substatutes). 1905. Reprinted as *"Du li cun yi" chongkanben* 讀例存疑重刊本, *A Typeset Edition of the "Tu-li ts'un-i,"* ed. Huang Tsing-chia (Huang Jingjia) 黃靜嘉, comp. Hsüeh Yun-sheng. 5 vols. Taipei: Chengwen, 1970.

Yang Lien-sheng 楊聯陞. "Chimi lun: Chuantong Zhongguo yizhong buxunchang de sixiang" 侈靡論—傳統中國一種不尋常的思想 (On extravagance: An extraordinary way of thinking in traditional China). Translated by Chen Guodong 陳國棟. In *Yang Liansheng Guoshi tanwei* 楊聯陞 國史探微 (Yang Liansheng's discussions of Chinese history), 169–88. Taipei: Lianjing, 1983.

Ye, Wa, and Joseph W. Esherick, comps. *Chinese Archives: An Introductory Guide*. Berkeley: Center for Chinese Studies, Institute of East Asian Studies, University of California, 1996.

Zeitlin, Judith T. *Historian of the Strange: Pu Songling and the Chinese Classical Tale*. Stanford, Calif.: Stanford University Press, 1993.

Zelin, Madeleine, Jonathan Ocko, and Robert Gardella, eds. *Contract and Property in Early Modern China*. Stanford, Calif.: Stanford University Press, 2004.

Zhang Guanzi 張冠梓. *Lun fa de chengzhang—Lai zi Zhongguo nanfang shandi falü minzuzhi de quanshi* 論法的成長—來自中國南方山地法律 民族誌 的詮釋 (The development of law—Interpretations of ethnographies on law from the mountains of southern China). Beijing: Shehui Kexue Wenxian Chubanshe, 2000.

Zhang Weiren 張偉仁 [Chang Wejen] et al., eds. *Zhongguo fa zhi shi shumu* 中國法制史書目 (The history of China's legal systems, a bibliography). Taipei: Zhongyang Yanjiuyuan Lishi Yuyan Yanjiusuo, 1976.

Zheng Qin. "Pursuing Perfection: Formation of the Qing Code." Trans. Guangyuan Zhou. *Modern China* 21.3 (1995), 310–44.

Zheng Tuyou 張土有 and Wang Xiansen 王賢森. *Zhongguo chenghuang xinyang* 中國城隍信仰 (The cult of the City God in China). Shanghai: Sanlian Shudian, 1994.

Zhongguo diyi lishi dang'an guan guancang dang'an gaishu 中國第一歷史檔案館 館藏檔案概述 (A general description of archival materials stored in the First Historical Archives of China). Beijing: Dang'an, 1985.

Zhou, Guangyuan. "Illusion and Reality in the Law of the Late Qing: A Sichuan Case Study." *Modern China* 19.4 (1993), 427–56.

Zhuang Jifa 莊吉發. *Gugong dang'an shuyao* 故宮檔案述要 (A general description of archival materials in the Palace Museum). Taipei: Gugong Bowuyuan, 1983.

Contributors

THOMAS M. BUOYE is associate professor of history at the University of Tulsa and research associate at the Center for Chinese Studies, University of Michigan. He is the author of *Manslaughter, Markets, and Moral Economy: Violent Disputes over Property Rights in Eighteenth-Century China* (2000) and co-editor (with Kirk Denton, Bruce Dickson, Barry Naughton, and Martin Whyte) of *China: Adapting the Past, Confronting the Future* (2003). He is currently working on two projects in legal and economic history: "Capital Punishment and Confucian Justice in Eighteenth-Century China" and "Ruler, State and Economy in Eighteenth-Century China: The Economic Role of the Qing Imperial Household Department"

KATHERINE CARLITZ is adjunct professor of early modern Chinese literature and culture at the University of Pittsburgh. She is the author of *The Rhetoric of Chin P'ing Mei* (1986), "The Daughter, the Singing-girl, and the Seduction of Suicide" (2001), "Style and Suffering in Two Stories by 'Langxian'" (1998), and other articles on Chinese fiction, drama, and gender. She is currently writing a book about the cult of women's virtue in sixteenth-century China.

CHIU PENG-SHENG is assistant research fellow at the Institute of History and Philology, Academia Sinica, Taipei. His book *The New Associations of Merchants and Artisans in Suzhou, 1700–1900 (Shiba, shijiu shiji Suzhou cheng di xinxing gongshangye tuanti)* was published by National Taiwan University in 1990. He is the author of several articles on organizational behavior, market innovation, and legal reasoning in early modern China. He is currently writing a book about the path of market evolution and the transformation of material culture in nineteenth-century China.

MARAM EPSTEIN is associate professor of Chinese literature at the University of Oregon. She is the author of *Competing Discourses: Orthodoxy, Authenticity, and Engendered Meanings in Late-Imperial Chinese Fiction* (2001), "Inscribing the Essentials: Culture and the Body in Ming-Qing Fiction," (1999) and "Reflections of Desire: The Poetics of Gender in *Dream of the Red Chamber*" (1999). She is currently writing a book on gender and the embodied representations and meanings of filial piety in eighteenth-century China.

ROBERT E. HEGEL is Liselotte Dieckmann Professor of Comparative Literature and professor of Chinese at Washington University in St. Louis, where he teaches courses on Chinese fiction and theater. He is the author of *The Novel in Seventeenth-Century China* (1981) and *Reading Illustrated Fiction in Late Imperial China* (1998), as well as numerous essays on various aspects of Ming-Qing writing. He is currently compiling a collection of translated crime reports from the Qing period, and is working on conceptions of justice in literature and legal writings in late imperial China.

PAUL R. KATZ is a research fellow at the Institute of Modern History, Academia Sinica, and a specialist in the history of Chinese religion and society. His leading publications include *When Valleys Turned Blood Red: The Ta-pa-ni Incident in Colonial Taiwan* (2005), *Images of the Immortal: The Cult of Lü Dongbin at the Palace of Eternal Joy* (1999), *The Cult of the Royal Lords in Taiwan* (in Chinese; 1997), and *Demon Hordes and Burning Boats: The Cult of Marshal Wen in Late Imperial Chekiang* (1995). He is currently writing a book on judicial rituals and dispute resolution in Chinese society.

KARASAWA YASUHIKO is assistant professor of history at Ritsumeikan University, Japan. His major publications are (in Japanese) "The Narrative in Legal Plaints in Qing China: Textual Analysis in Historical Studies" (2001), "Legal Plaints and their Writers in the Qing" (1998), and (in English) "From Oral Testimony to Written Records in Qing Legal Cases" (2007). He is currently completing his doctoral dissertation, "Orality, Textuality, and Reality: Legal case records in nineteenth-century China."

MARK MCNICHOLAS is a doctoral candidate in history at the University of California at Berkeley. He is currently completing his dissertation on forgery and impersonation in the Qing period.

JONATHAN OCKO is professor and department head in the Department of History, North Carolina State University, and Adjunct Professor of Legal History at Duke University Law School. He is co-editor (with Madeline Zelin and Robert Gardella) of *Contract and Property in Early Modern China* (2004), which contains his essay "The Missing Metaphor: Applying Western Legal Scholarship to the Study of Contract and Property in Early Modern China." His numerous publications on Chinese law include "Using the Past to Make a Case for Law" (2000), and "I'll Take It All the Way to Beijing: Capital Appeals in the Qing" (1988).

JAMES ST. ANDRÉ is lecturer at the Centre for Translation and Intercultural Studies and the Centre for Chinese Studies, University of Manchester, UK. He is the author of "'But Do They Have a Notion of Justice?' Staunton's 1810 translation of the Penal Code" (2004) and "Picturing Judge Bao in Ming Fiction" (2002), as well as articles on translation theory and practice. He is currently working on a book-length project on translation, spurious translations, and writings in Chinese-English Pidgin in nineteenth-century Britain.

JANET THEISS is associate professor of Chinese history at the University of Utah. She is the author of *Disgraceful Matters: The Politics of Chastity in Eighteenth-Century China* (2004), "Female Suicide, Subjectivity, and The State in Eighteenth-Century China" (2004), and "Managing Martyrdom: Female Suicide and Statecraft in Mid-Qing China" (2001). She is currently working on a book about an eighteenth-century sex and corruption scandal.

DANIEL YOUD is Luce Jr. Professor of Chinese at Beloit College, where he teaches Chinese language, literature, and culture. His main interests are in Ming and Qing dynasty fiction and comparative literature. His current research involves the placement of eighteenth-century European translations of Chinese literature in the broader context of early modern global exchange.

Index

A Ying, 256–57n35
abortion, 175
accidental injury, 114, 115, 117, 118
Accounts of Proof of Divine Retribution, 171
accusation, 64–65, 69–70
administration of laws, 15
Administrative Disciplinary Regulations, 268, 272
adultery. *See* illicit sex
alcohol use, 32–34, 40, 50
Alford, William P., 179, 237, 240
almanacs, 145, 147, 149–51
amnesty, imperial, 31, 35, 36, 38, 86, 201, 202, 213n47
appeals of capital sentences, 237, 244, 252, 273–75
archives: local, 4, 8, 64–65, 69–71; Qing imperial (Beijing), 3, 8, 9, 20n1; Qing imperial (Taipei), 4, 8
argumentation, rhetoric of, 66–72, 76–78, 81–100, 109–23
assault on parent, 109, 110, 111, 112–13, 114–15, 116–19
audience response. *See* conventions

authority, official, 144, 146–47, 151, 156
Autumn Assizes (*Qiushen*), 17, 49, 115, 117, 119; as closed community of interpretation, 278; functions of, 110–11, 275–76

Ba County Archives (*Baxian dang'an*), 65, 70
Bai Bingbing (Pai Ping-ping), 170
Bai Xiaoyan (Pai Hsiao-yen), 170
banks (*piaohao*), 125
Bao, Judge (Bao Longtu), 19, 69, 72, 76, 79, 80n33, 264, 265, 278. *See also Bao Longtu pan baijia gong'an*
bao (requital), 265; in contrast with *renqing*, 226, 229, 230; in *Wanli yehuo bian*, 218–19; in *Xing shi yinyuan zhuan*, 217–18
Bao Gong. *See Bao Longtu pan baijia gong'an*
Bao Longtu: idealized, 199, 201–2, 208–9, 217, 219, 236, 254; criminal motivation, 194–95; criminals, 196–97, 204; moral or religious themes, 197, 208–

332

9, 265; punishment, 201–2; sexual
  themes, 193–94, 195–96; structure
  and organization, 192–93; torture,
  199, 208; unjust sentences, 199–200;
  victims, 202; violence, 196
Bao Longtu pan baijia gong'an (Judge
  Bao's Hundred Cases), 189–214
  passim, 232n24
Bao Zheng, 189, 217. See also *Bao Longtu
  pan baijia gong'an*
baoying (retribution), 208
beating, as punishment, 12, 34, 36, 49,
  57, 62n15
biji xiaoshuo (informal writings), 9, 83,
  93–95, 216
"blocking the palanquin to express a
  grievance" (*lanjiao shenyuan*), 163, 164,
  167, 182n21
blood covenants (*xuemeng*), 183n42
Board of Civil Office (Libu), 14, 126
Board of Personnel, 14, 126
Board of Punishments (Xingbu), 8, 16,
  49, 51, 57, 88, 241, 268, 273–76
Bourgon, Jérôme, 179, 181n7
brokers and brokerage (*jingji* or *jihang*),
  125, 130–31; entitlement system, 128;
  insolvency, 128; receipts, certified, 129
Brook, Timothy, 75
Buddhist precepts, 64, 69–70, 208–9
Buoye, Thomas, 253
The Bureaucrats: A Revelation, 274
business firms: cotton, 125; silk, 125
"bypassing the magistrate" (*yuesong*),
  270

calendars. See almanacs
capital sentences, 262; appeals of, 237,
  244, 252, 273–74; revisable after
  assizes, 275
case memorials. See crime reports
cash, private casting of, 145, 147
celestial codes (*tianlü*), 178
Censorate (*duchayuan*), 16
censors (*du yushi*), 16

Certeau, Michel de, 98
Chao, Yuen Ren, 69
characterization, of persons in legal
  writing, 5, 7–8, 18, 27–42, 44–62, 64–
  78, 83. See also filiality
The Chart of Good and Evil, 173
chastity cult, 45–46
Chen Huaixuan, 220, 233n25
Chen Huizu, 89
Cheng Deliang, 176
chicken beheadings (*zhan jitou*), 161, 164,
  168, 169, 170, 173
Chien Shuo-ch'eng, 183n35
Chufen zeli (Administrative Disciplinary
  Regulations), 268, 272
city god (Chenghuang), 161, 161–69 passim, 171–78 passim, 185n69
civil law, 12, 17
civil service examinations, 13–14, 66–67,
  100, 106n46
civil suits, 12, 17, 45, 73, 130
"clear-sky" (*qing tian*) officials, 217, 264,
  265
Clear Words to Instruct the World, 172
clerks, 203, 204, 207
clichés, 65, 66, 70, 71, 76–77, 79n11, 90,
  92, 96; "became anxious," 112, 116, 117,
  118
*Collected Discourses while Rambling in the
  Garden*, 174, 185n69
Collection of Concealed Trivia, 185n69
Collection of Doubtful Cases, 192, 210n2
*Collection of Enlightened Judgments by
  Famous Officials*. See *Minggong shupan
  qingming ji*
*Combined Edition of the Tang and Ming
  Codes*, 145
commercial law, 125–38
commodities brokers, 125–36
commoners, depicted in history and
  fiction, 200, 202–3, 206
*Complete Book Concerning Happiness and
  Benevolence*, 109
Complete Records of Yanshan, 176

Index 333

confessions. *See* testimony, recorded
Confucian influence on law, 118, 119, 120, 123
Confucianism as social order and morality, 70, 73–74
Confucius, 48, 100, 103n14
conventions: of reading, 6, 19, 66, 75, 81–84, 92–93, 96–97; of writing, 5–7, 9, 12, 17–18, 27–42, 44–62, 64–78, 110–23, 128–38. *See also* narrative: elements; rhetorical questions
coroners, 240
corruption, 203–4
cosmic justice. *See* divine justice
counterfeiting (*wei*), 146, 152; of almanacs and calendars, 145, 149–50; of copper cash, 145, 147; of official seals, 144, 145, 148–50, 153; of precious metals, 147. *See also* forgery
Country Codger's Words of Exposure, 28
court-case genre (*gong'an xiaoshuo*), 12, 68, 72–78, 79, 80n25, 220–25, 232n24, 263–65; and popularization of legal knowledge, 220, 234, 253–54, 263–64
Cover, Robert, 278–79
crime reports (*xingke tiben*), 17, 44, 49, 51–61, 81–88, 215, 216; agency in, 28, 33–36, 37–38, 39–40; characterization in, 28–29, 30–33, 35–41; compositional features of, 27–28, 29–30, 33–34; confessions in, 144, 152, 154; depositions in, 29–30, 31, 32–33, 35–36, 39–40; emotions in, 29–33, 35–37, 38, 40, 41, 44–45, 48–62; emplotment, 27, 29–31, 32, 33, 35, 40–41, 144, 151–52, 154–56, 157, 271, 272, 276; rhetoric of indignation in, 153, 270; set phrase "normally harmonious," 29, 31–33; set phrase "unexpectedly," 31, 36, 42; substatutes resulting from, 153, 272–73; summaries, 27, 29–30, 31–34, 37, 38, 40, 41–42; unpacking by appellate officials, 273–74; use of direct speech, 32, 37

crime tales. *See* court-case genre
criminal motivation: "local glory," 150; poverty, 144, 152, 154
criminality: contrasting views on, 202–6; theories of origin, 204–6
critical approaches to law and writing, 4–8, 9–10, 19–20
Critical Legal Studies, 6
cultural imaginary, 227
cursing, 29–32, 118, 121
customary law (*xiguan fa*), 179

dark indictment (*yinzhuang*), 171
Davis, Natalie Z., 35, 67
defense of parents, 110–11, 112–13, 114–15, 116–17
Dickens, Charles, 211n20
diction and narrative effects, 235, 243, 249
diminution or aggravation of punishment (*churu*), 272
disguise, ritual, 165, 174
disguising cause of death, 30, 53
divine justice, 10, 94–95, 137–38, 161–85 passim, 234–35, 246–47, 252, 264–65
divorce, 193
Dizang, Bodhisattva (Dizangwang pusa), 161, 162, 175; as Ksitigarbha, 168–69
Dizang Abbey (Dizang An), 162, 170, 175, 177, 179
documents of grievance (*yuanwen*), 169
domestic violence. *See* homicide: of wife; wife beating;
Dou E yuan (Injustice to Dou E), 265
Dragon Lake Temple (Longhu gong), 175
Dudbridge, Glen, 184n67
due care principle, 134
Duke Yan (Yangong), 173
Dukes of Response (Youying gong), 170
Duli cunyi (Remaining Doubts after Reading the Substatutes), 273

Dupian xinshu (*A New Book for Aiding in the Eliminating of Deceptions as Based on What Has Been Experienced and Witnessed in the Great Wide World*), 228, 229, 254; personal responsibility in, 221, 222, 227; preface, 220; relation to *gong'an* model, 220–25

dyeing shops, 133–35

Earth God (Tudi gong), 167, 169, 171, 182n29

economic crimes, 143–44, 147–49, 153–54, 156. *See also* petty crimes

eight-legged essay (*bagu wen*), 66–67

elite men, 7, 13, 32–33, 36, 42–43n10, 66, 75, 89–100

Emperor of the Eastern Peak (Dongyue dadi), 161, 165, 168, 173, 174, 177, 179

emperors, 109–10; as interpretive community of one, 278. *See also* imperial moral leadership

encyclopedias for daily use (*riyong leishu*), 131

Enlightened Judgments. See *Minggong shupan qingming ji*

Epstein, Maram, 46

Ernü yingxiong zhuan (Tale of Heroic Lovers), 28

Ershi nian mudu zhiguai xianzhuang (Strange Events Eyewitnessed over Twenty Years), 248, 256n32

Ershisi xiao (Twenty-four Exemplars of Filial Piety), 32

Erxin (Hearsay), 168

ethical standards, 11, 13–14, 28, 45, 47, 61–62, 82, 87–88, 96–97, 109, 123. *See also* filiality

exaggeration of facts in a case, 64–66, 70

execution, 11, 28, 34, 35, 37–38, 49, 55, 86, 275–76. *See also* strangulation

exile, as punishment, 12, 34, 36

exposé literature, 277

fabrication, 64–66, 83–84

fairness in administration, 15. *See also* ethical standards

fatal spots, 50, 51, 52, 56, 57

fate, 35, 55, 128; and socio-economic status, 137–38

fathers, 28, 33–35, 36–37, 40–41

fathers-in-law, 49, 54

fault, 27, 46–48, 111, 113, 116, 119–20

female chastity, 28

Feng Menglong, 95, 99, 172, 231–32n13

fengshui, 239, 246

Fengzhen shi (Styles of Interrogation), 114

fetus ghosts, 175

fiction, 9, 11, 18–19, 21n14, 44, 46, 72–78, 82–84, 93–95, 100, 106n45; elements of, 65–66, 69; and law, 28–29, 30, 41; stereotypes, 70–73

filiality (or lack of), 16, 27–32, 41–42, 44, 45, 48, 49, 54–61, 73–74, 90, 112, 262; in daughters, 29, 38–41; in rhetoric, 29–30, 31–32, 34; in sons, 28, 30–38, 267

fines, as punishment, 36

Fish, Stanley, 261

Five Emperors (Wudi), 166

Flowers in the Mirror, 28

forensic medicine, 114, 117, 119

forgery: of identification certificates, 150, 156; of imperial decree, 153; of letters, 153; of Peking gazette announcement, 153; of rice tickets, 148; as symbolic usurpation of state authority, 156; of tax remittance receipts, 144; of travel permits, 144

formulaic composition of crime reports. *See* conventions: of writing

frugality, 137–38

Fuhui quan shu (A Complete Book Concerning Happiness and Benevolence), 109

Fulehun, 89–90, 96

Fuma Susumu, 66

Index 335

Gang Yi, 274
Gao Jin, 135
Gates, Hill, 184n50
ghosts, as agents of justice, 265
Ginzburg, Carlo, 75
gong'an xiaoshuo (crime tales). *See* court-case genre
Great King of Vast Blessings (Guangfu dawang), 169
greed, 194, 195, 197, 206, 207
Guan Gong, 177
Guanchang xianxing ji (The Bureaucrats: A Revelation), 274
Guandi, 176, 177
Gui Wangrong, 190, 210n2
guidebooks for judicial administrators, 8, 9, 11, 14–15, 19, 23n40, 23n42, 47–48, 66, 82, 84, 101n5, 109–10
guilds (*huiguan*), 125
Gujin xiaoshuo (Stories Old and New), 95

Hanan, Patrick, 193, 256n21, 257n38, 279n6, 279–80n11
Hansen, Valerie, 178
Hanxuan lou, 238
He Meng, 192, 210n3
He Ning, 192, 210n3
Hearsay (Erxin), 168
heaven and earth interconnected, 236, 264–65
Ho, Virgil Kit-yiu, 182n15
homicide, 28–42, 44–62, 82, 84–87, 102n7, 102n10, 113–23; child, 39; father, 28; husband, 39–41; Qing Code, 49–50, 61; revenge killings, 36–38, 41; uncle, 34–35; of wife, 29–33, 50–61
Hong Mai, 167
Honglou meng (Story of the Stone), "Mandarin's Life Preserver" in, 264
Hsu Dau-lin, 255n5
Hu-Xiang yan lue (Summaries of Judgments from Hubei and Hunan), 180
Huang, Philip C. C., 179

Huang Liuhong, 8, 101n5, 102n7, 109, 176, 184n57, 273
Huanxi yuanjia (Lovers Who Cause Both Joy and Pain), 72–73
Huizhou merchants' judicial records, 279n9
Huizui bian (Collection of Concealed Trivia), 185n69
Hunan substatutes, 134
husbands: authority over wives, 46–48; use of violence by, 46–61; as wife killers, 44–61
Huters, Theodore, 248

ideology, 109, 112, 119; and law, 110, 115, 117, 120, 122, 123
illicit sex, 11, 36–37, 39–40, 64–78, 85–89, 193–97, 200, 211n15; linked to greed, 195
illiterates, 77–78, 78n7
imminent danger (*zai weiji*), 113, 114, 115, 118, 119
imperial moral leadership, 45, 96–97, 126
impersonation, 143–44, 145, 149, 150, 156
independent judiciary, lack of, 236
indictments, ritual (*fanggao* or *gao yinzhuang*): against other members of the living, 165–73; against spiritual forces, 175–76; by spiritual forces, 173–75
infant spirits (*yingling*), 175
Injustice to Dou E, 265
insolvency, 126–31, 133, 138; broker, 128; intentional, 130; legislation, 136; "not allowed by Heaven and Earth," 128
intent to kill, 115, 118
interpretive community, 216; autumn assizes as, 276; defined, 261–63; emperor as community of one, 278; external and internal, 276; framing of a case, 268, 270, 274; Guangdong as, 254; and intertextual interaction, 261, 267, 274; magistrates as best example

336 *Index*

of, 273; reviews and appeals, 274; role of novels and newpapers, 274, 277
interpretive space, 157
interrogation, 15, 85–87, 88–93, 98–99, 114, 215. *See also* testimony

Ji Yun, 94–95, 98–99
Jianghu lilan dupian xinshu. See *Dupian xinshu*
Jiangsu substatutes, 133–35
Jiangxi substatutes, 133–36, 137
Jin Ping Mei (The Plum in the Golden Vase), 215
Jing fu xin shu, 235; accurate legal procedure in, 240–43; authorship and publication, 238; *bao*, or requital, 242; diction, 243; justice hero in, 239–40, 243; layout and illustration reinforcing judgment, 243; legal language in, 241; plaint in, 241–42
Jinghua yuan (Flowers in the Mirror), 28
Jiu ming qi yuan (The Strange Case of Nine Murders), 234, 235, 247–52, 265; based on *New Warning*, 249; constructs rational reader, 251; deus ex machina in, 264; diction in, 249; indictment of superstition, 248, 252; indictment of Yongzheng emperor and Manchu rule, 249, 251; modernizing agenda of, 248; psychological motivation and realism, 251; representation of subjectivity, 250–51; as textbook on appellate process, 274; use of modern typography, 249; vision of human potential, 252
Journey to the West, 265
Judge Bao's Hundred Cases. See *Bao Longtu pan baijia gong'an*
judges (*panguan*), 165
judicial continuum, 164, 166, 167, 179, 180
judicial interpretations, 12, 28–30, 31, 33–42, 47, 50–53, 61–62, 117–23
judicial review, 12, 16–17, 23n36, 34, 35, 49, 57, 83, 86, 109–10, 112, 115, 117–19;

and Surveillance Commissioners, 92; and Three Judicial Offices, 31
judicial rituals (*shenpan yishi*), 61, 162, 169, 176, 178, 179; and blood covenants, 183n2; and oaths, 161; and trials of the insane, 174. *See also* chicken beheadings; indictments
justice anti-hero, 219
justice hero, 217, 219; defined, 237

Kang, Xiaofei, 175
Kangxi emperor, 96
Kao, Karl, 217, 256n21
Karasawa, Yasuhiko, 33
karma and karmic retribution. See *bao*
killing: in an affray, 117; in defense of one's parents, 109, 112
Kinkley, Jeffrey C., 181n5
kinship, 113, 120
Kong Yuxun, 240
Ksitigarbha, Bodhisattva. *See* Dizang, Bodhisattva
Kuhn, Philip A., 168

Lai Ming-hsien, 170, 182n34
Lan Dingyuan, 8, 91–93, 176
A Lantern for the Crossroads, 28
Lao Can youji (The Travels of Lao Can), 274
law (*fa*), 205; as divine justice, 10, 94–95, 235–36, 246–47, 252, 255n5, 264–65; as historically secular, 235–36; and literature, 4–7, 189, 209; as modern and rational, 251; as paradigm for fiction, 235, 254; popular knowledge of, 10–15, 116–17, 220, 234, 253–54, 263–68, 277
legal codes, 8, 11, 14, 15, 28, 48–49, 60, 62–63n15, 86, 89, 97, 109–23, 130–31, 134. *See also* Qing code
legal judgments (*pandu*), 179
legal knowledge, popular, 10–15, 116–17; and court-case fiction, 220, 234, 253–54, 263–64, 277; and novels, 11–12, 263–68

Index   337

legal reasoning, 109, 114
legal secretaries (*muyou*), 9, 14–15, 18, 83, 91, 99, 116, 166
legal specialists, 65–66, 78n8
legal terminology, 18, 65–67, 78n6, 84, 100, 102n6
legal writing, 4–8, 65–78
legislation: central government, 134–36; commercial, 136–37
legislators, 136–37
leniency, 12, 113–15, 118–19; Autumn Assizes, 276; formal request for, 109–11, 114, 115, 117, 119; informal appeal for, 109; magistrates' preference for, 272; path to failure in *Sanguo zhi yanyi*, 265; Qianlong emperor and, 265, 275
li (principle), 205, 226–27, 230, 276; defined, 225
Li Baojia, 248
Li Boyuan, 274
Li Le, 128
Li Lüyuan, 216, 227, 228, 229
Li Yu, 216
Liability, 130–33
Liang Qichao, 248
Liang Tianlai gao yu zhuang (Liang Tianlai Brings His Complaint to the Emperor), 235, 244; legal language in, 245–46; plaints in verse, 245; plot contrasts with *New Warning*, 246–47
Liang Zhiping, 179
Liaozhai zhi yi (Liaozhai's Record of the Strange), 93
Liaozhai's Record of the Strange, 93
licentiates, 66
Ling Mengchu, 216
Ling Tao, 129–30
"list of grievances" (*yuandan*), 167
literacy, 13, 32–33, 42n10, 69, 78n8
literary devices, 67–69
litigants: fictional, 196–98; urban and rural, 197–98
litigation masters (*songshi*), 9, 14, 66–67, 200, 262, 263, 277, 279n4; treatises for, 3, 6, 10, 78n8, 80n19, 80n20
litigation mongers (*songgun*), 66, 78n8, 270, 279n8
Liu, James T. C., 190, 210n1
Liu Heng, 273
Lord of the Hordes (Dazhong ye), 162, 169, 170, 175
Lord of the Red Banner (Hongqi gong), 183n34
Lovers Who Cause Both Joy and Pain, 72–73
Lüyuan conghua (Collected Discourses while Rambling in the Garden), 174, 185n69

Ma, Y. W., 253
Ma Shutian, 169
Macauley, Melissa, 278n8
Macgowan, John, 168, 184n66
Magic Mirror for Solving Cases, 210n2
magistrates (*zhixian*), 11–12, 14–15, 18, 33, 45, 50–62, 64–71, 79n10, 85–88, 99, 111–23; casebooks, 273, 275, 278; editing of case record, 272; outsiders to their districts, 204; and reading of petitions, 271
"maledictions" (*zu*), 170, 183n41
Mandarin language (*guanhua*), 18
marital conflict, 44–62; in fiction, 46; official views of, 49–53
marriage, harmonious, 29–31, 50, 53, 54–57. See domestic violence
Marriage Bonds to Awaken the World. See *Xingshi yinyuan zhuan*
Marshal Wen (Wen Yuanshuai), 165, 166, 180, 181n11
masculinity: ideals of, 45–48; official assumptions about, 49, 61–62; violence and, 44–62
McKnight, Brian, 151, 190, 210n1
McMahon, Keith, 30, 46
Mencius, 47, 207
merchant or craftsmen associations (*huiguan*), 125

merchants, 125, 129–38; far from home (*jilü yuan shang*), 126, 127–28, 136; manuals for, 127
Ming Code, 145
Minggong shupan qingming ji (Collection of Enlightened Judgments by Famous Officials), 189–214 passim; classification of cases, 192; criminality caused by social conflicts, 204; depiction of magistrates in, 198–99; duration of cases, 195; false accusations in, 200; landed property in, 194–95; "legal" text, 193; leniency in, 201; official collusion in, 208; officials reluctant to judge cases, 201; relatives and neighbors in, 196; sexual themes in, 194; structure and organization of, 188–93; supports scholar-official views, 202–4; torture in, 198–99; violent crimes in, 196
"Minzhai jushi" (Resident Scholar of Sagacity Studio), preface to *A New Warning about Wealth*, 238
mixin (superstition), 248, 252
money exchanger (*qianzhuang*), 125
monks, Buddhist, 64–78; lack of filiality among, 73–74; lascivious or licentious, 64–65, 71, 76–77, 80n22; sinful, 64–65, 69, 71
Monks and Nuns in a Sea of Sin, 45
Moskowitz, Marc L., 175
mothers, 31–36, 38, 51–52
Mulian operas, 162
muyou. See legal secretaries

"naming the crime" (*zuiming*), 27
nanyin, 235, 244
narrative: elements, 64, 67–73, 75–78; fashioning, 66–67; skills, 66–67; strategies, 66, 73, 75
negligence, 126, 130–38
nephew killing an uncle in an affray (*zhi ou qiqin boshu shasi zhe*), 119
A New Book for Aiding in the Eliminating of Deceptions as Based on What Has Been Experienced and Witnessed in the Great Wide World. See *Dupian xinshu*
New Fiction, 248, 249
A New Warning about Wealth. See *Jing fu xin shu*
Nian Fu, 251
Nian Gengyao, 251
Nine Ministers (Jiuqing), 35, 49
notaries, 65, 68, 79n10
Notes from the Studio for Careful Scrutiny, 94–95

oaths (*lishi*), 161, 176
Ocko, Jonathan, 237
official malfeasance, 89–93
One Hundred Court Cases Adjudicated by Bao Longtu, Completely Supplemented. See *Bao Longtu pan baijia gong'an*
Outlaws of the Marsh. See *Shuihu zhuan*

Parallel Cases from under the Pear-tree, 190, 210n2
pardons, 109–11, 115. See also amnesty, imperial
parent-ordered (*zhuling*) attack, 111, 114, 115, 118
pawnbrokers, 132–38
pawnshops (*dangpu* or *diandang*), 125, 132–34, 135, 137
Peking gazette, 153
penal codes. See legal codes
petitions of penance (*shuzui zhuang*), 174
pettifoggers, 65. See also litigation mongers
petty crimes, 145, 151, 156; substatutes on, 148–50. See also economic crimes
plaints or petitions, legal, 13–14, 64–76, 78n7, 268–70; in fiction, 241–42, 245, 251, 266–67; form (*zhuangzhi*), 65–66, 79n10; model, 68, 69–70, 71, 79n10; in religious indictment rituals, 163–64, 170; representation of reality in, 68, 71, 76; writers and, 65–66, 71

Index   339

Plaks, Andrew, 217, 218
plausibility, 64, 67, 68, 75
plot, 65, 70–71, 72–73
popular fiction (*tongsu xiaoshuo*), 9, 11, 83, 95. See also Bao, Judge; fiction; *Shuihu zhuan*
Posner, Richard, 5, 20nn3–4, 20nn6–7
poverty, 137–38; in confessions, 144, 152; as criminal motivation, 144, 152, 154; as rhetorical device, 154–56, 157
prefects (*zhifu*), 16
private (legal) secretaries (*muyou*), 9, 14–15, 18, 83, 91, 99, 116
procedures, legal and judicial, 12, 15–17
property, 193–97, 203, 205, 206, 211n17
Propp, Vladimir, 29
provincial substatutes, 132–36
Pu Songling, 93
punishments, 11, 14, 15, 16, 28, 30–32, 34–41, 48–49, 70–71, 73, 86, 87, 89, 109, 121–23, 130–36; "execution warranted" (*qingshi*), 110; "immediate execution" (*lijue*), 110; "imminent" decapitation (*zhan lijue*), 119; "imprisonment awaiting strangulation" (*jiao jianhou qiu hou chujue*), 117, 119; "indefinite stay" (*huanjue*), 110; "left at home to care for aged parents" (*liuyang*), 110; "worthy of compassion" (*kejin*), 110

qadi justice, 109
Qian Chun, 180
Qianlong emperor, 45, 95–97, 126, 128–29 136, 138, 141n47, 226; mocks leniency at Autumn Assizes, 265, 275
Qilu deng (A Lantern at the Crossroads), 28
qing, 227; as "actual state of affairs," 219, 225, 276; range of meaning, 225–26
Qing Code, 8, 11, 13, 15, 27–28, 30, 31, 37, 86, 89, 98, 109, 111, 115, 118, 120, 126, 226, 261, 272, 281n40; circumvention of, 152–54; commentary on, 145–48; Confucian bias of, 28, 41, 42; on consumption of property received in deposit, 131–34; on domestic violence, 48–50, 61; on illegally earning interest, 130; on obtaining property by deceit and cheating, 130; political orientation of, 150–51; on spousal homicide, 49–50, 60, 61, 62n15; *zhawei* statutes in, 145–46
Qingming ji. See *Minggong shupan qingming ji*
Qiushen bijiao tiaokuan (Rules of Comparison), 275
Quan bu Bao Longtu pan baijia gong'an. See *Bao Longtu pan baijia gong'an*

"Receiving Good News in Prison" (Tong guita jianxin deng huo, nao lingyu jiebao qi ling), 226–27
Record of the Listener and Recorder, 167, 171
Record of Trivial Things Heard, 176, 177
reduction of sentence, 49, 86
religious beliefs and practices, 9–10, 13, 103n14. See also divine justice; fate
Remaining Doubts after Reading the Substatutes, 273
renqing (feelings), 205, 226, 229, 230
renqing fiction, 225, 226, 254
representation of crime, 109, 113, 117. See also conventions: of writing
rhetoric of persuasion, 65–72, 76–78, 81–100, 132–36; textual framework, 66, 68, 75–76; textual manipulation, 65; as theater, 97–100
rhetorical maneuvers in crime reports, 44–61, 65–67
rhetorical questions, 81–100 passim, 216
righteous anger (*yiji*), 49
Rowe, William, 226
Royal Lords' Offering (*Wang jiao*), 167
Rules of Comparison, 275
Rulin waishi (The Scholars), 28

Sanguo zhi yanyi (The Three Kingdoms), 264, 265
The Scholars, 28
Seidel, Anna, 173
Sengni niehai (Monks and Nuns in a Sea of Sin), 75
senior relatives, 119, 122
sentencing, 113, 115, 117–20; and "naming the crime," 27; provisional sentencing, 110, 111; reduction of, 29, 31, 34–35. *See also* fault
Sequel to "What the Master Did Not Speak About," 178, 180
Shakespeare, 277
Shan E Tu (The Chart of Good and Evil), 173
Shen Defu, 218
Shen Zhiqi, 131, 146–48
Shenbao, 274
shengyuan (licentiates), 35
shifting the blame for crime, 12, 34, 44, 50, 87–88
"Shiwu guan xiyan cheng qiaohuo" (Fifteen Strings of Cash), 217, 231–32n13
shrewish wives, 29–31, 44–62, 267
shrewishness: definition of, 44–45; in fiction, 46; judicial constructions of, 52–60
Shuang jietang yongxun (Simple Precepts from the Hall Enshrining a Pair of Chaste Widows), 47
Shuihu zhuan (Water Margin, or Outlaws of the Marsh), 11–12, 19, 265; Li Kui as agent of justice in, 264
signposts, documentary and rhetorical, 155–56
Simple Precepts from the Hall Enshrining a Pair of Chaste Widows, 47
social and economic inequality, 137–38
Song Penal Code. See *Song xing tong*
Song xing tong, 190, 191, 192, 196
soul-stealing (*jiaohun*), 168
spectacle, judicial procedures as, 15, 87

Spence, Jonathan, 184n57
spontaneous response (*yishiqing jie*), 111, 113, 114, 115, 118
spousal homicide. See homicide: of wife
standardization of form in crime reports, 32, 33, 35, 65–66
standardization in legal writing. See conventions: of writing; language style in legal documents
Stories Old and New, 95
Story of the Stone, 264
storytelling, 65, 67–68, 69, 71, 79n11, 98
stove god, 173
The Strange Case of Nine Murders. See *Jiu ming qi yuan*
strangulation, as punishment, 30, 31, 34–37, 49, 55, 86, 89, 113, 117, 119
streamlining of reporting, 109, 114. See also conventions: of writing
substatutes (*li*), 111, 113, 115, 118, 132–36
suicide, 267, 281n40; female, 45; male, 95
Supreme Court of the United States, 274, 282n58
Surveillance Commissioners (*anchashi*), 16, 86, 92
Suzhou, 129–30
Szonyi, Michael, 182n17

Tale of Heroic Lovers, 28
tanci, 244
Tang Code, 149, 211n8
Tang Ming lü hebian (Combined Edition of the Tang and Ming Codes), 145
Tang Suizu, 149
Tang yin bi shi, 190, 210n2
Tang Zhen, 127
ten abominations (*shi'e*), 30
testimony, recorded (*kougong*), 11–12, 17–18, 31–33, 36, 37, 38–41, 43n19, 50–60, 64, 84–103, 109, 113–18, 120, 121
theft, 193, 194, 195
Theiss, Janet, 183n39

Three Courts of Revision. *See* Three Judicial Offices
Three Judicial Offices (Sanfasi), 16, 31, 34, 57, 115
The Three Kingdoms, 264, 265
Tian Tao, 279n9, 281n45
tianli (will of Heaven), 208, 226
tiaokuai system, 263
time limits for judicial procedures, 16–17
tongyangxi (child bride), 57
torture, judicial, 15–16, 23n35, 41, 84, 89, 90–92, 95, 102n7, 198–99
transaction costs, 128; for bargaining and decision, 129; for information, 129; for policing and enforcement, 129–30
The Travels of Lao Can, 274
trials of the insane (*shen fengzi*), 174
tropes, 126, 127, 128, 136, 137. *See* conventions: of writing
truth, 65–66, 67, 68
Twenty-four Exemplars of Filial Piety, 32
typography, and visual impact: in modern novels, 249; in traditional novels, 243; "woodblock effect" for traditional materials, 257n36

underworld bureaucracy, 236, 255n6
urban-rural divide, 197–98

verdicts overturned, 199–200
vernacular novel: modern, espoused by Liang Qichao, 248; traditional, linear narrative progression in, 235
violence, and criminal intentionality, 50–61

Wang Danwang, 89–90
Wang Huizu, 14, 47–48, 53, 61, 62n3, 78n2, 137, 176, 273
Wang Kentang, 145
Wang Lingguan, 169
Wang Xiansen, 169

Wanli yehuo bian, 218–19
The Washing Away of Wrongs, 236, 241
Water Margin. *See Shuihu zhuan*
wealthy people, 126, 136; social responsibility and contributions of, 137–38
weapons, use of dangerous or lethal, 111–16, 118–19, 121
Western criticism of Chinese law, 111, 119
What the Master Did Not Speak About. *See Zibuyu*
White, James Boyd, 5, 20n6
wife beating, 29, 30, 31, 32, 33; magistrates' views of, 51–52; in Qing Code, 49–50
"wifely way" (*fudao*), 269
wives' conflicts with mothers-in-law, 49, 56, 57–61
women, as perpetrators of crime, 7, 9, 38–41, 44–62
wronged relatives and creditors (*yuanqin zhaizhu*), 175
Wu Jianren. *See* Wu Woyao
Wu Woyao, 234, 235, 247–48
Wudashan, 153–54

Xi you ji (Journey to the West), 265
Xi yuan lu (The Washing Away of Wrongs), 236, 241
Xin xiaoshuo (New Fiction), 248, 249
Xingke tiben. *See* crime reports
Xingshi yinyuan zhuan (Marriage Bonds to Awaken the World), 46, 216, 218–19, 232n17, 265, 266–67
Xinzheng lu (Accounts of Proof of Divine Retribution), 171
Xu Changzuo, 176
Xu Qing, 171
Xu Zibuyu (Sequel to "What the Master Did Not Speak About"), 178, 180
Xue Yunsheng, 145, 273

Yan Youxi, 133
Yang Naiwu, 237, 274

Yanshan conglu (Complete Records of Yanshan), 176
Ye Mengzhu, 127
Yesou puyan (Country Codger's Words of Exposure), 28
Yongzheng Emperor, 45, 137–38, 141n47
yi (righteousness), 205
Yi yu ji, 192, 210n2
Yijian zhi (Record of the Listener and Recorder), 167, 171
Yu Yue, 185n69
Yuan Mei, 172, 175
Yuewei caotang biji (Notes from the Studio for Careful Scrutiny), 94–95
Yushi mingyan (Clear Words to Instruct the World), 172

Zeng Jing, 137
Zhan Yanfu, 189, 202
Zhang Boxing, 128
Zhang Guanzi, 169, 181n6
Zhang Yingyu, 220, 254
Zhang Zhupo, 226
Zhao Yi, 129
zhawei (forgeries and counterfeiting): cases, 143–44, 153–54; political crime, 145, 151; statutes, 145–46, 151, 156–57
Zhe yu gui jian (Magic Mirror for Solving Cases), 210n2
Zhejiang legislation, 132–36
Zhen Xishan, 191
Zheng Ke, 210n3
Zheng Tuyou, 169
Zheng Zhongkui, 168
Zhenwu, 176
Zhiwen lu (Record of Trivial Things Heard), 176, 177
Zhouli, 183n41
zhu (self-mastery or self-containment), 53; in fiction, 46
Zhu Fengyun, 79n10
Zhu Xi, 224
Zibuyu (What the Master Did Not Speak About), 172, 173, 175, 177, 178

ASIAN LAW SERIES

1. *The Constitution of Japan: Its First Twenty Years, 1947–67*, edited by Dan Fenno Henderson
2. *Village "Contracts" in Tokugawa Japan*, by Dan Fenno Henderson
3. *Chinese Family Law and Social Change in Historic and Comparative Perspective*, edited by David C. Buxbaum
4. *Law and Politics in China's Foreign Trade*, edited by Victor H. Li
5. *Patent and Know-how Licensing in Japan and the United States*, edited by Teruo Doi and Warren L. Shattuck
6. *The Constitutional Case Law of Japan: Selected Supreme Court Decisions, 1961–70*, by Hiroshi Itoh and Lawrence Ward Beer
7. *Japan's Commission on the Constitution: The Final Report*, translated and edited by John M. Maki
8. *Service Regulations in Korea: Problems and Recommendations for Feasible Reforms*, by Young Moo Shin
9. *Order and Discipline in China: The Shanghai Mixed Court 1911–27*, by Thomas B. Stephens
10. *The Economic Contract Law of China: Legitimation and Contract Autonomy in the PRC*, by Pitman B. Potter
11. *Japanese Labor Law*, by Kazuo Sugeno, translated by Leo Kanowitz
12. *Constitutional Systems in Late Twentieth Century Asia*, edited by Lawrence W. Beer
13. *Constitutional Case Law of Japan, 1970 through 1990*, edited by Lawrence W. Beer and Hiroshi Itoh
14. *The Limits of the Rule of Law in China*, edited by Karen Turner, James V. Feinerman, and R. Kent Guy
15. *Legal Reform in Taiwan under Japanese Colonial Rule (1895-1945: The Reception of Western Law*, by Tay-sheng Wang
16. *Antitrust in Germany and Japan: The First Fifty Years, 1947–1998*, by John O. Haley
17. *The Great Ming Code / Da Ming lü*, translated and introduced by Jiang Yonglin
18. *Writing and Law in Late Imperial China: Crime, Conflict, and Judgment*, edited by Robert E. Hegel and Katherine Carlitz
19. *Law in Japan: A Turning Point*, edited by Daniel Foote

www.ingramcontent.com/pod-product-compliance
Lightning Source LLC
Chambersburg PA
CBHW021817300426
44114CB00009BA/207